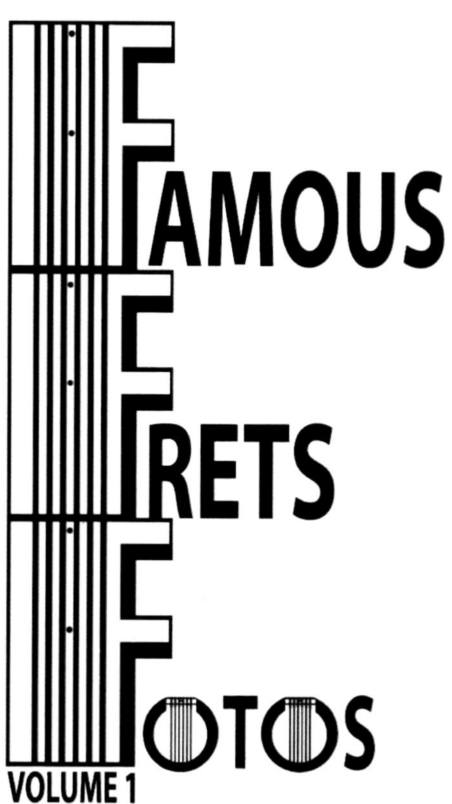

Famous Frets Fotos

VOLUME 1

by Steve Clarke

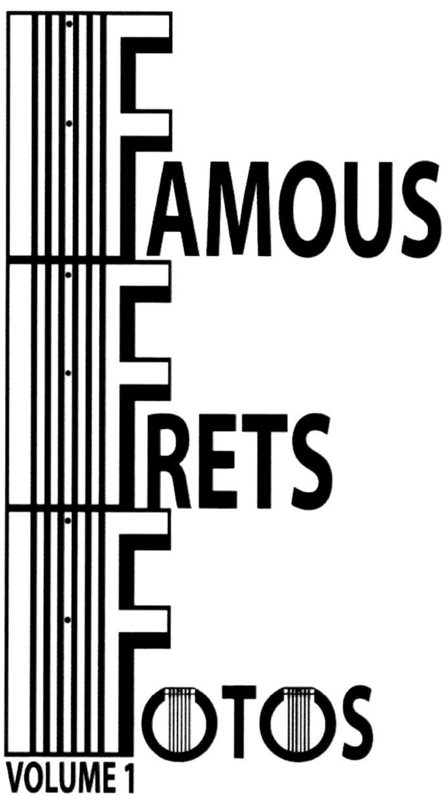

Famous Frets Fotos

VOLUME 1

by Steve Clarke

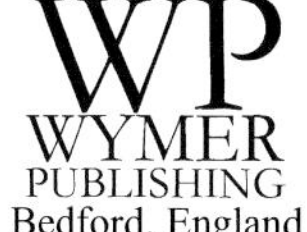

WP
WYMER
PUBLISHING
Bedford, England

First published in 2024.
Wymer Publishing
Bedford, England www.wymerpublishing.co.uk Tel: 01234 326691
Wymer Publishing is a trading name of Wymer (UK) Ltd

Every effort has been made to trace the copyright holders of the
photographs in this book but some were unreachable. We would
be grateful if the photographers concerned would contact us.

A catalogue record for this book is available from the British Library.

Book design by Steve Clarke and Danny Lee.
Front cover design by Steve Clarke.
Printed and bound in England by Halstan & Co. Ltd, Amersham.

Photo credits

All photos by Steve Clarke except as follows:

p10: Eddy Westveer; p26: Malcolm Park / Alamy Stock Photo; p32, p45, p93, p101 & p102: Alan Perry Concert Photography; p48: (left) Alamy Stock Photo, (right) Mark Meredith / Alamy Stock Photo; p49: unknown; p64: Tim Fleming / Alamy Stock Photo; p69: Robert Knight; p73: Suzy O'Hara; p74: Steve Rapport; p75: unknown; p 81 & p83: courtesy of Bonhams; p104: Jamie Lorriman / Alamy Stock Photo; p107: Odile Noel / Lebrecht Music & Arts / Alamy Stock Photo; p110: Richard Faulks; p115: Pictorial Press Ltd / Alamy Stock Photo; p125: unknown; p126: dpa picture alliance / Alamy Stock Photo; p130: unknown.

Contents

Introduction

In my first book ***Famous Frets*** I took a forensic deep dive into many famous guitars and I included detailed specifications of their construction with supporting photographs.

I would firstly like to thank anyone that purchased the book and for all the feedback, comments and opinion which I received gratefully. I also appreciate the many emails I received encouraging me to venture towards a second book. This book ***Famous Frets Fotos'*** is Volume One in a series of two.

In this book, I have decided to focus more on the images of the guitars rather than the very detailed approach that I used for the first book. There are many reasons for this change. As part of my role as a guitar consultant, I may be invited to view a single guitar or, as was the case with Peter Green and KK Downing, there were entire collections to assess, and in some instances, repair guitars in a very short time. So deep dives were not always possible.

With the Peter Green collection I looked at one hundred and fifty guitars and also his banjos, four-string Turkish lutes, amps and mandolins! That collection was so large it was located across two sites in London and Oxford. I did however manage to take more intricate details on a few of the most known guitars, some from his Splinter Group period. I am so very lucky to have had such opportunities.

For me personally there were a number of 'pinch me' moments, for example looking at the Graffiti Yellow Strat owned by Jeff Beck. Thank you for purchasing this book, I hope you enjoy it.

Steve Clarke

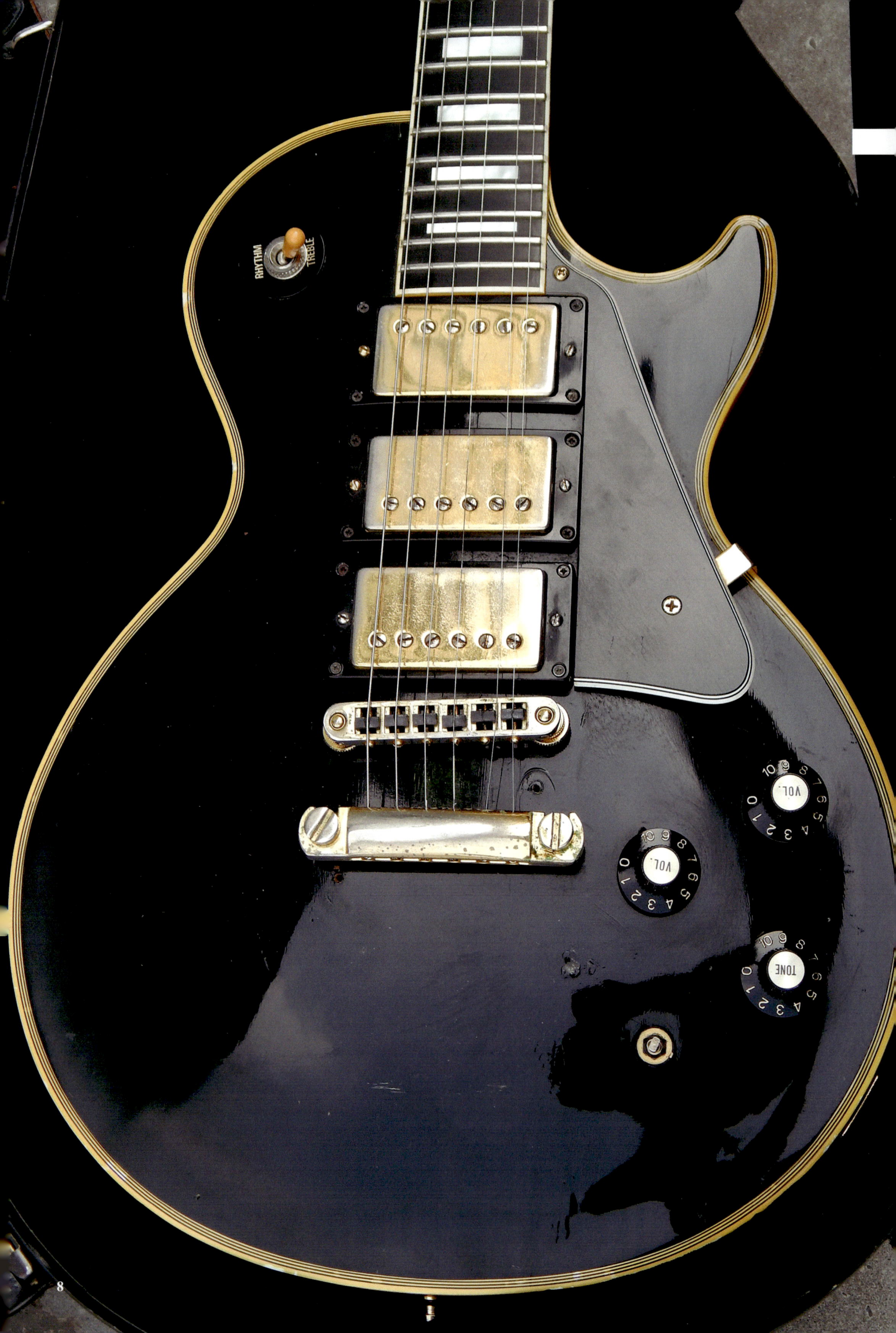

RHYTHM
TREBLE
VOL.
VOL.
TONE

Jan Akkerman – '57 Reissue
1995 Gibson Les Paul Custom

Since his early days in Focus Jan Akkerman has always been associated with a Black Les Paul Custom. He didn't have it long before he modified the '68 Custom by fitting a Gretsch pickup in the neck. Soon after that he put a Gretsch Filtertron pickup in the bridge position. In 1973 he is seen with a '54 Black Custom (at Live at the Rainbow Theatre, London) with the combination of a P90 pickup in the bridge position and P90 Staple pickup in the neck position. This gave a unique tone not to be found in the Humbucker equipped version.

Other than a handful of one night shows, Jan had a long lay off from touring but eventually went to the UK in 1997. He took with him a Black three pickup Les Paul Custom Reissue. I was lucky enough to get to a gig which was at the Floral Pavilion Theatre, New Brighton on 15th November 1997. It was an incredible gig and Akkerman was on top form.

When I went over to Holland to see his guitars, I was thrilled to find five of his guitars to look at. This was at the factory where his signature Brandin model was being built. In my first book, Famous Frets, I spoke about his Les Paul Personal in great detail.

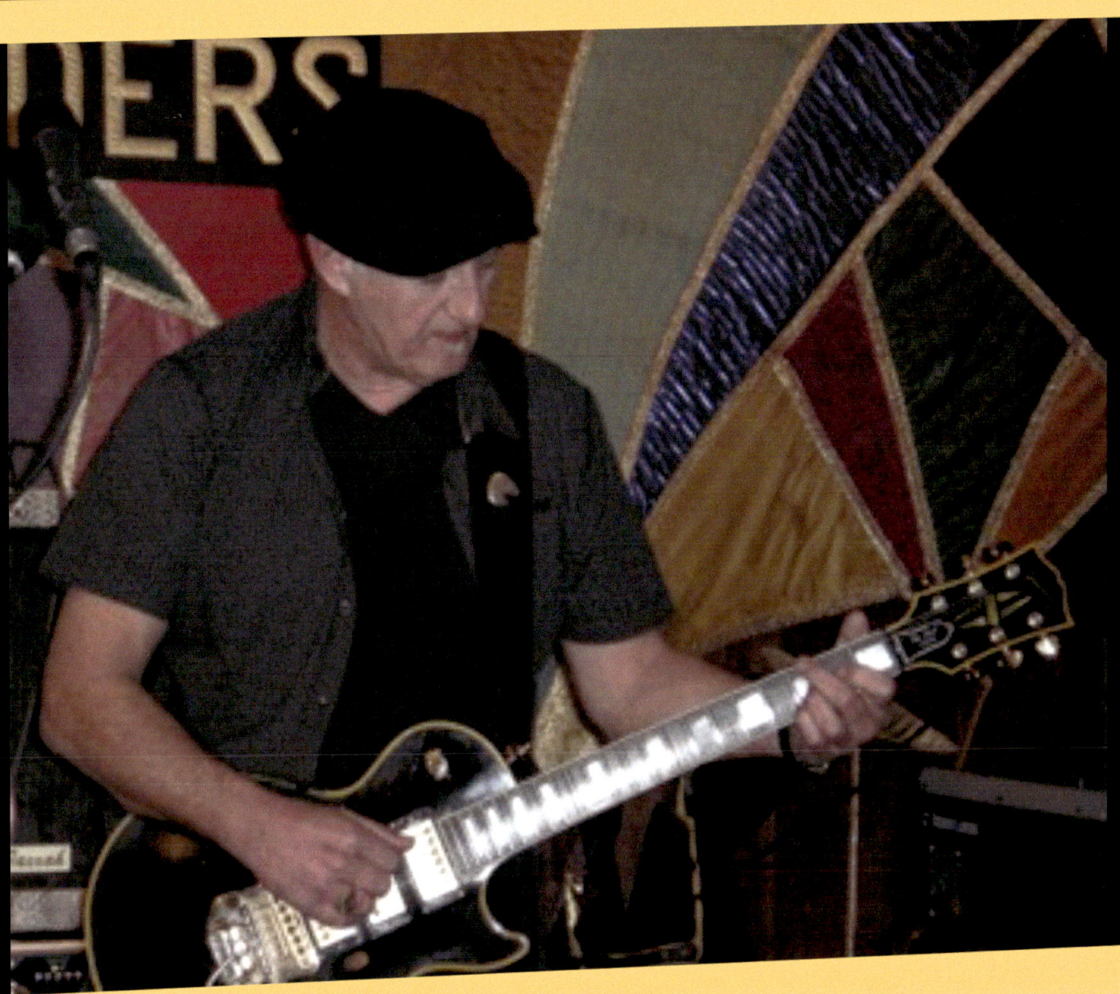

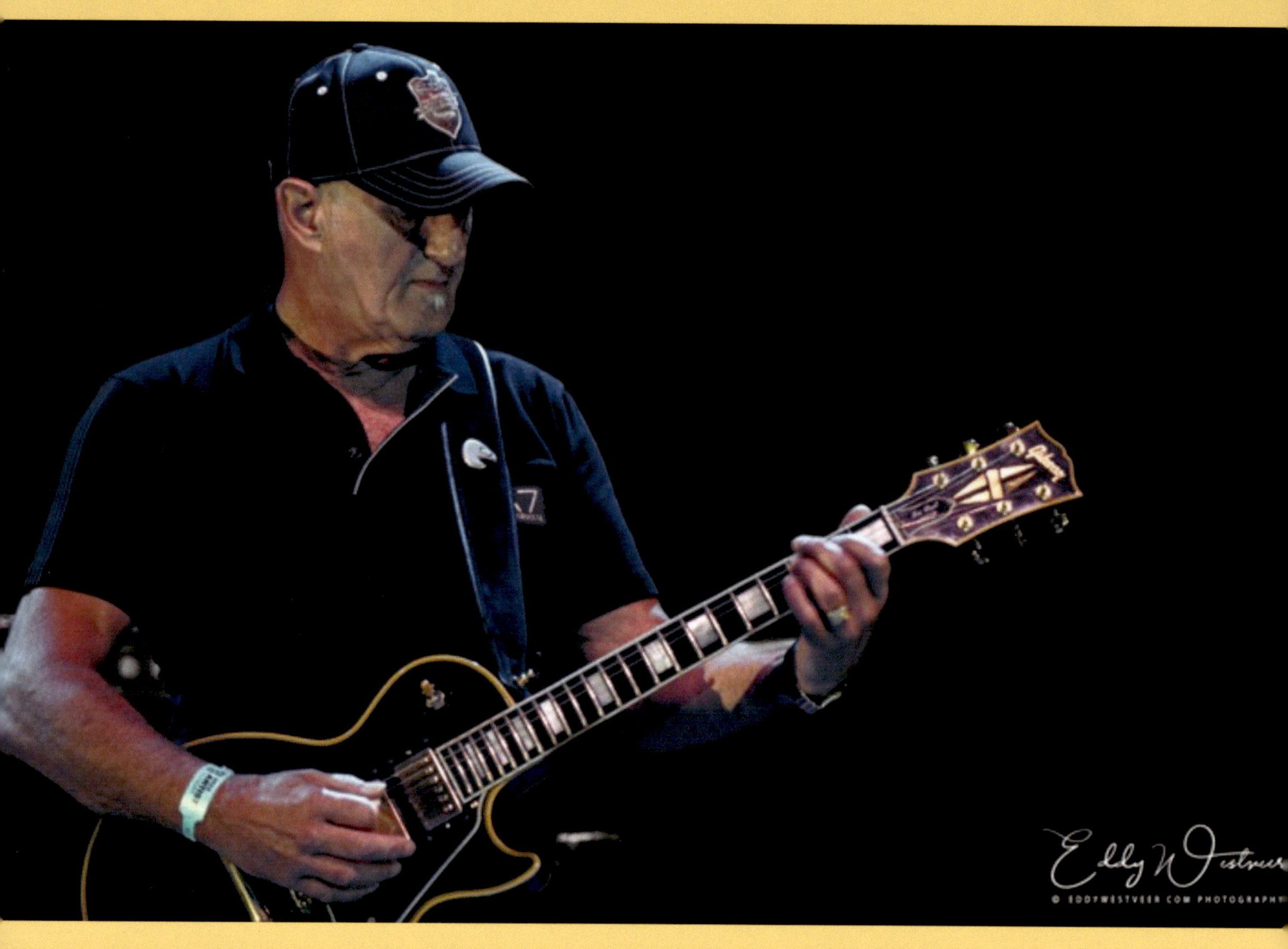

One of the other guitars I looked at whilst at the factory, was this three pickup '57 Reissue which he still uses to this day along with the Les Paul Personal. He also has a '54 Les Paul Custom Reissue (Limited Edition) that Gibson built especially for him. The Custom and the Personal Guitar both had the Stetsbar Trem System fitted but they were removed some time later when Jan returned to the Stop tailpiece look. This Black Custom although similar in wiring to the Personal Les Paul has a very different voice

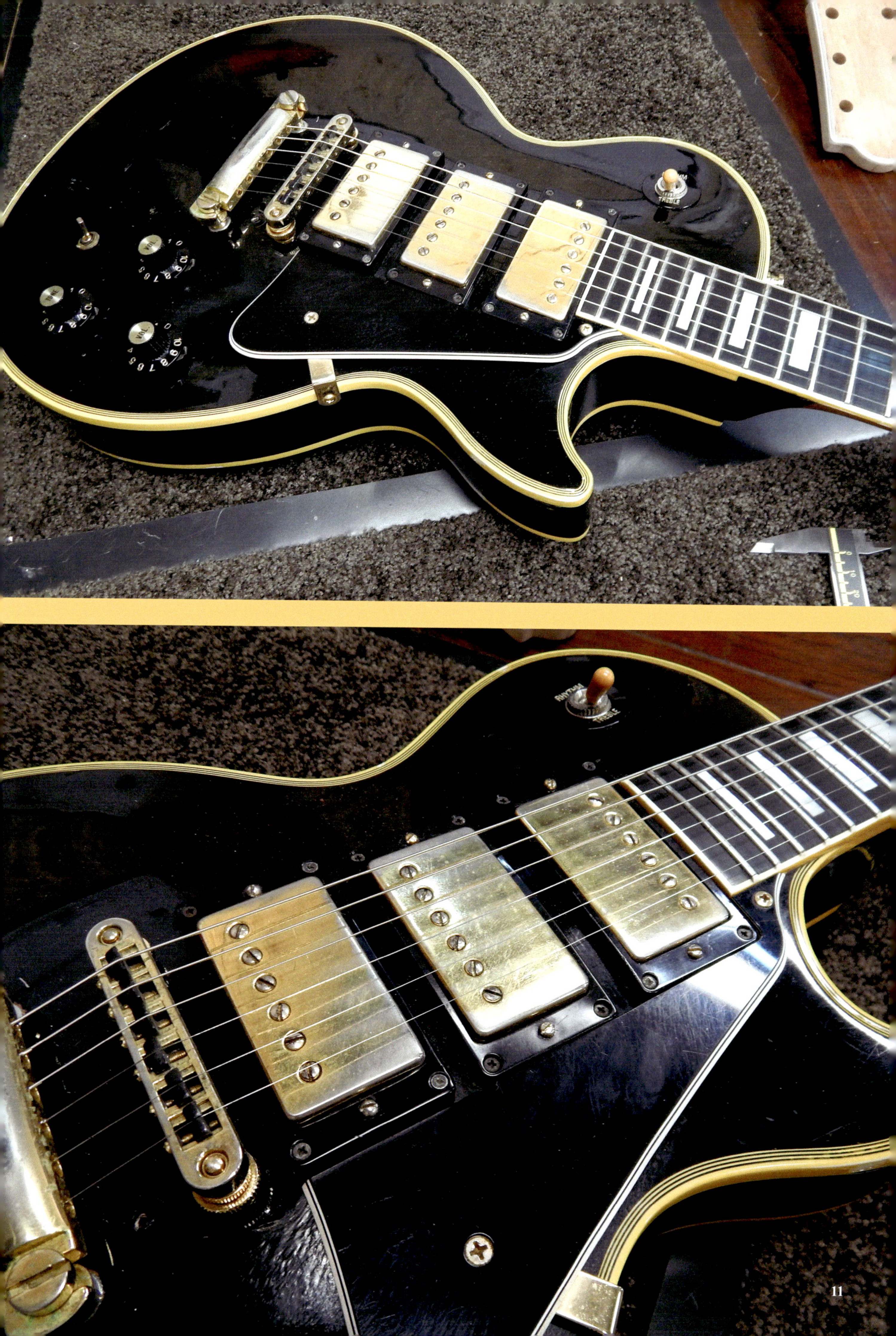

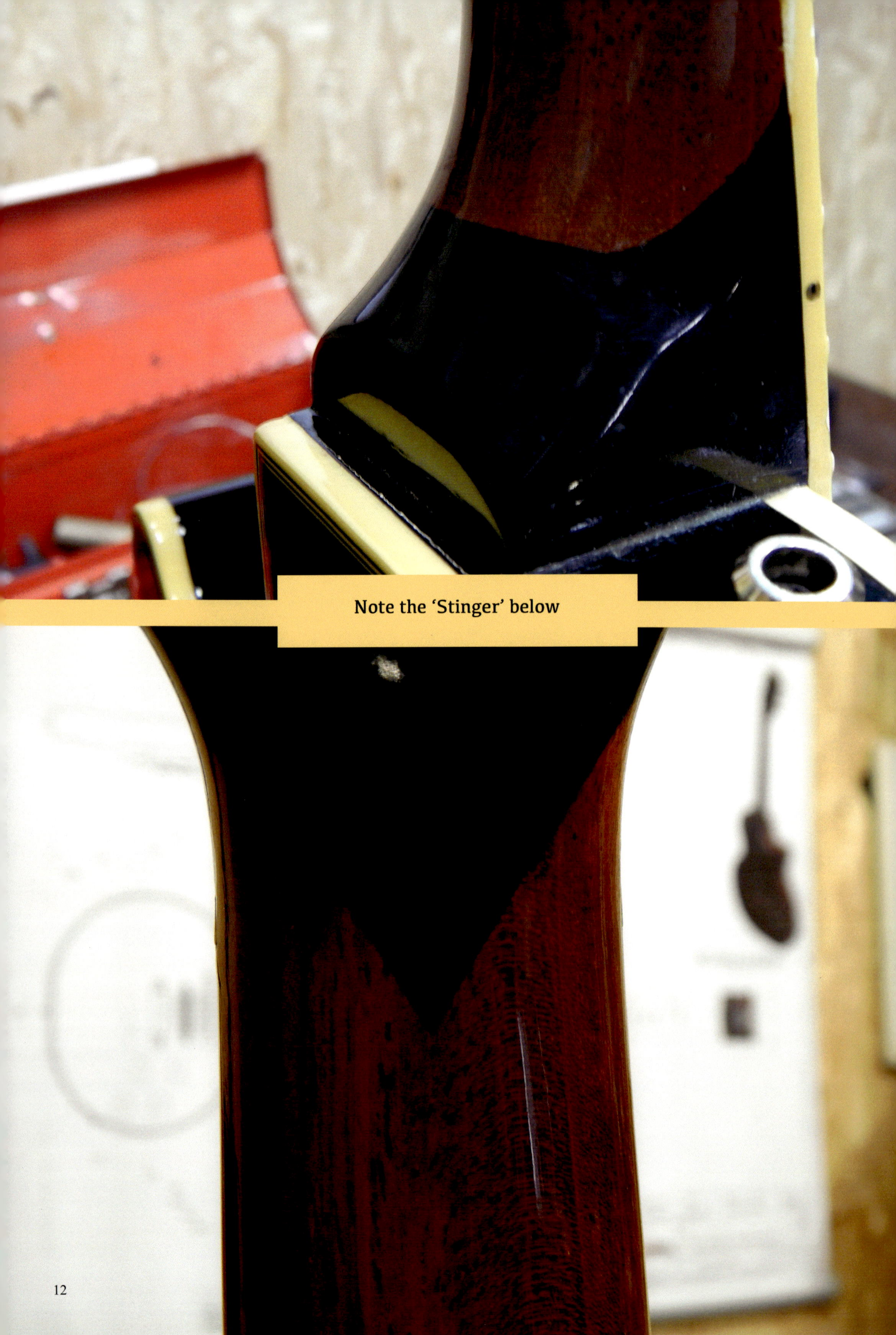

Note the 'Stinger' below

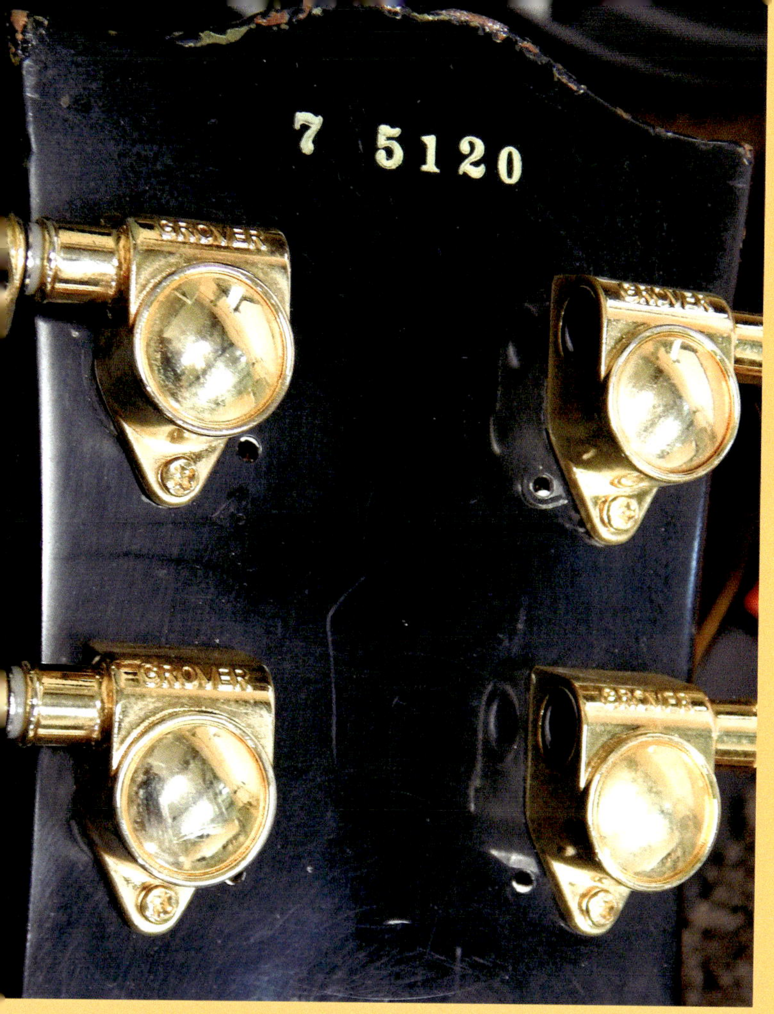

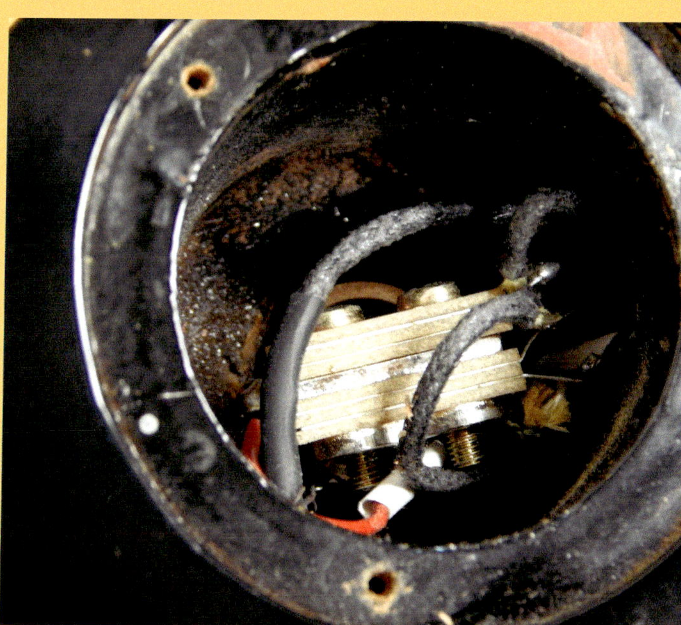

Grover Machine heads replaced the previous Waffle back tuners.

Toggle cavity

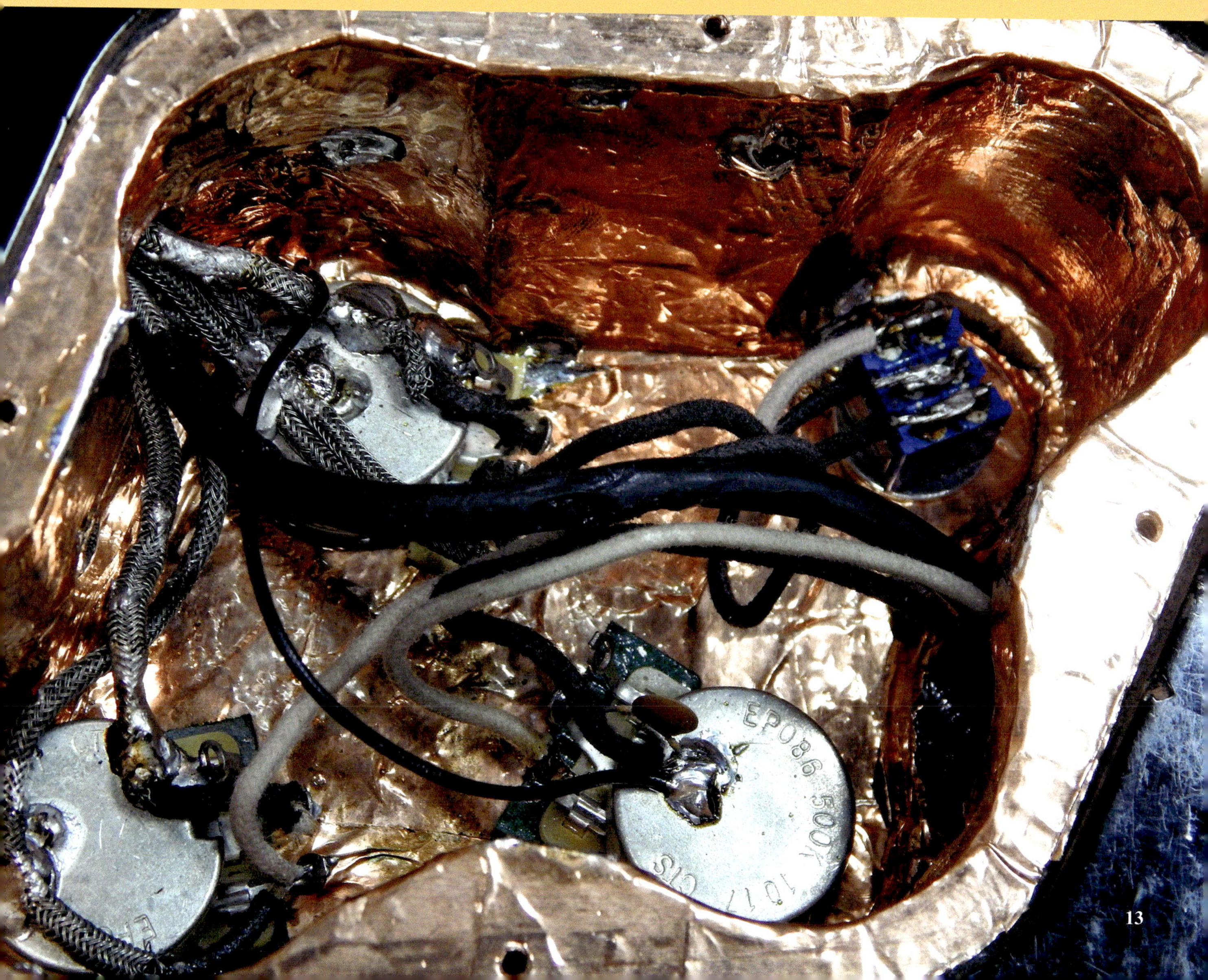

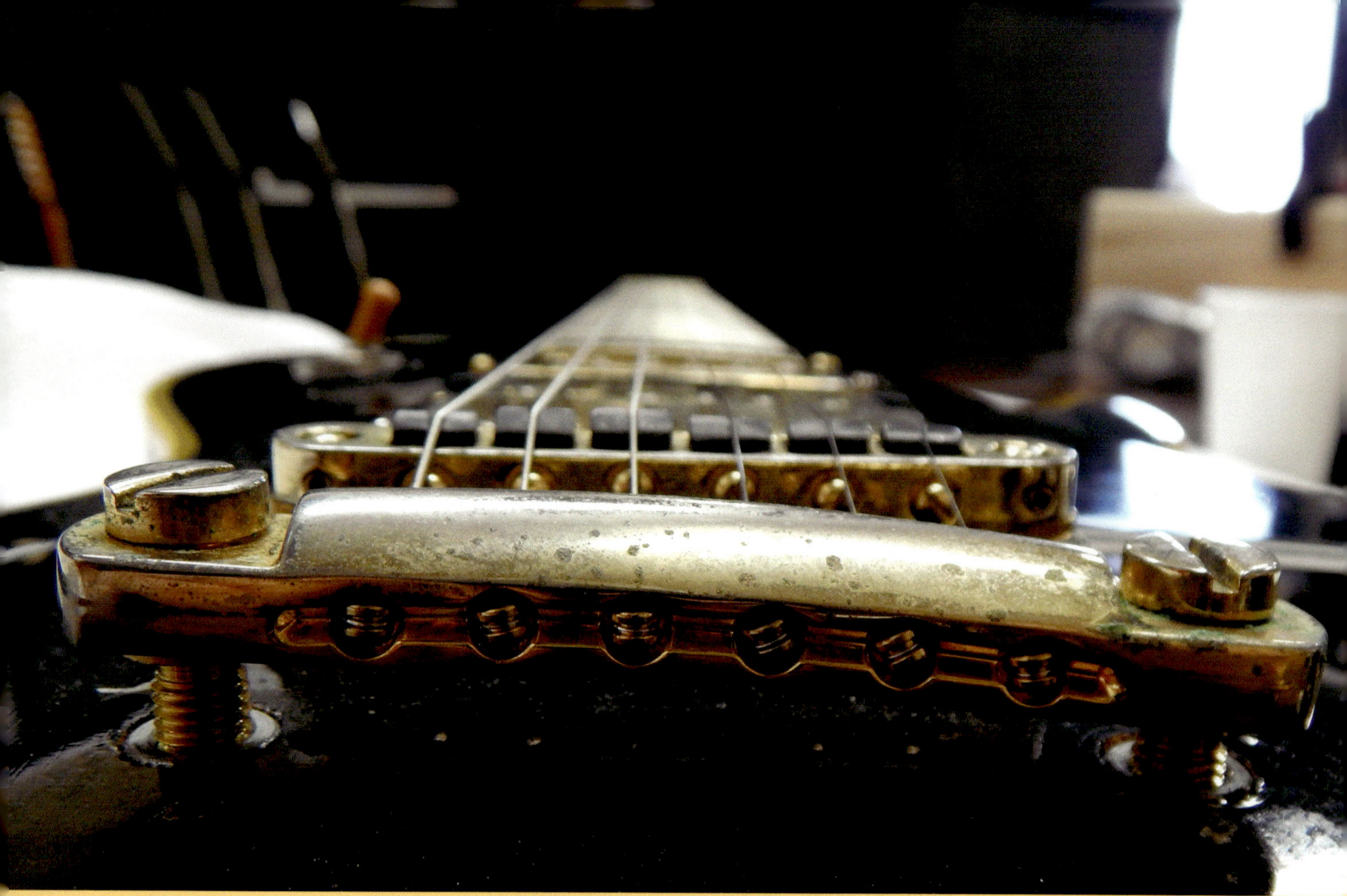

Bass side raised tailpiece

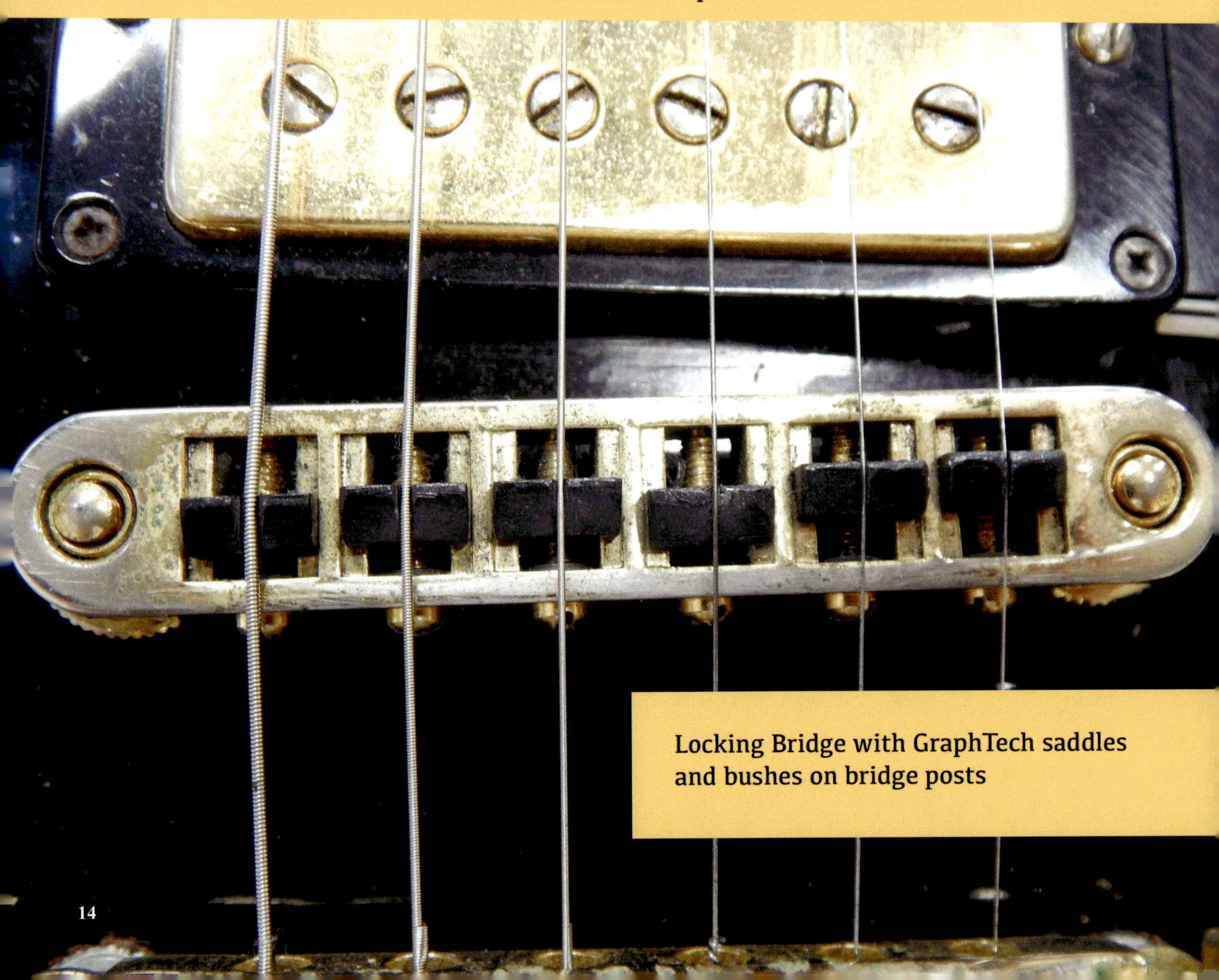

Locking Bridge with GraphTech saddles and bushes on bridge posts

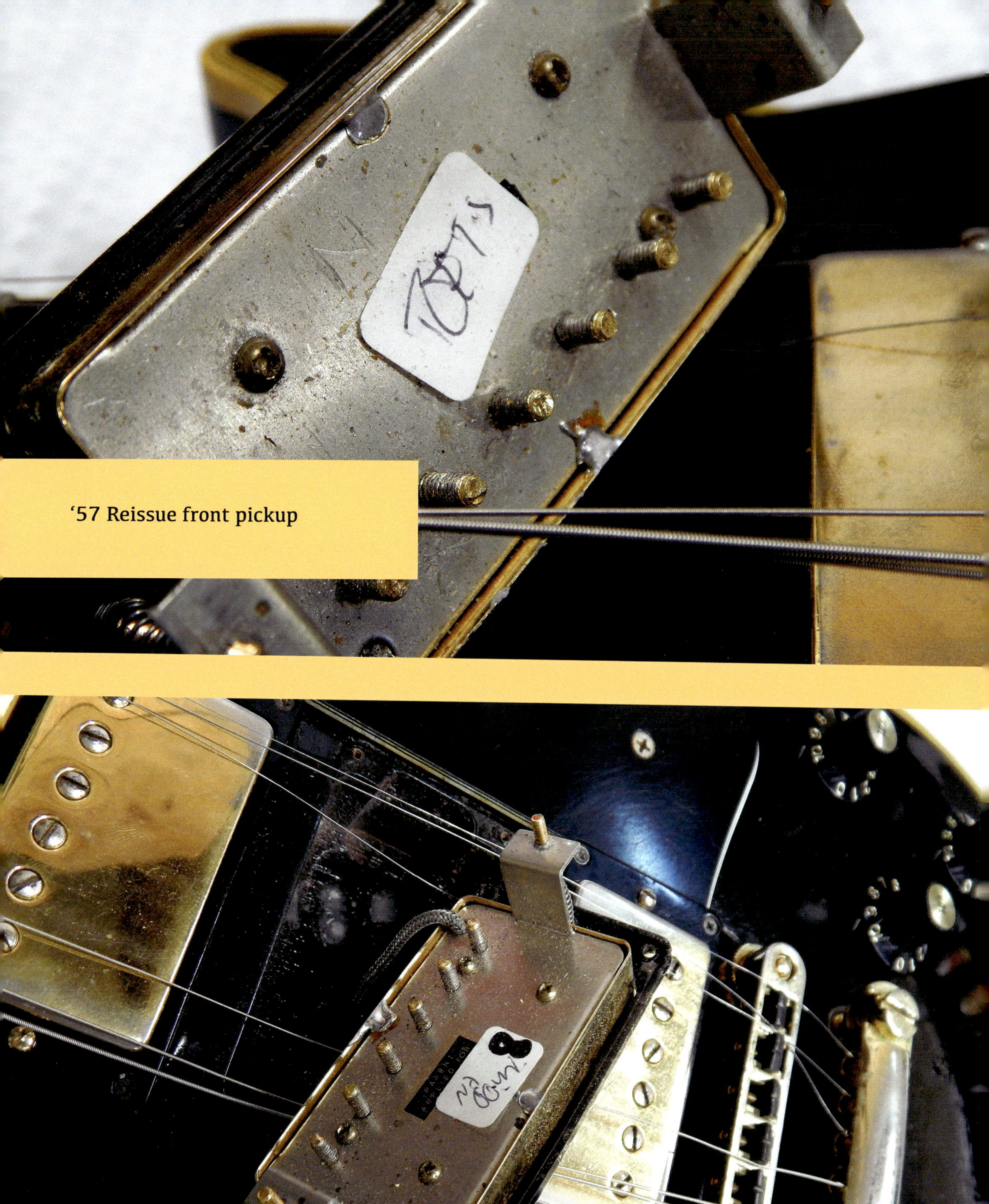

'57 Reissue front pickup

'57 Reissue mid pickup

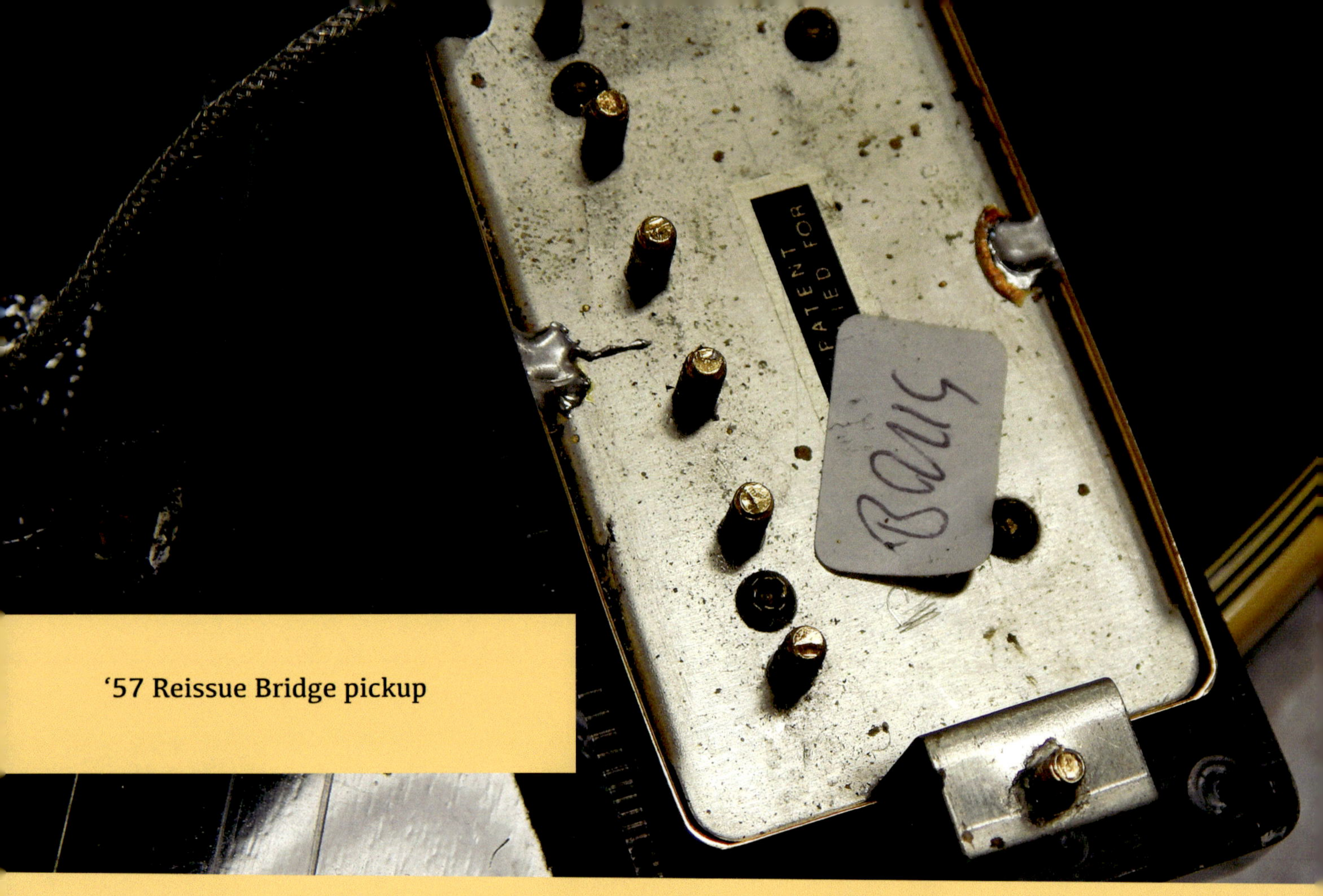

'57 Reissue Bridge pickup

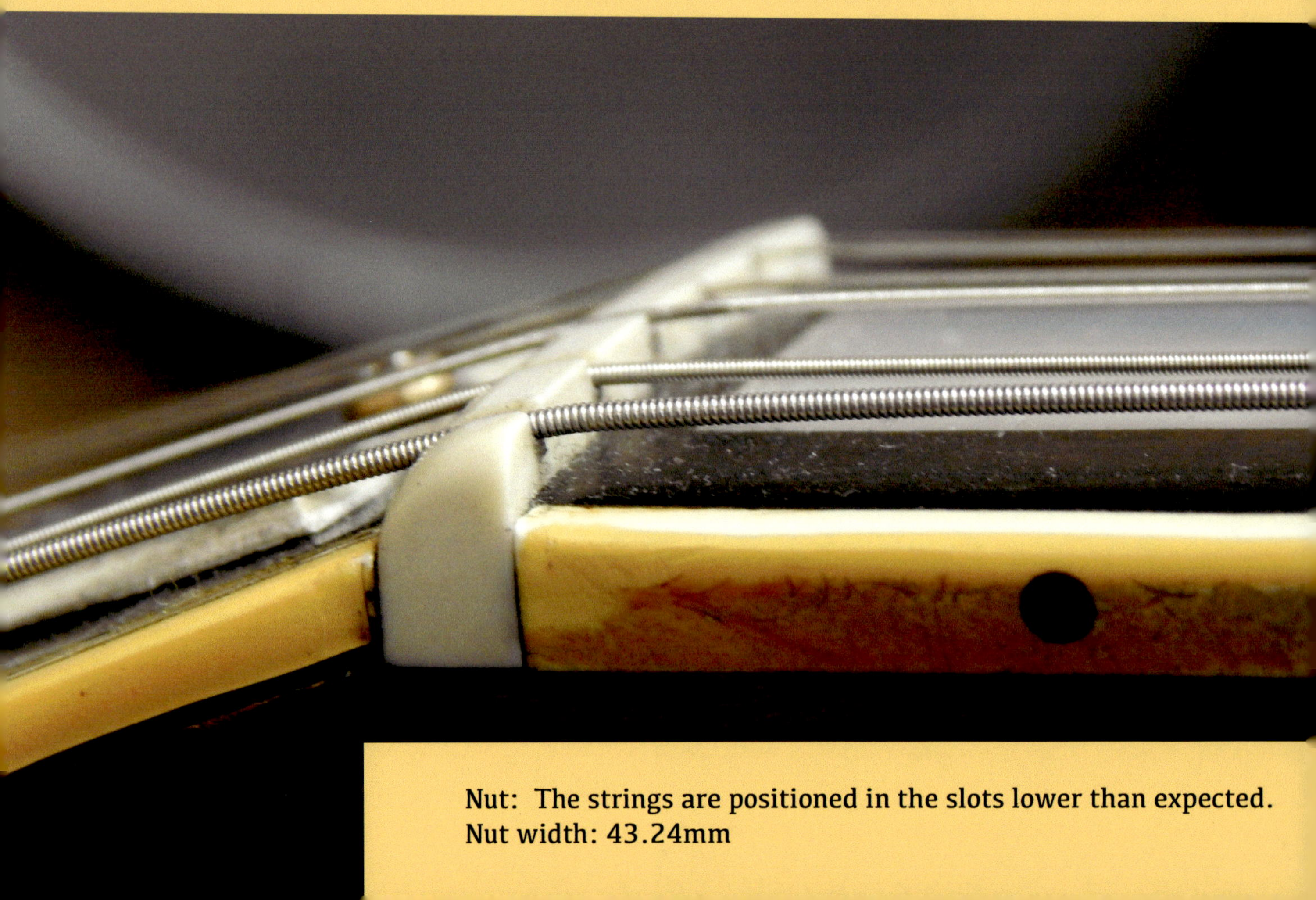

Nut: The strings are positioned in the slots lower than expected.
Nut width: 43.24mm

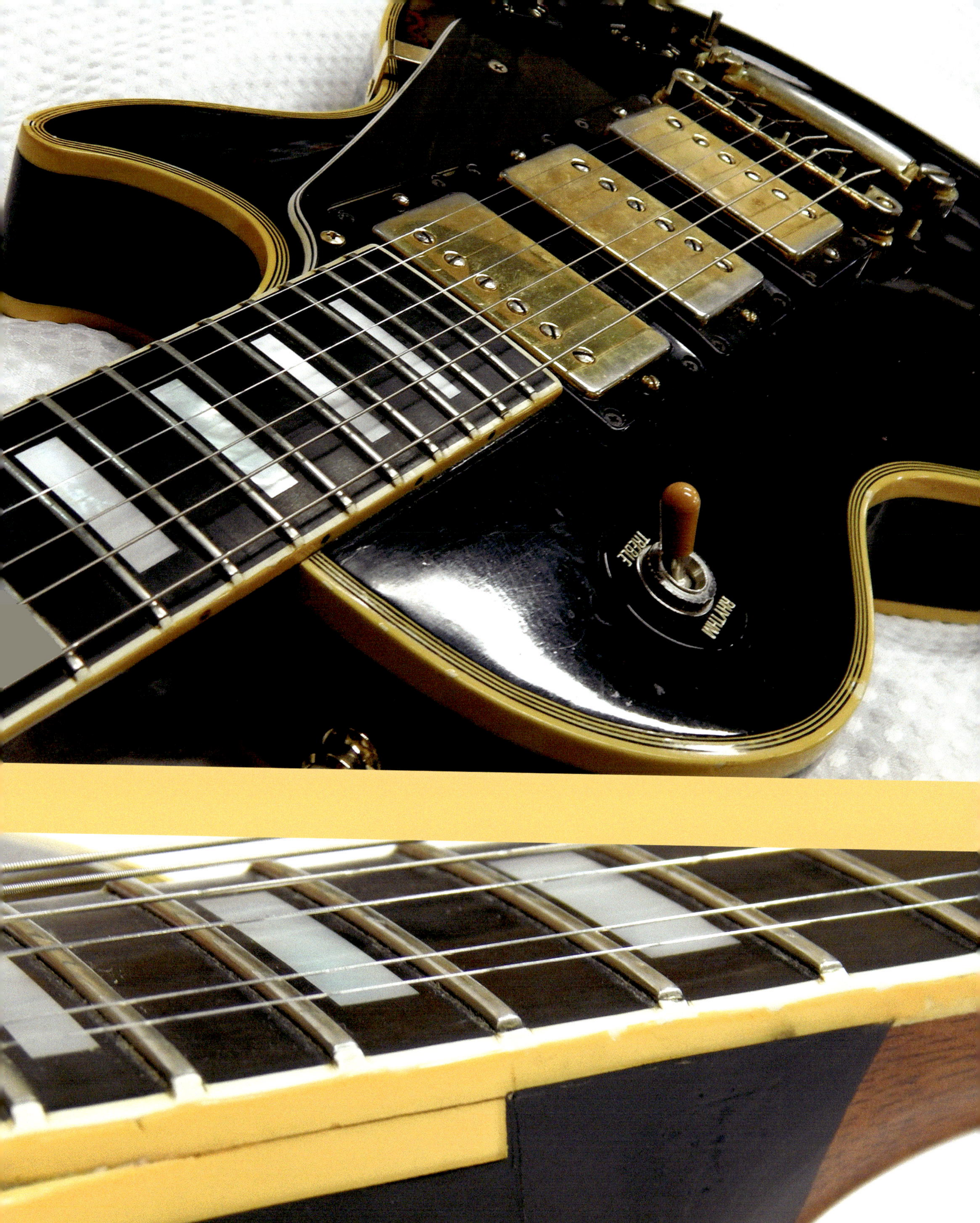

Original Frets: you can see where the nibs have worn on the treble side.

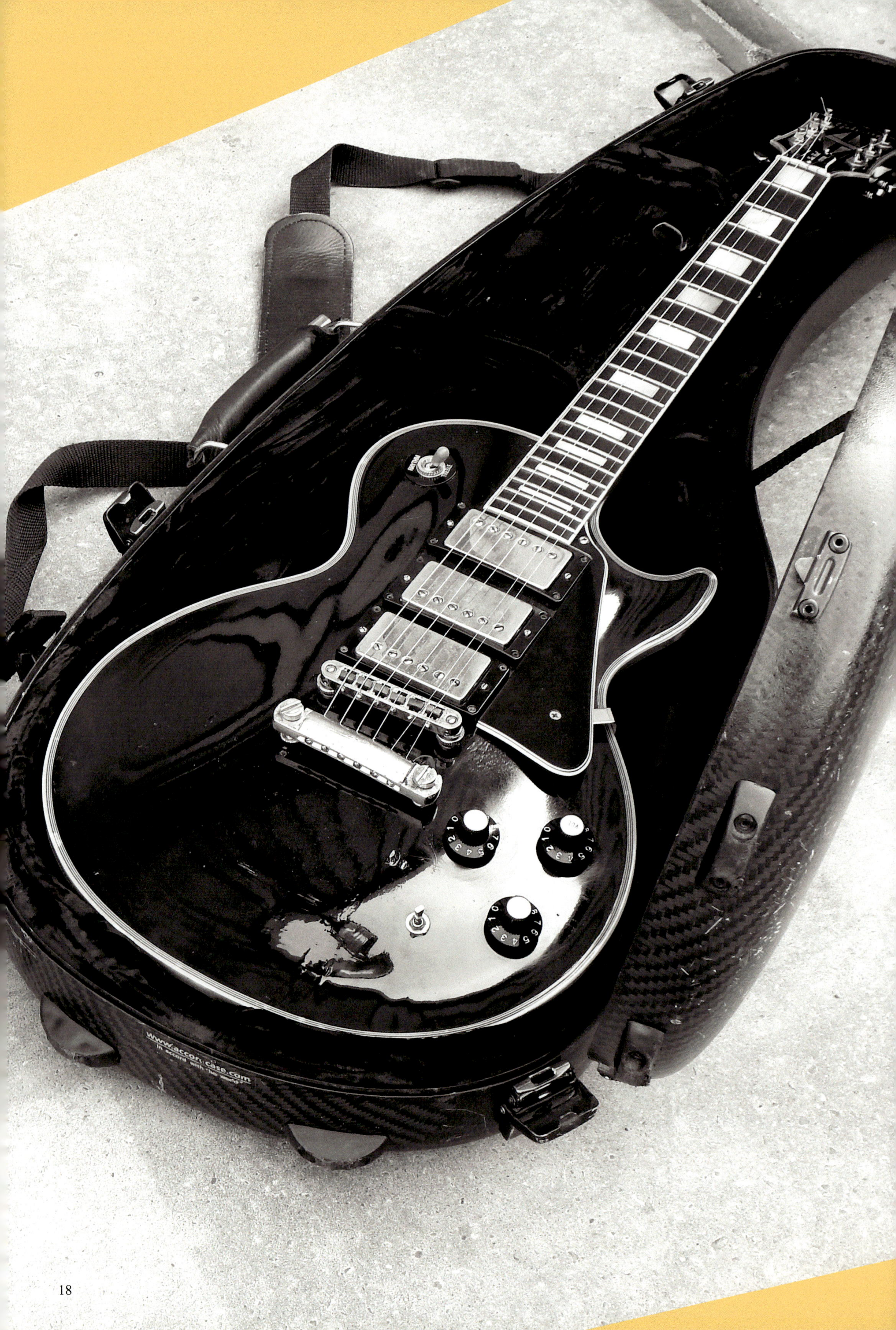
www.accordcase.com
in accord with the world

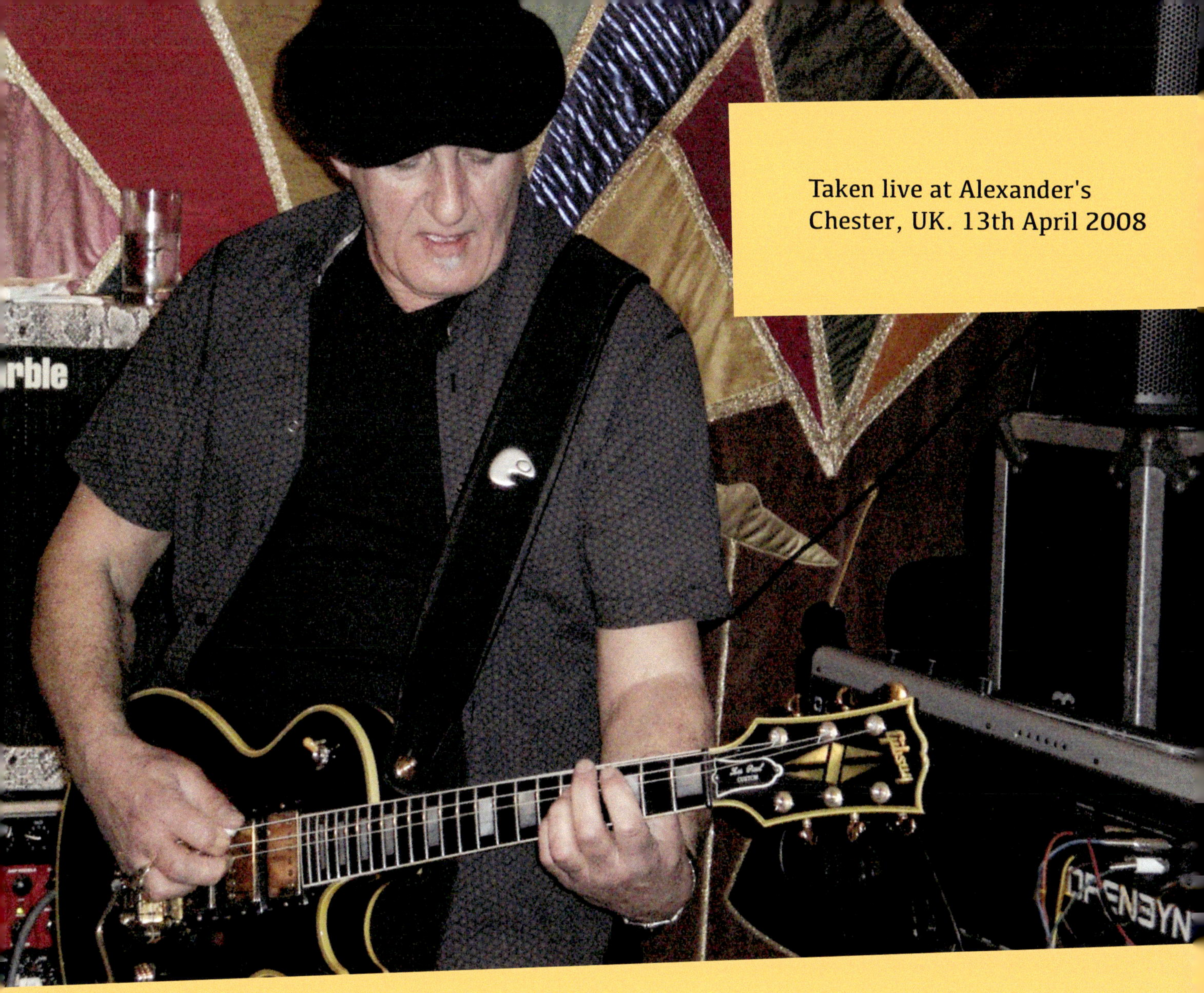

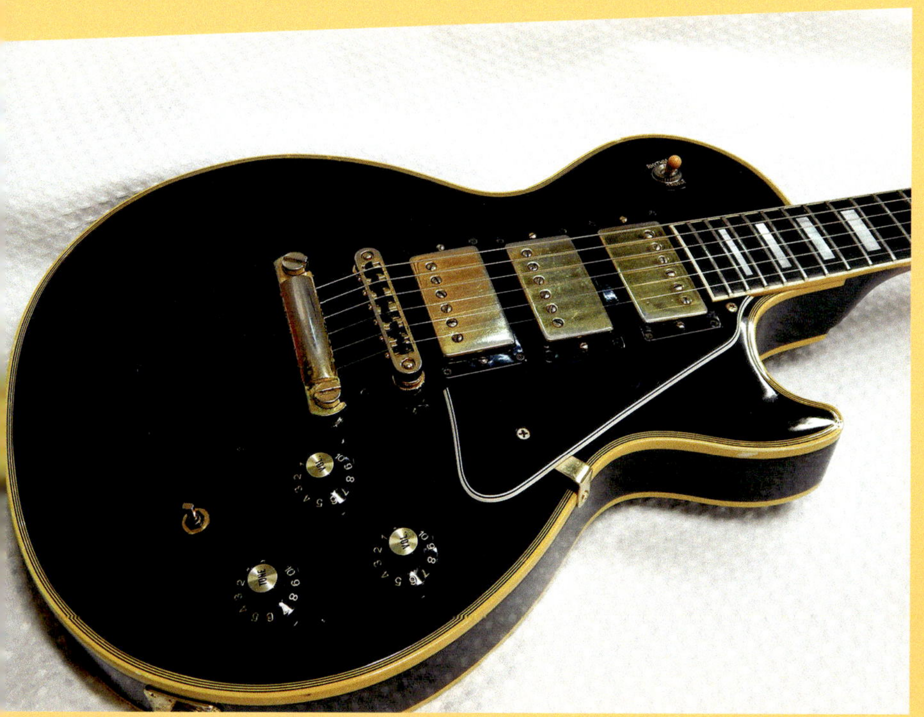

Above, with Stets Bar fitted. The control knobs were called 'Ringos' but these were later changed back to the 'Witches Hat' style knobs (left).

Famous Frets Specs

Nut: 43.24mm and 53.23 at 12th fret
Bridge: 13.95 mm width, 85.48 mm length
Pickups: Bridge 7.78 ohms - Neck 7.71 ohms - Mid 8.06 ohms
Coil tapped: 3.93 ohms in bridge position and 3.91 ohms in neck position
Frets: 2.43mm
Weight: 9.74 lbs
Machine heads: Gold plated Grover
Body thickness: 49.61 mm
Control Cavity: 500k CTS pots
Headstock: 16.23 mm low E side – 14.65mm at D string
Serial Number: 7 5120
Fingerboard: Ebony
Toggle switch: Switchcraft
Pickup surround: M69 stamped on the neck pickup surround
Capacitor: 223Z ceramic
CTS pots: EPO-86 500k (only one cap in control assembly)

Neck pickup has white label stuck on it covering a PAF sticker
'57 Reissue Humbuckers Mid has PAF sticker and white label
with what looks like an '8' and 'Mid' written on Bridge PAF sticker
and label with 'bridge' written on it

All pickups have brass Phillips screws to secure pickup bobbins

Famous Frets SPECS

Framus Akkerman White

Model no: 10970
Weight: 9.22lbs
Machine heads: Made by Kolb, with a hole in centre of post like a Fender machine head.

Body thickness: 62.75mm
Thickness at 'F' hole: 10.06 mm
Nut width: 43.57mm
Headstock width: 77.57mm
Headstock thickness: 16.46mm
12th Fret Neck: 56.26mm
Control knob: Width 24.89mm (16.58mm tall)
Bridge length: 99.86mm
Bridge width: 20.21mm
Pickup bridge: 9.55 ohms
Neck pickup: 9.84 ohms
Pickup Length: 83.04mm
Pickup Width: 37.05mm
Frets: 1.91mm
Stud length: 38.10mm

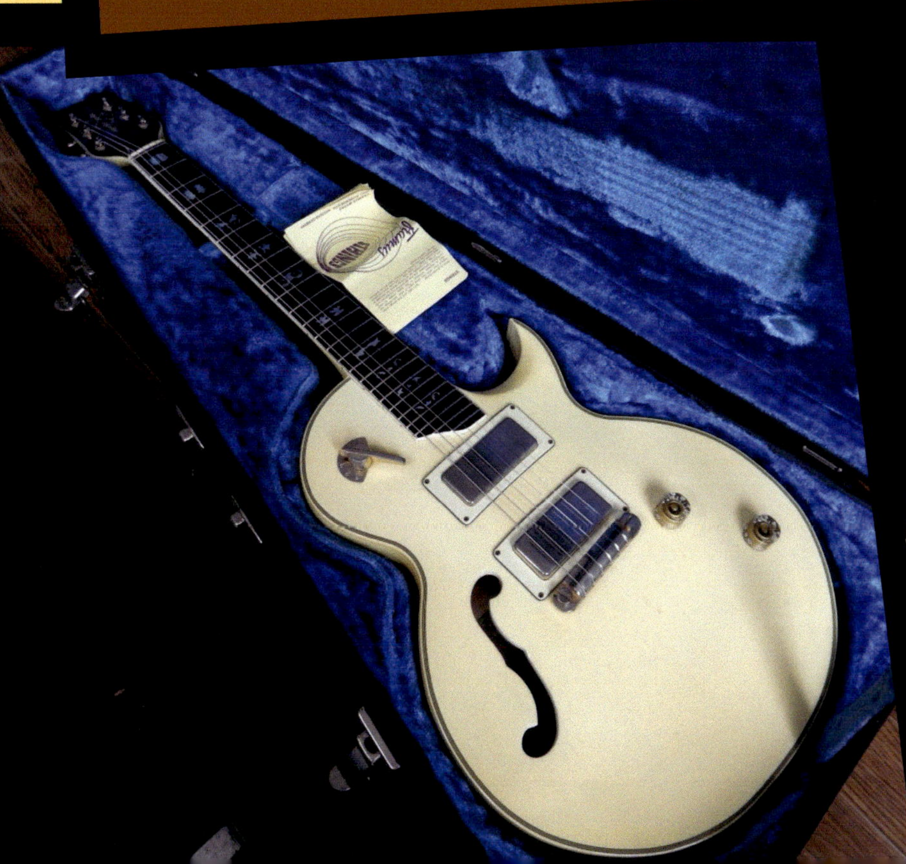

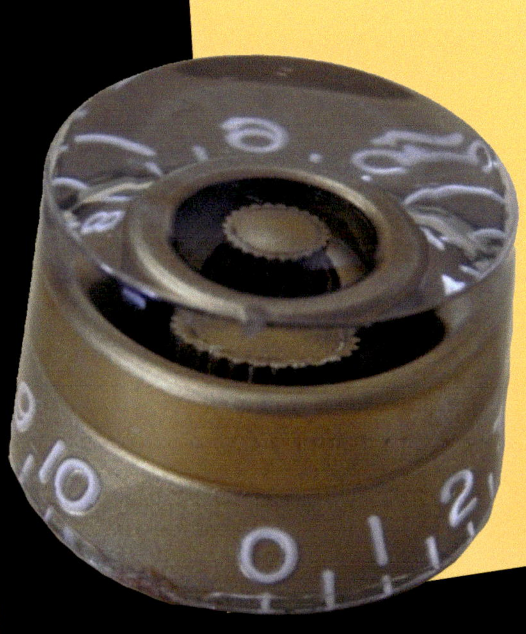

Framus Akkerman Sunburst

This is the 1974 Jan Akkerman Signature model built by Framus.
The catalogue only referred to Sunburst and Black but a handful
of very rare white ones were also made.
The catalogue had an error showing model as 10950,
It's actually 10940.
Black 10980 and very rare white 10970.

Model no: 10940
Weight: 8.98lbs
Machine heads: Made by Kolb (no split shaft)
Body thickness: 60.90mm
Thickness at 'F' hole: 7.09mm
Nut width: 44.28mm
Headstock width: 77.50mm
Headstock thickness: 16.67mm
12th Fret Neck: 55.33mm
Control knob: 24.89mm
Bridge length: 99.95mm
Bridge width: 19.92mm
Pickup bridge: 9.72 ohms
Neck pickup: 9.52 ohms
Frets: 1.87mm

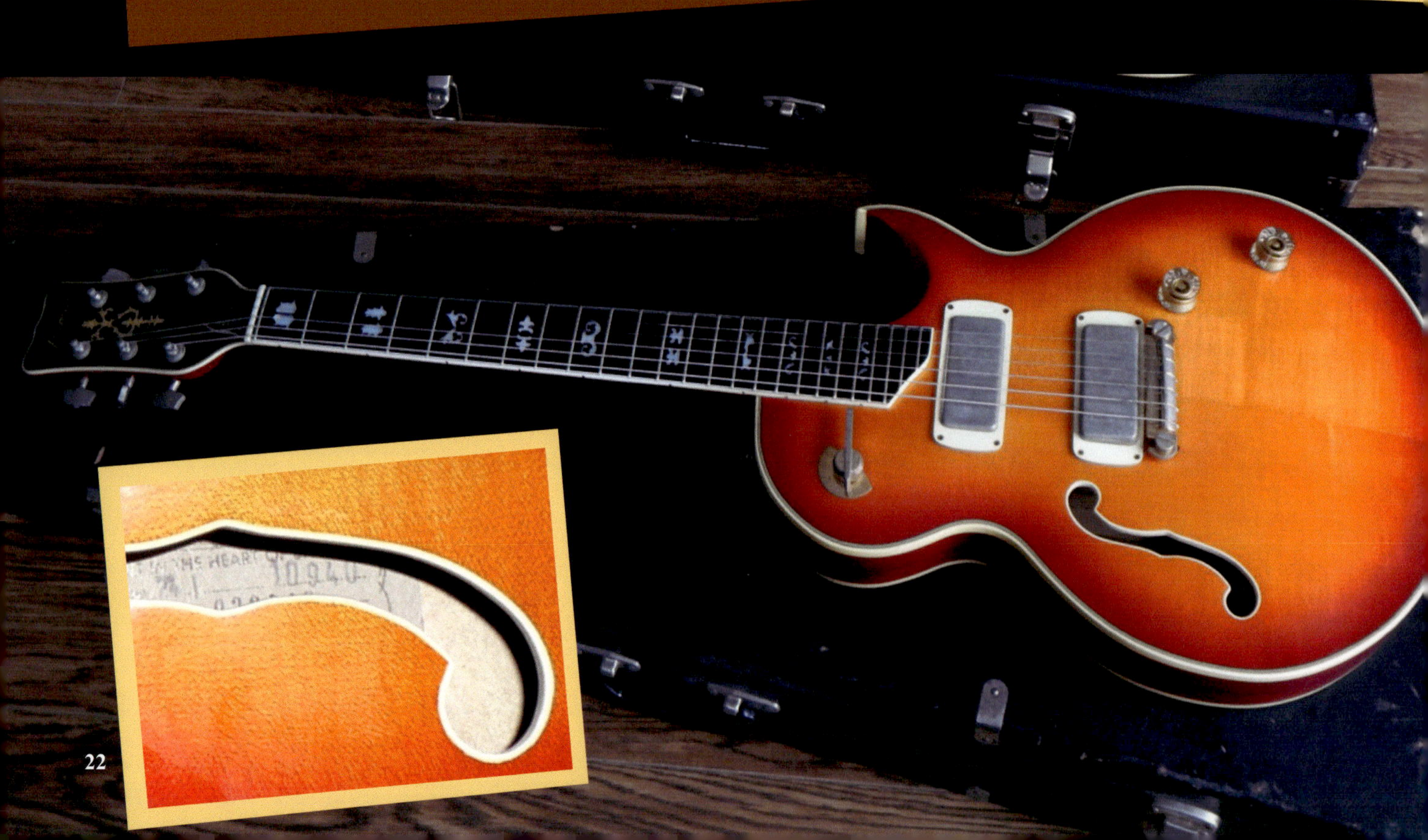

Harvey Goldsmith
1991 Gibson Les Paul
Hall of Fame Deluxe Edition

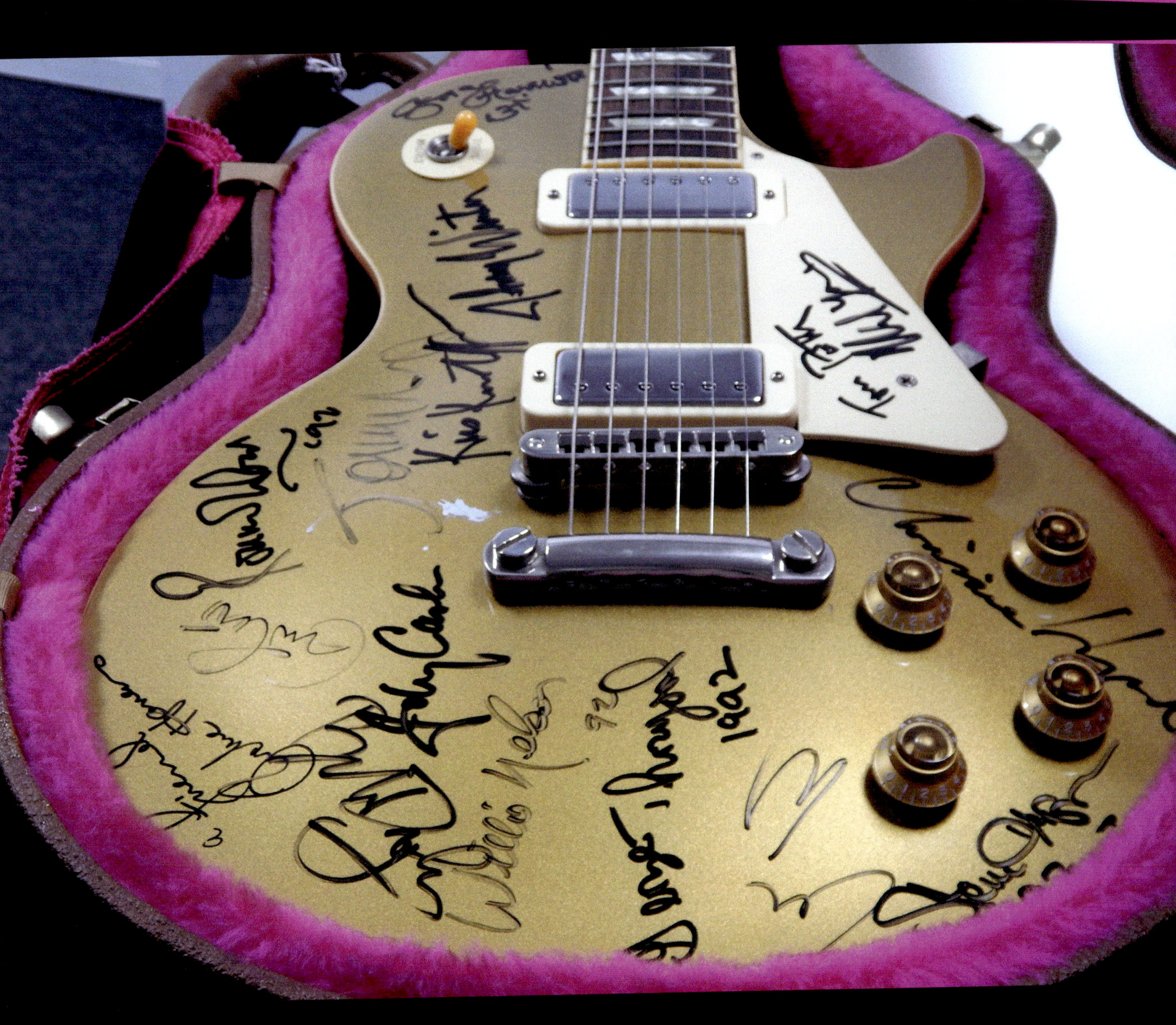

Concert promoter and producer Harvey Goldsmith was responsible for bringing together some of the biggest concerts and live shows ever. What is not widely known is that he is also a huge collector of pop memorabilia. Many pieces in his collection were given to him by the artists he worked with and this signed Les Paul was from the 30th Anniversary Concert to celebrate the career and music of Bob Dylan held at Madison Square Garden, New York City. Six weeks before the concert was scheduled, Bob Dylan personally called Harvey Goldsmith for help with the concert idea. There was to be a huge and impressive line up. Harvey accepted the job and ensured it was organised and managed properly.

Many of the acts had already been approached by Dylan's team to perform, but when they knew that Harvey was to be the promoter they agreed they would be available to play. The concert was a huge event for Bob Dylan, it was also an important anniversary concert as it became one of the first big events of its kind to happen in the U.S.A. This guitar was signed by various artists on the night including Bob Dylan, Eric Clapton, George Harrison, Willie Nelson, Johnny Cash, Chrissie Hynde, Tom Petty, Ronnie Wood, Johnny Winter, Kris Kristofferson, Neil Young and Stevie Wonder.

Only 200-250 of these guitars were produced during 1991 and some of these were fitted with Seymour Duncan 'Antiquity' P90 pickups instead of the mini humbuckers.

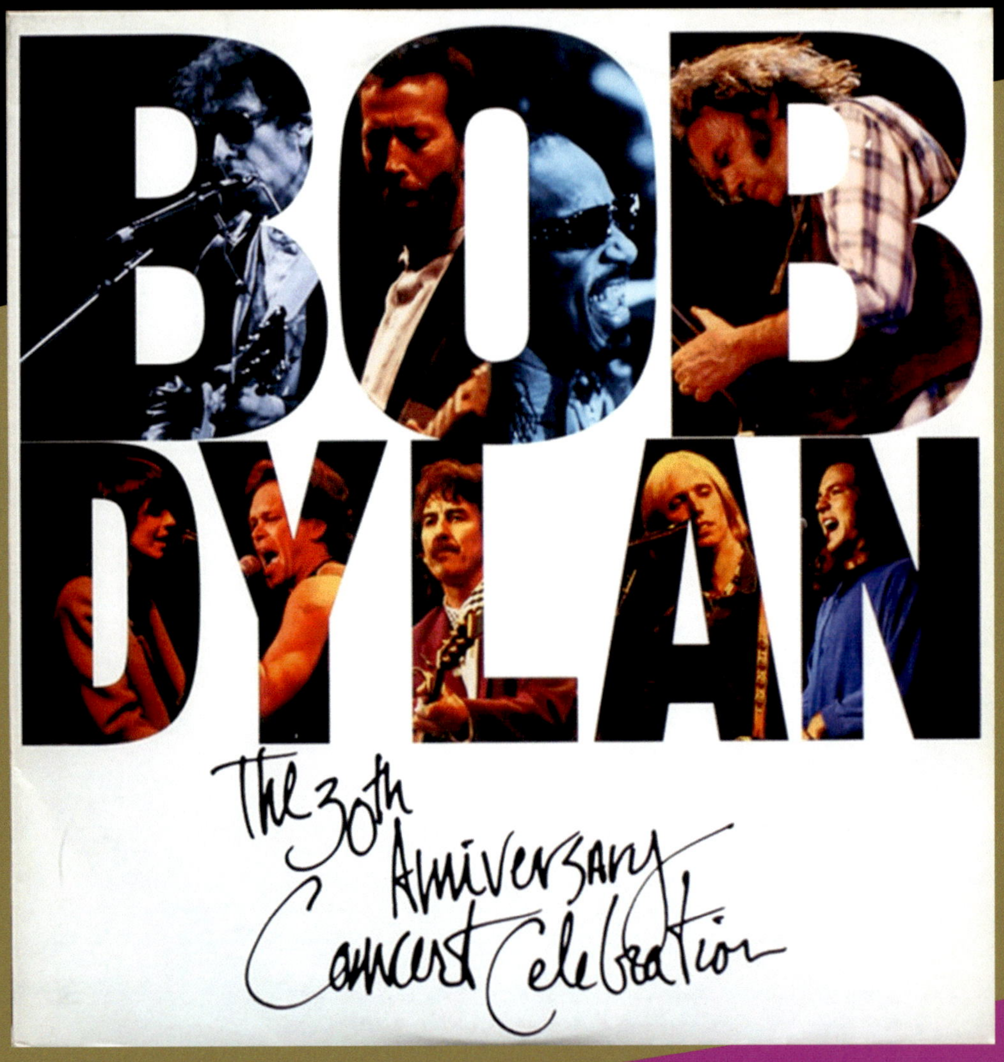

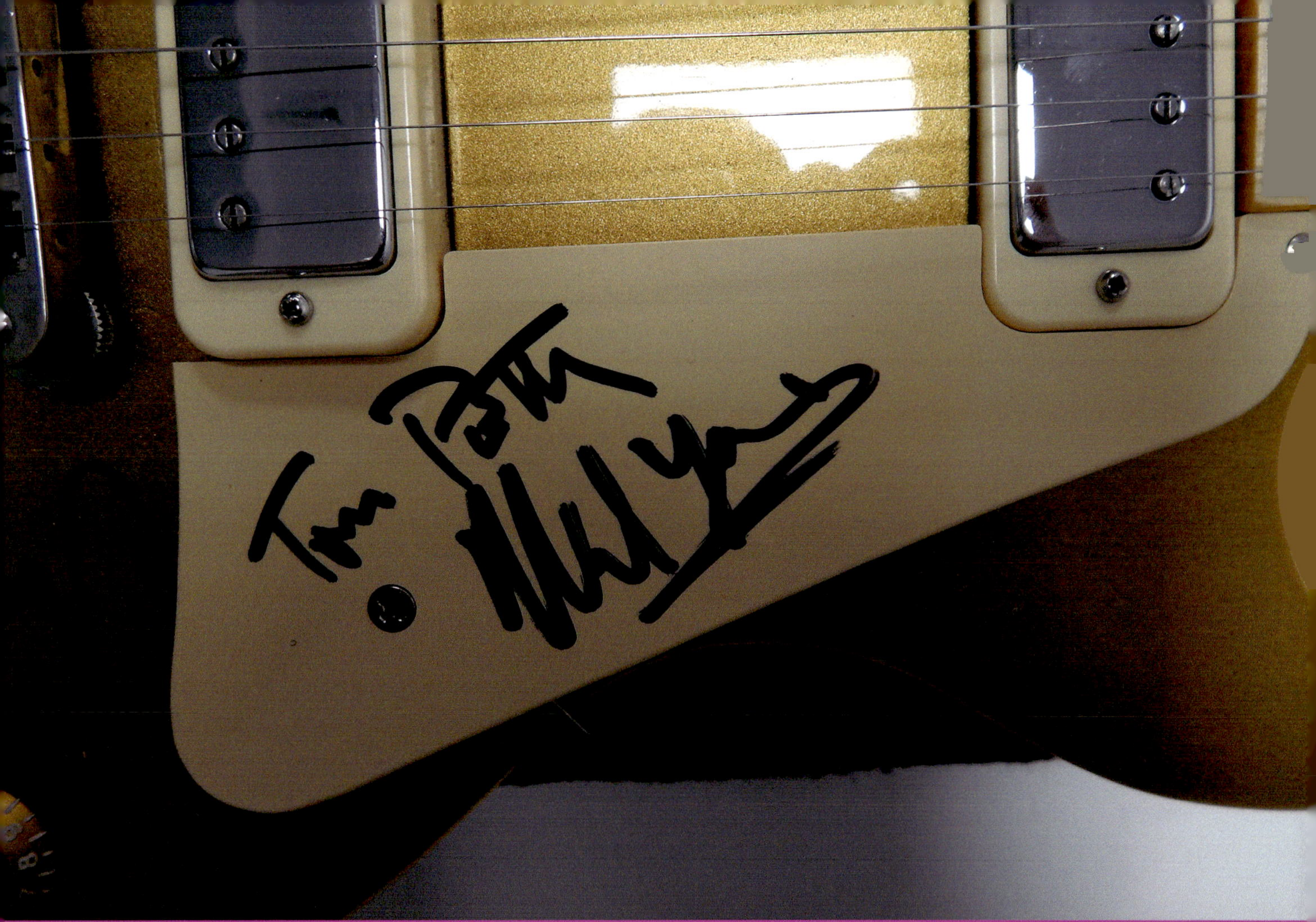

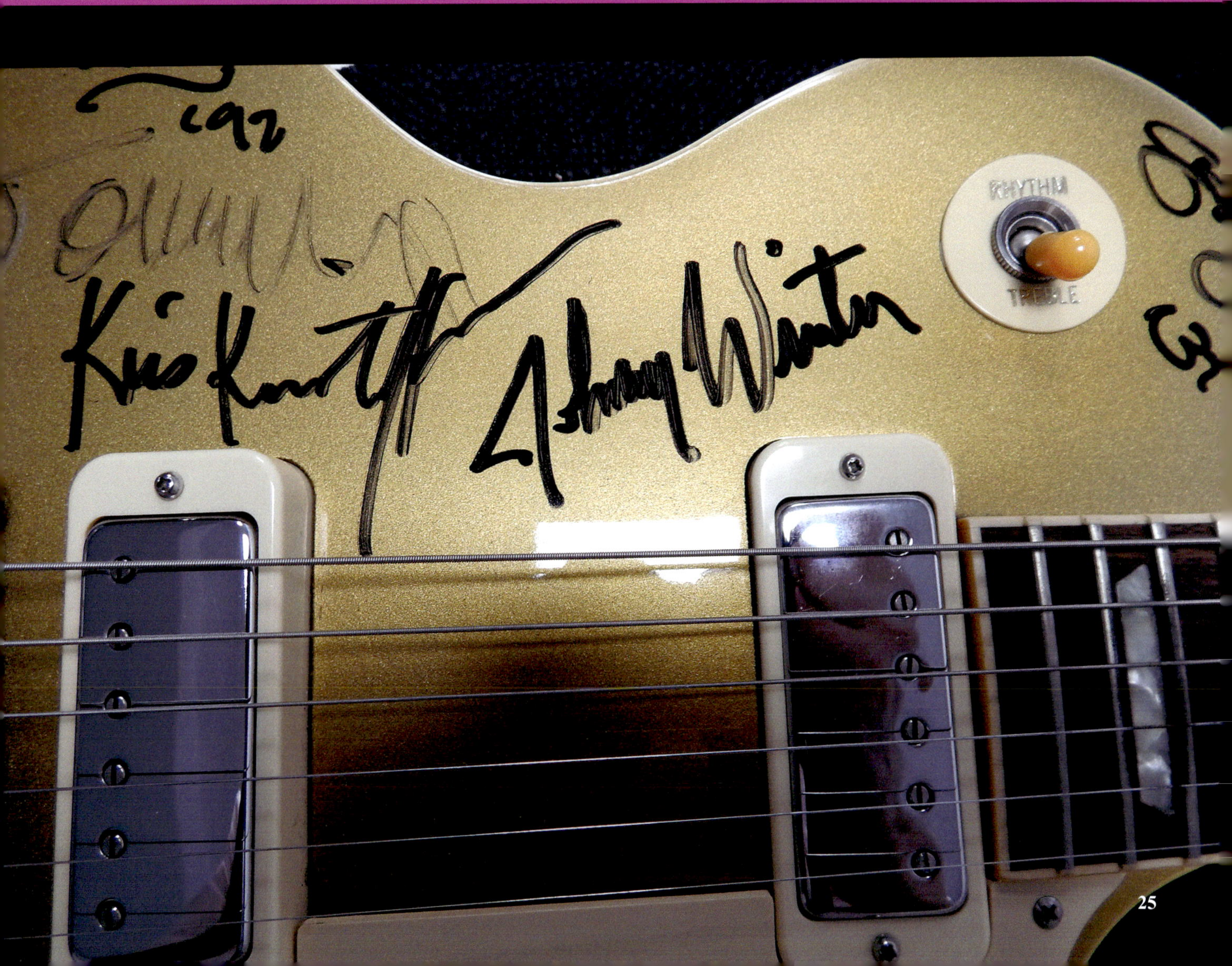

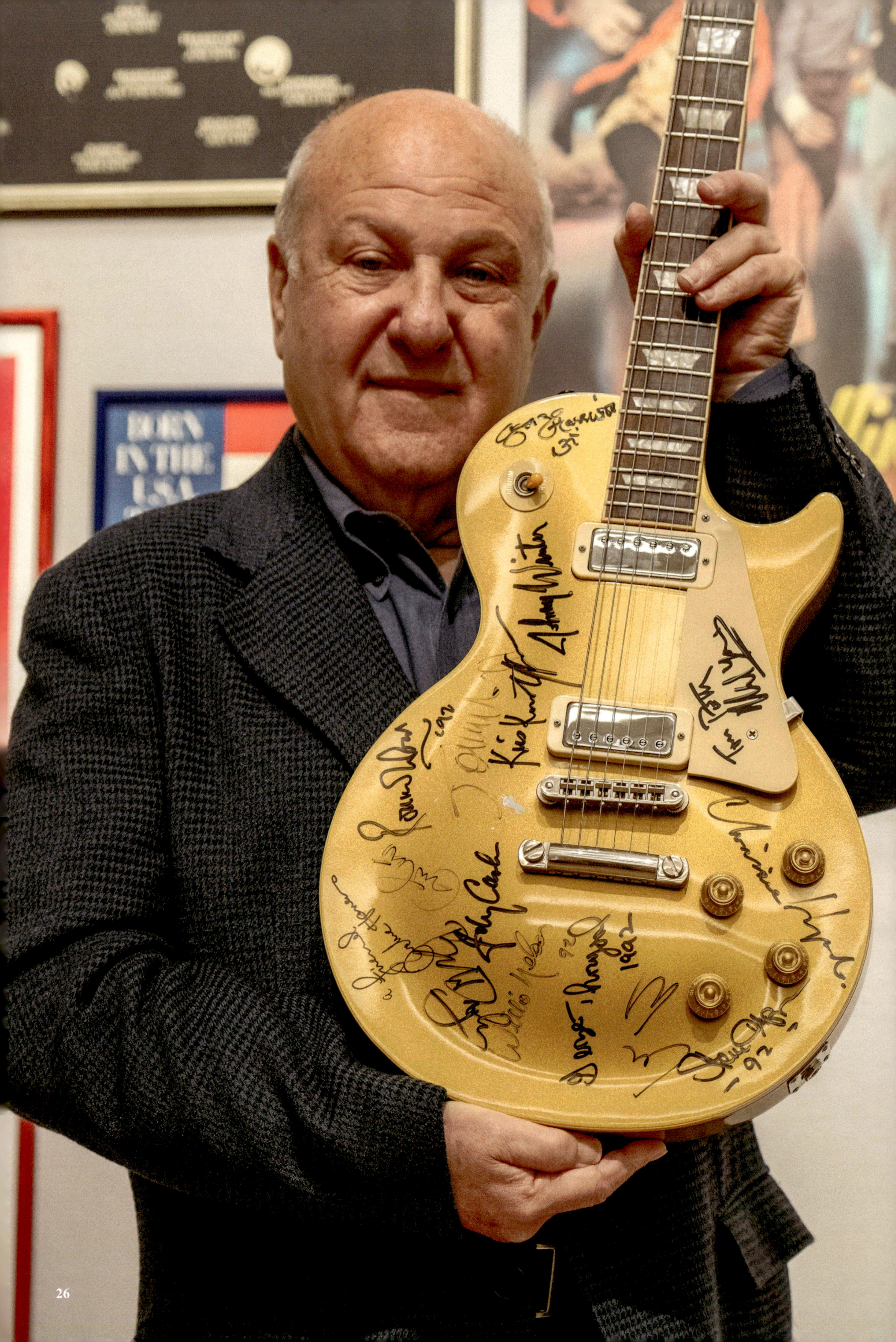

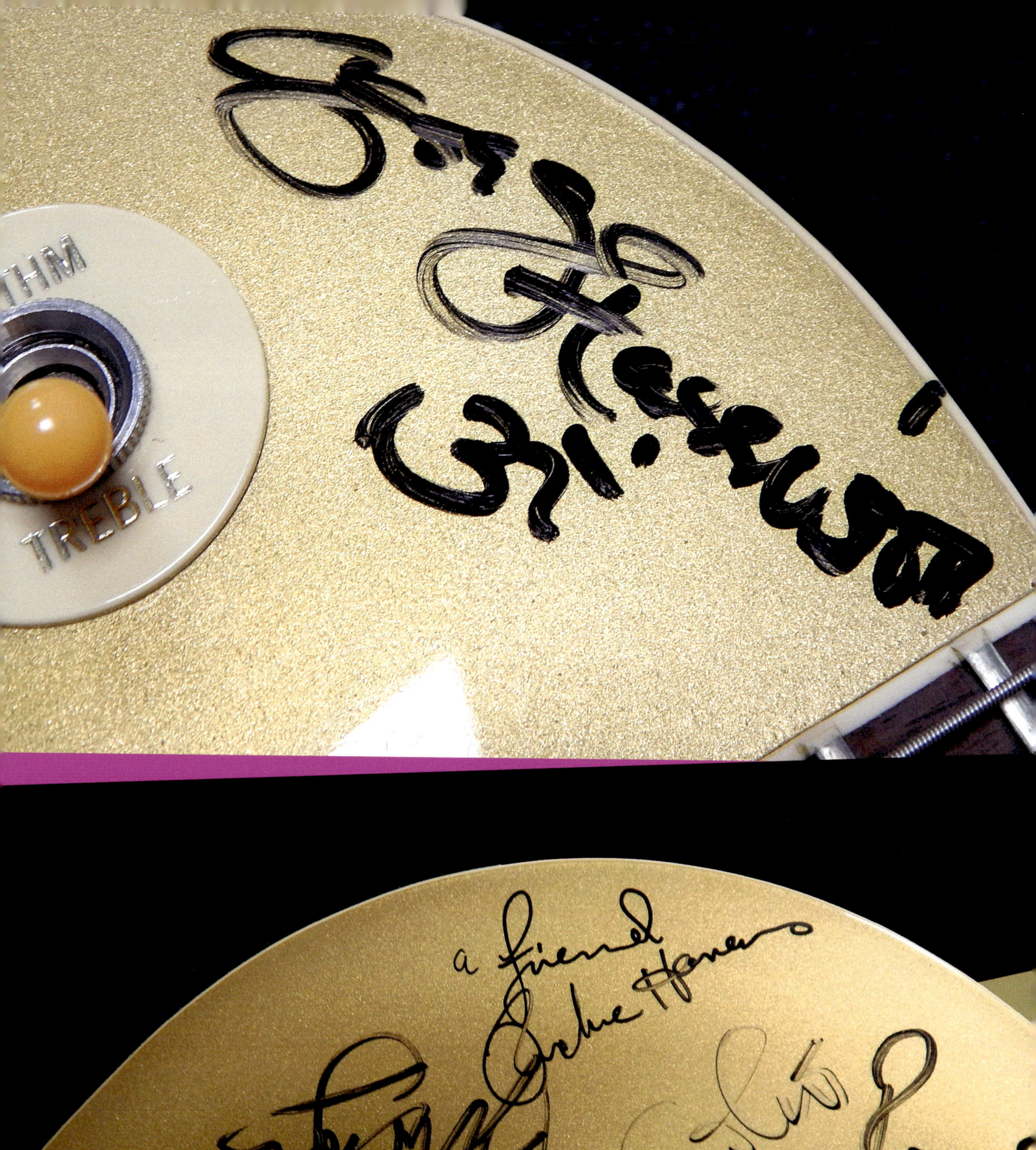

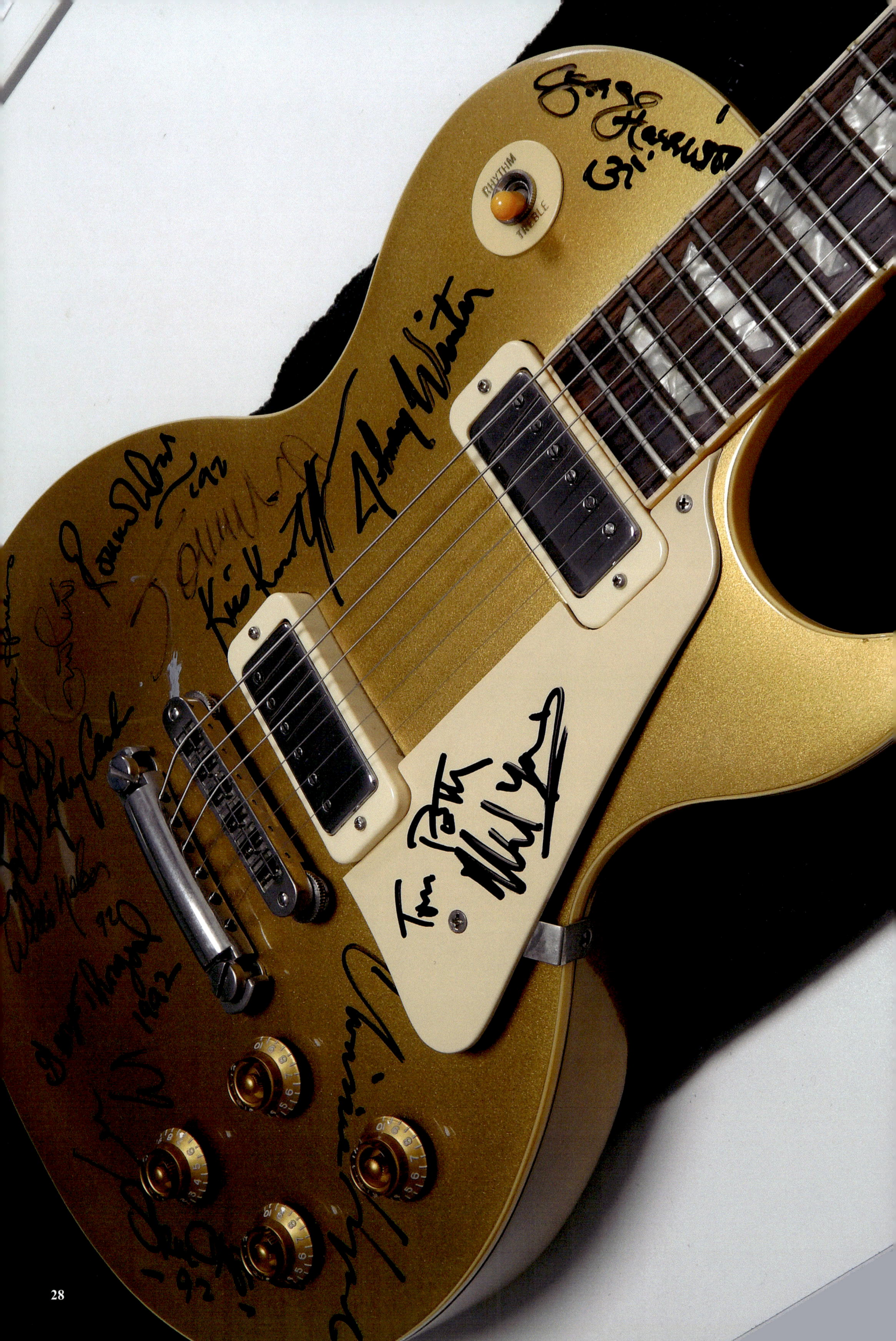

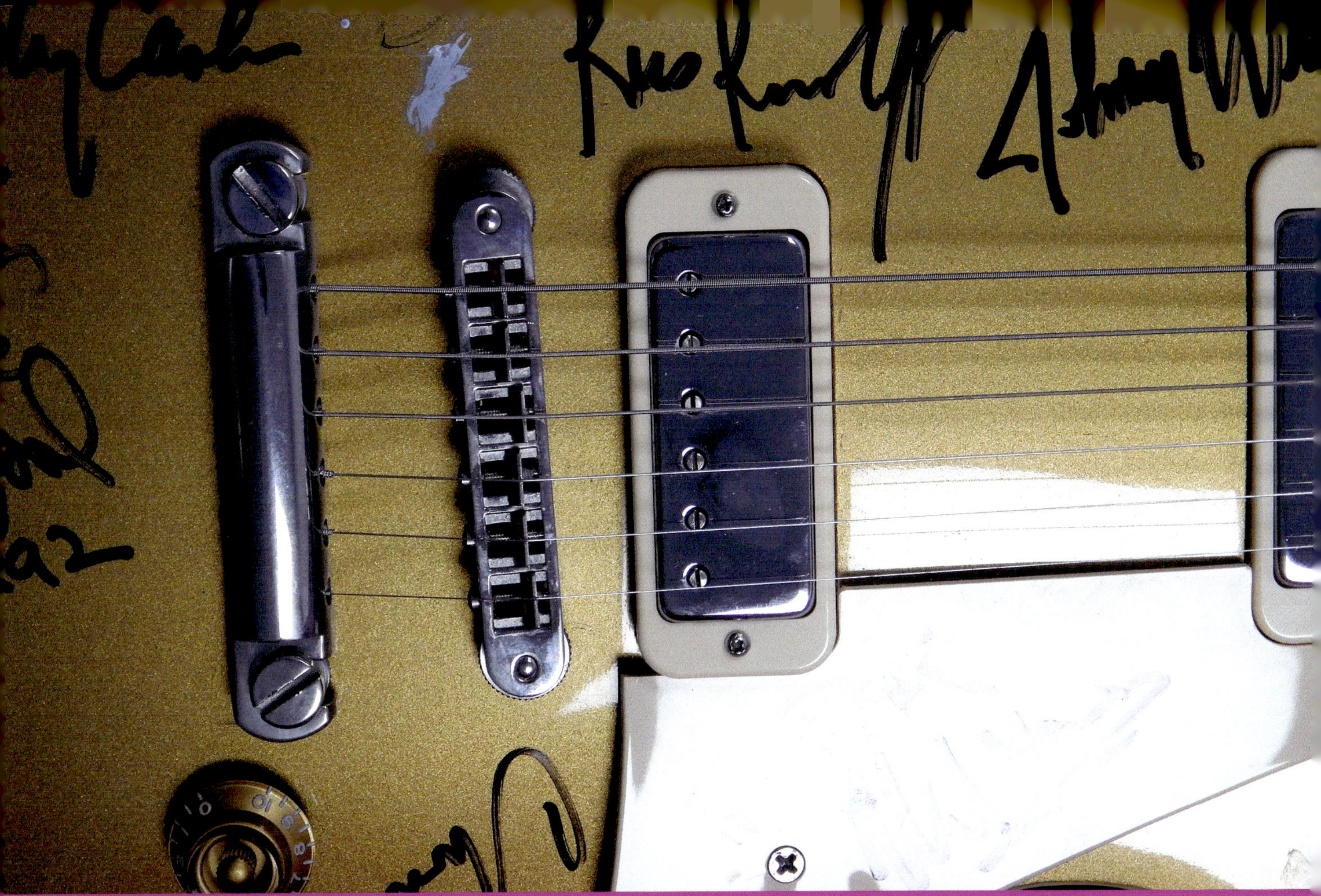

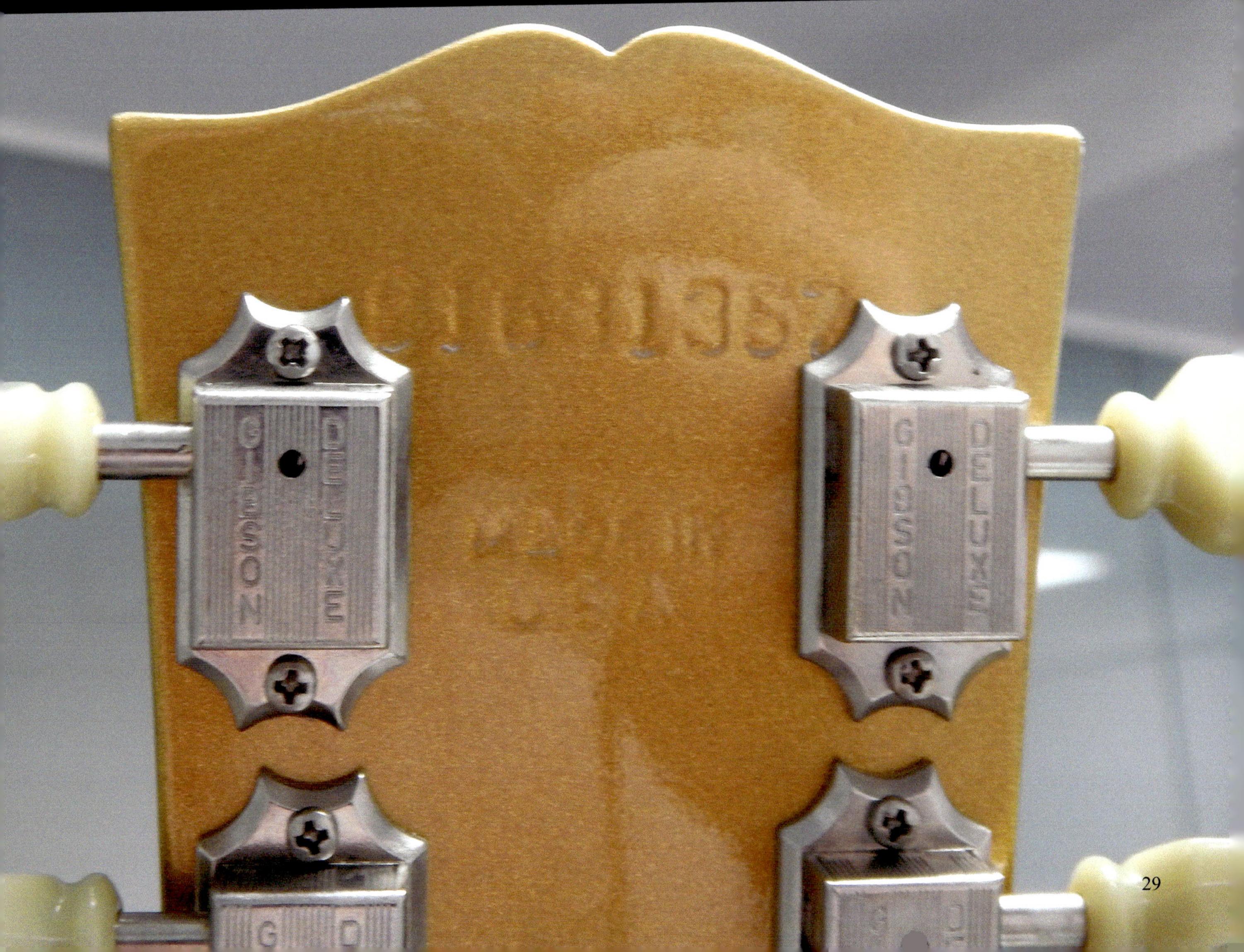

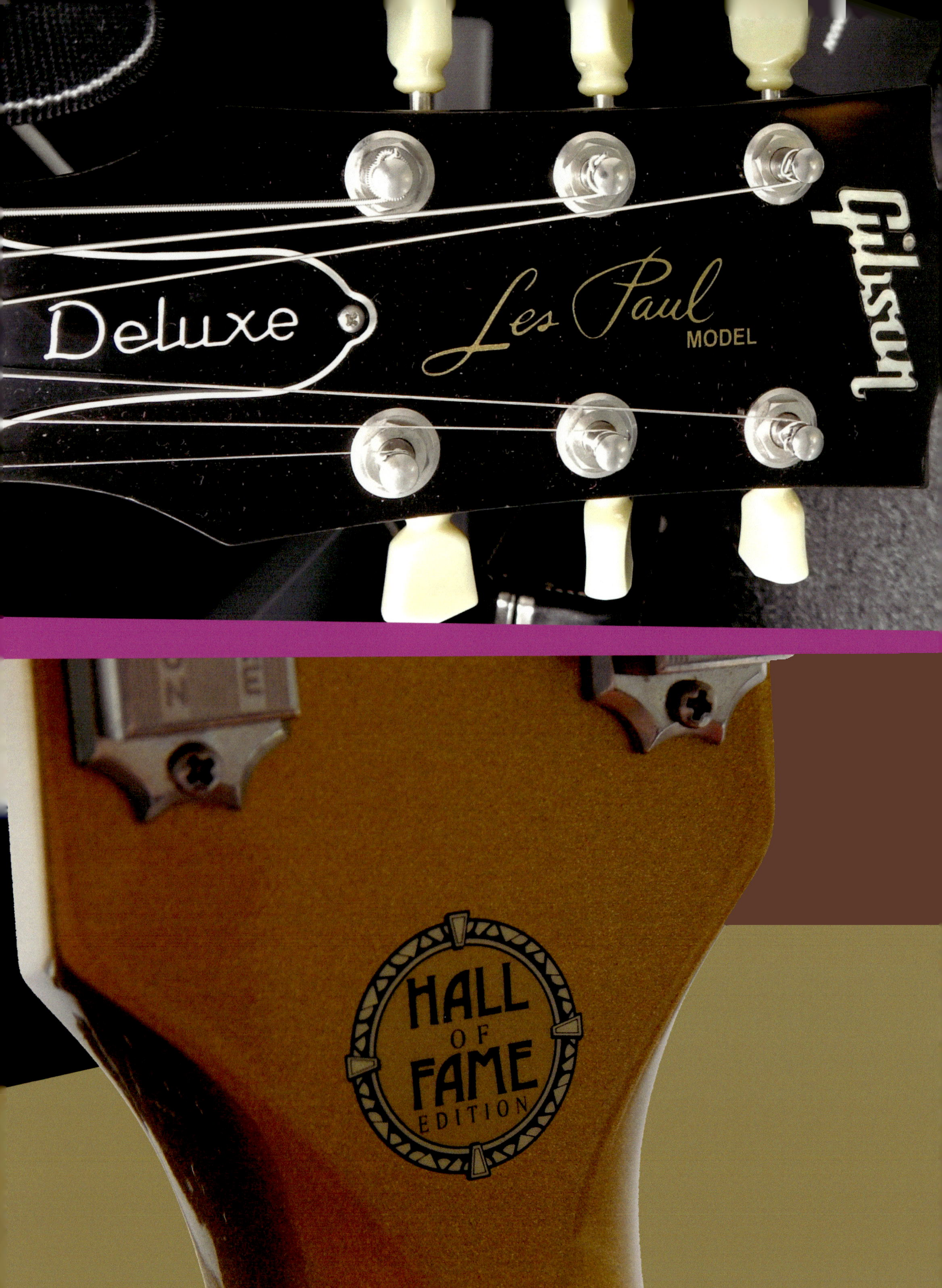
Deluxe
Les Paul
MODEL
Gibson
HALL
OF
FAME
EDITION

There was slight cracking in the lower horn where the maple neck meets the mahogany body, but the volume and tone controls worked fine and no neck adjustment was necessary.

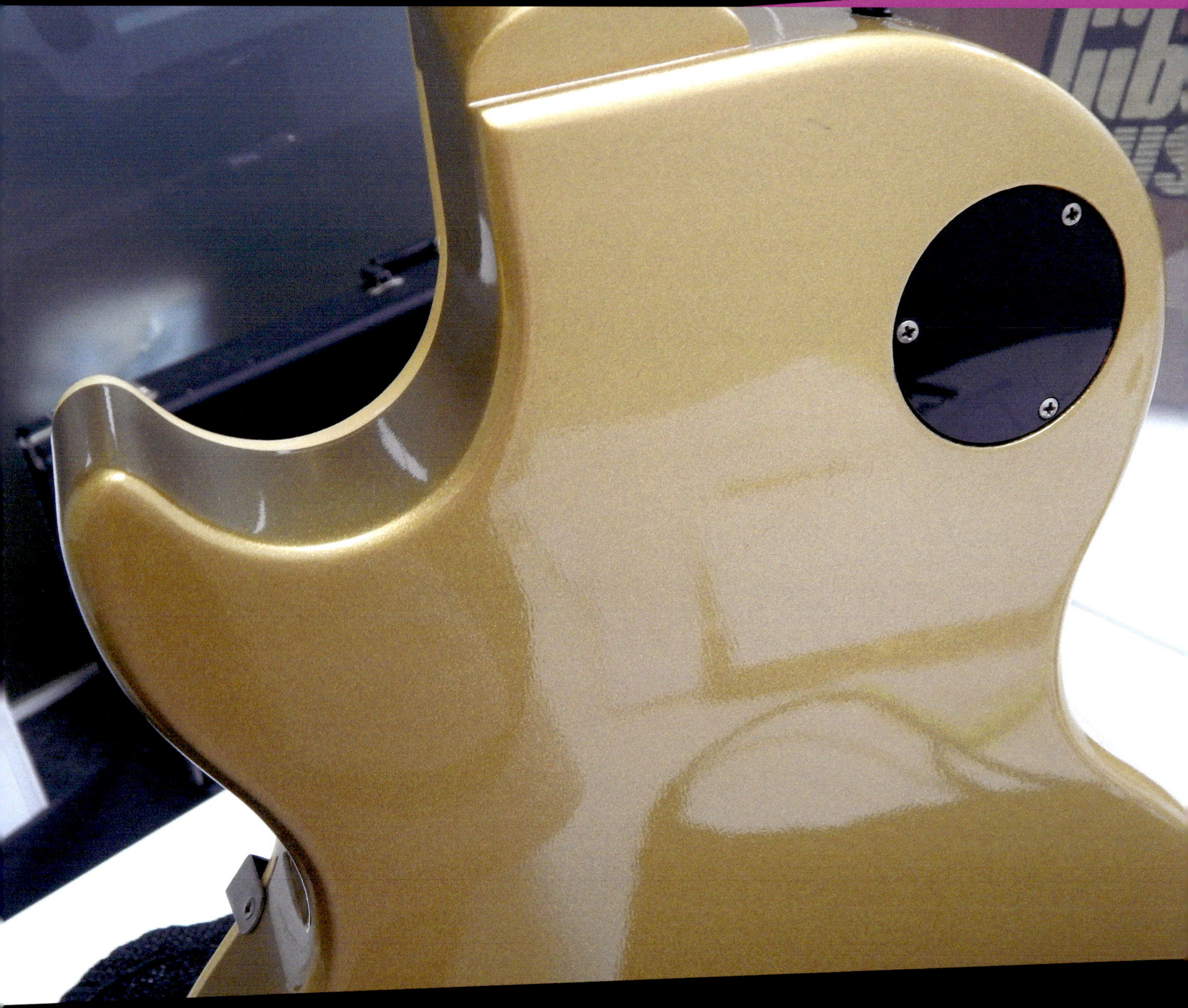

From the Bob Dylan 30th Anniversary Concert Celebration, Recorded on October 16, 1992, at Madison Square Garden in New York City

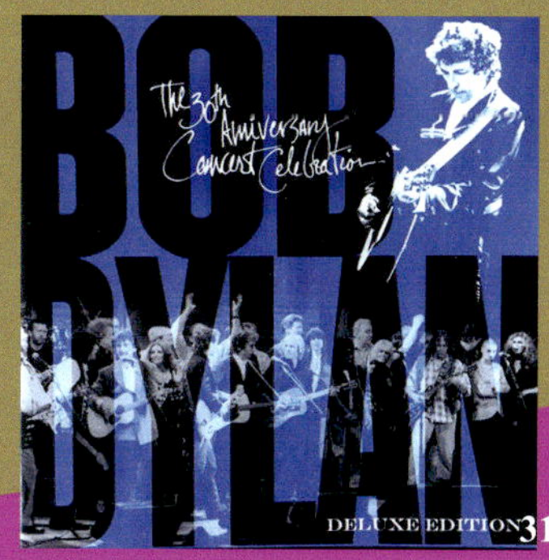

KK Downing – Judas Priest

KK Downing is one of the founding members of heavy metal band Judas Priest. He left the band after 40 years in 2011. He has always been associated with the Flying V guitar and has used various custom maker models over the years. Some of his guitars were included in an auction at Bonhams Knightsbridge in December 2018 and I was lucky enough to take a look at some of them and take some measurements prior to sale. The gold Hamer V also sold at a later auction.

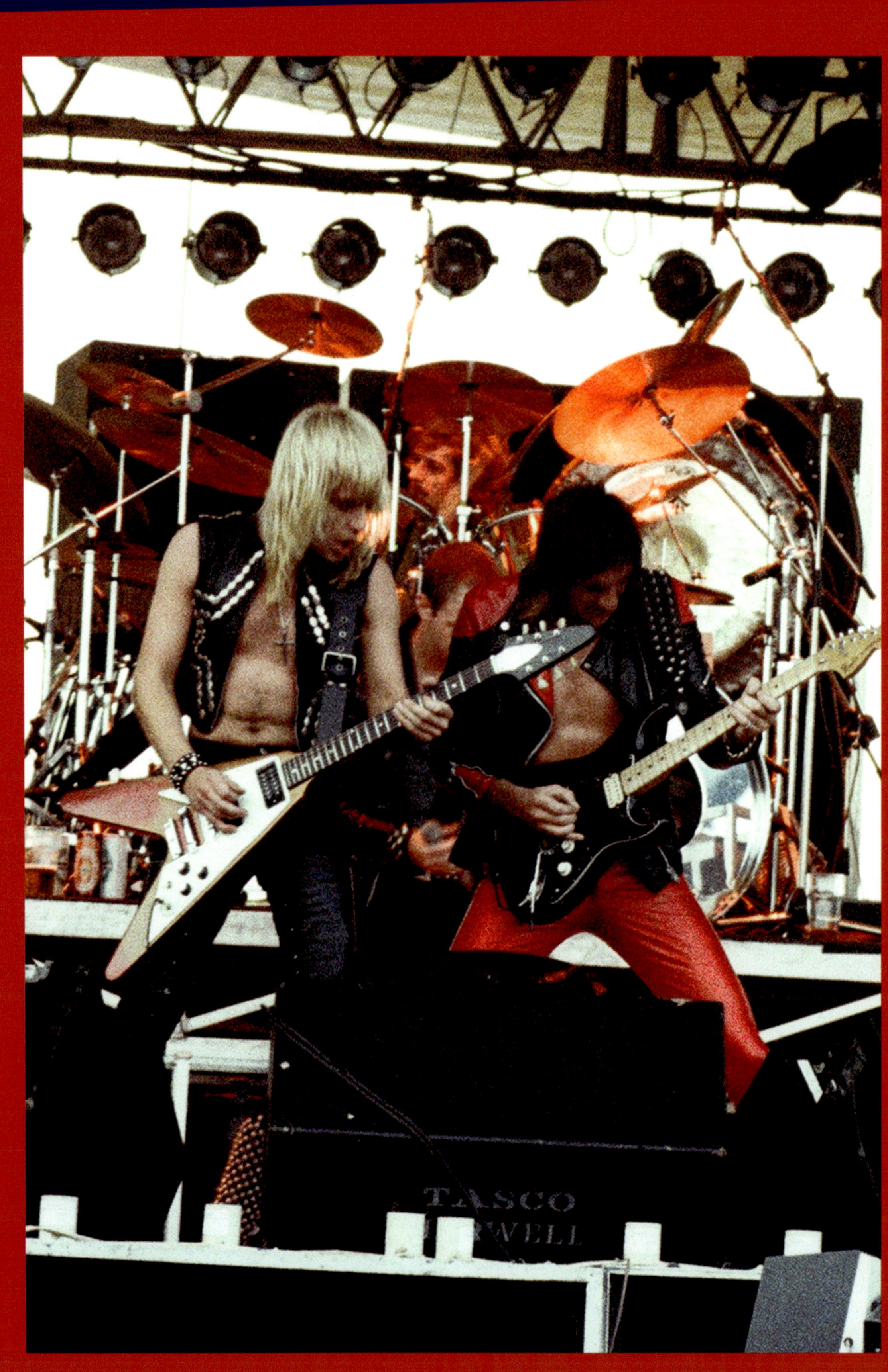

Paul Hamer (Hamer guitars) approached KK with the idea of producing a Flying V for him. Touring with his 1967 and 1971 Gibson Flying V's was becoming a worry, in the case they got lost or were stolen. KK very much liked this idea. He played this guitar a lot and it was used on 'The Defenders of Faith' album. Floyd Rose also came to visit KK in Seattle and brought with him a prototype bridge claiming Eddie (Van Halen) had the other one. Hamer then fitted this on the V and KK was more than happy with the result.

1971 Gibson Flying V

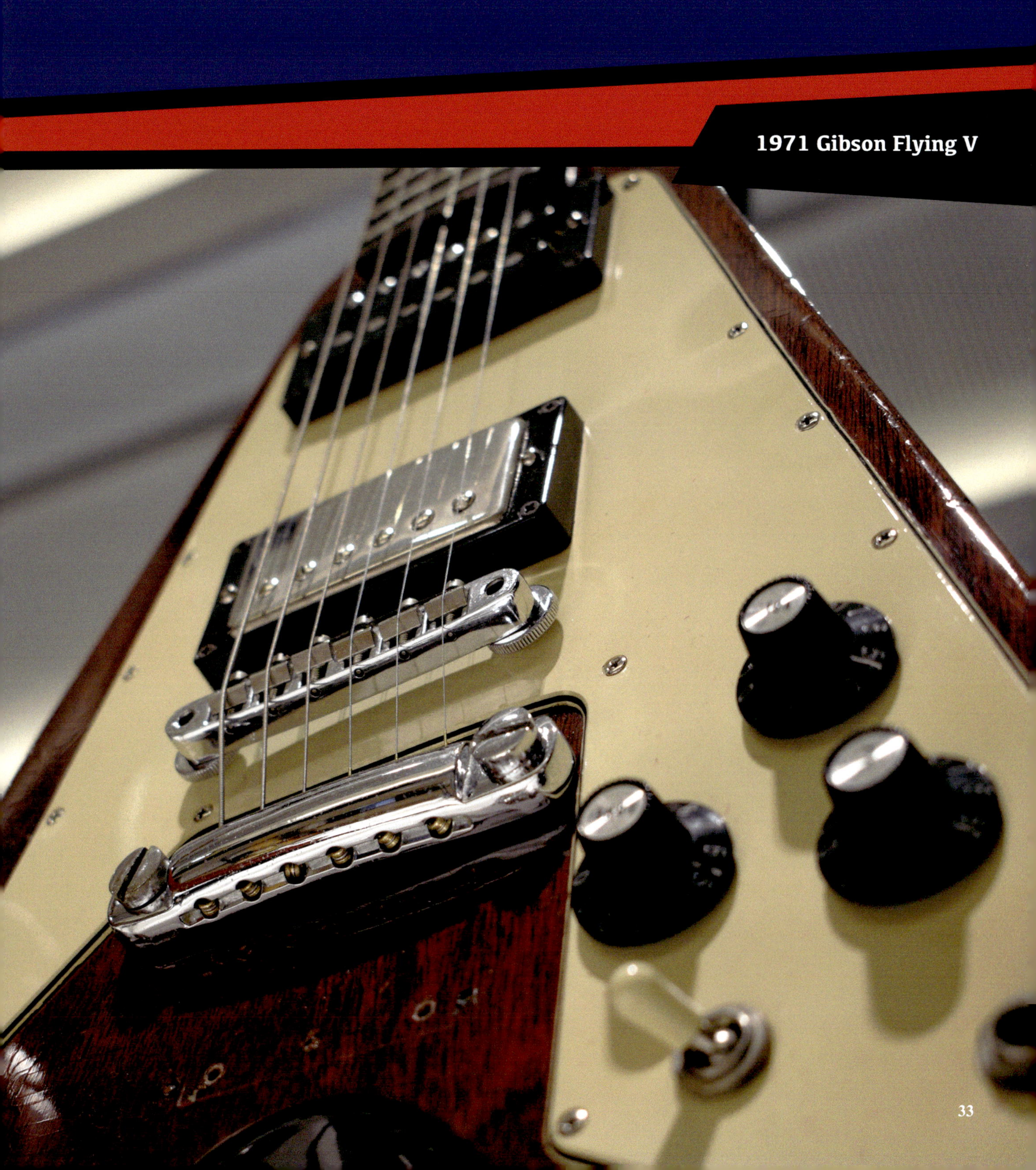

The 1971 Flying V was bought from a guy in the South of England. It is part of a limited edition series of 500 made between 1970-71. This one is number 233. He changed the machine heads to Grovers and there is a scarf joint across the back of the headstock, just below the two E Tuners. You can also see it is a different piece of wood.

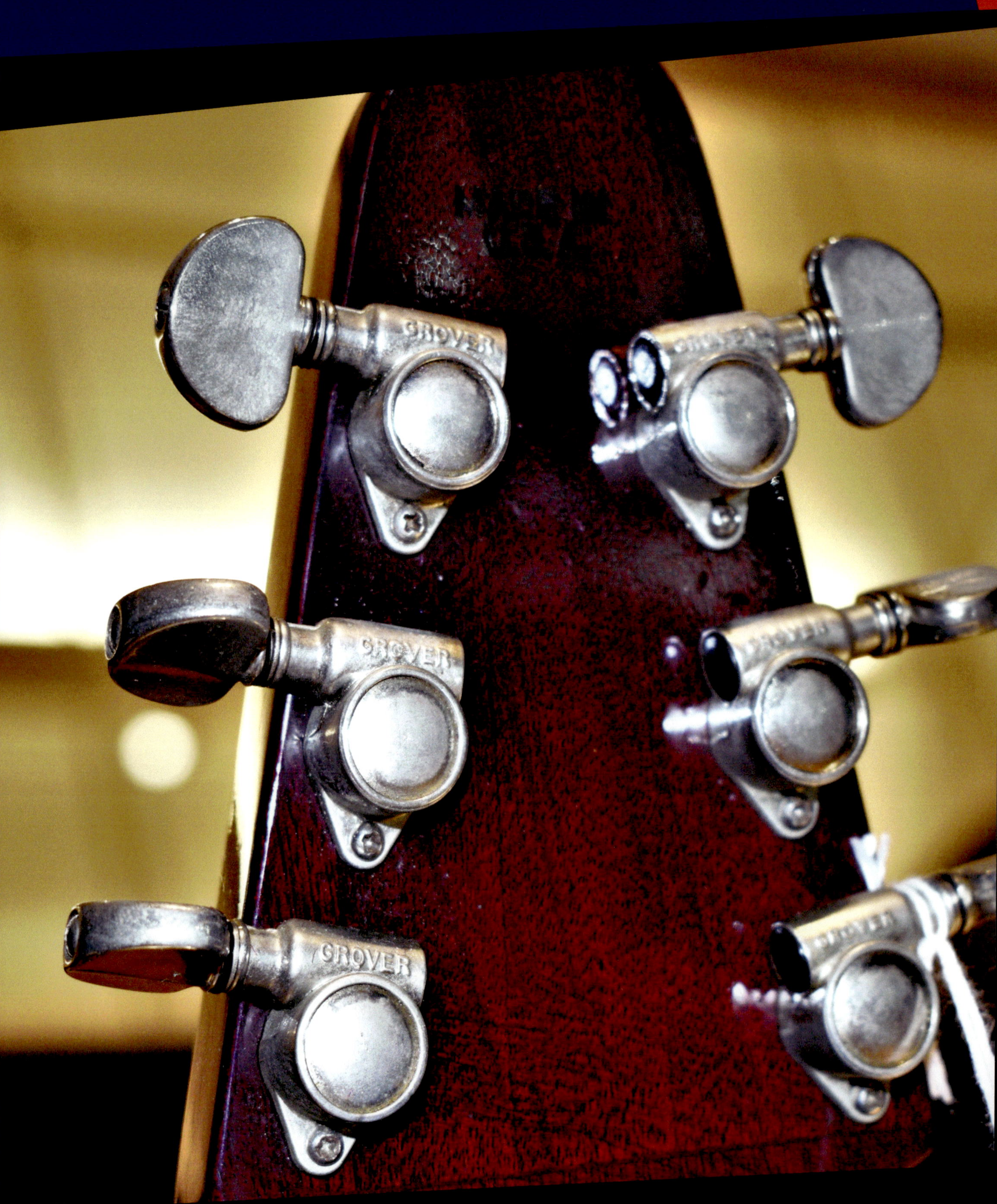

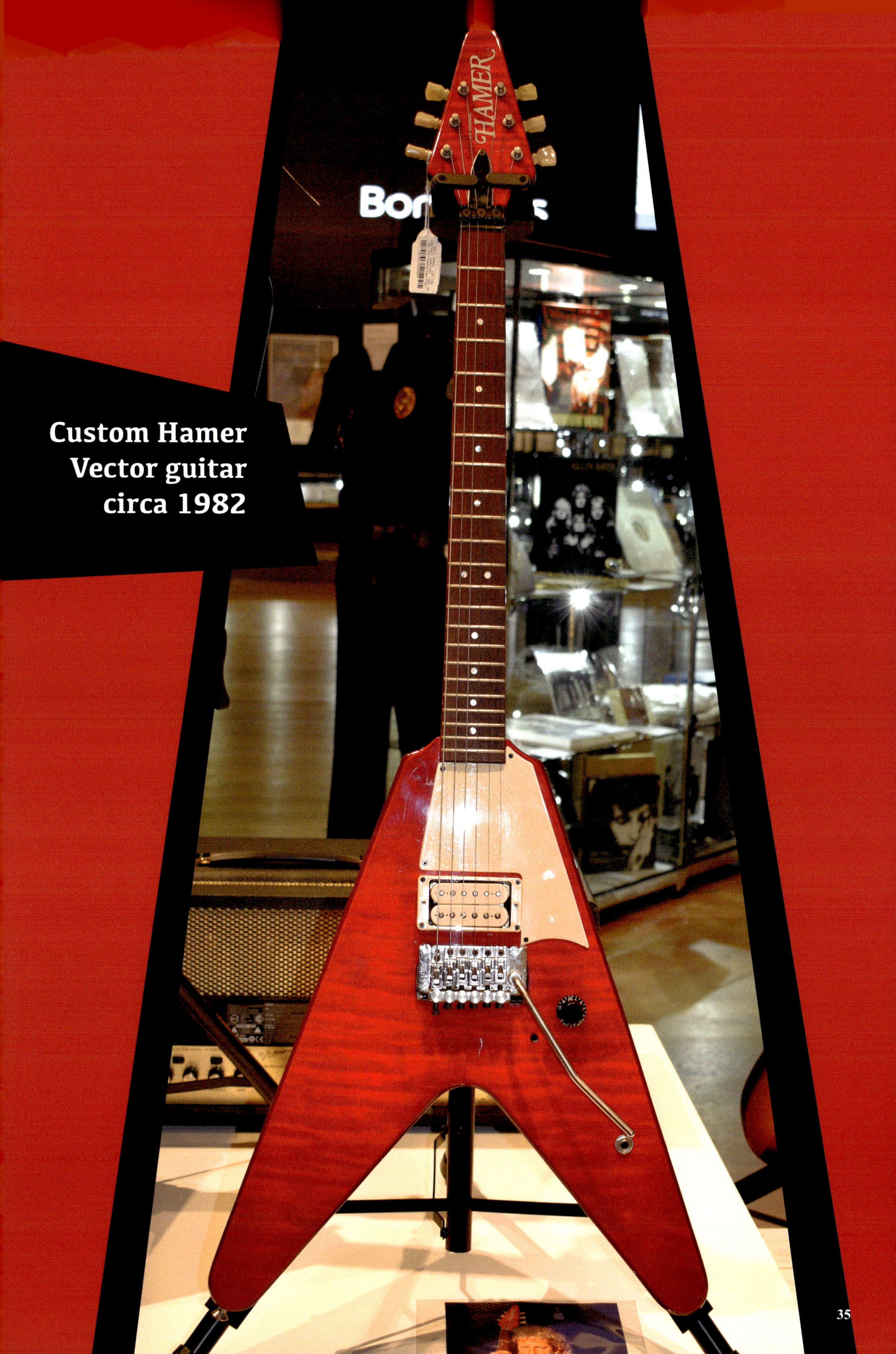

Custom Hamer Vector guitar circa 1982

DiMarzio Humbucker
13.27 ohms

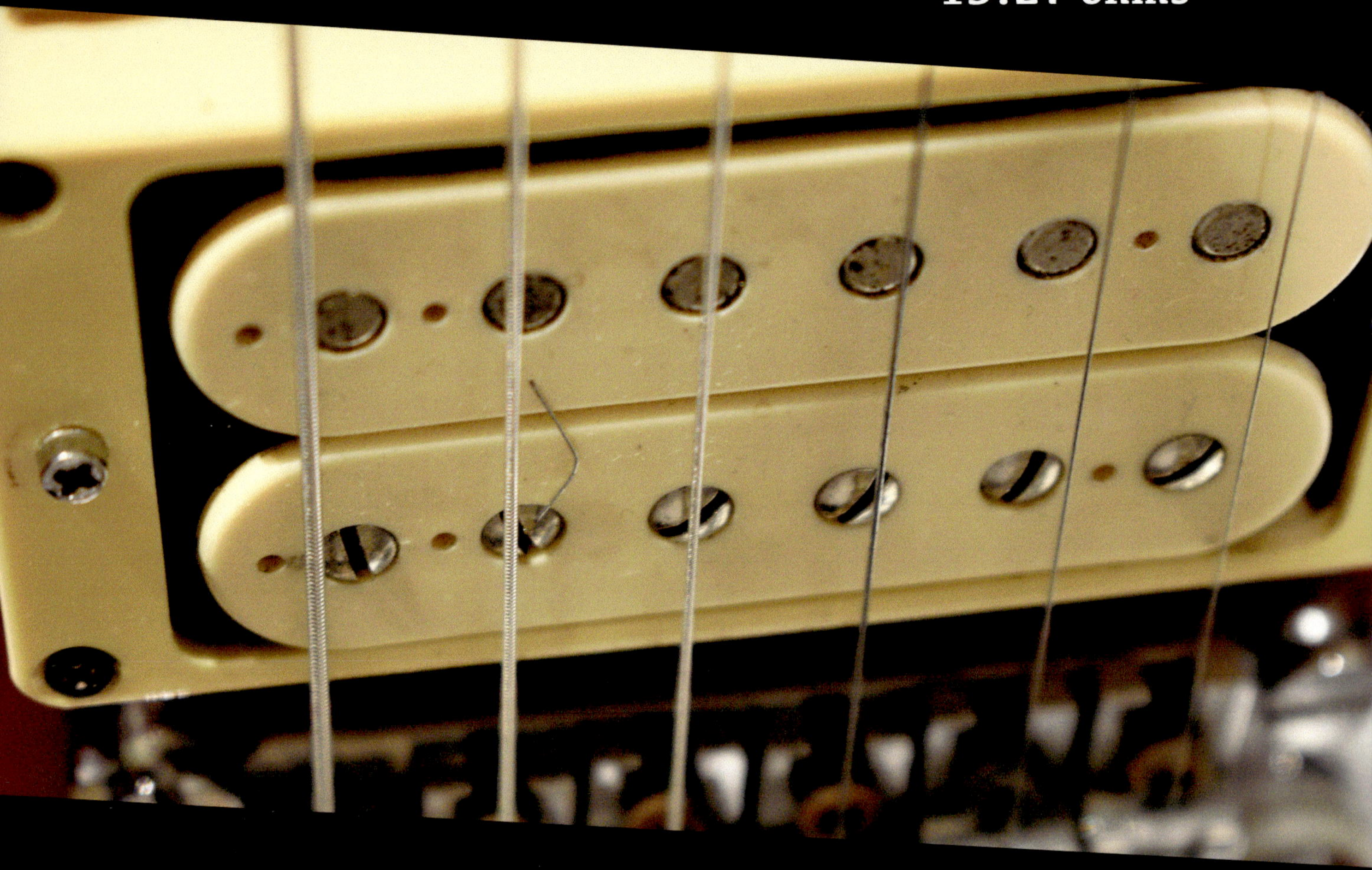

Floyd Rose Bridge
(Prototype)

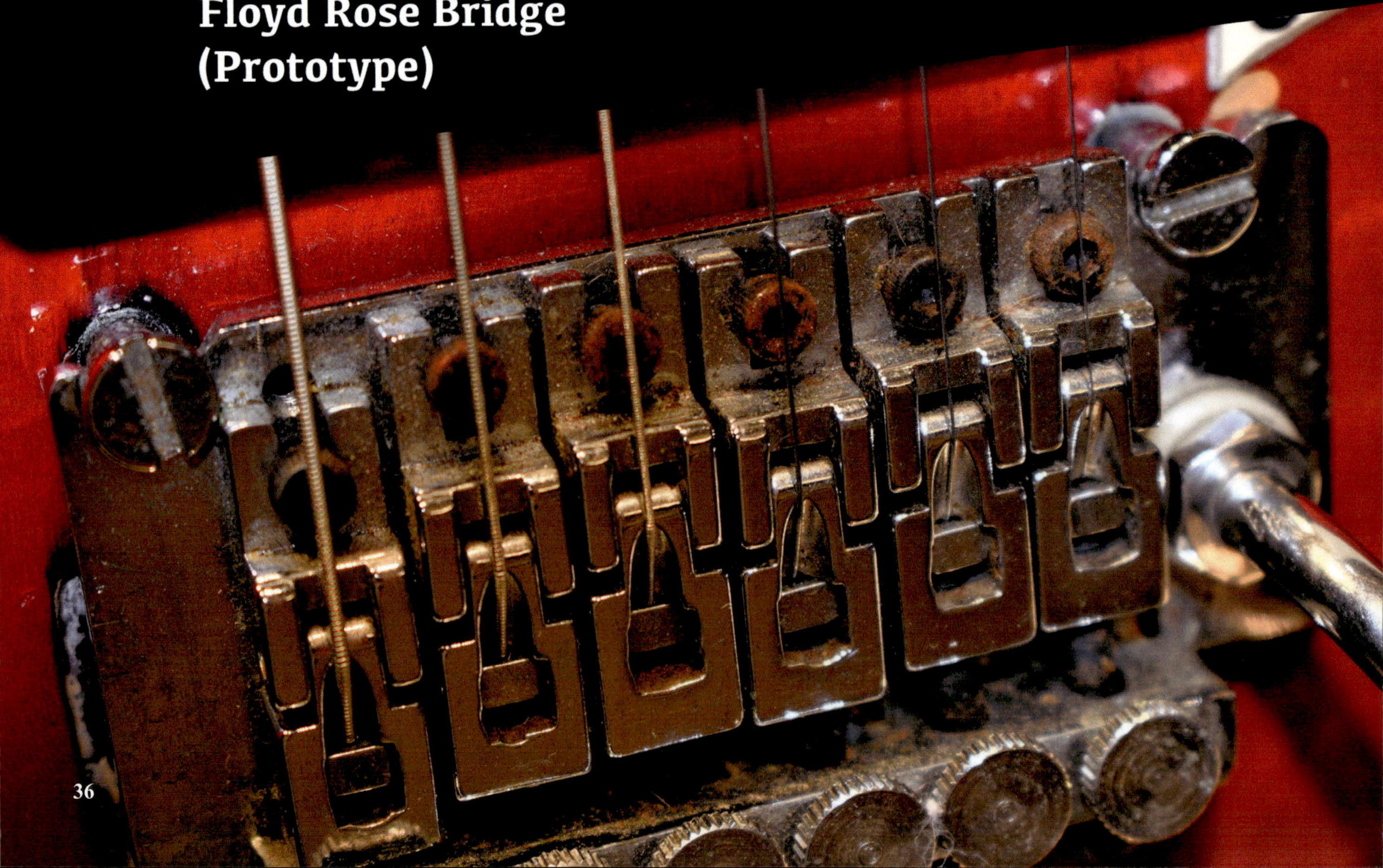

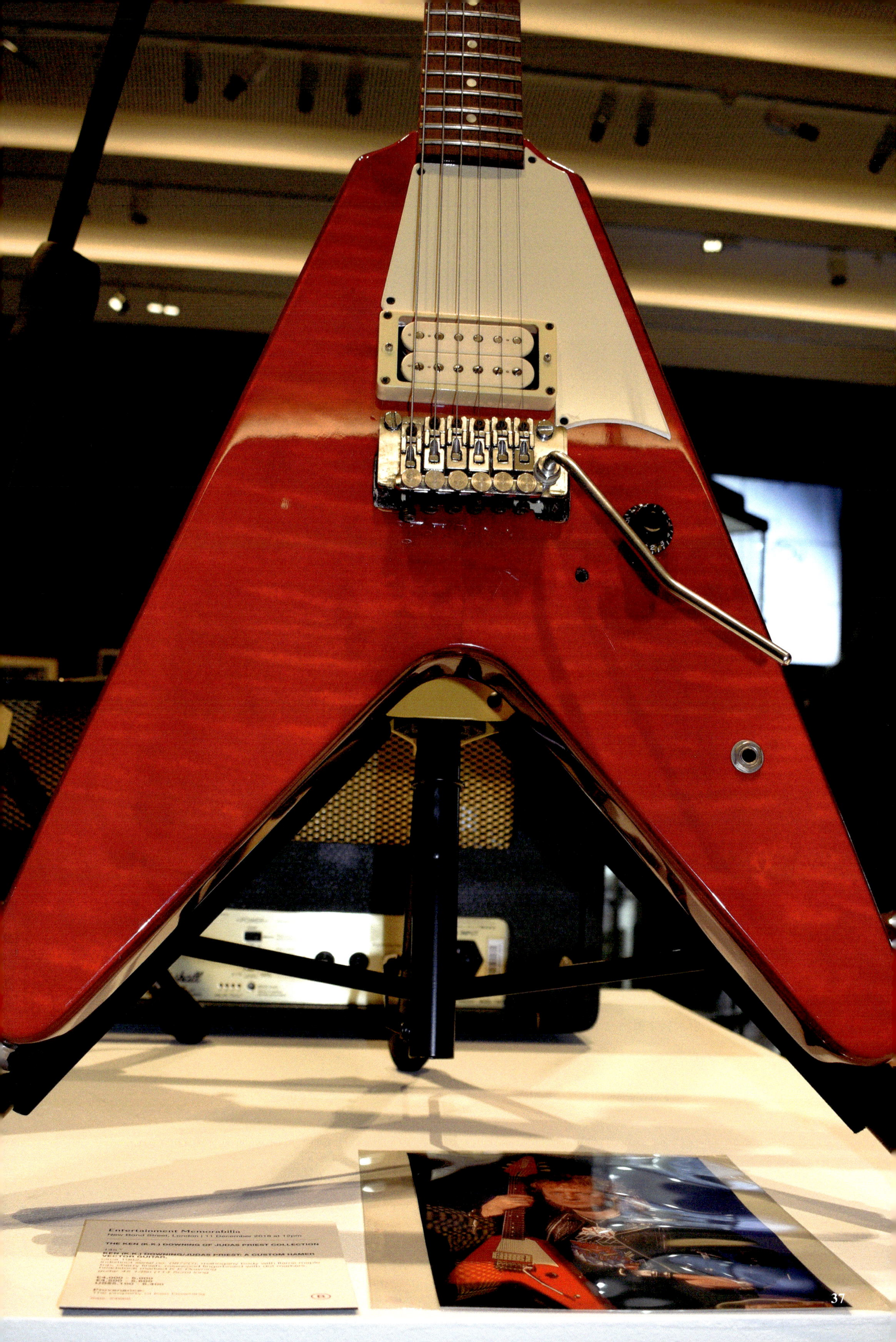

Entertainment Memorabilia
New Bond Street, London | 11 December 2018 at 12pm
THE KEN (K.K.) DOWNING OF JUDAS PRIEST COLLECTION
KEN (K.K.) DOWNING/JUDAS PRIEST: A CUSTOM HAMER VECTOR GUITAR,

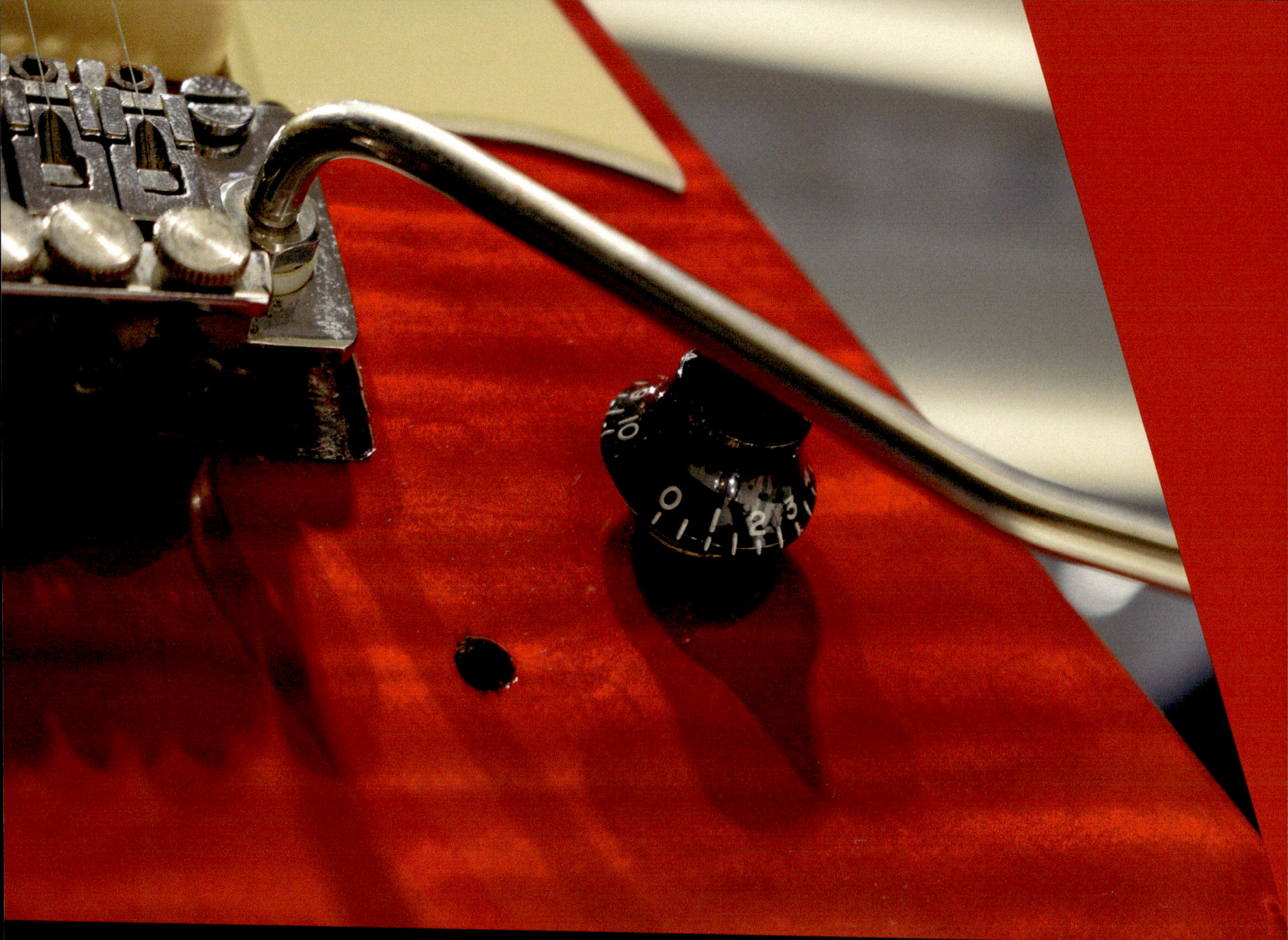

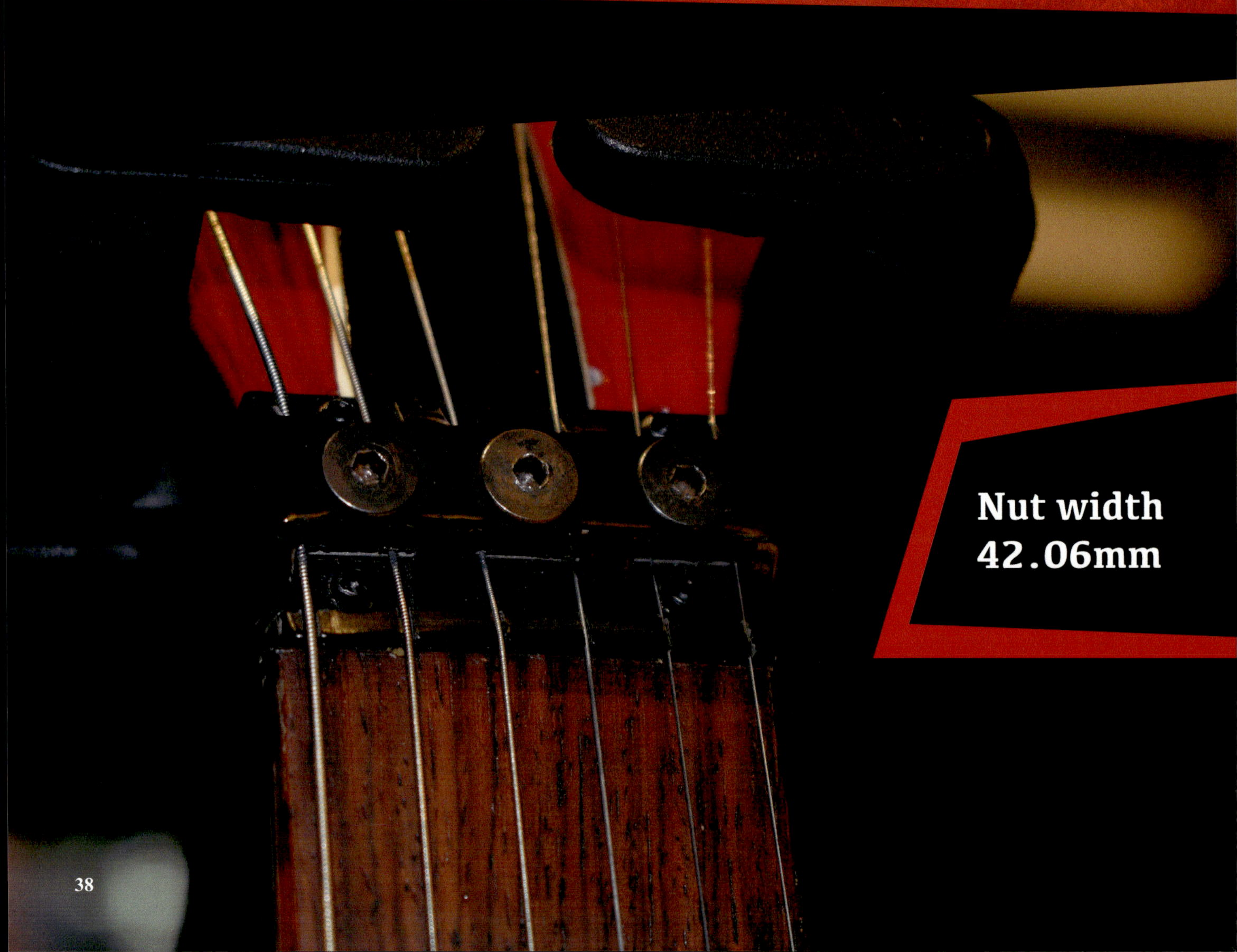

Nut width
42.06mm

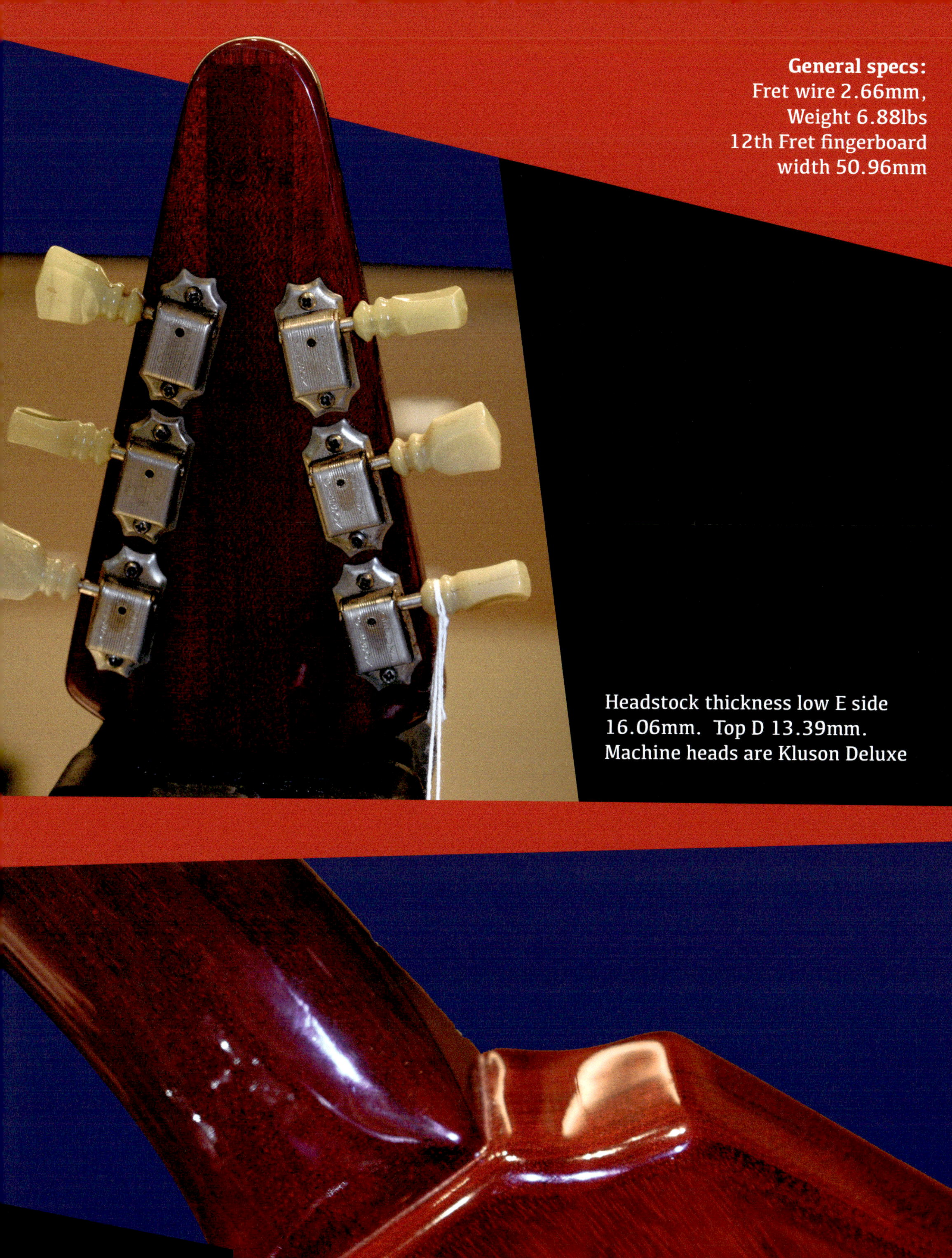
General specs:
Fret wire 2.66mm,
Weight 6.88lbs
12th Fret fingerboard
width 50.96mm

Headstock thickness low E side
16.06mm. Top D 13.39mm.
Machine heads are Kluson Deluxe

Body thickness at
upper horn near
strap button is
42.52mm

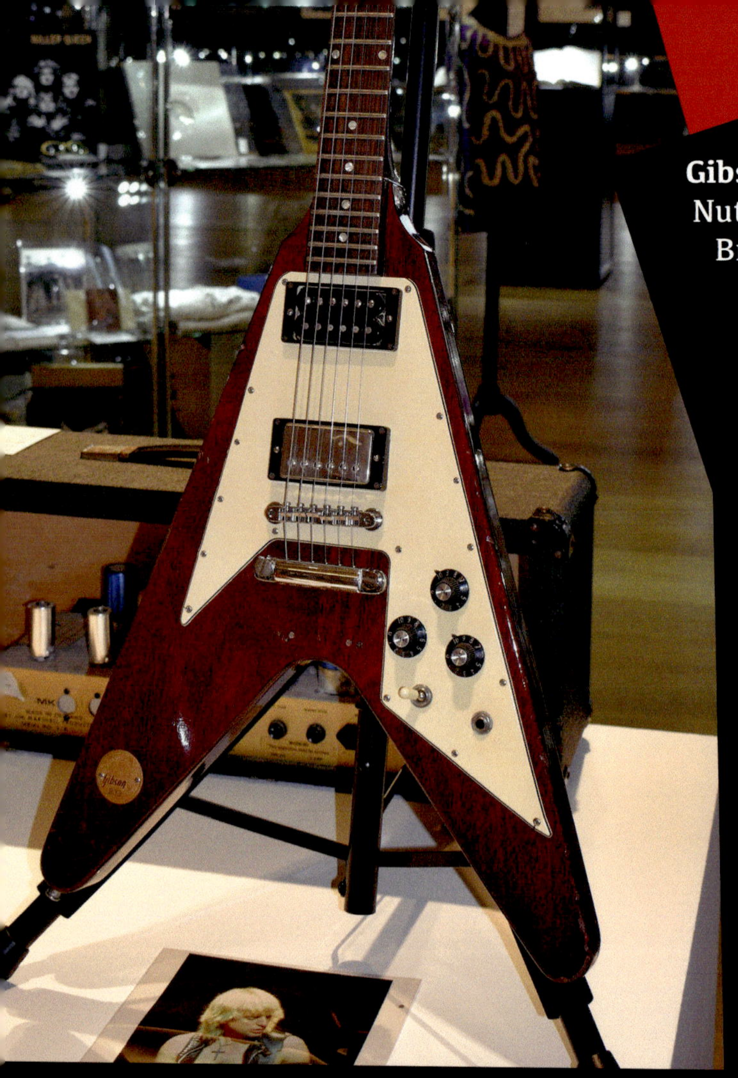

Gibson Flying V 1971:
Nut: 40.16mm
Bridge pickup: 8.21 ohms
Neck pickup: 8.13 ohms
12th fret fingerboard:
width 50.46mm
Headstock thickness:
Low E 16.92mm & Top D 16.40mm,
Weight: 6.52lbs
Machine heads: Grover
Upper body thickness:
34.37mm and lower horn 34.78mm
There was some damage on the back
of the headstock resulting in
localised re-spray.

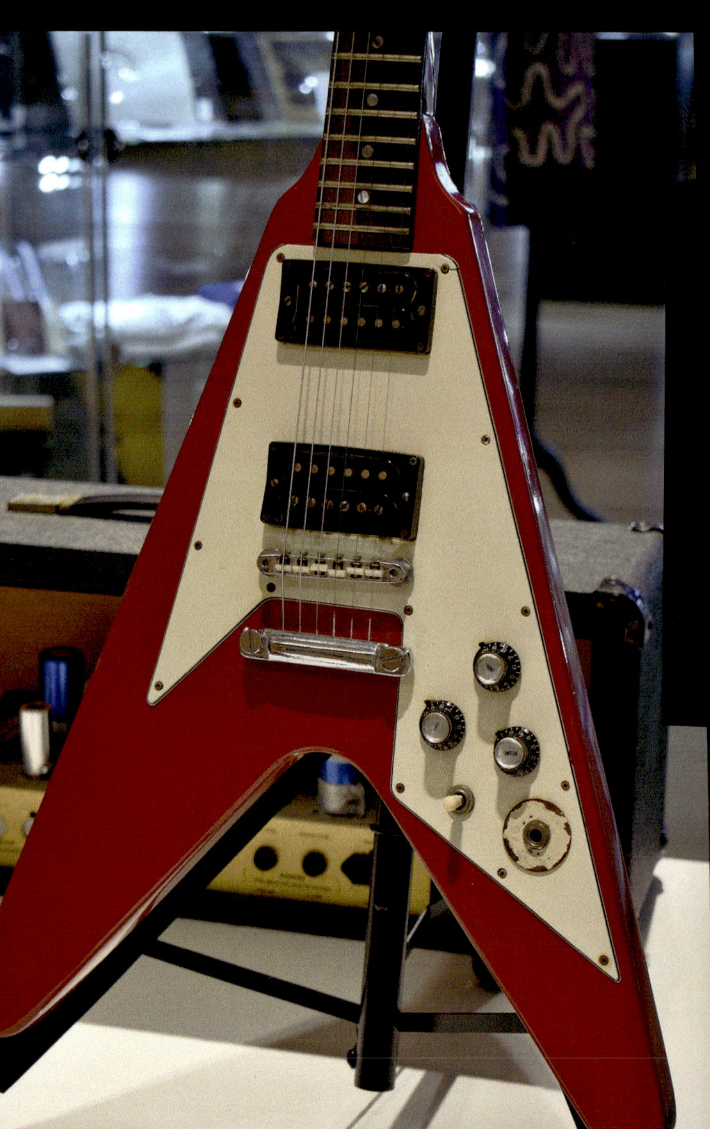

Gibson Flying V 1967:
Nut: 39.82mm
Electric fault so no readings for pickups.
12th fret fingerboard width: 50.54mm
Upper neck body thickness: 34.02mm
Lower horn body thickness: 33.15mm
Headstock thickness:
Low E tuner is 13.84mm
Upper D tuner is 14.15mm
Weight: 6.34lbs
Machine Heads: Kluson Deluxe
Bridge: ABR-1 Tune-O-Matic with nylon saddle

KK Downing says the 1967 Flying V was originally
Candy Apple Red, it faded so he had it refinished
hoping it would be the colour he wanted. When it
came back he said "it was this mucky brownie red
colour". He was disappointed but got used to it over
time. Gibson made a reissue of it after taking a lot of
measurements.

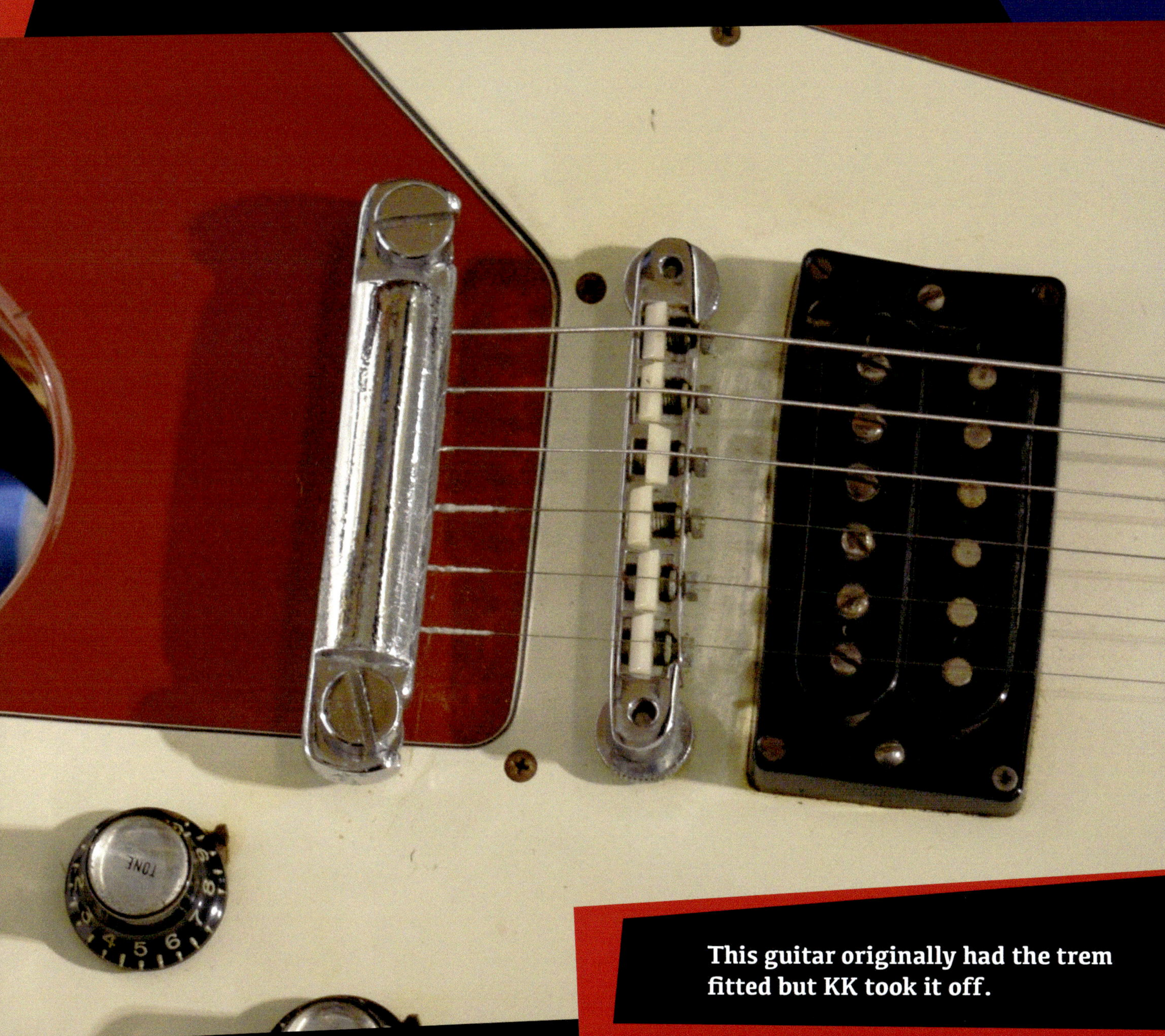

This guitar originally had the trem
fitted but KK took it off.

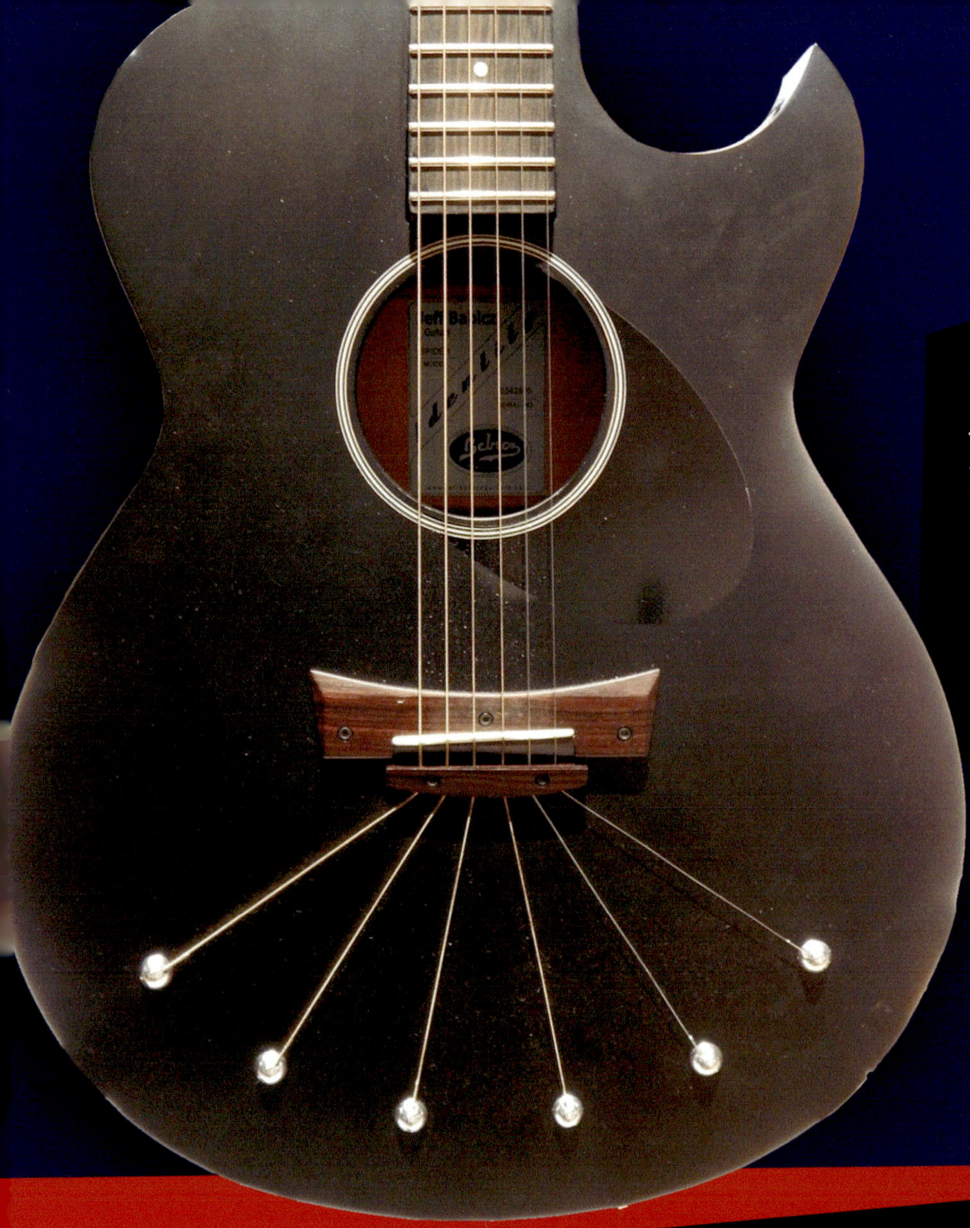

KK Downing;
Jeff Babicz Identity Series Spider
Acoustic Guitar circa 2006
Nut 43.32mm
Body thickness 95.09mm
12th fret fingerboard width
52.82mm
Headstock at Lower E 16.61mm
Headstock at D 16.42mm

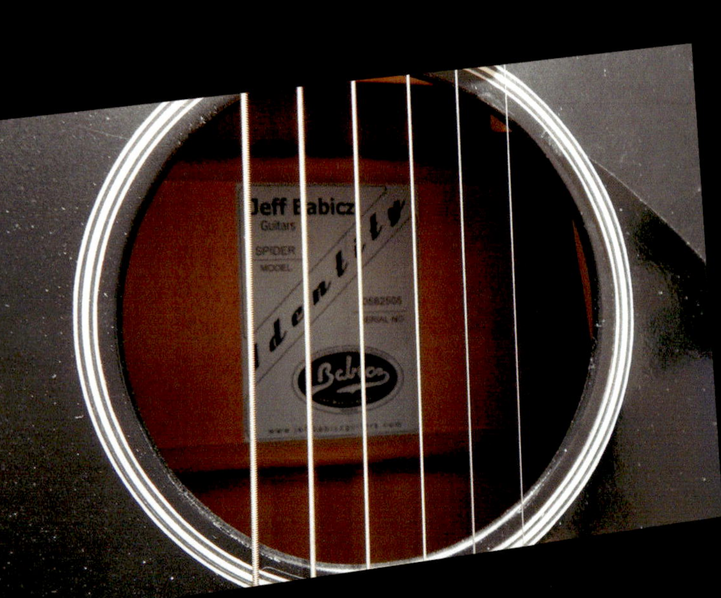

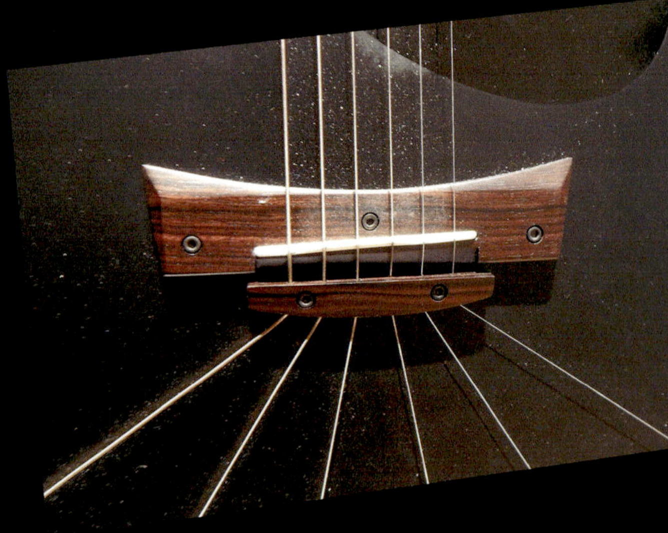

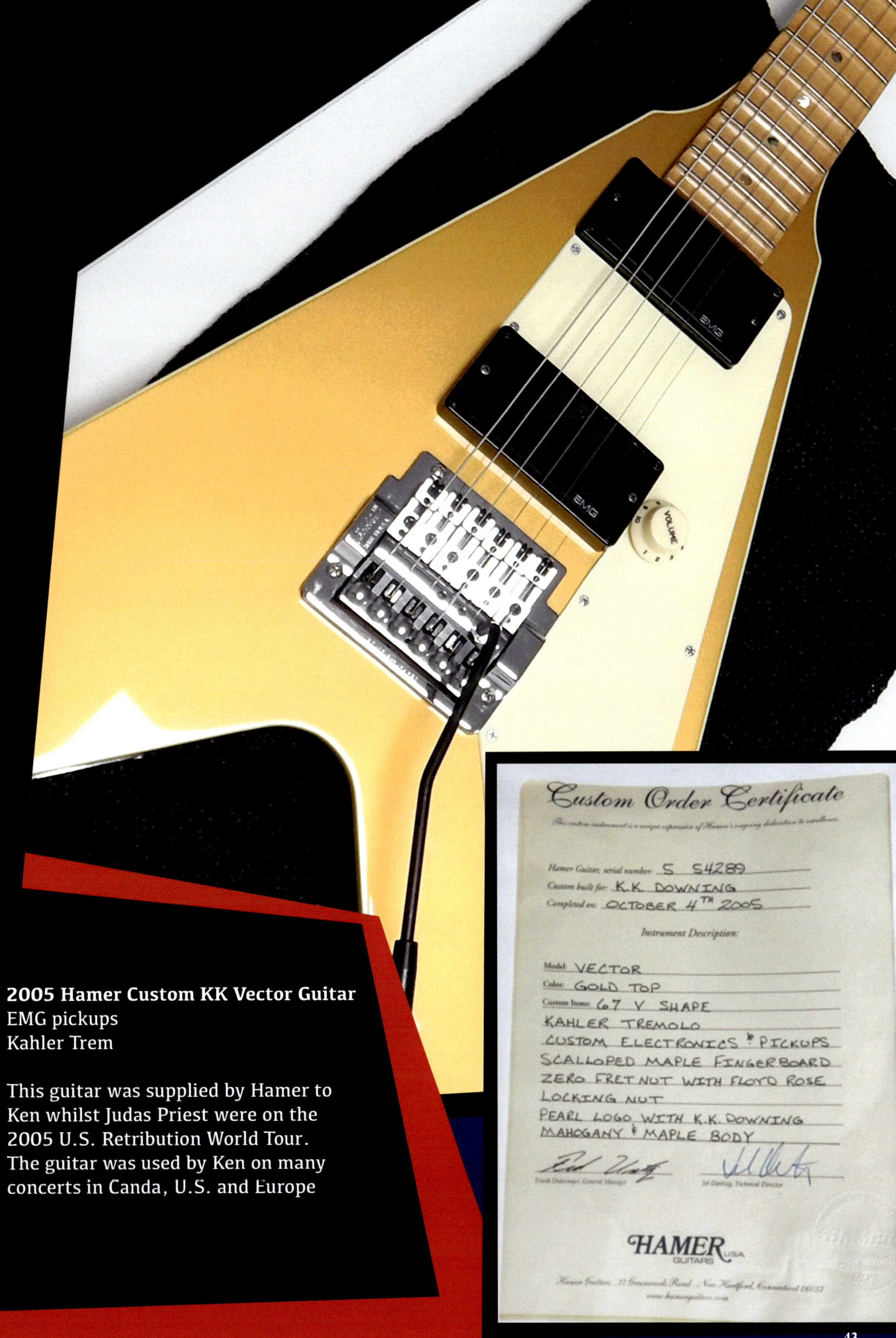

2005 Hamer Custom KK Vector Guitar
EMG pickups
Kahler Trem

This guitar was supplied by Hamer to Ken whilst Judas Priest were on the 2005 U.S. Retribution World Tour. The guitar was used by Ken on many concerts in Canda, U.S. and Europe

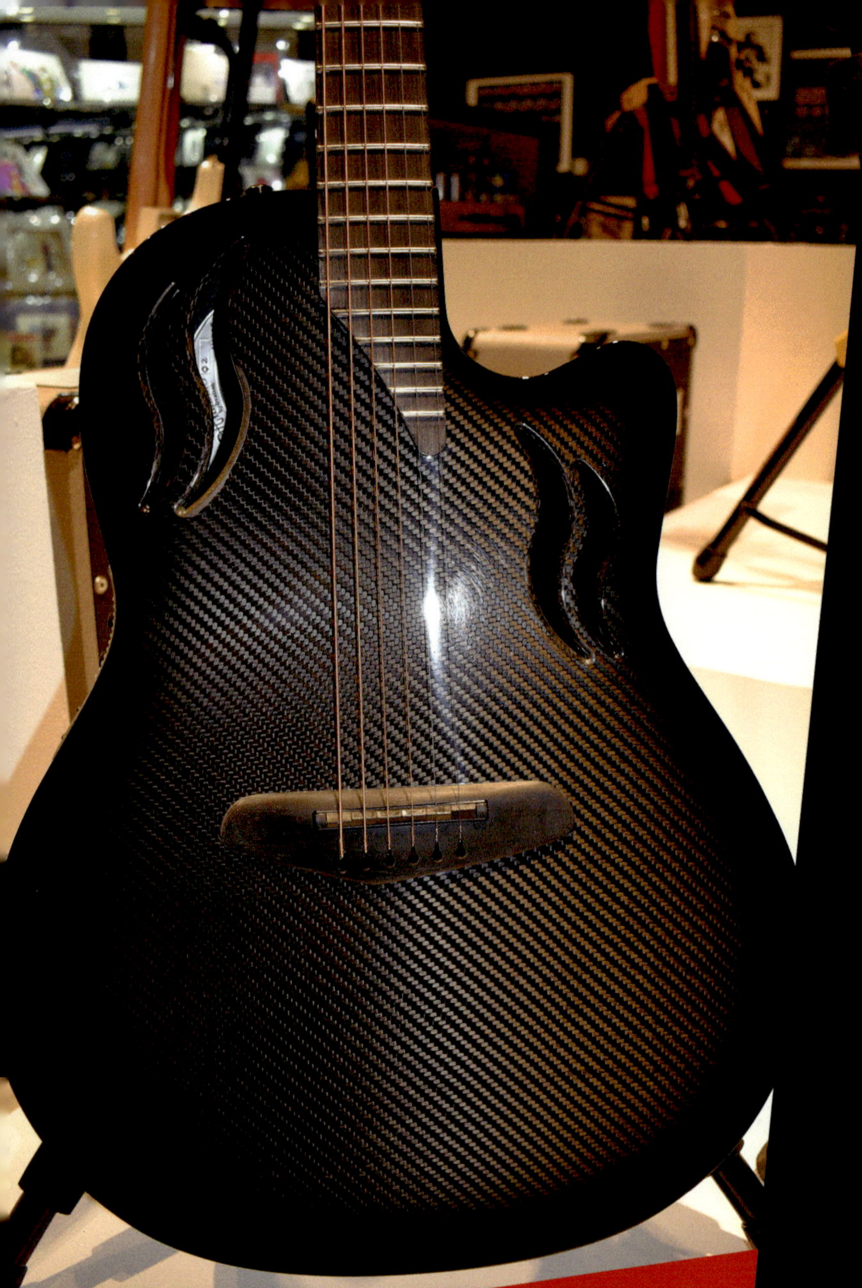

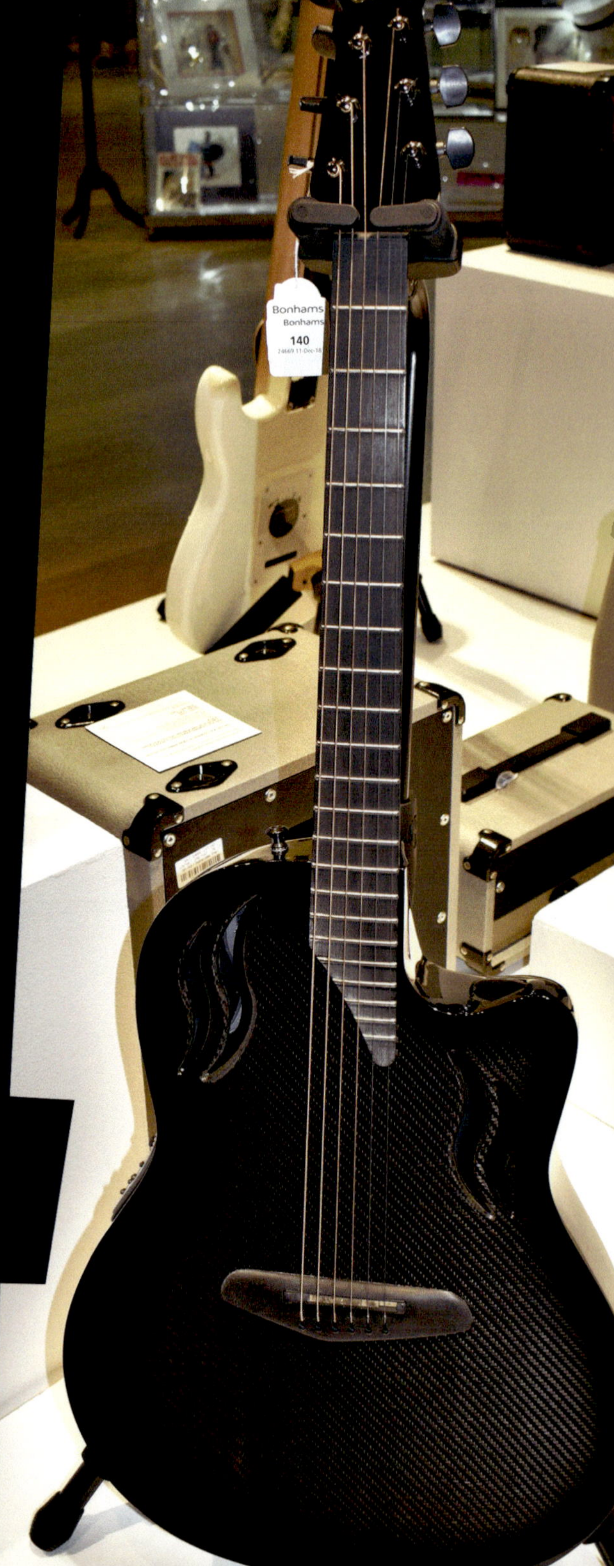

Nut width 43.07mm
12th fret fingerboard width 52.61mm

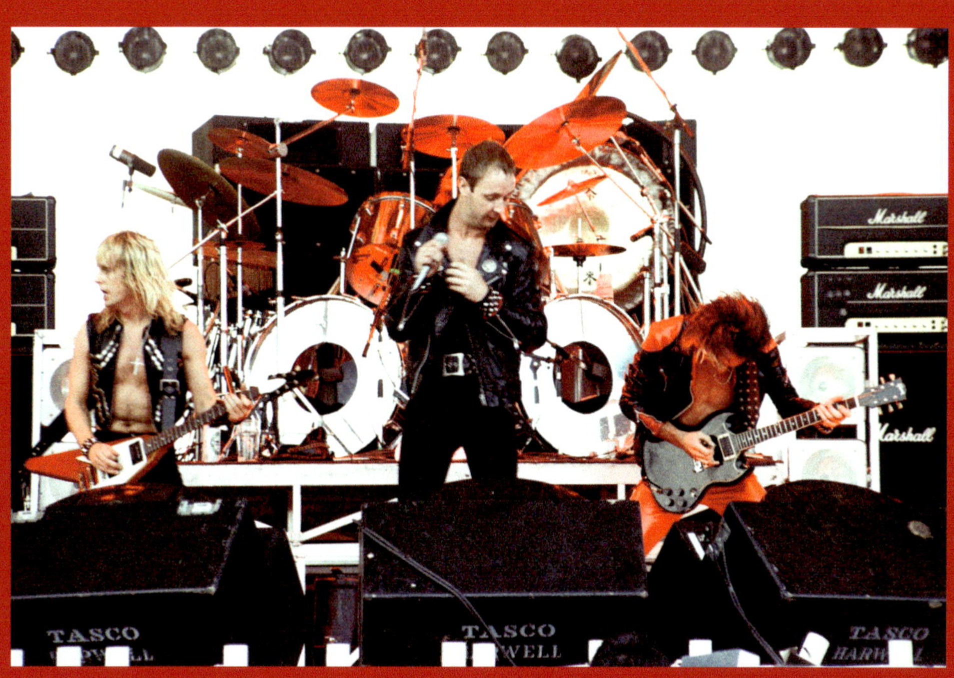

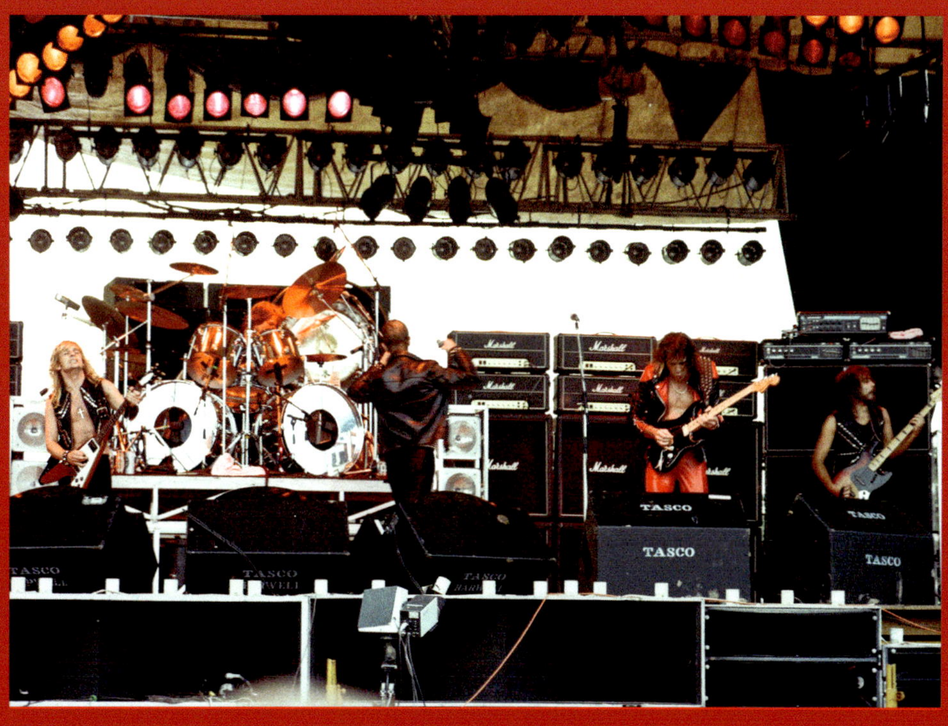

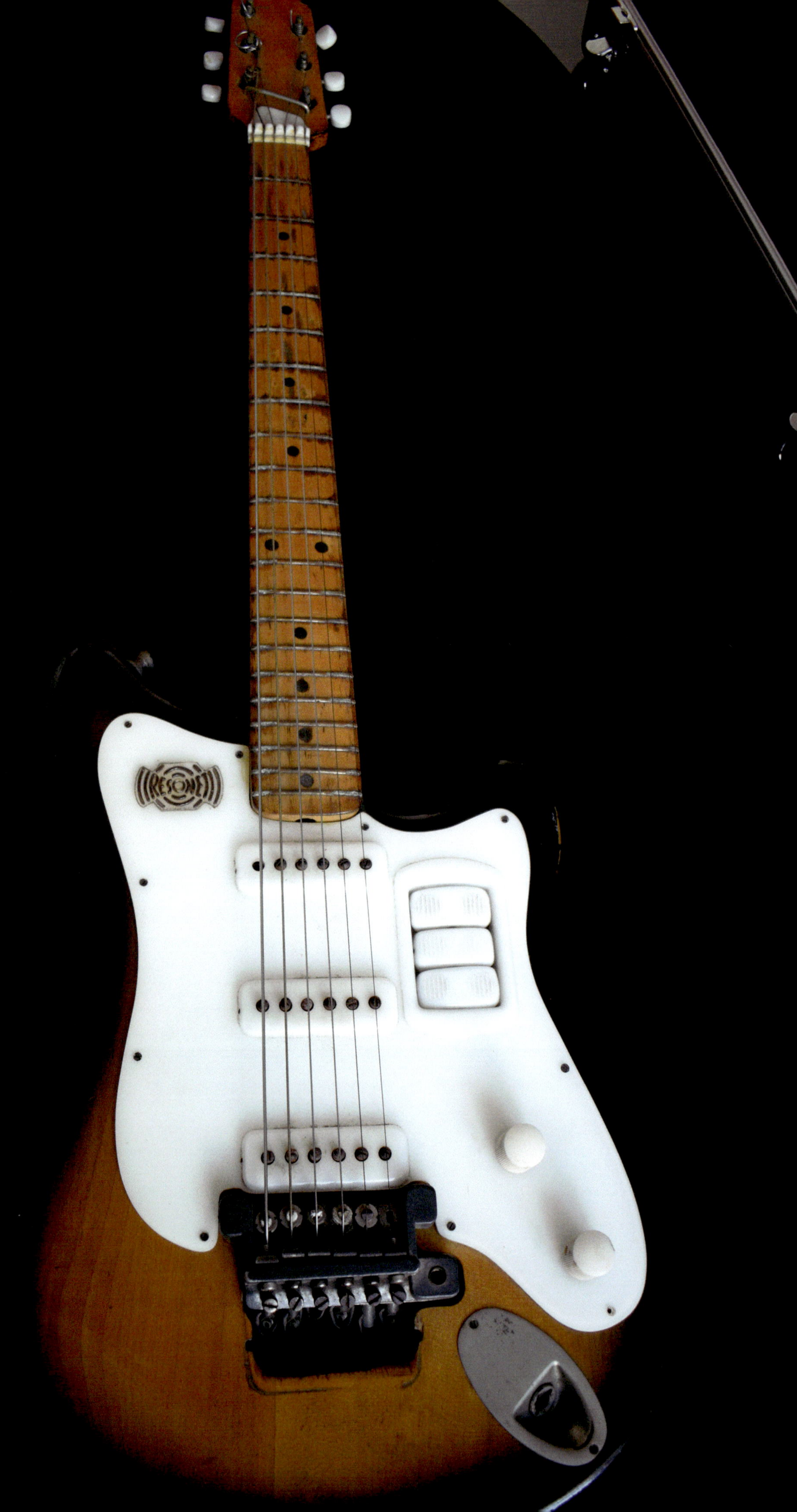

RESONE))

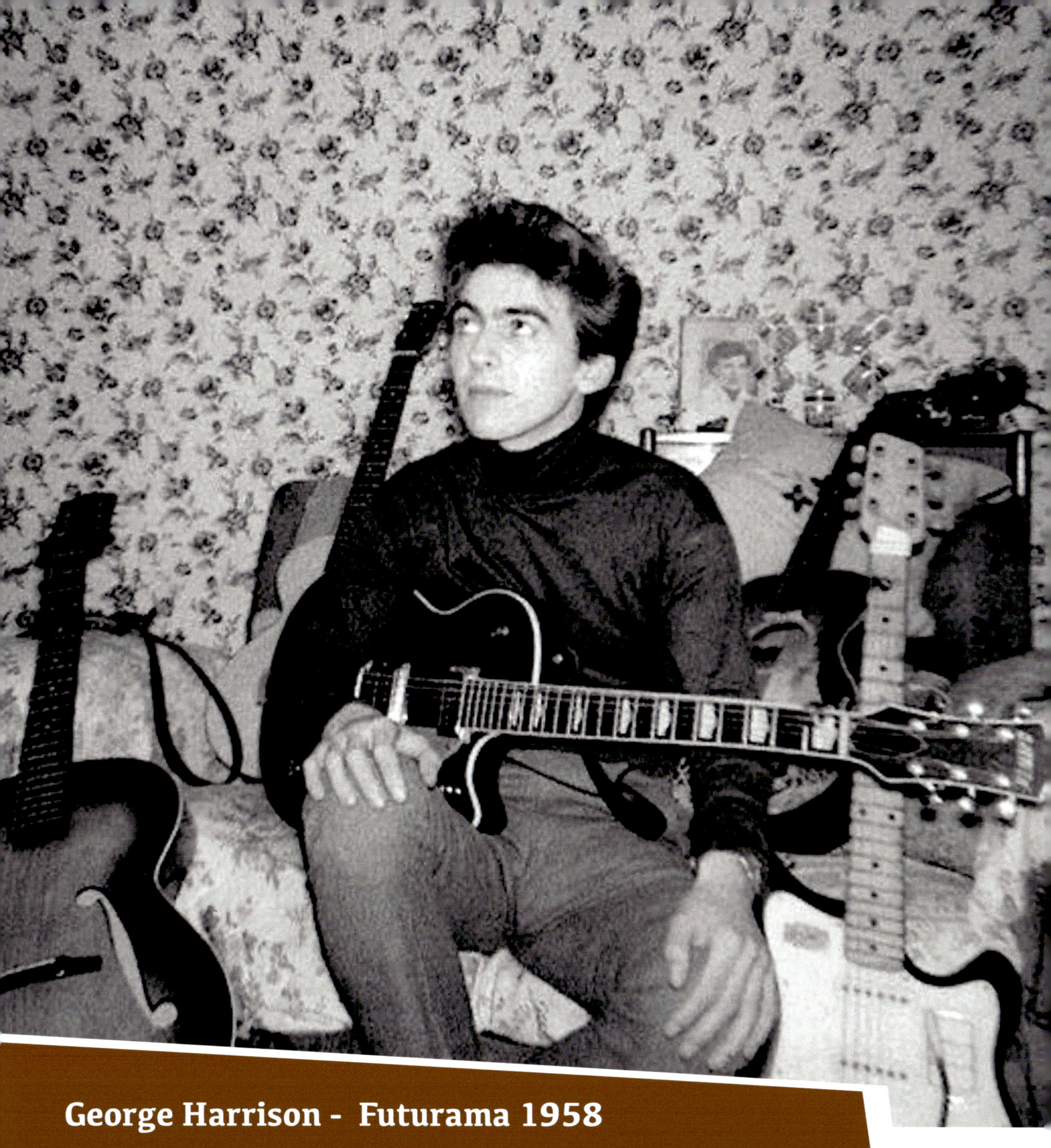

George Harrison - Futurama 1958

George Harrison bought this guitar from Hessy's Music Shop in Liverpool in November 1959. As Harrison was only 16 at the time his mother had to sign the purchase agreement for George. The balance was paid later by Brian Epstein, when he became the Beatles manager.

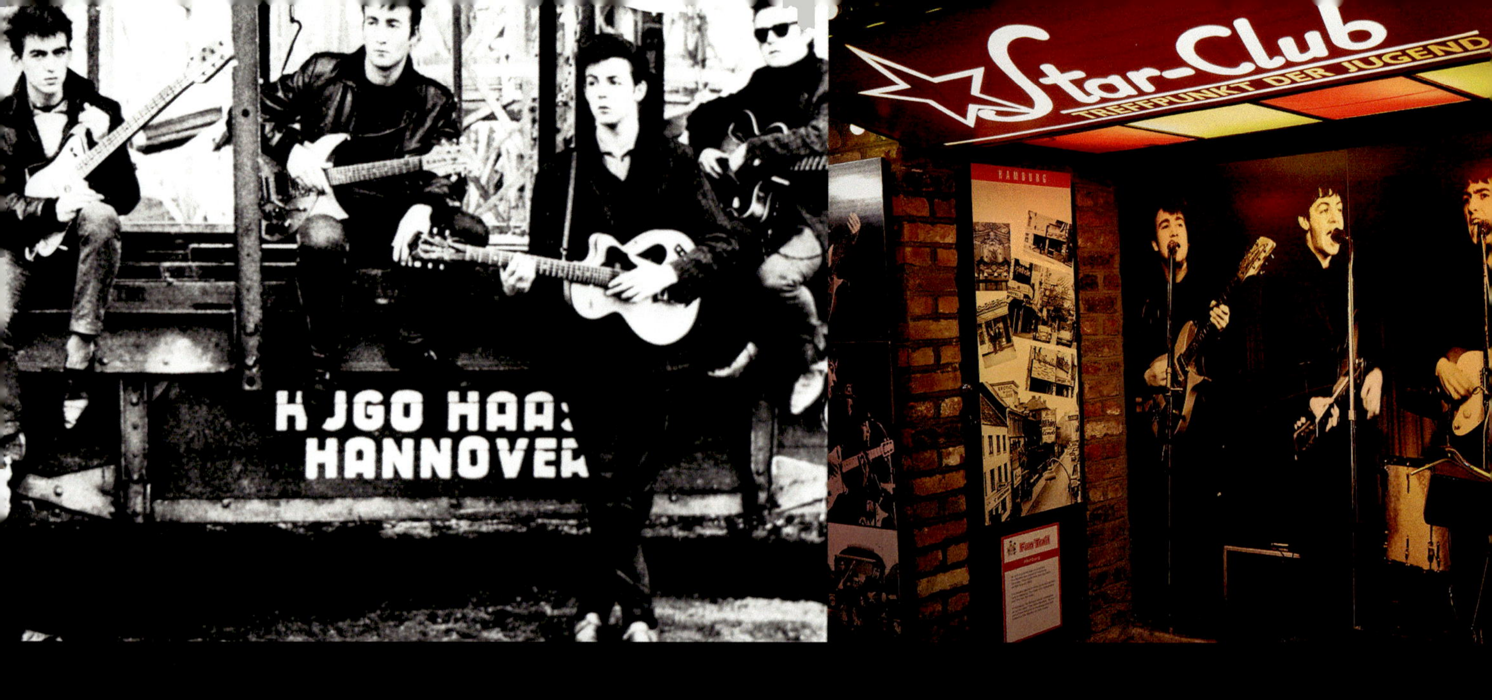
HUGO HAASE
HANNOVER
Star-Club
TREFFPUNKT DER JUGEND

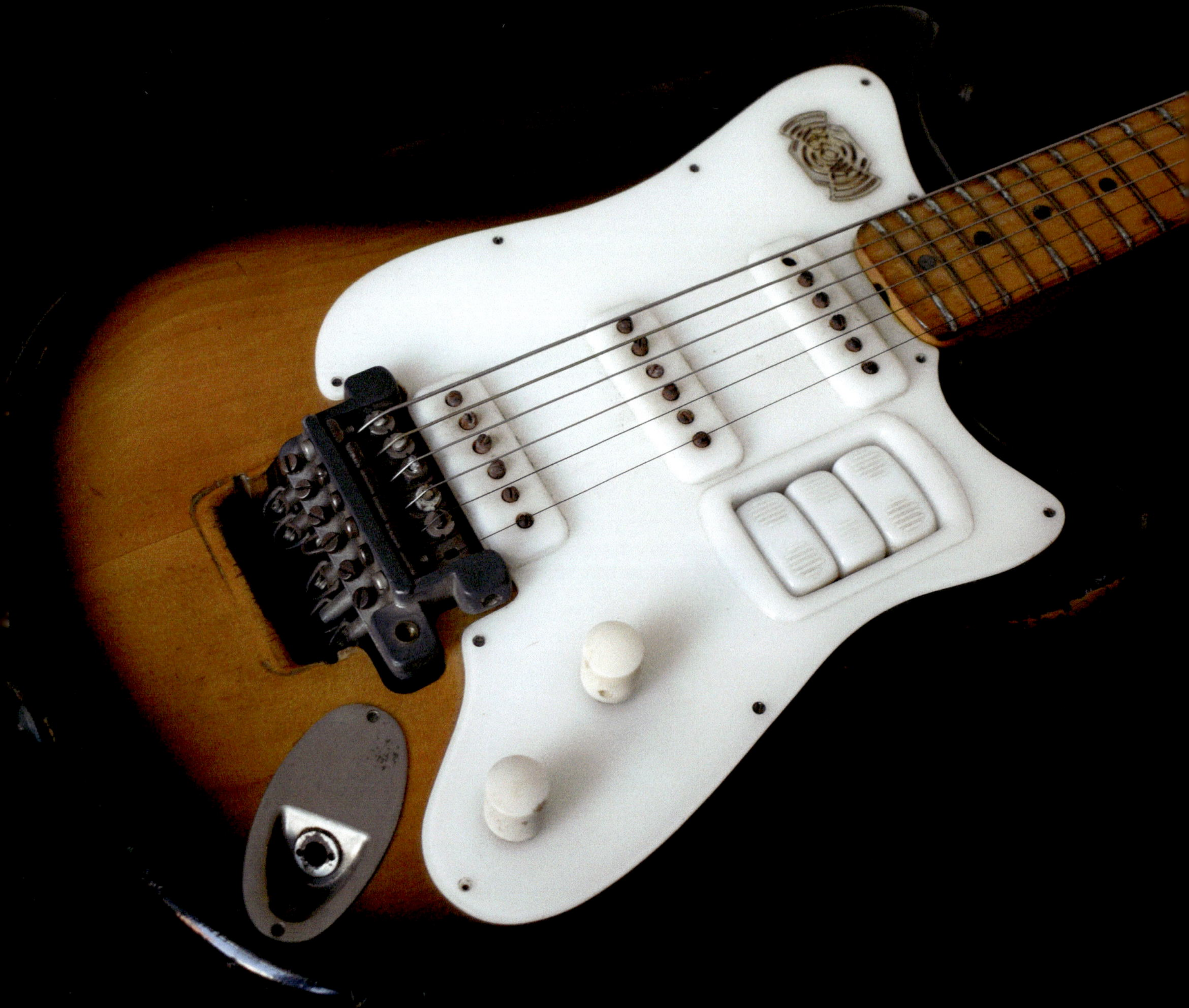

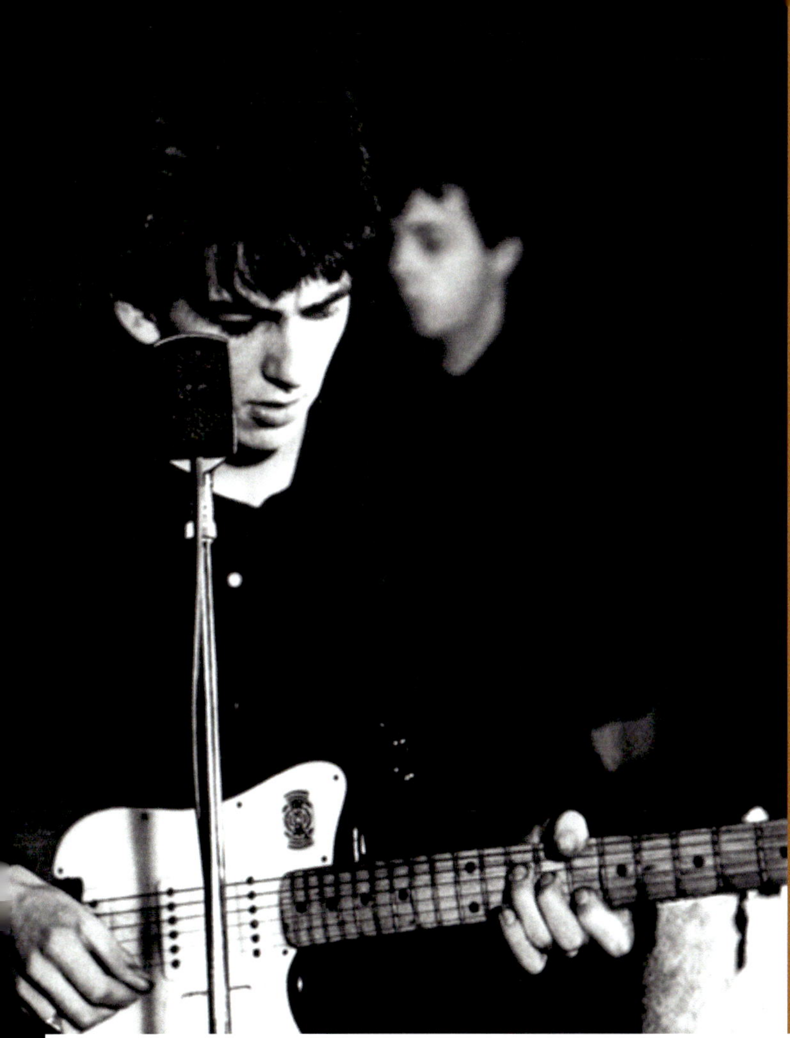

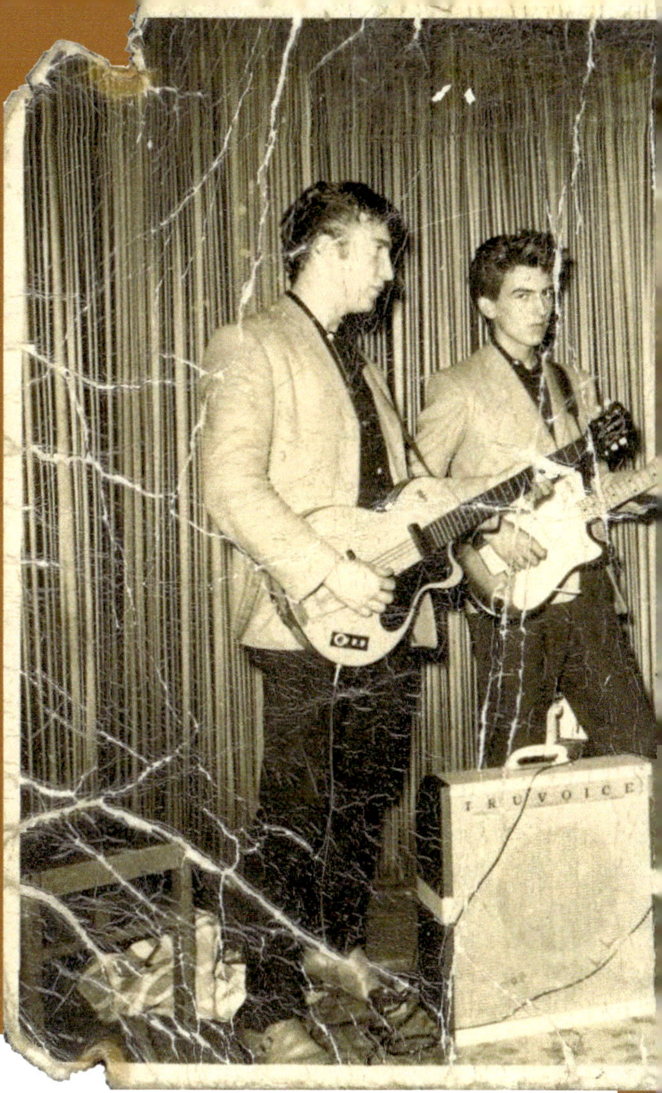

The guitar was used during the Beatles two lengthy club residences in Hamburg in 1960 and 1961. It was also played on numerous gigs throughout a period of 18 months.

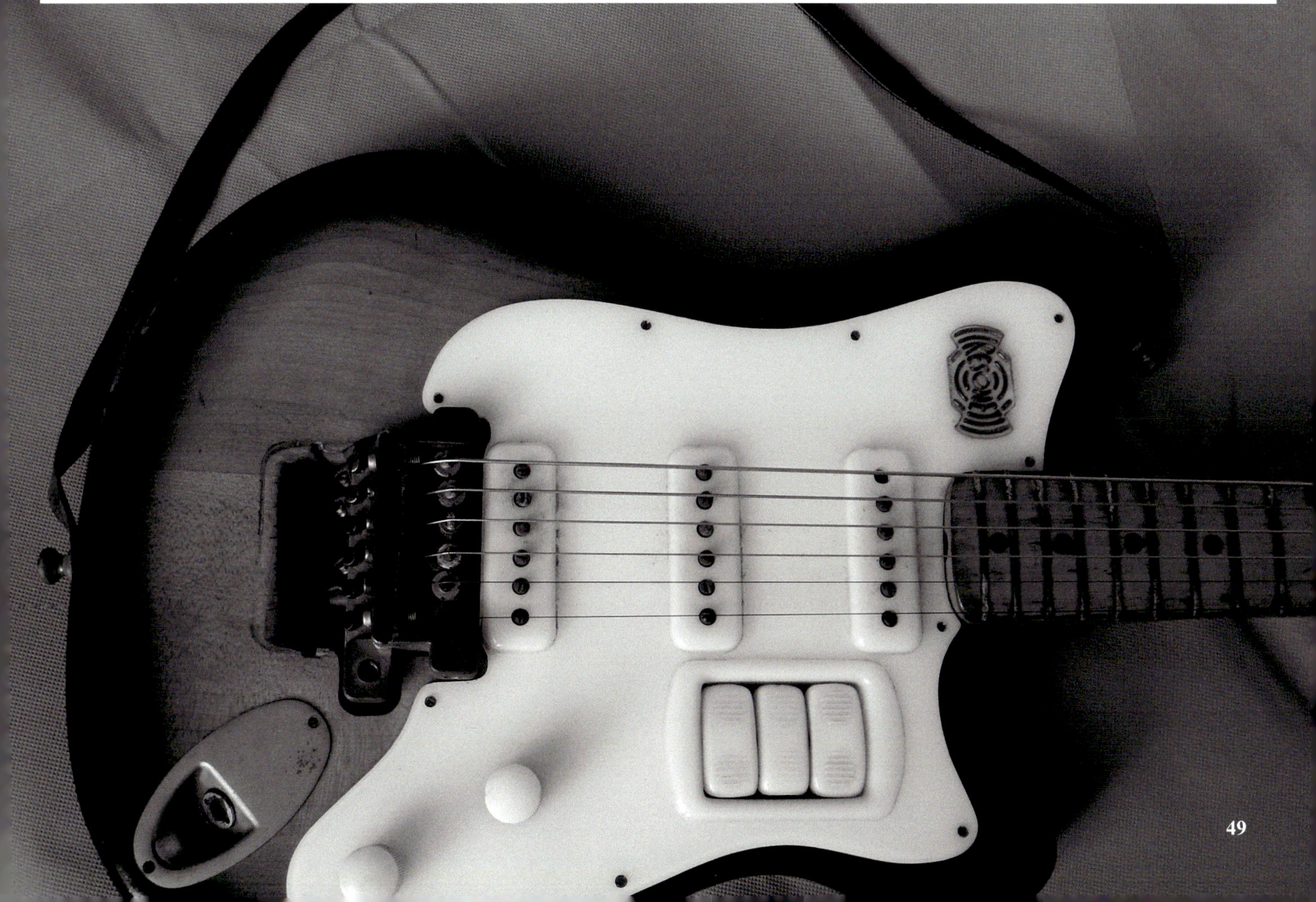

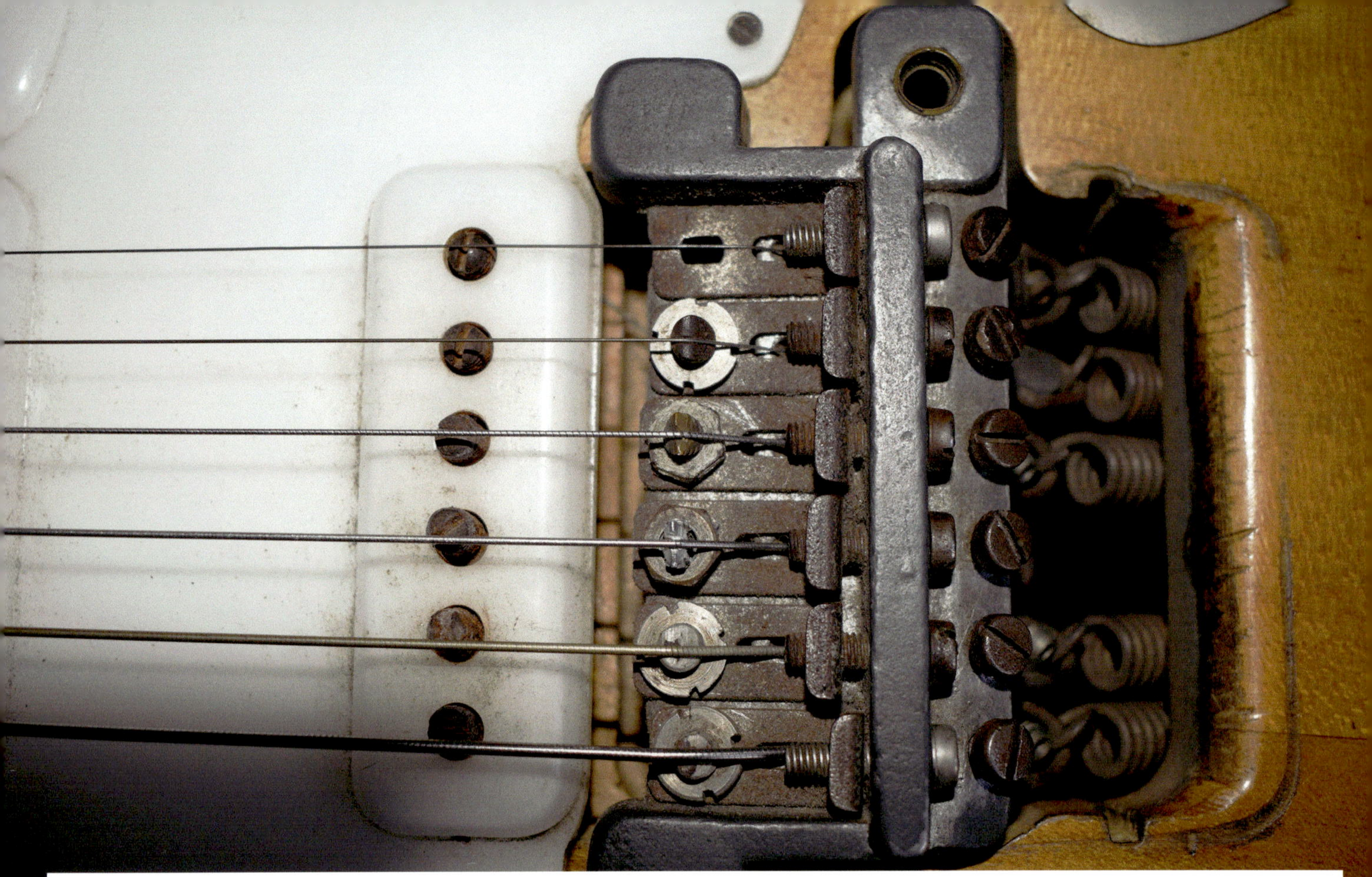

The Resonet Grazioso guitar was made for a very short time in the late 1950's by the Drevokov Co. in what was then Czechoslovakia, it was clearly inspired by the Fender Stratocaster and had pickup switching that could enable all three pickups to be used at once as well as a complex tremolo unit.

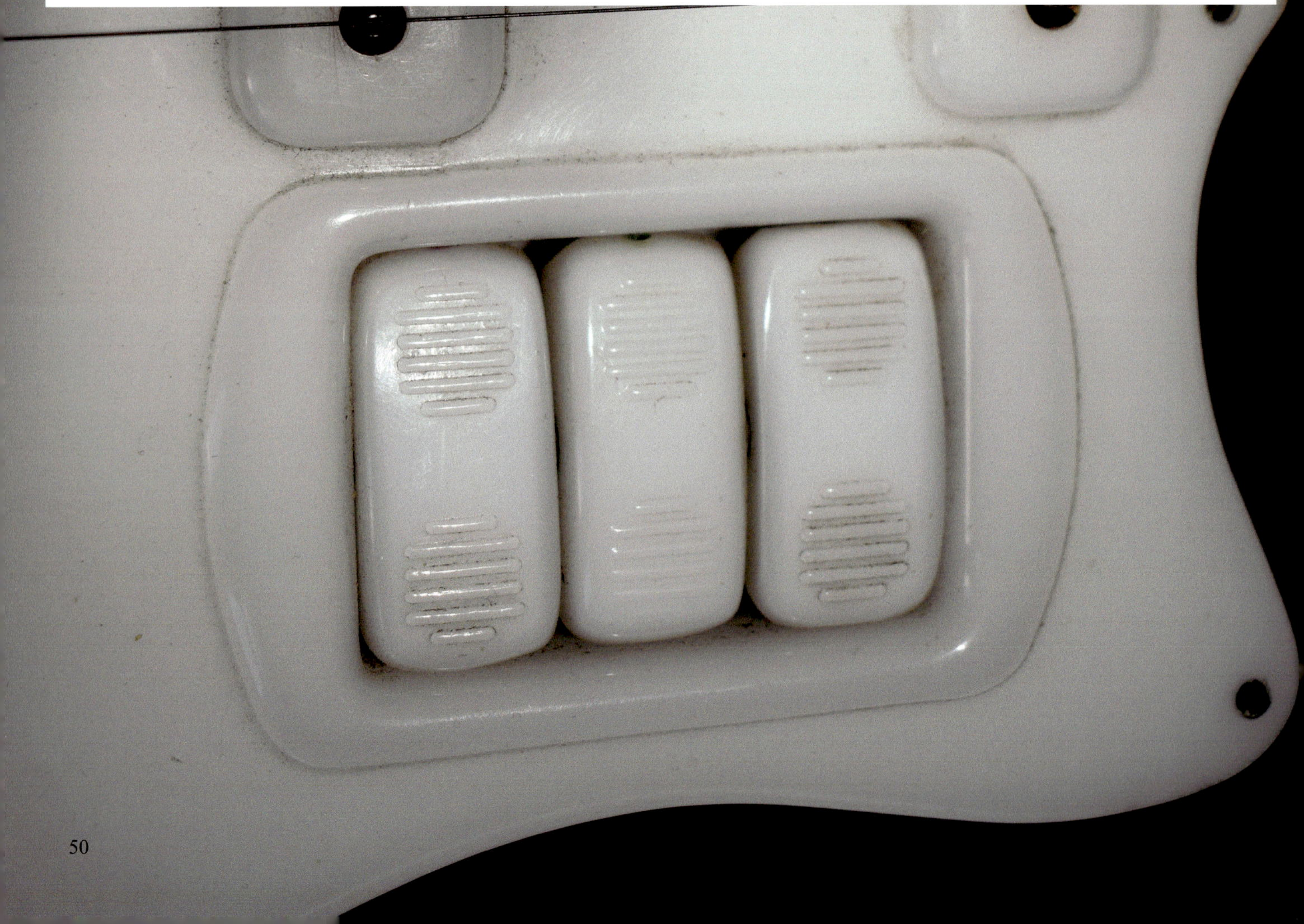

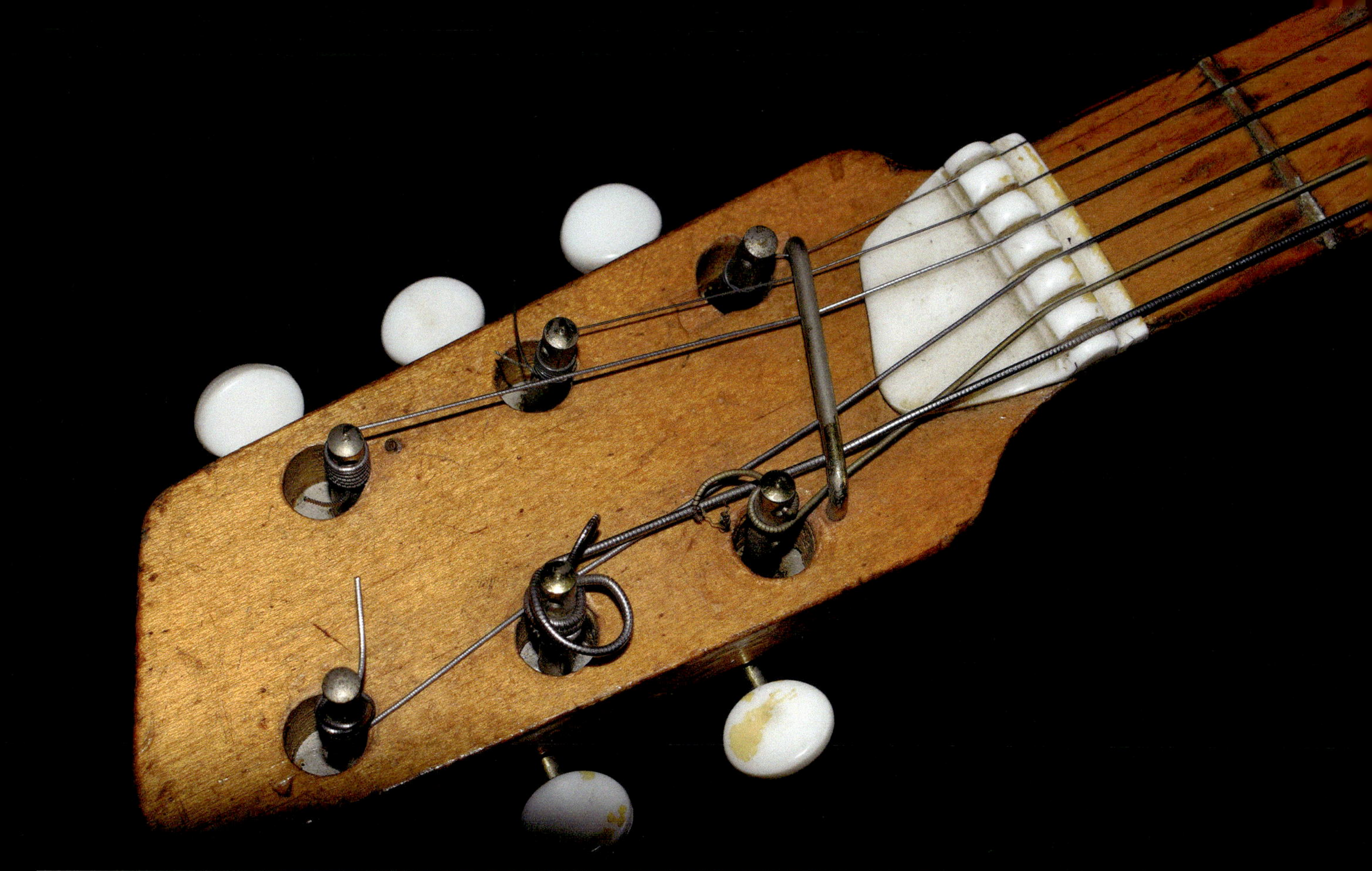

The guitar was imported by the Selmer Company in London at a time when there was an embargo on American made goods. The guitar name was changed to 'Futurama' and many players such as Jimmy Page and Albert Lee played them.

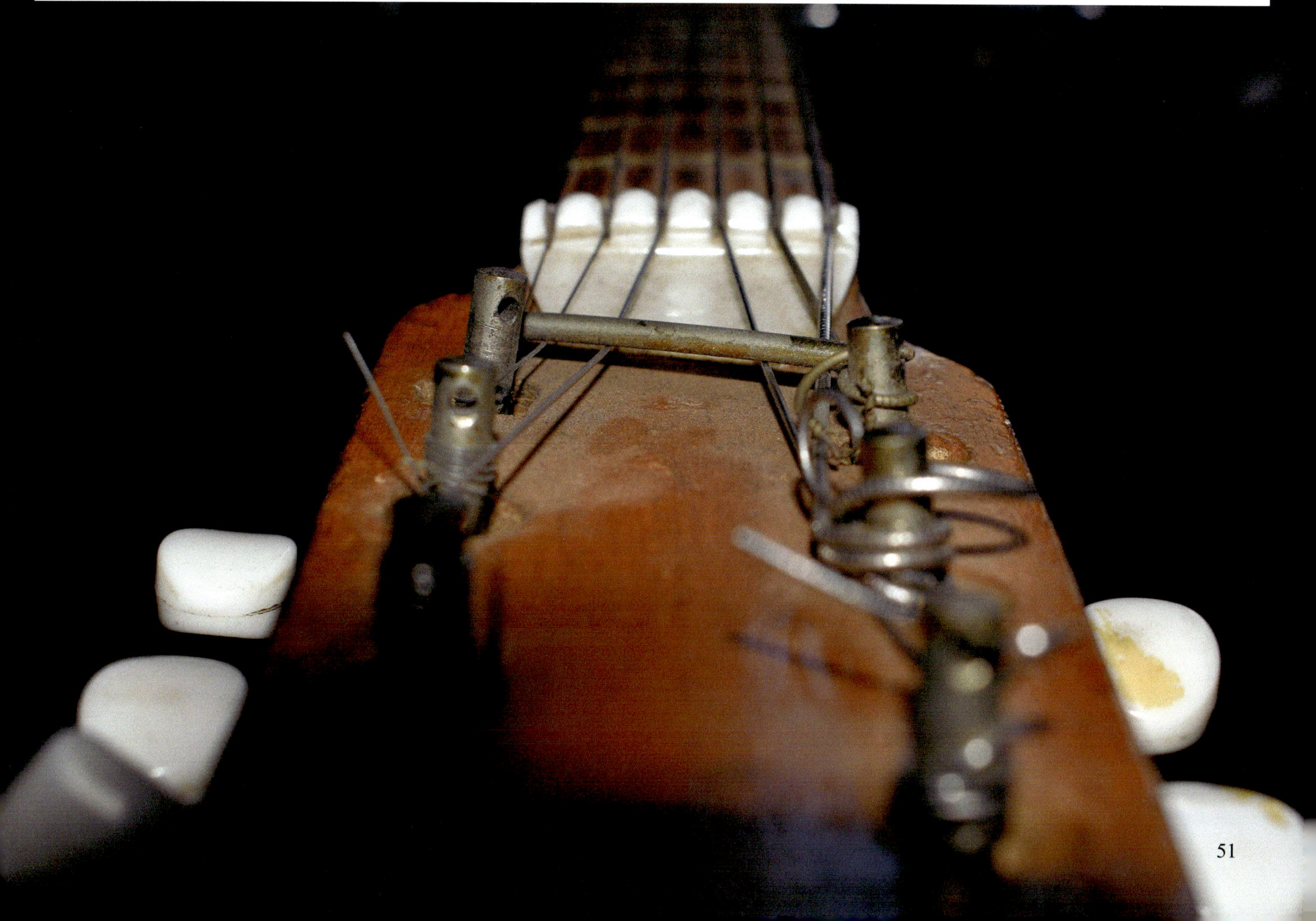

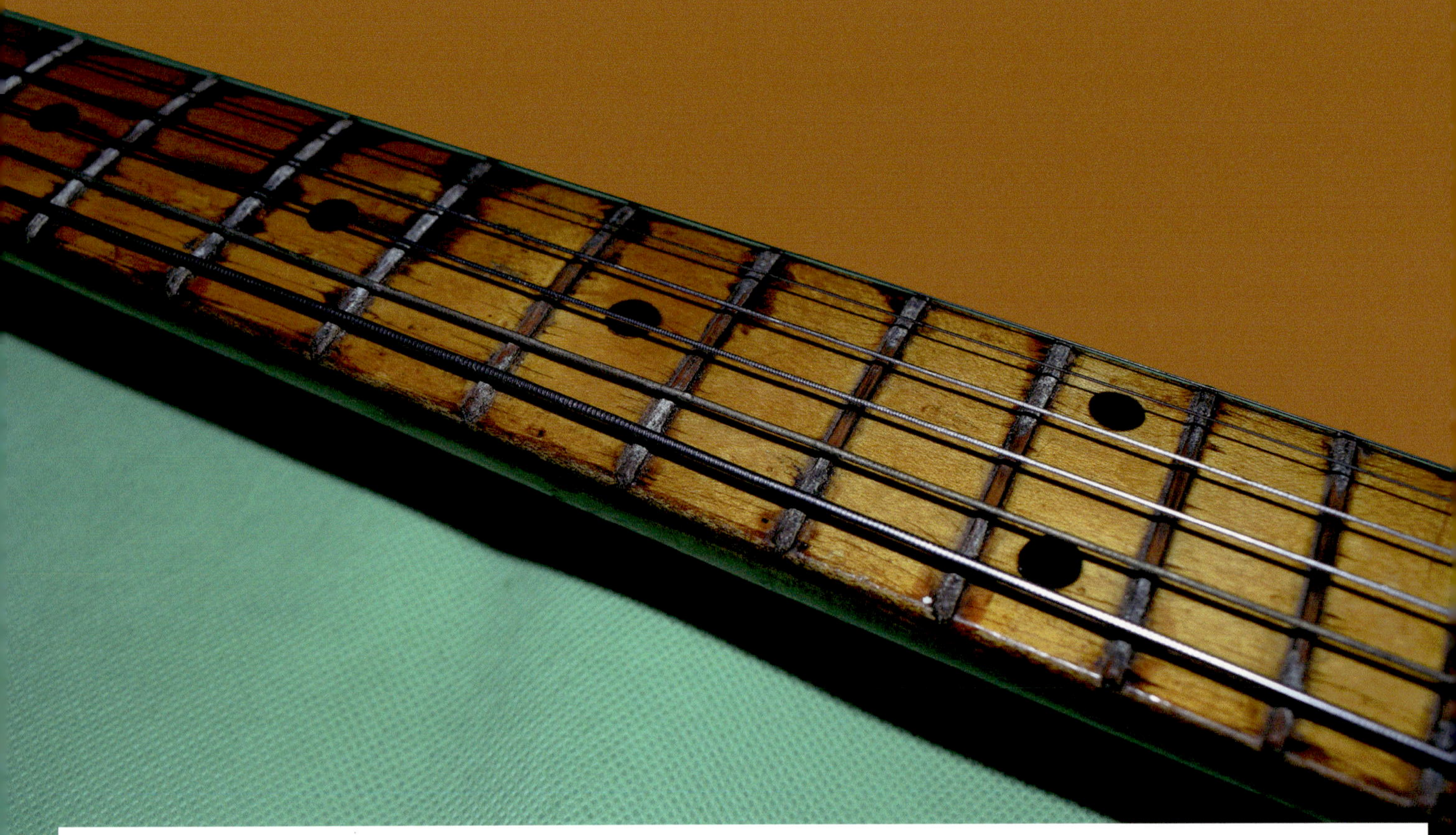

12th fret measurement taken is 50.84 mm. Headstock thickness low E side: 13.83 mm and at the D tuning peg 14.50 mm. Frets 2.26 mm

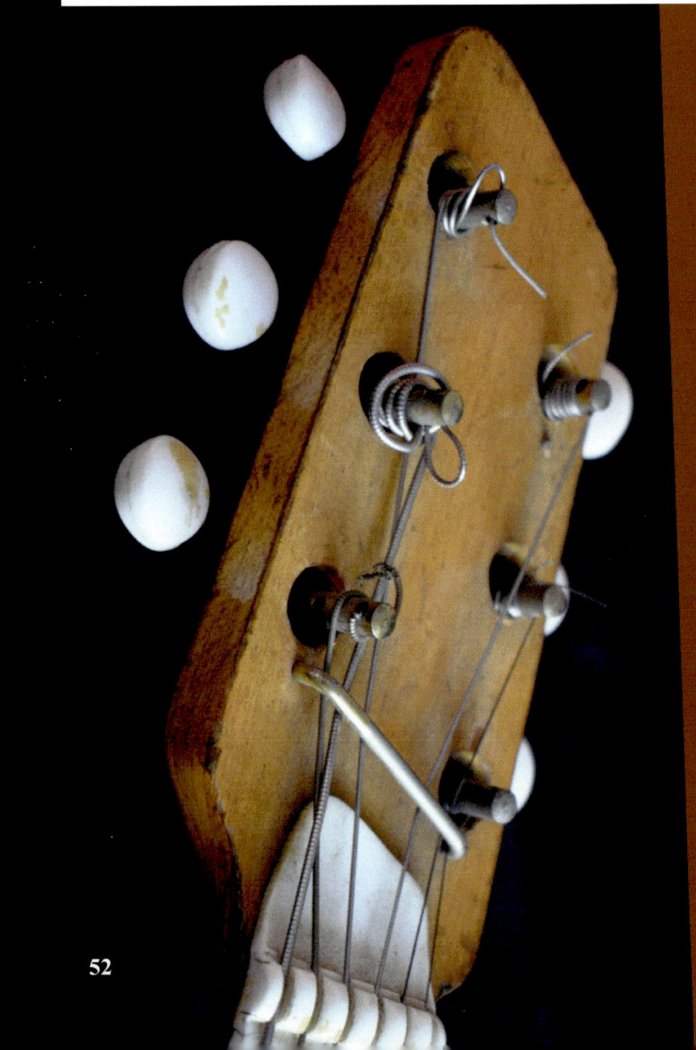

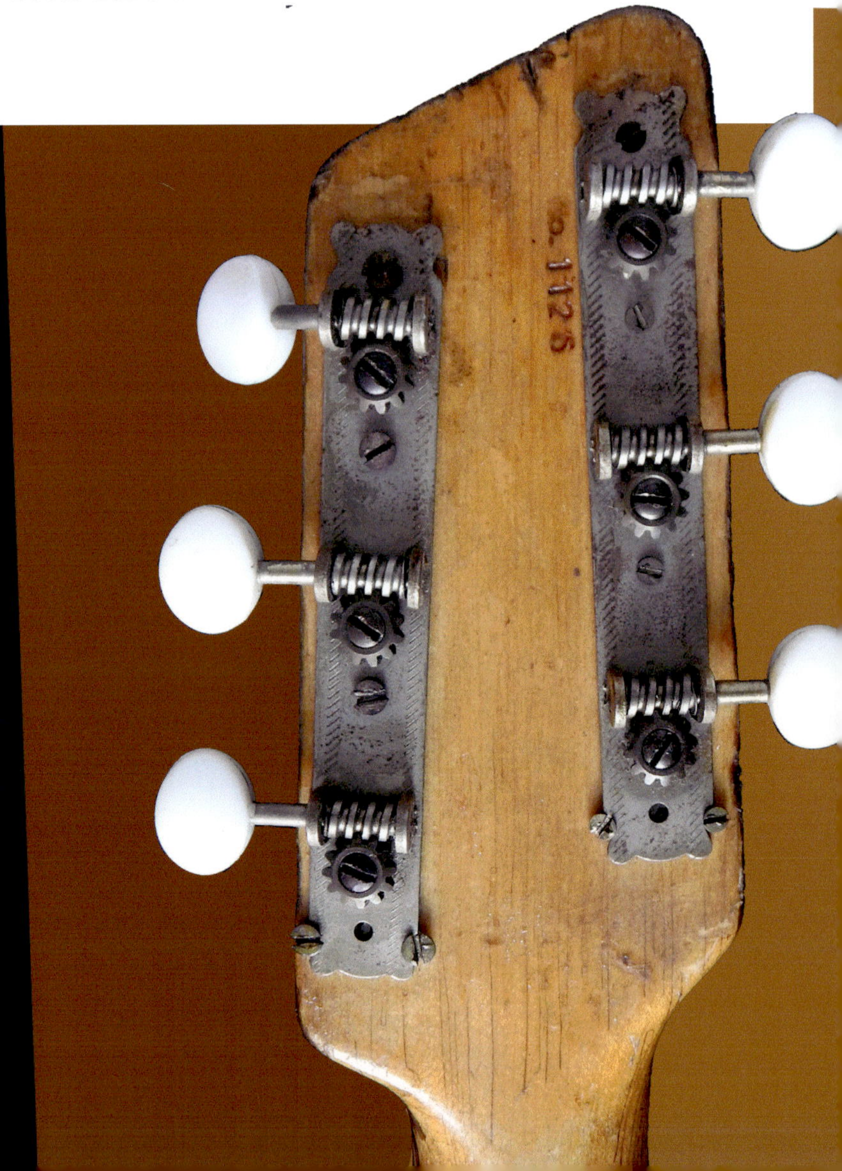

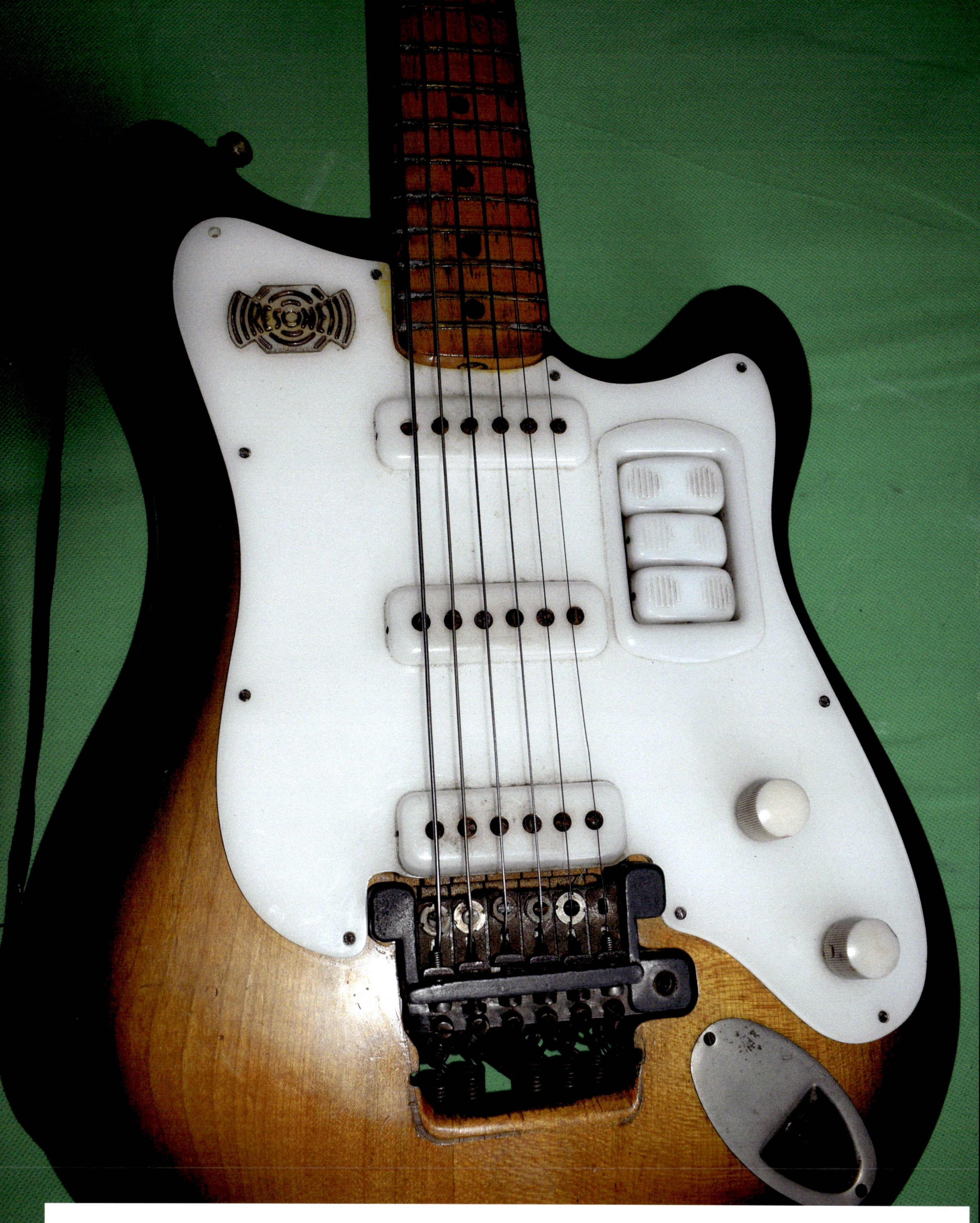

Pickups: Front 6.35 ohms, Mid 6.39 ohms, Bridge 6.16 ohms

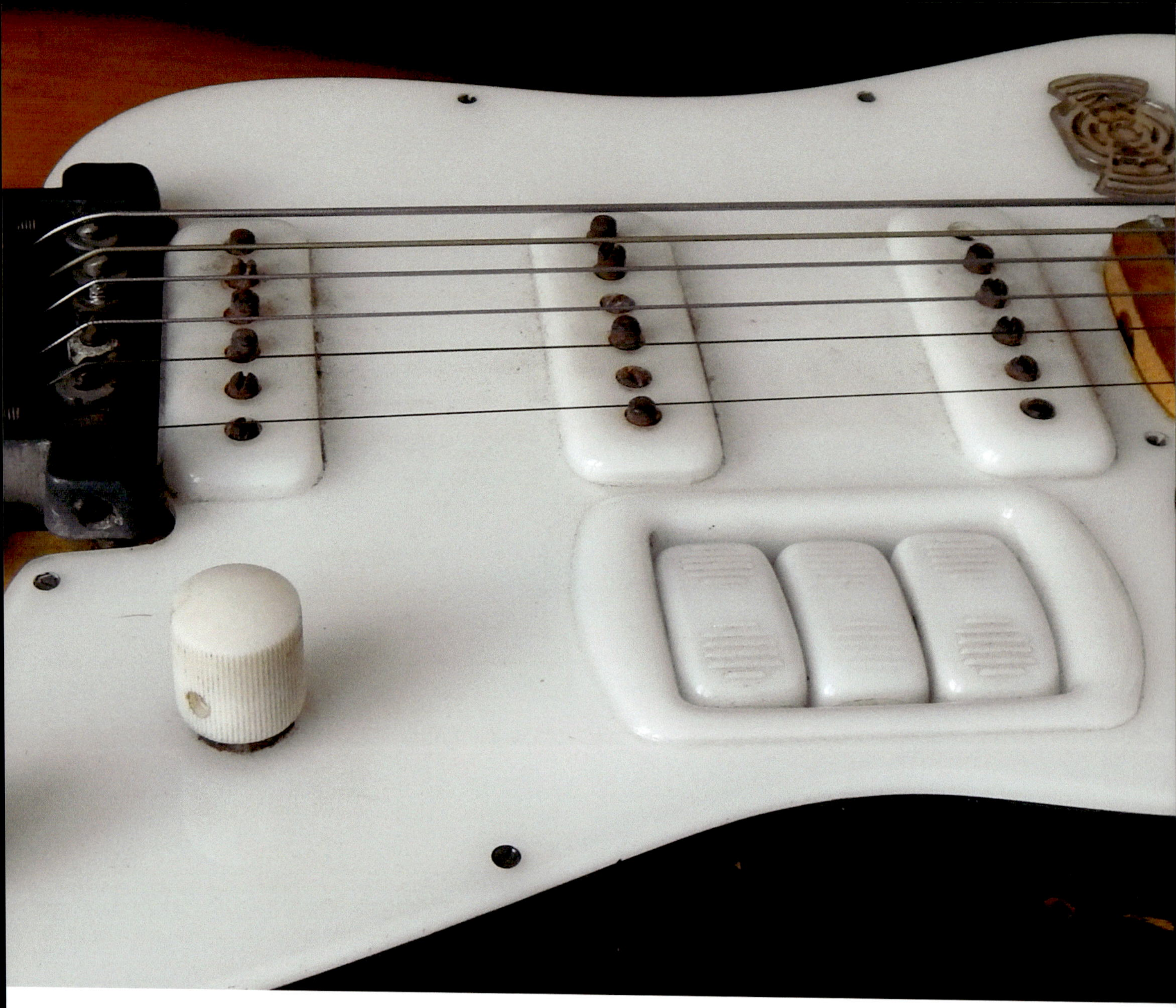

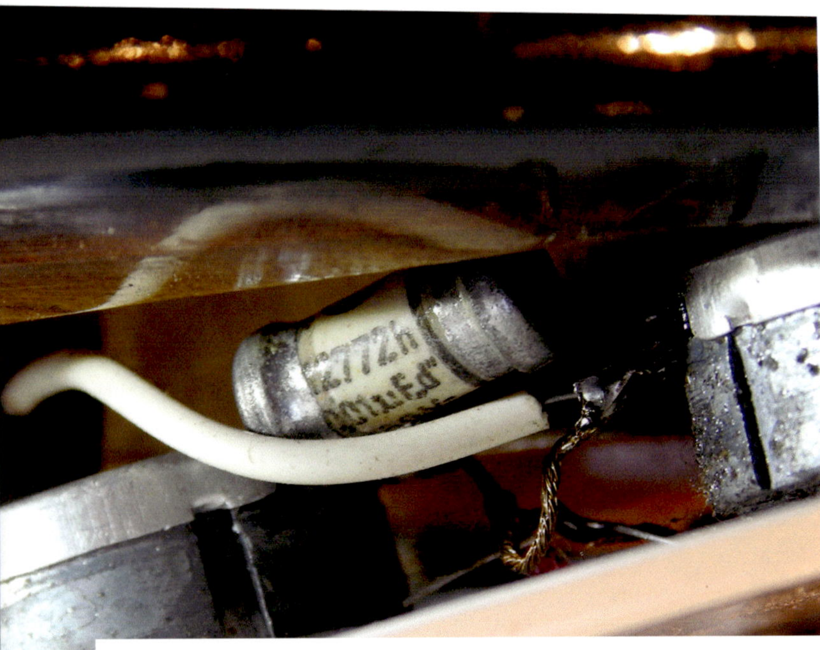

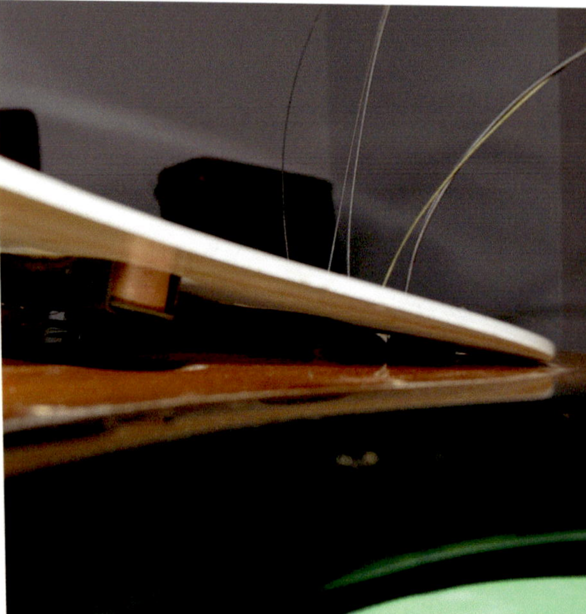

Pickup width is 26.48 mm and length is 75.5 mm. The whole plastic cover goes over
the pole pieces as it is all one single moulded cover.

The scratchplate is just one moulded piece and the pickup pole pieces just come through the plastic, but when taking the scratchplate off they fall inside the guitar cavity underneath. I left the assembly in place as the jack input wires are very tight due to the short length used and they are also soldered to the volume control. I still managed to have time to look underneath and see the volume and tone control values and part number. The capacitor looks to be Russian made and the neck pocket is clean but tight with the figures '61' stamped on top, but this does not mean it was made in 1961 though. The neck is clearly very worn and photos show distinctive marks on the fingerboard from when George used it.

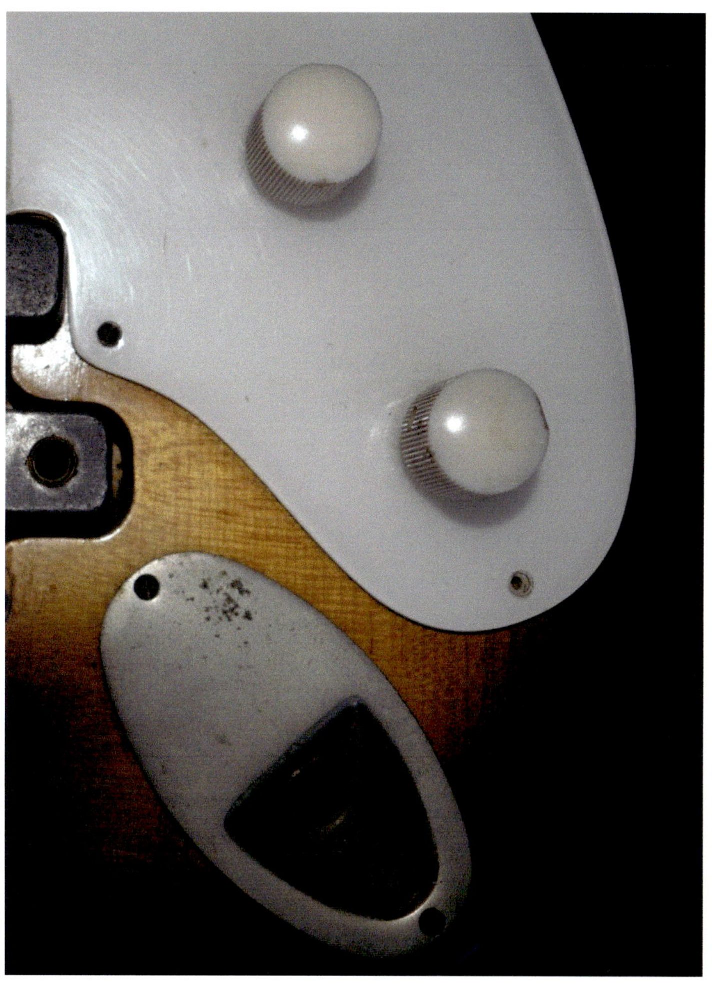

Control knobs diameter 18.83mm

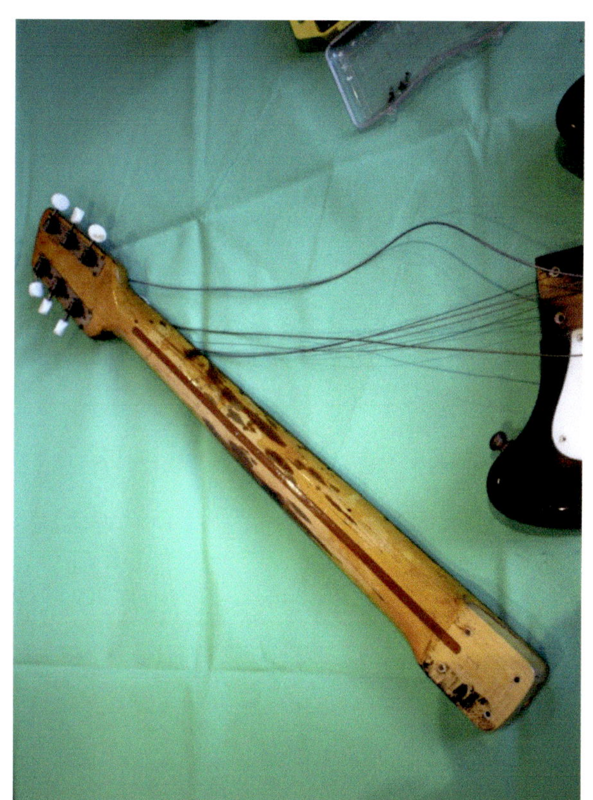

Neck is well worn. 1st fret thickness is 23.47mm & at 12th fret 25.74mm.

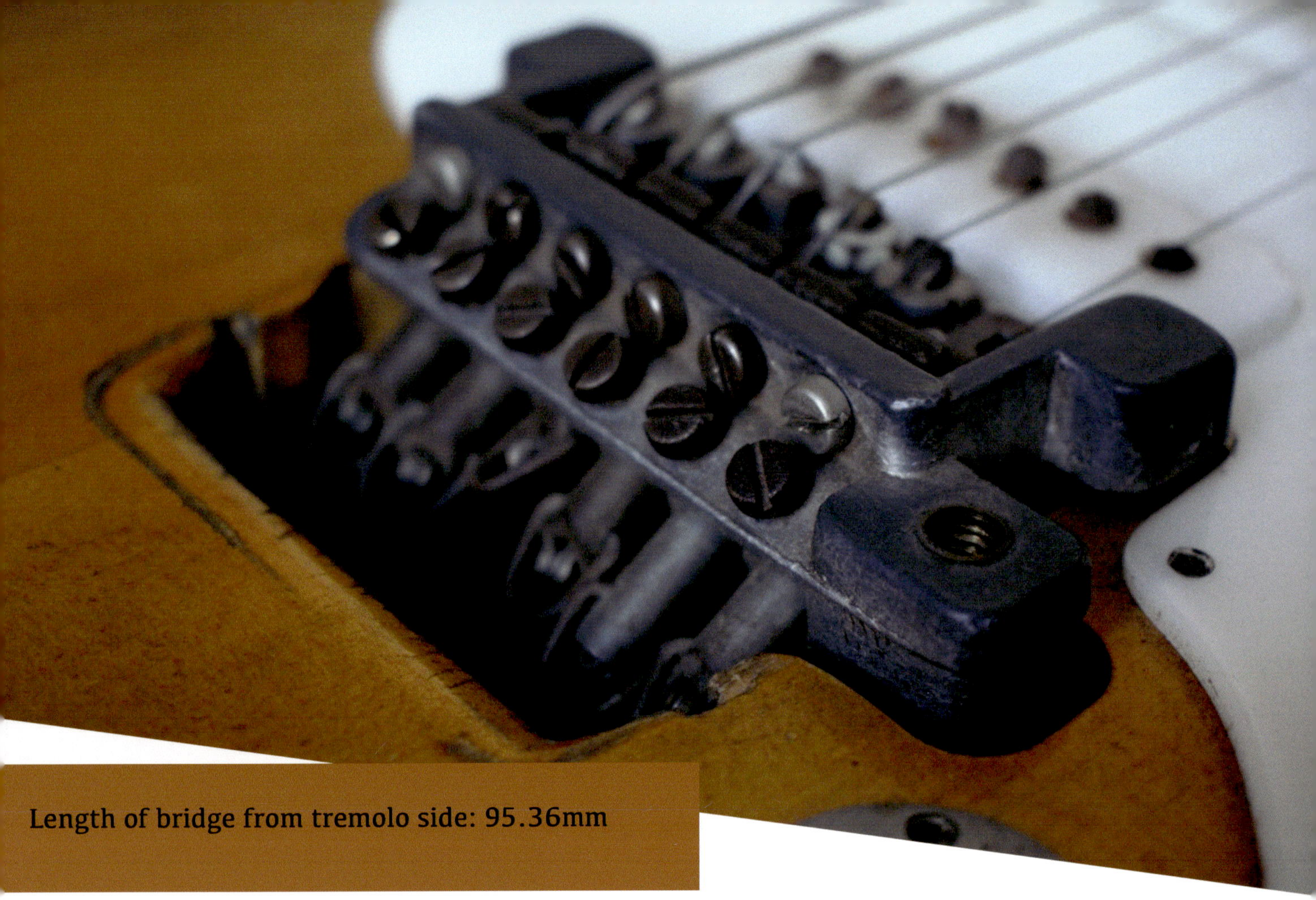

Length of bridge from tremolo side: 95.36mm

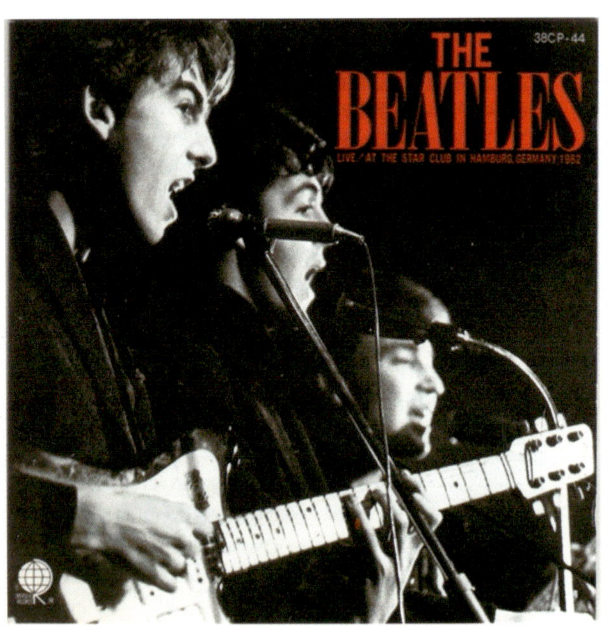

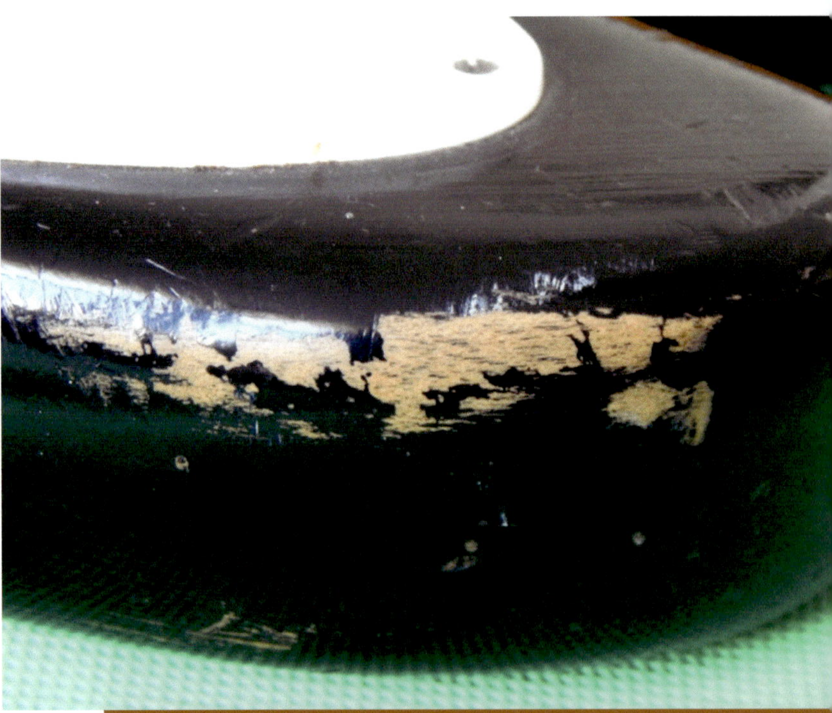

Body thickness at lower cutaway :
38.58 mm

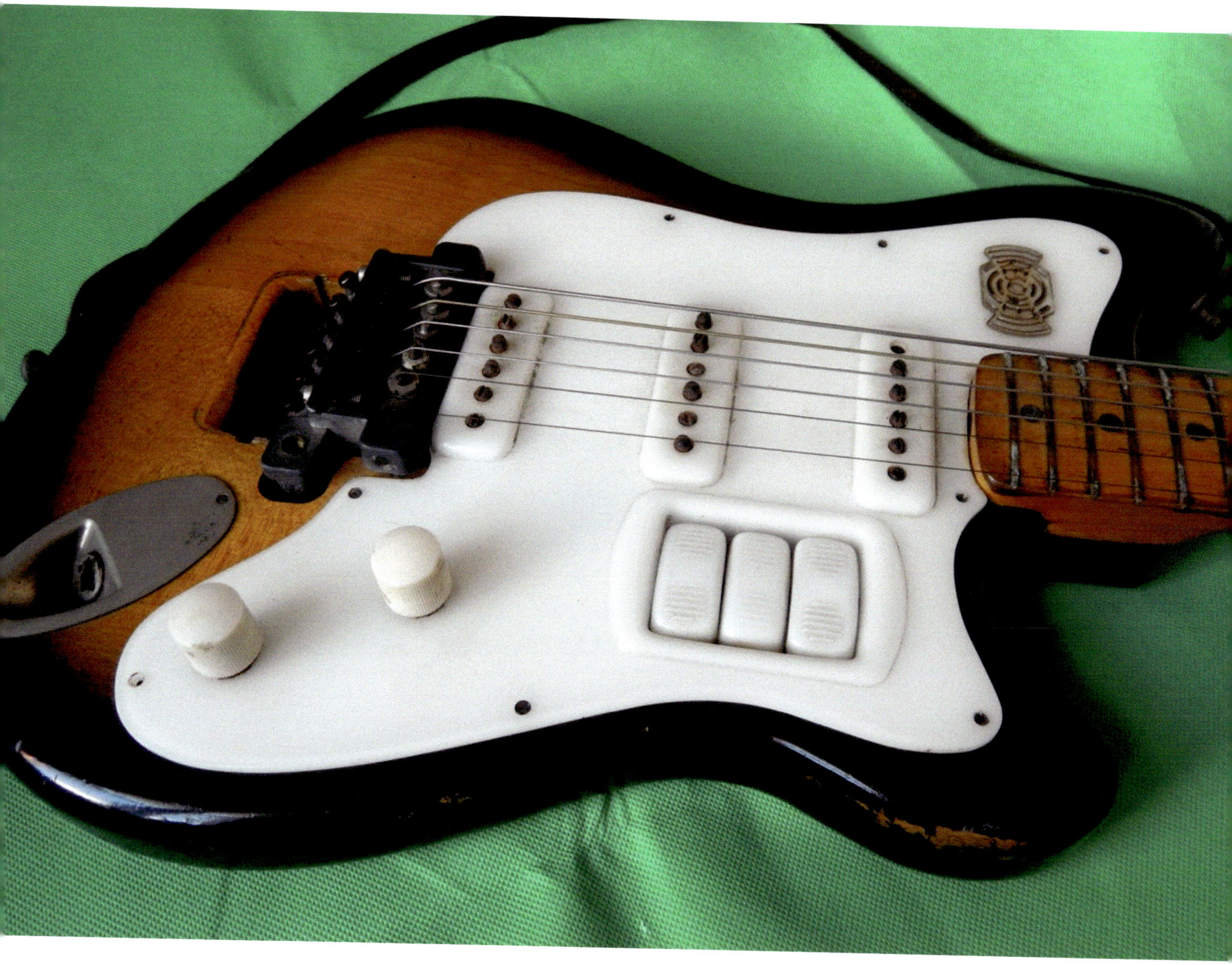

Body thickness at the middle waist: 27.06 mm and at the upper cutaway: 38.74mm.

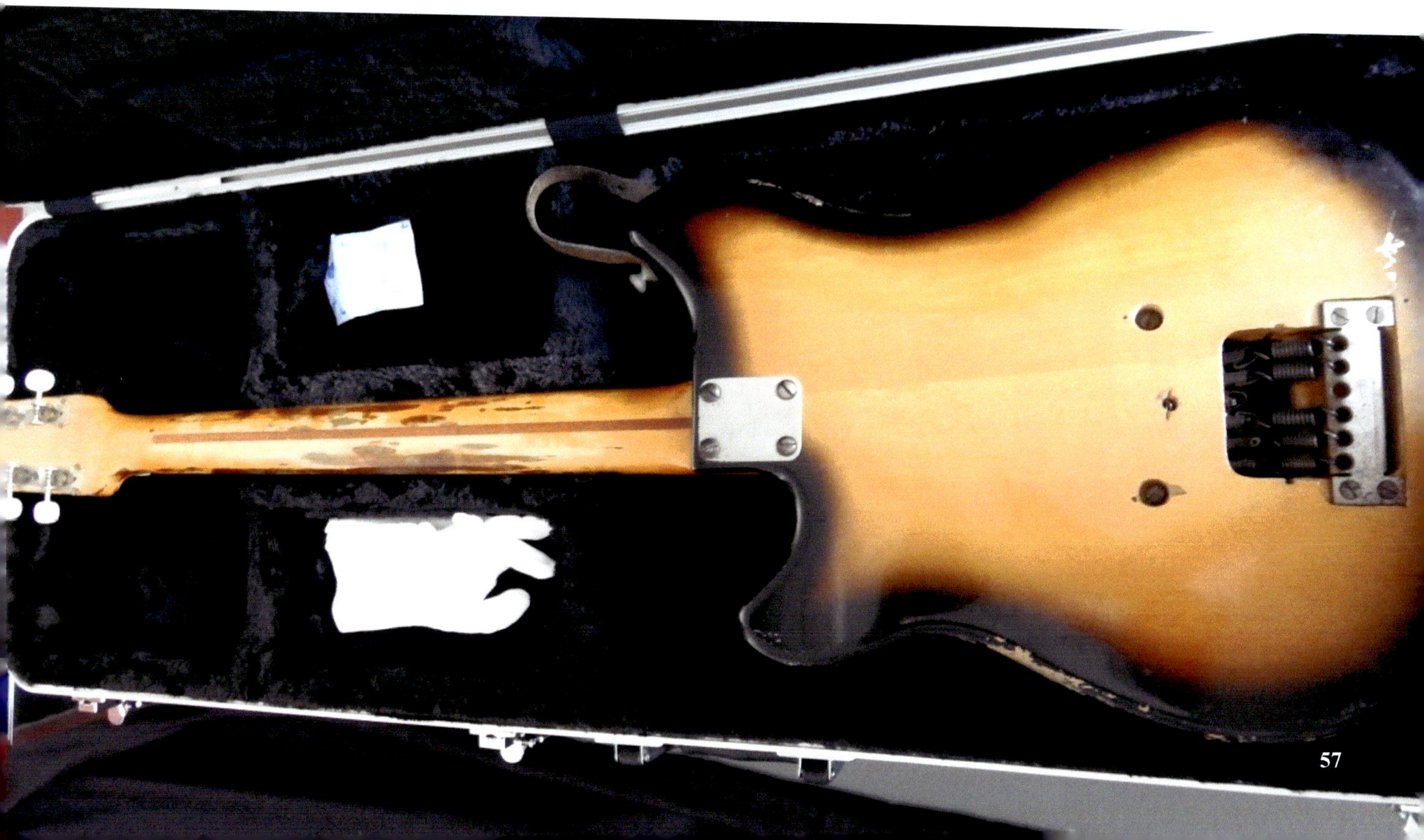

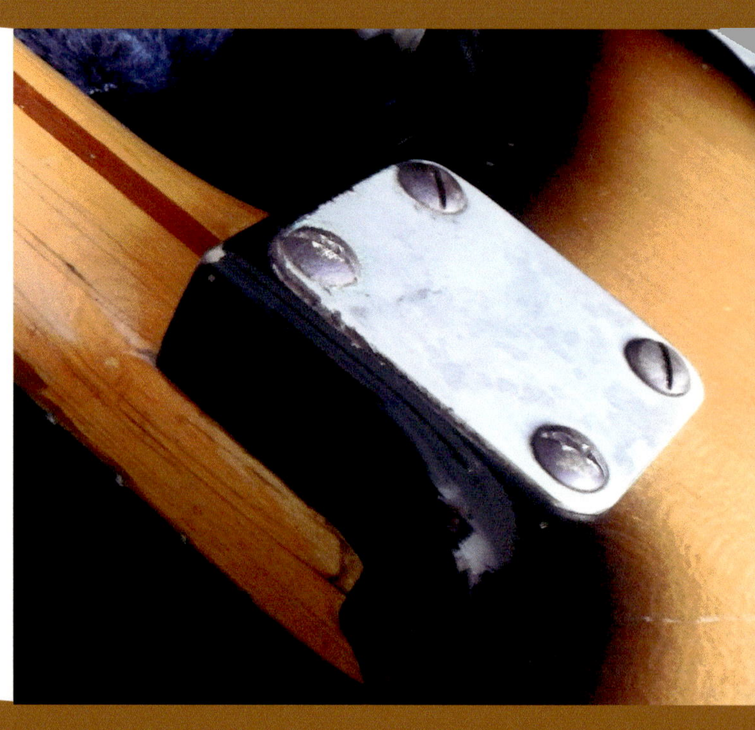

Length of bolts securing
the neck 41.56 mm.
The collar at the top above the
thread is 4.95 mm.
Truss rod end of the neck
thickness 26.75 mm.

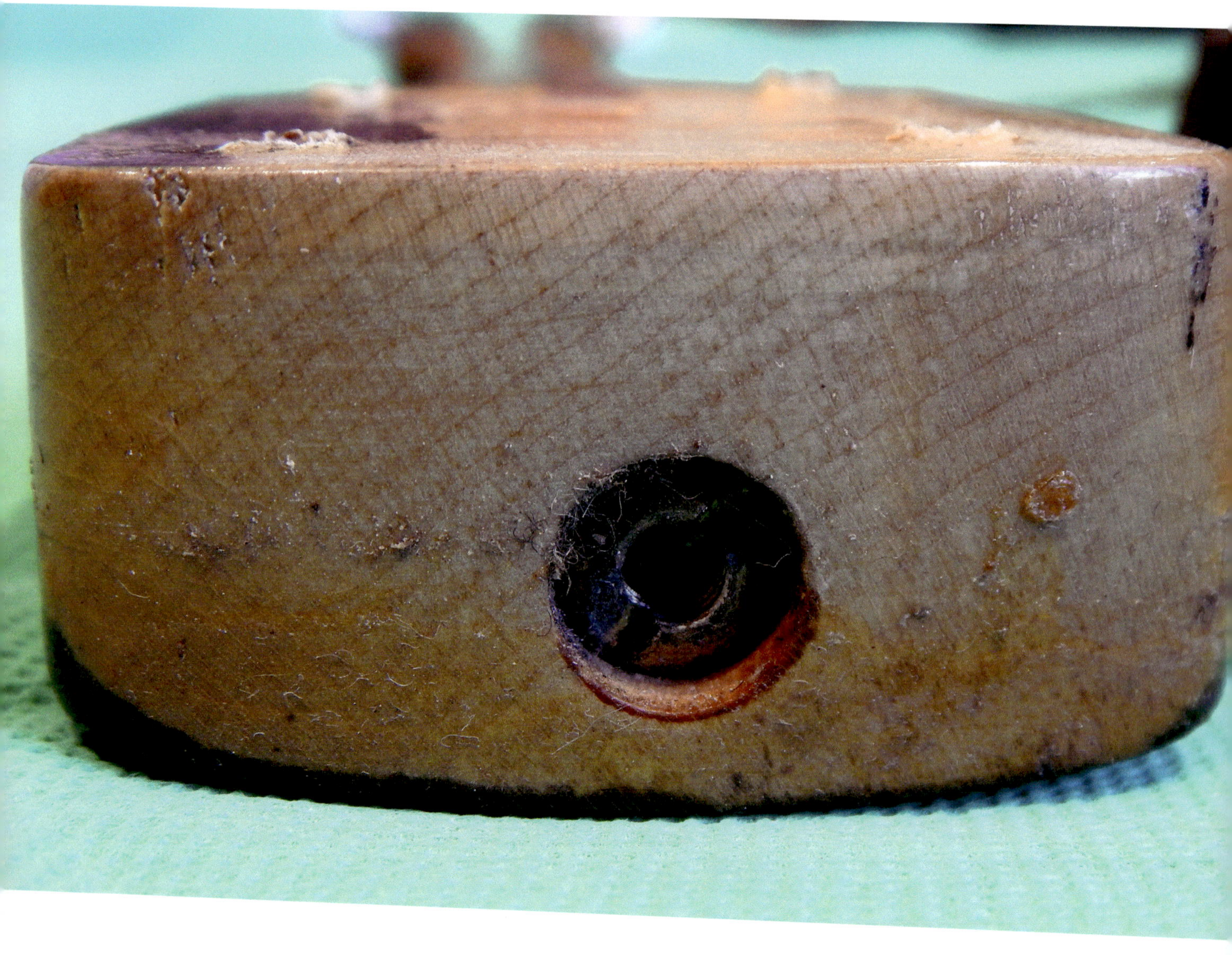

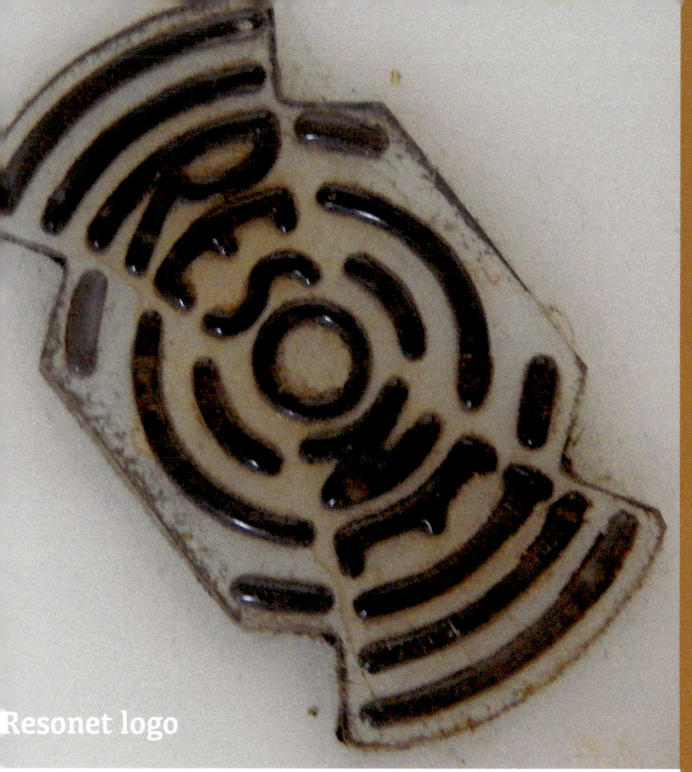

Resonet logo

Weight: 7.42 lbs
Case sticker for Hamburg

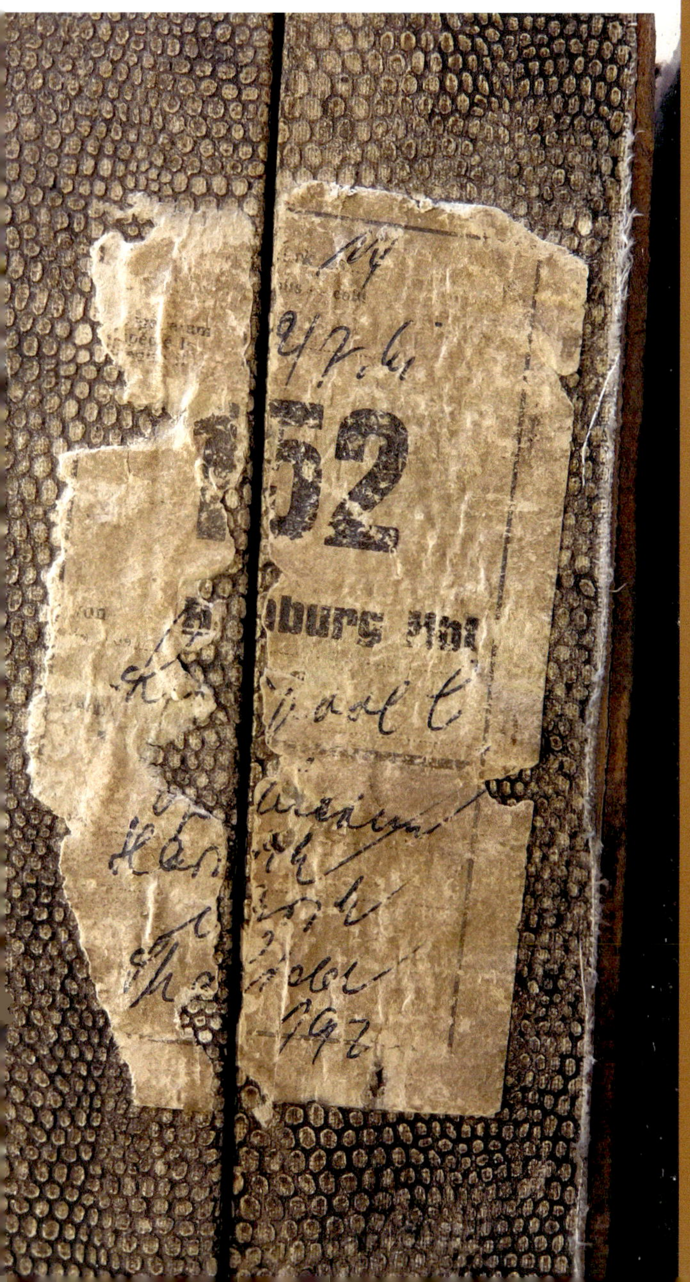

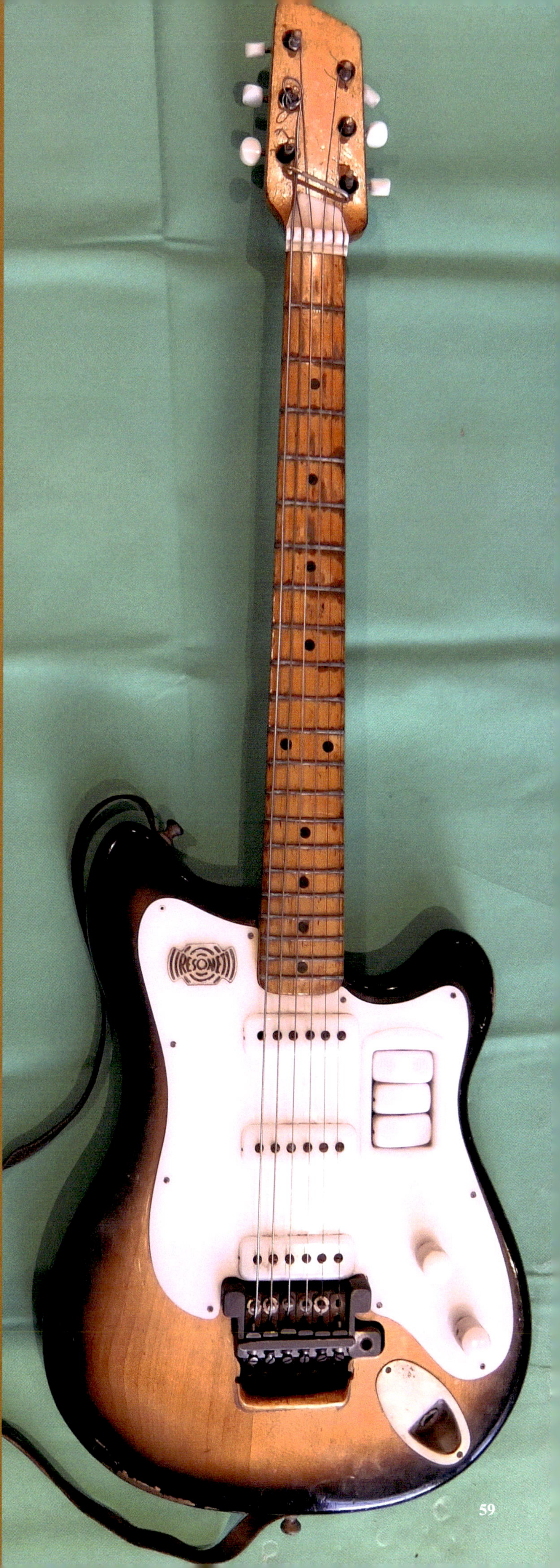

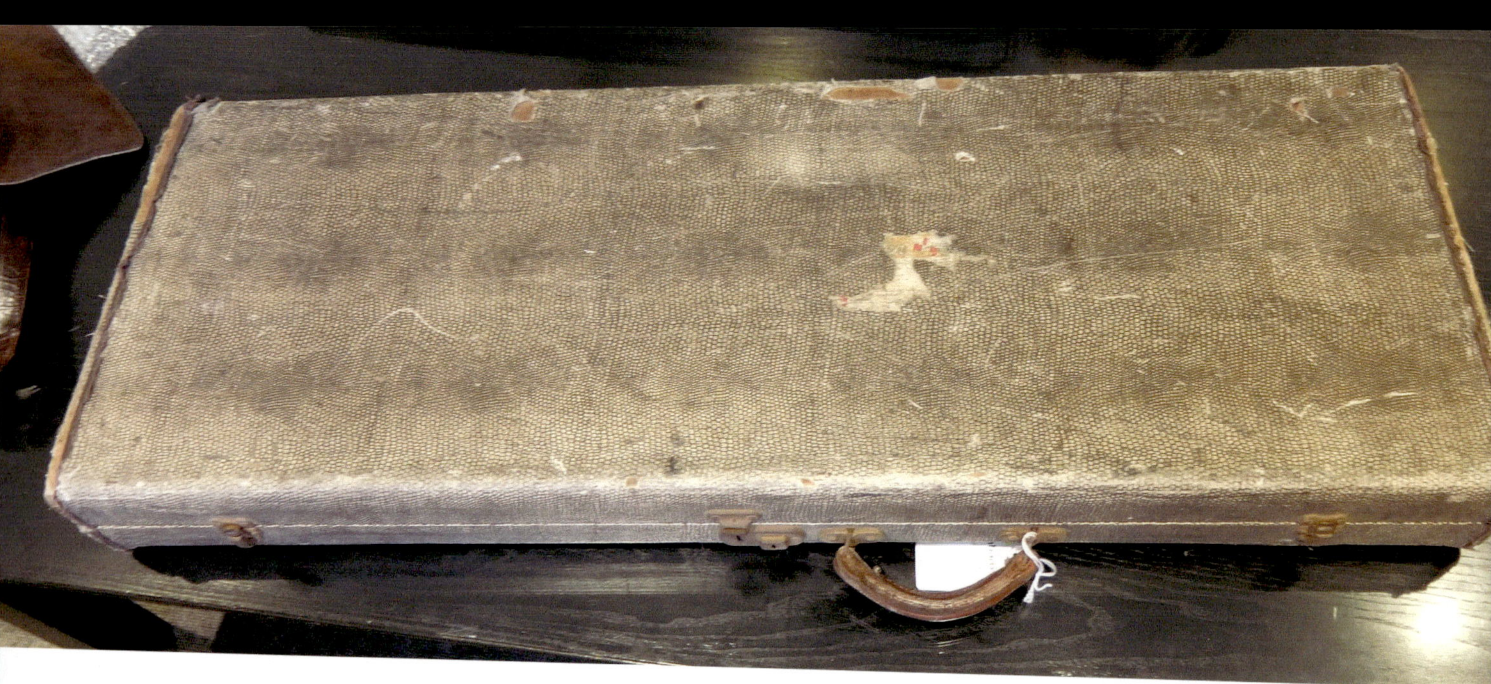

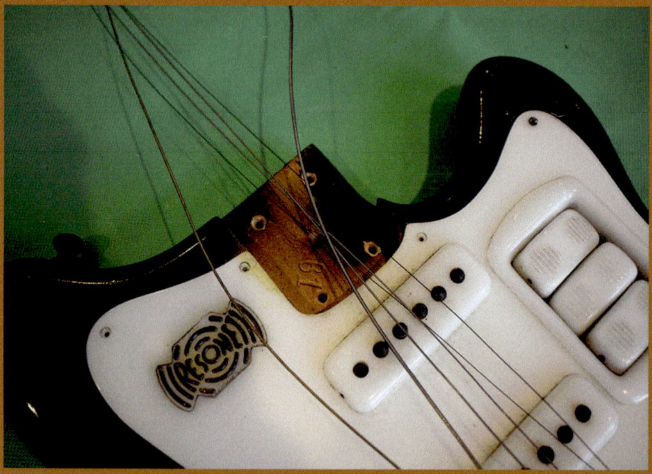

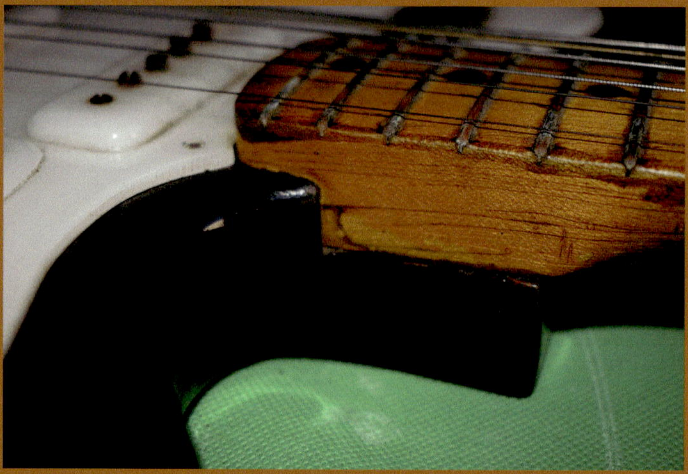

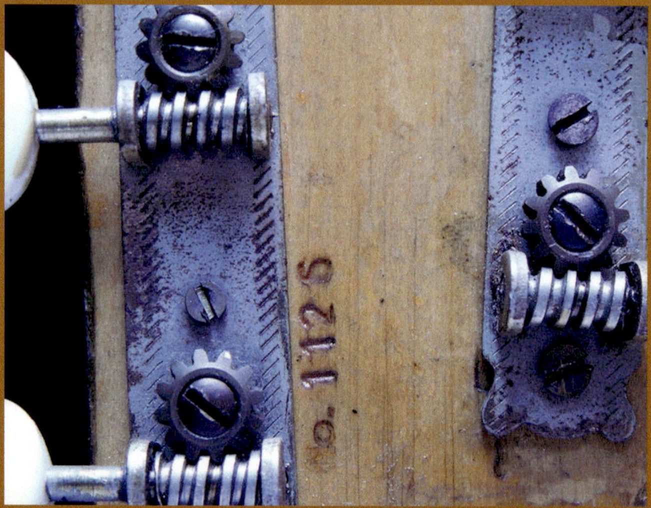

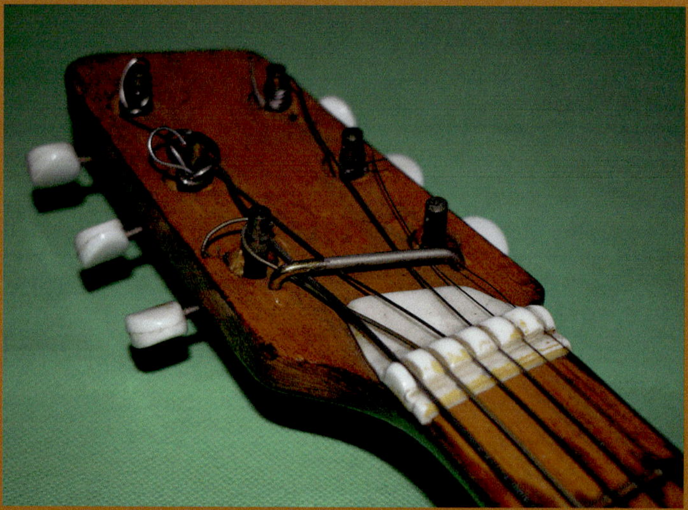

These guitars were made of either Beech or Maple

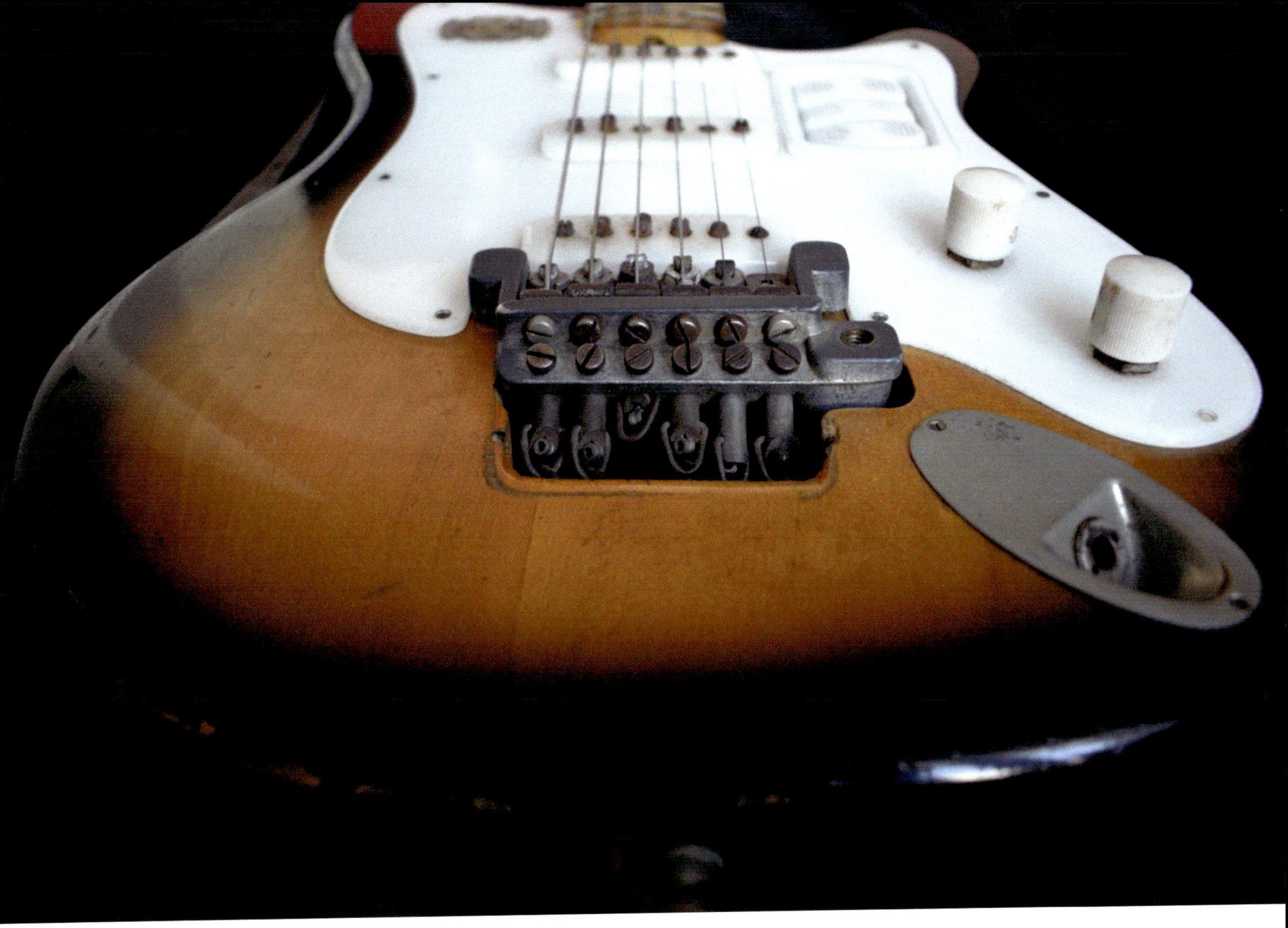

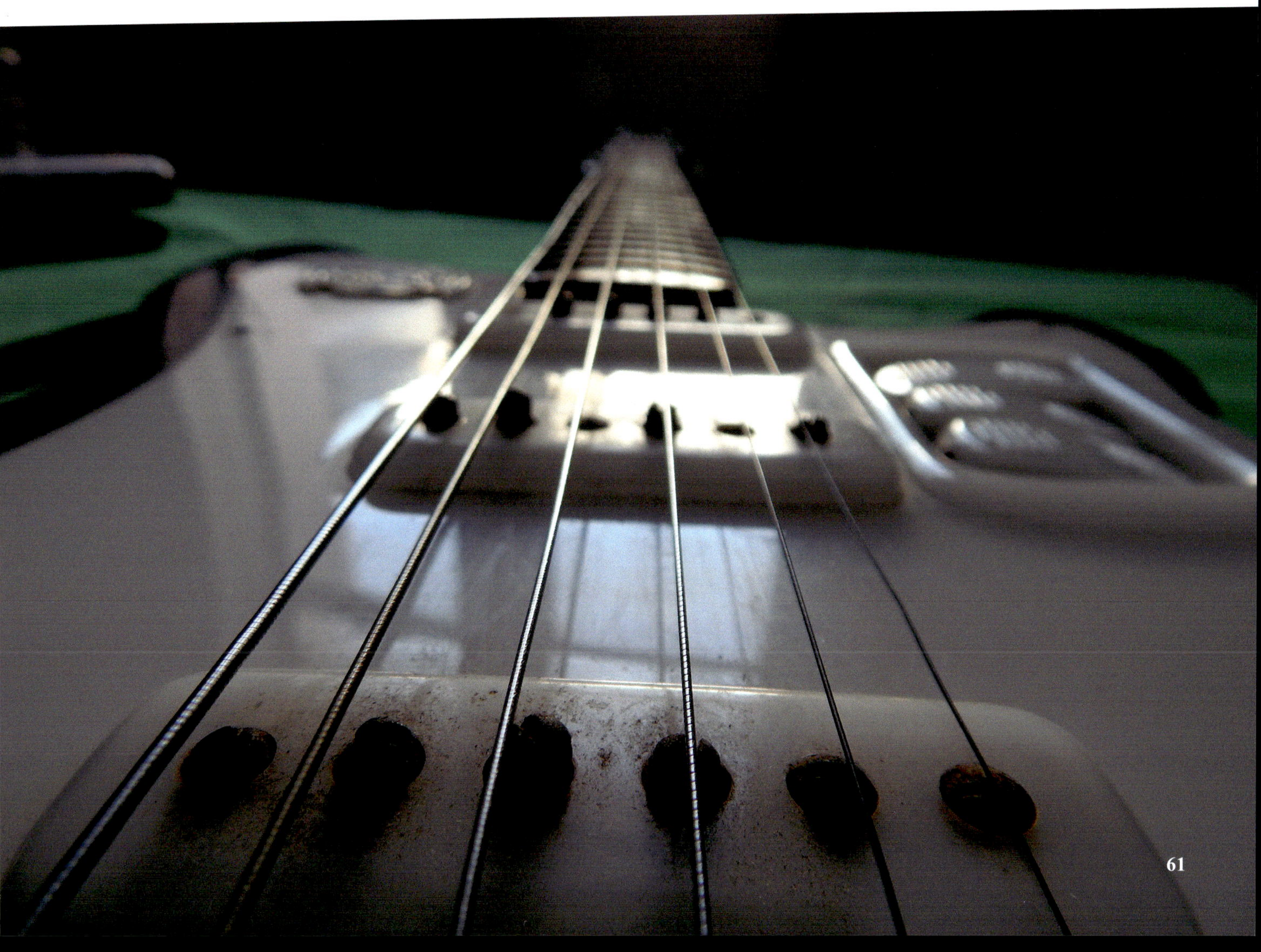

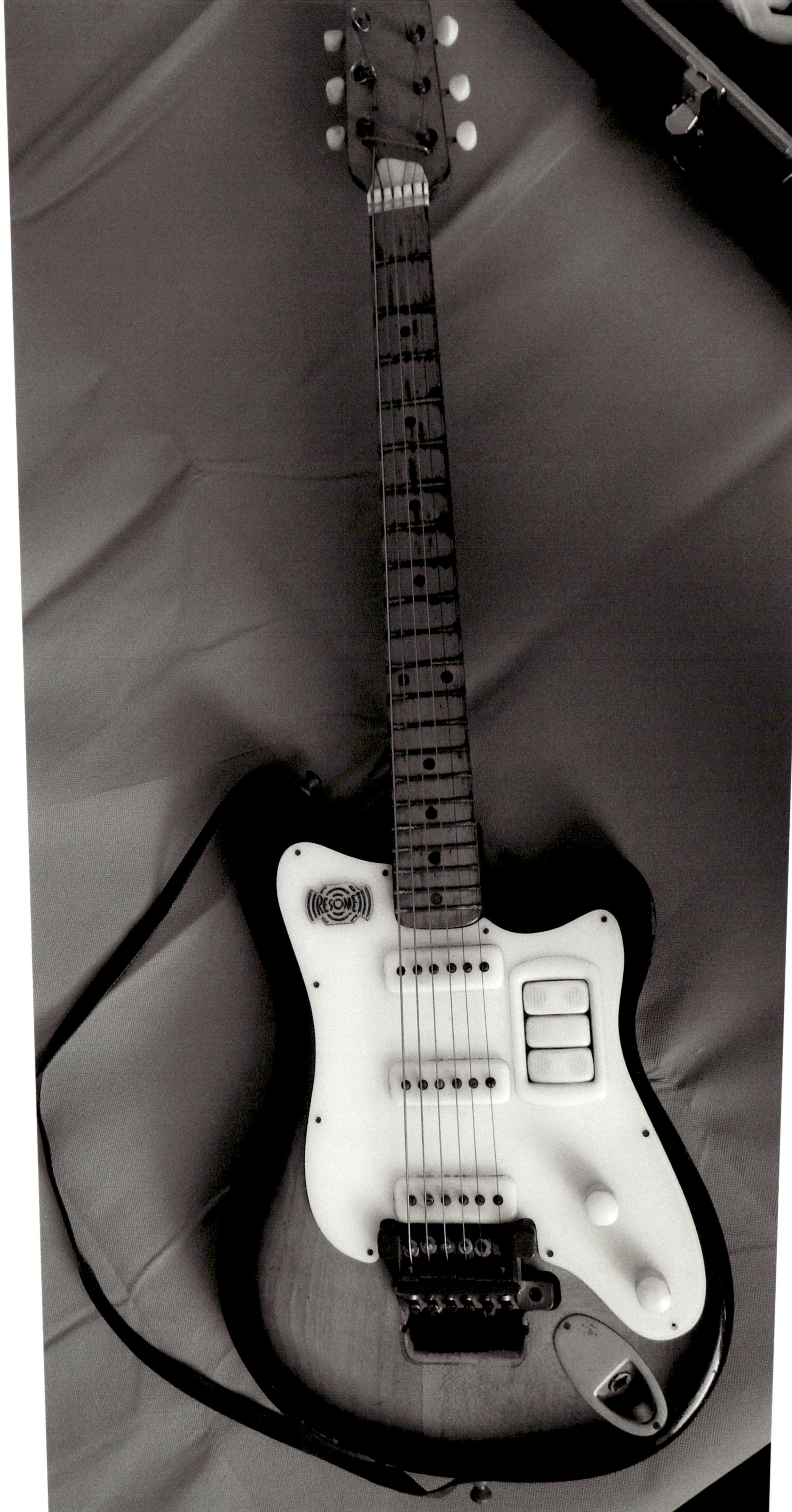

RESONET

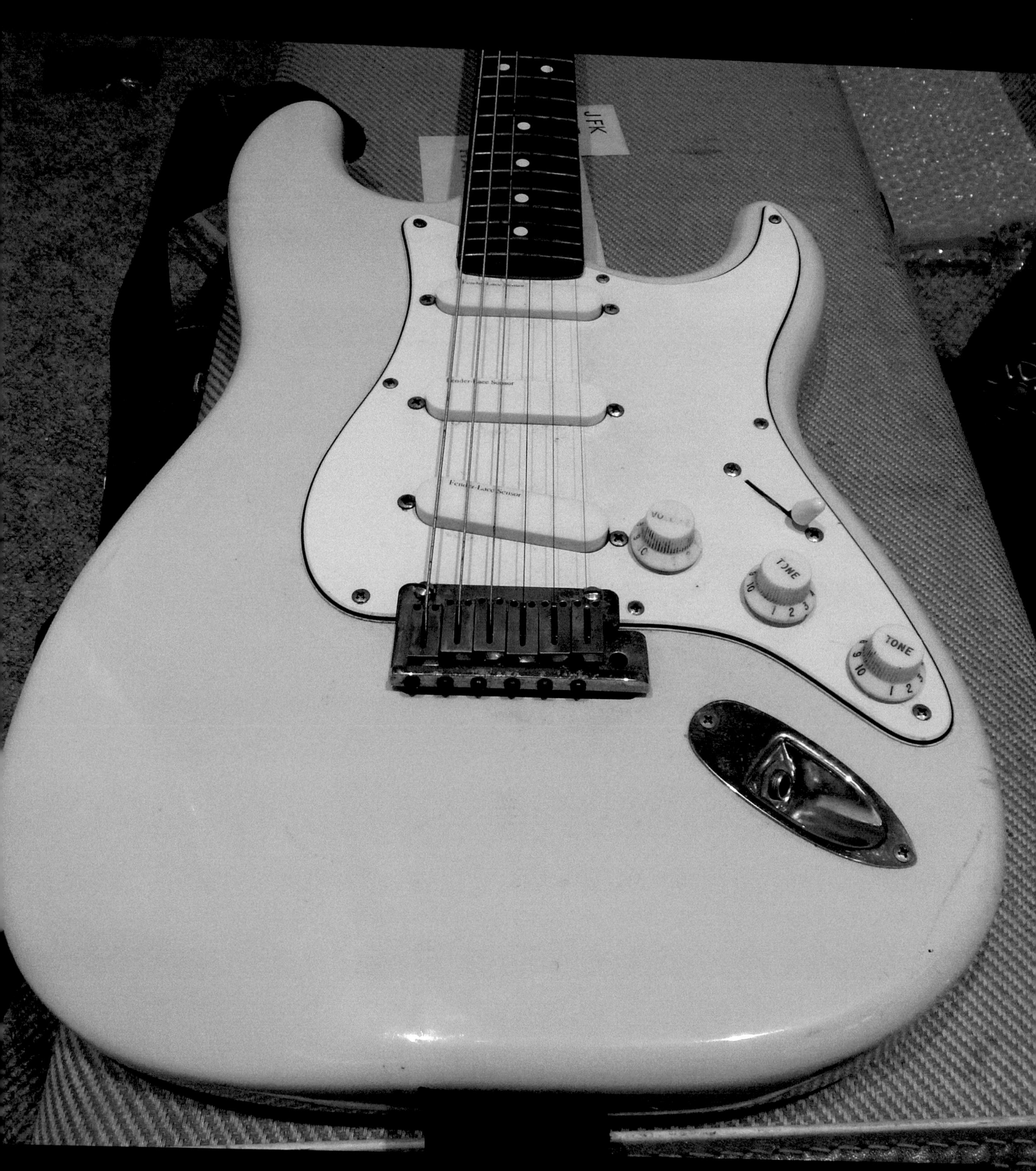

Jeff Beck - Graffiti Yellow Fender Stratocaster 1986

Jeff Beck has been described by many as one of the most influential guitarists of all time. The respect from his peers is testament to his innovation and uniqueness that elevated him to much more than just a rock guitarist. Jeff never had the signature songs in the way Eric Clapton had Layla or Jimmy Page had Stairway to Heaven but what he did have was the maverick genius and ability to take known songs and transform them in his own way: take Nitin Sawney's 'Nadia' as an example.

This graffiti yellow Strat typifies Jeff's idea and suggestion to Fender to build him a '62 spec Strat for his forthcoming Japanese tour in 1986. It was through a meeting in the UK organised by John Hill, Fender's Brand and Artists Relations Director bringing together a party to celebrate the very first Stratocaster that came to the UK: the red Strat of Shadows guitarist Hank Marvin. (this guitar is featured in Famous Frets book one) The idea was to get the most celebrated guitarists in the world to use Fender as part of a re-launch of the brand. Eric Clapton, David Gilmour, Hank Marvin and Jeff Beck were some of the people John Hill brought to the Hilton Hotel.

Some time afterwards Jeff asked Fender for a new Stratocaster with a huge neck and a '62 spec for his tour of Japan. He requested that the colour was the same shade of yellow as the 1932 Ford Hotrod Coupe that had featured in the 1973 movie 'American Graffiti'.

Around 5 or 6 yellow guitars were made at Fender. It was George Blanda who built the neck for Jeff and wrote on the end of it "Jeff Beck's Neck".

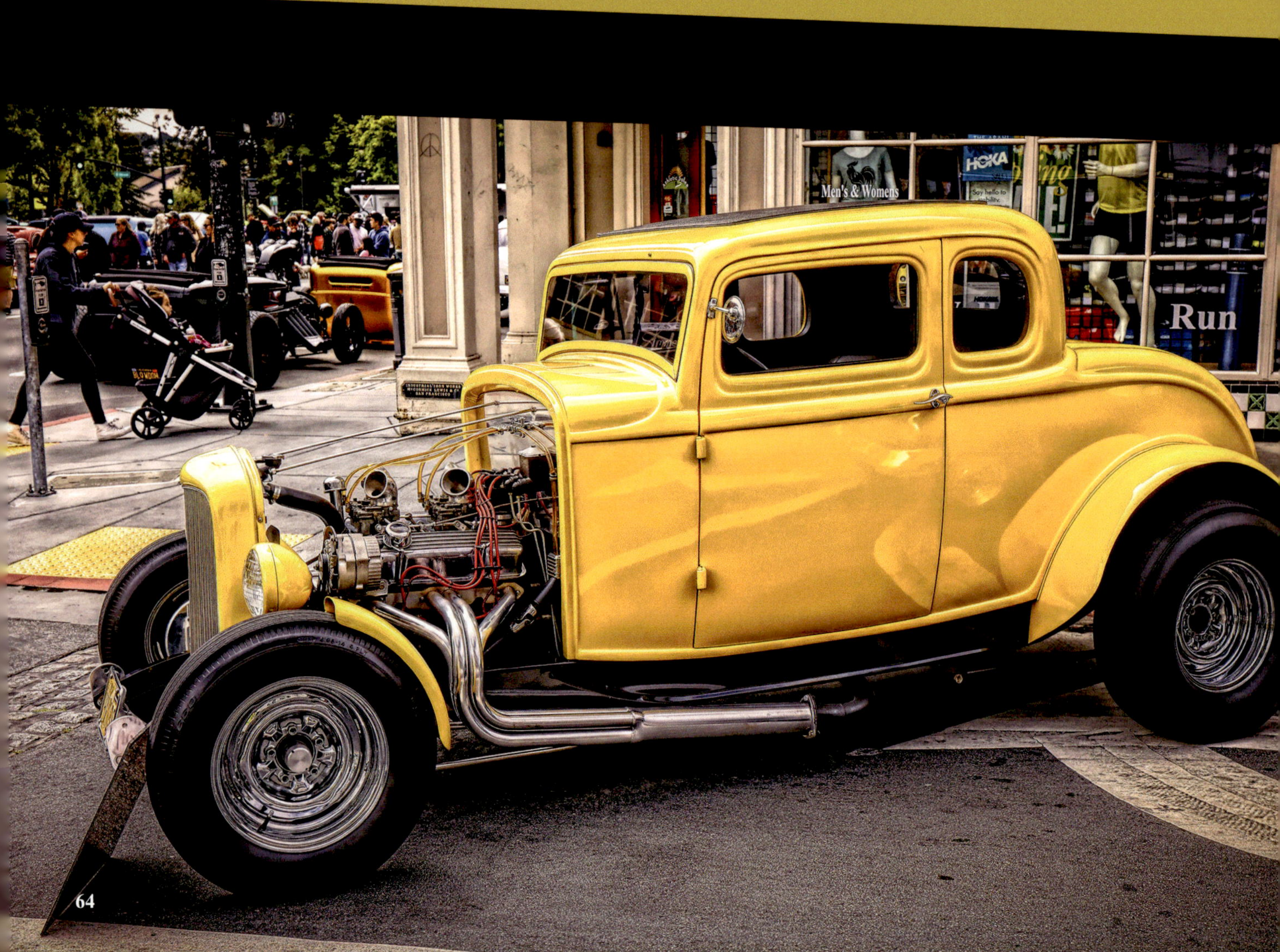

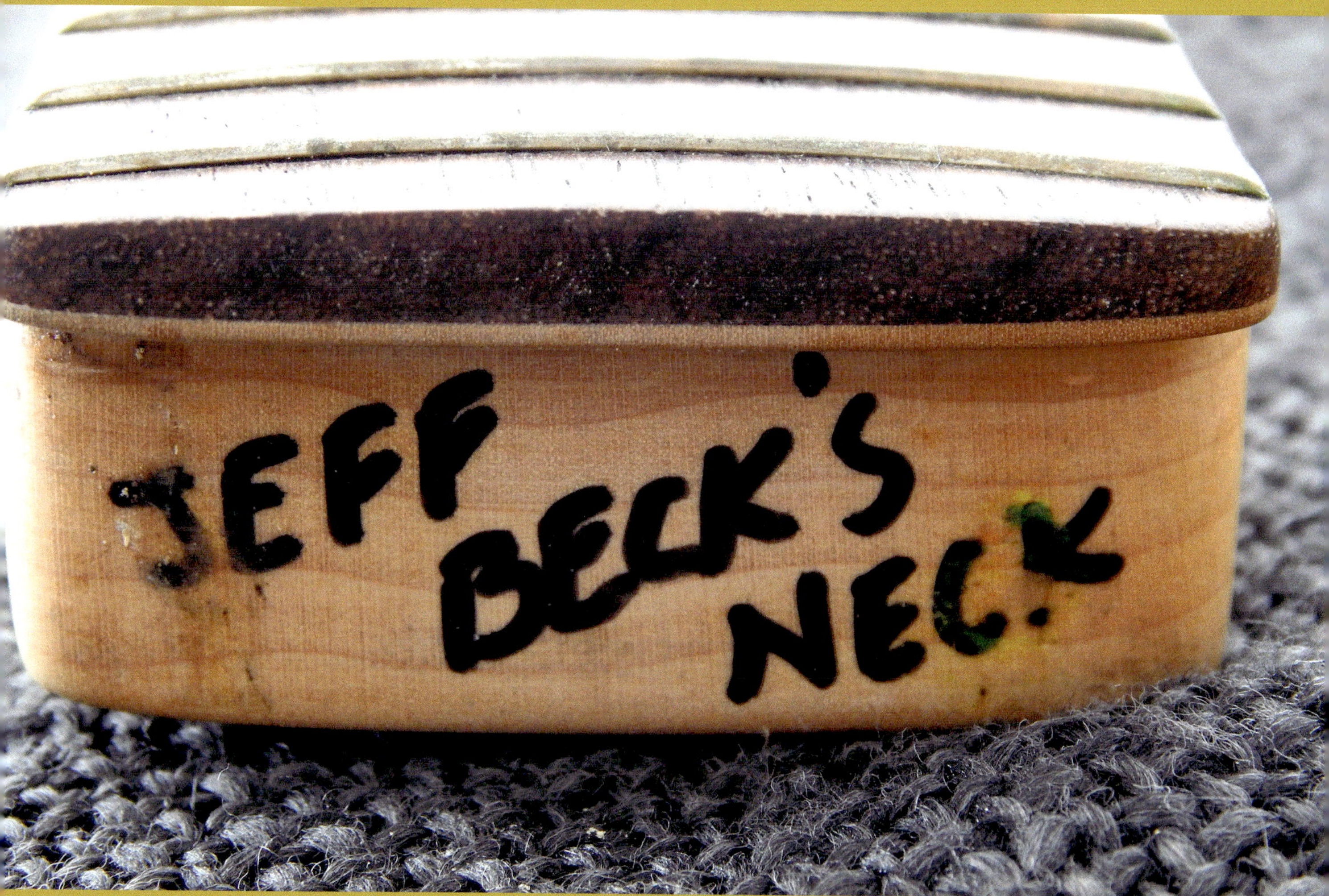

JEFF BECK'S NECK

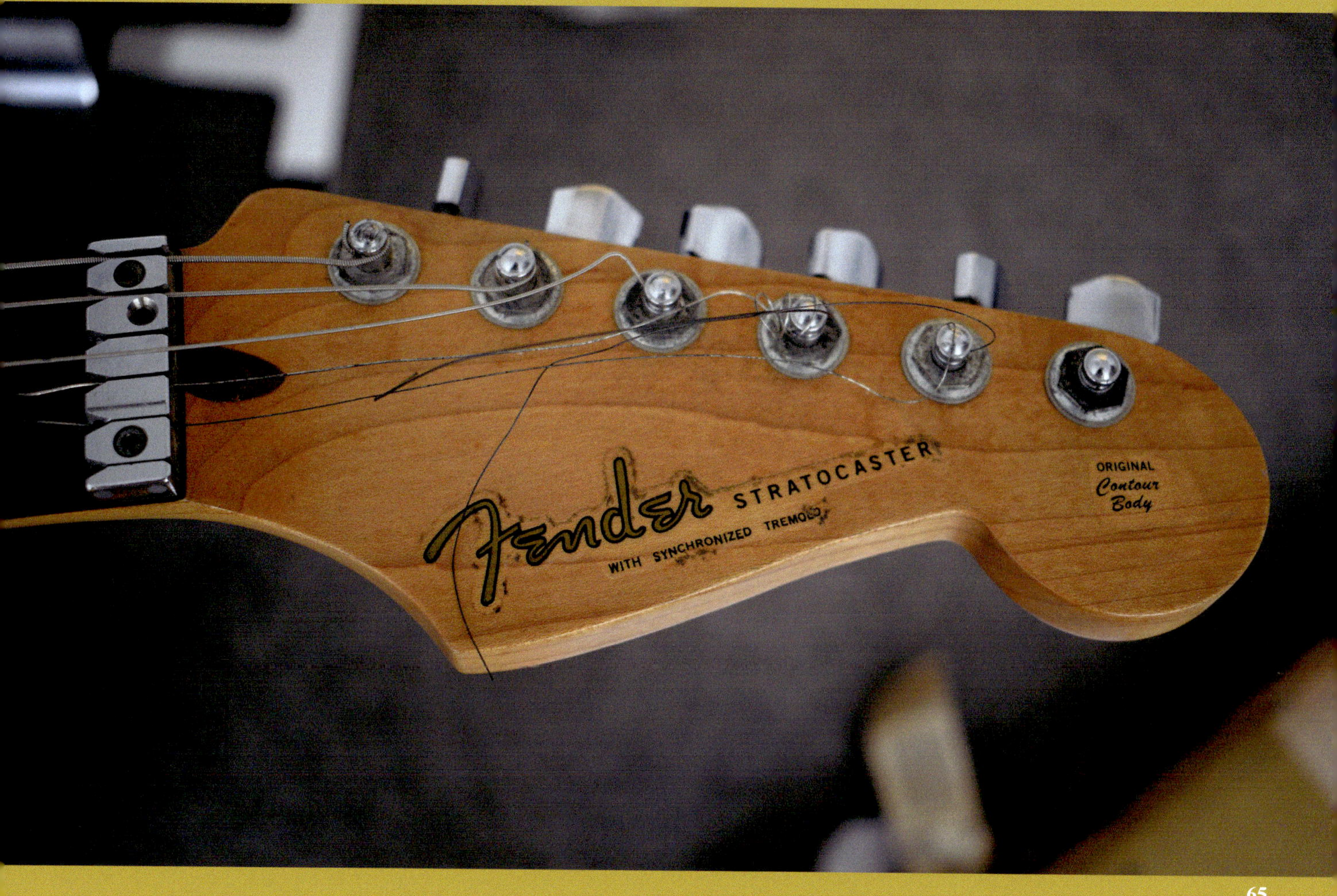

Fender STRATOCASTER
WITH SYNCHRONIZED TREMOLO
ORIGINAL
Contour
Body

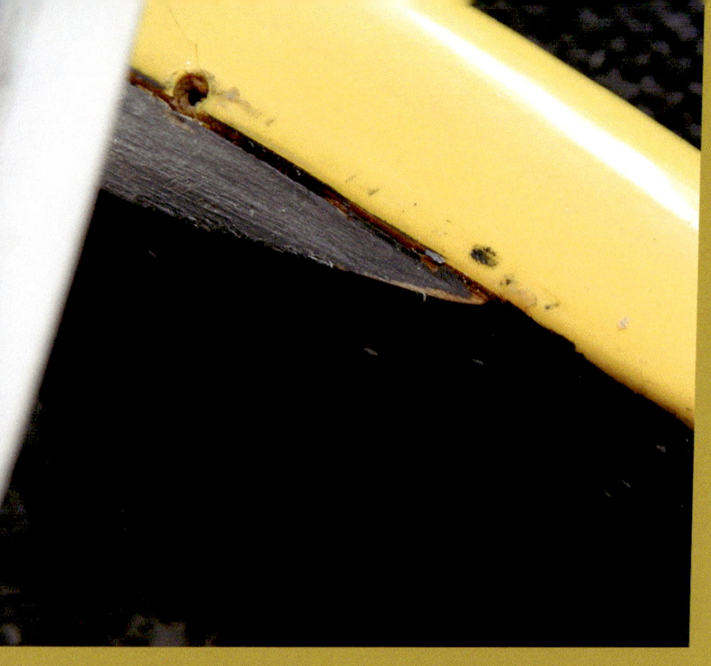

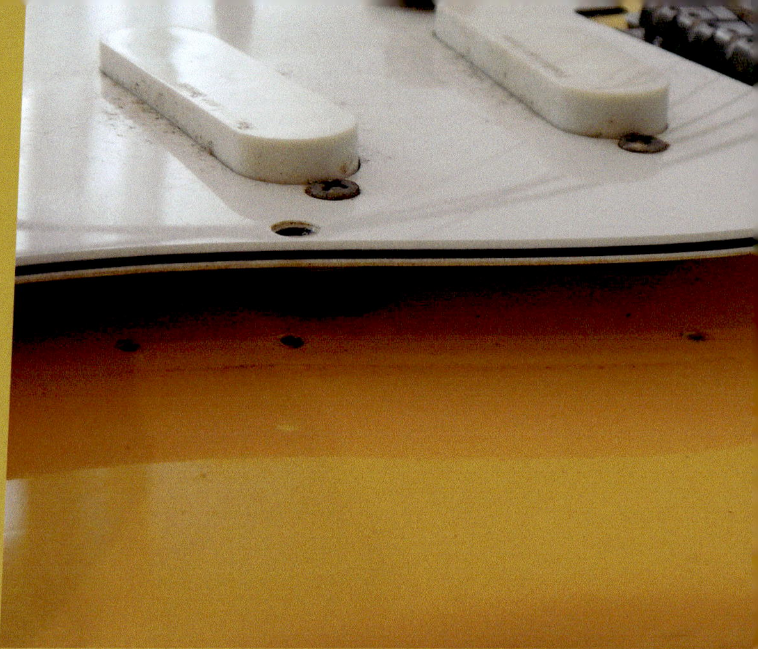

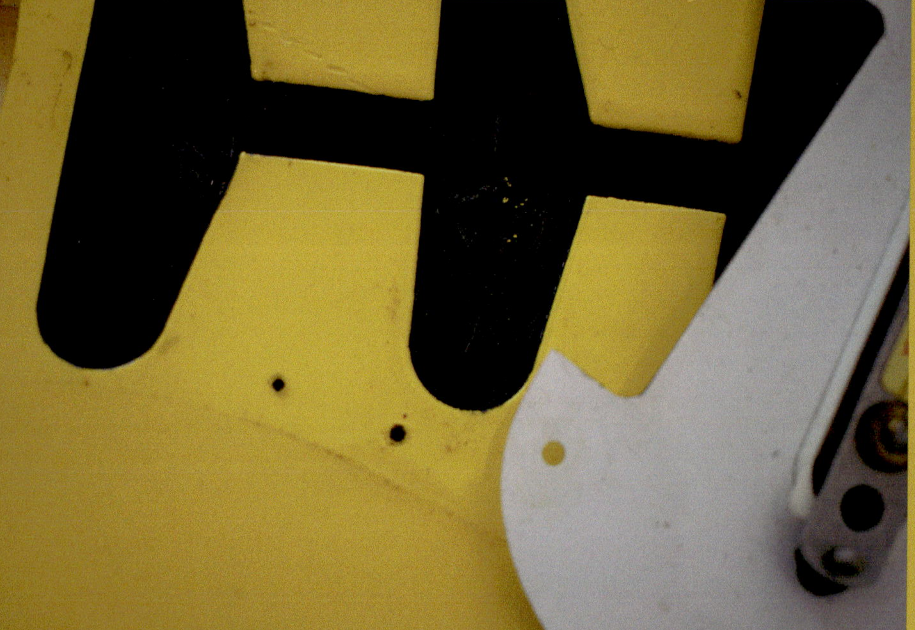

Here you can see the original screw holes from the 11 screw pick guard and the wood insert to accommodate the 8 screw pick guard.

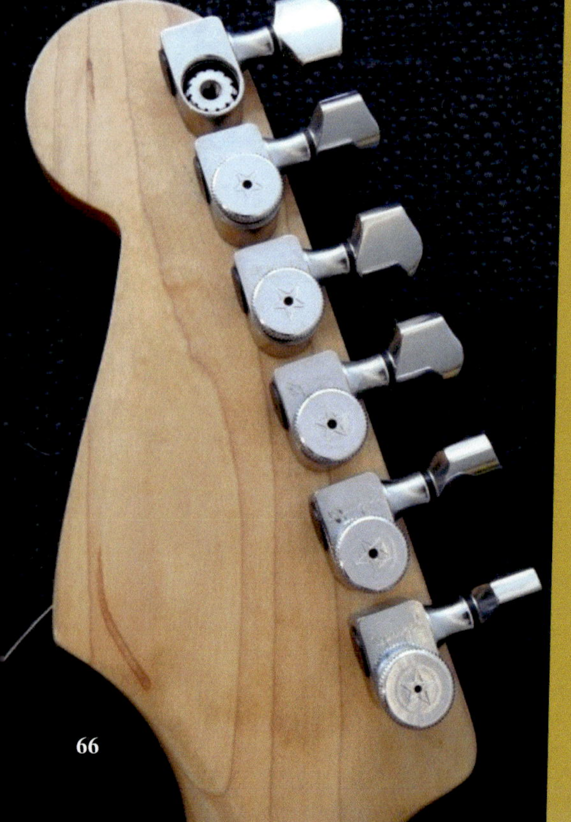

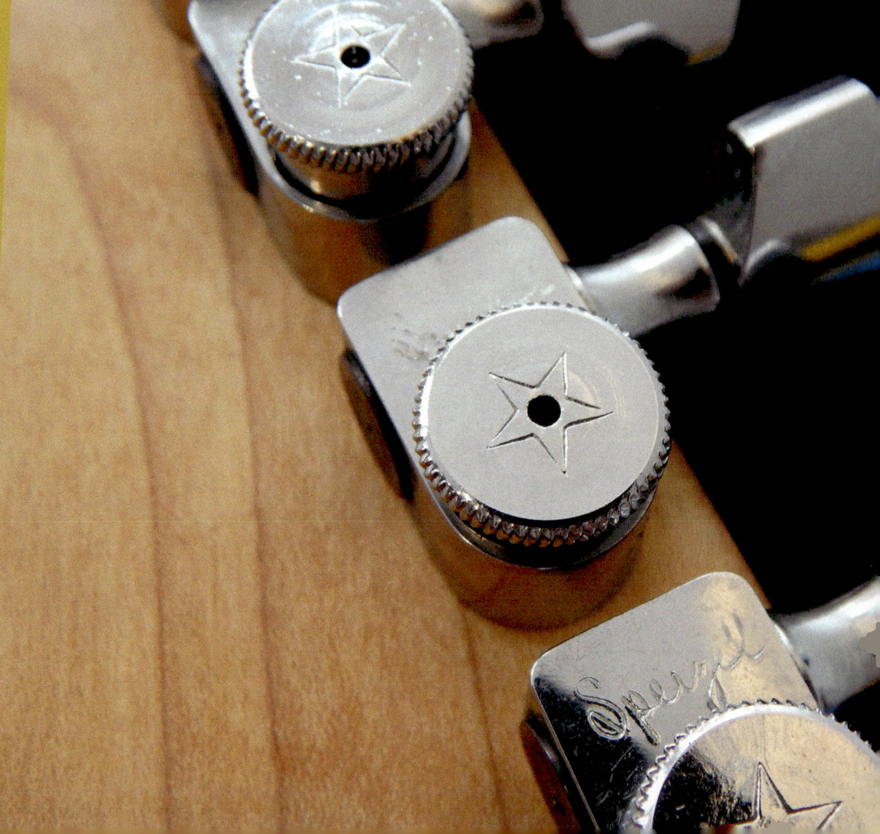

In the summer of 1986 the guitar was sent back to Fender for some additional modifications. The vintage style bridge was removed and replaced with a proto of the two-pivot tremolo that they took off the American Standard Prototype. It was at that time that a new, oversized neck with a Brazilian Rosewood fingerboard was fitted. The 3-ply eleven hole pick guard was replaced with a 3-ply eight hole one. This neck was fitted probably in early 1987 with what are now the very rare Sperzal Star locking tuners and the new 1st generation Trevor Wilkinson Roller nut. Trevor told me that he sent Fender maybe 10 of these at that time but when Fender first fitted the Roller nut Jeff complained that there was a rattle coming from one of the strings near the nut. The curious extra hole that can be seen between the A and D strings was probably due to Fender thinking that it needed to be secured more to the headstock but in actual fact it was not fitted correctly. Once the error was rectified Jeff was thrilled with the result and the tuning stability if offered.

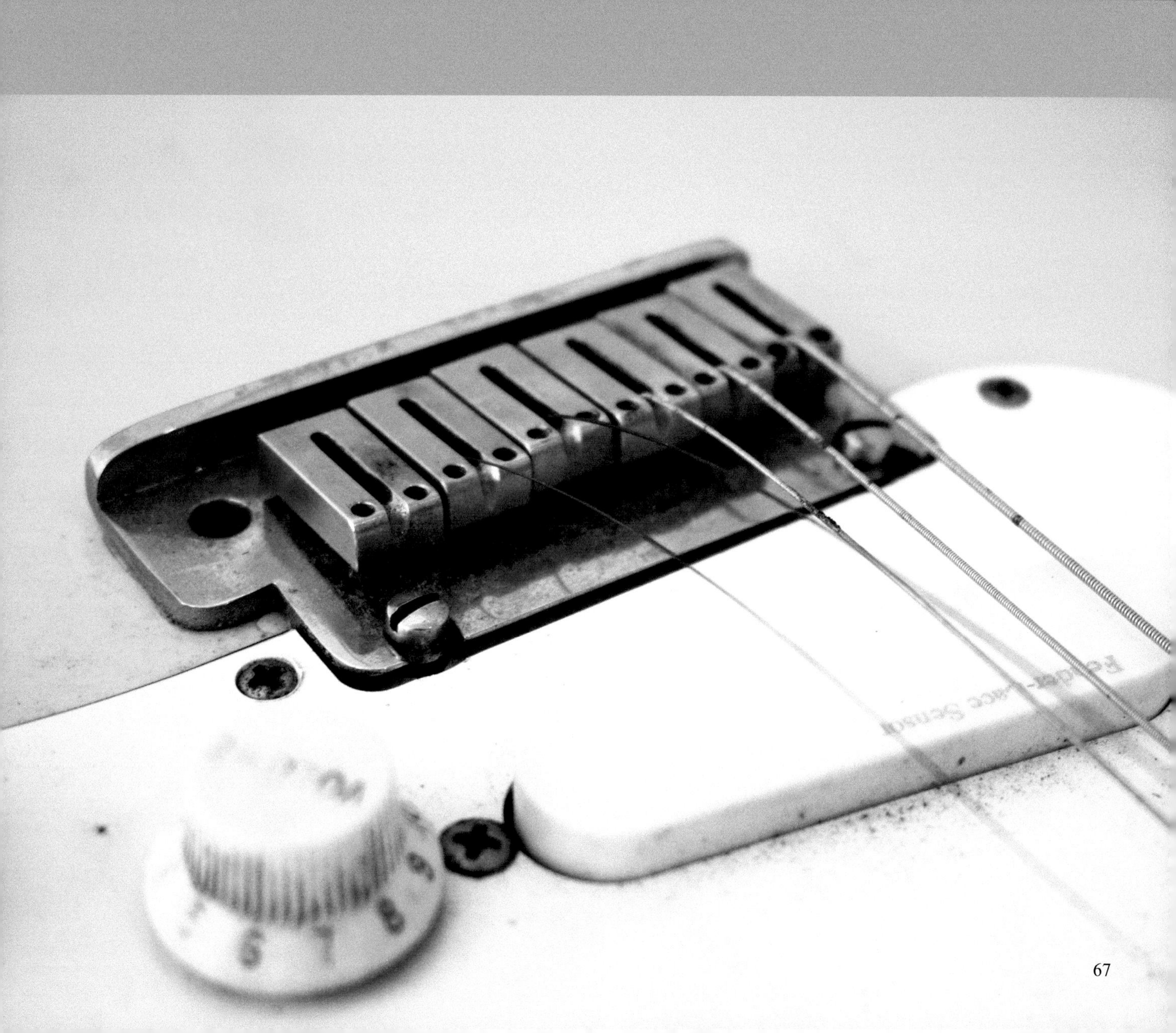

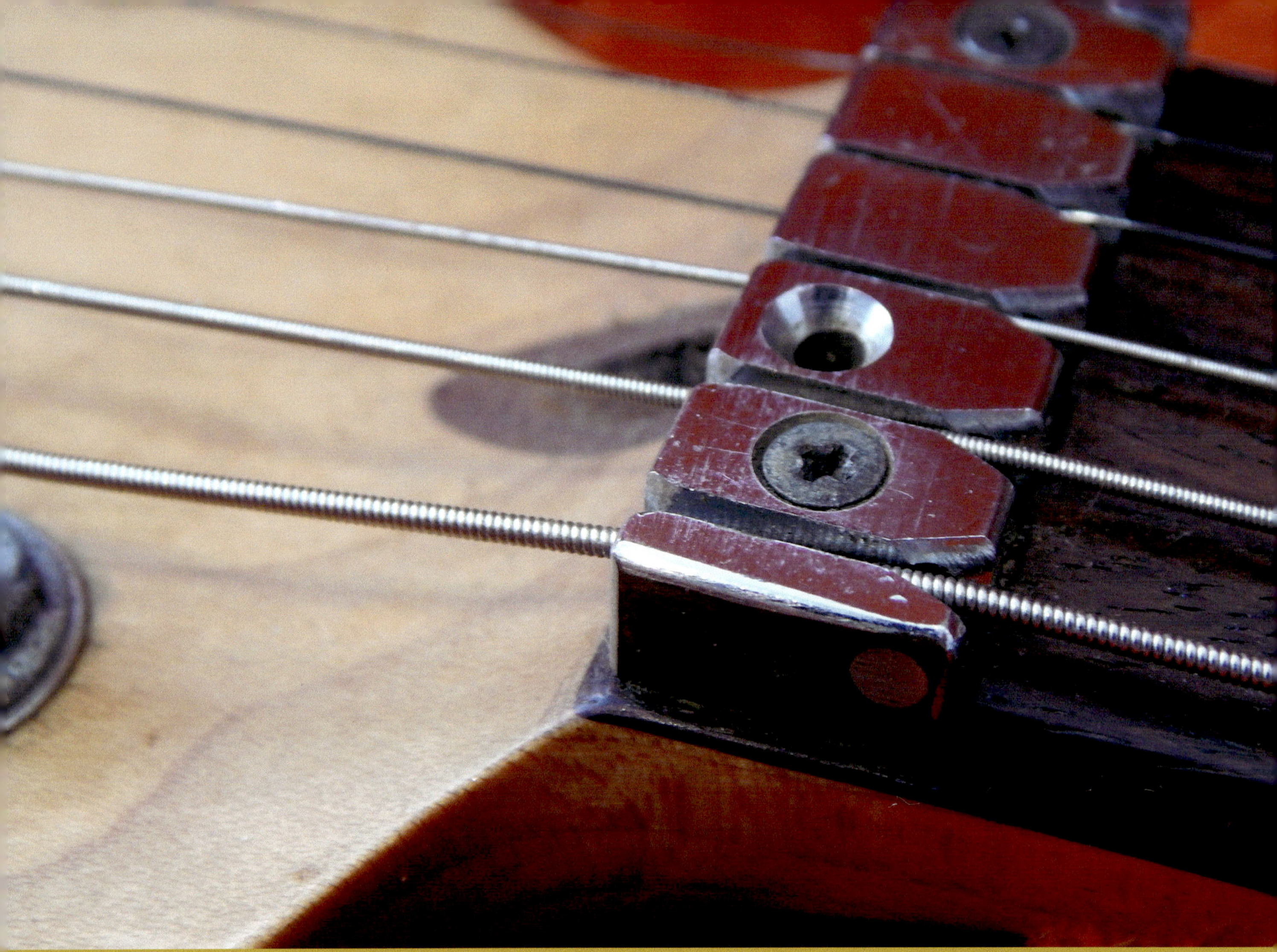

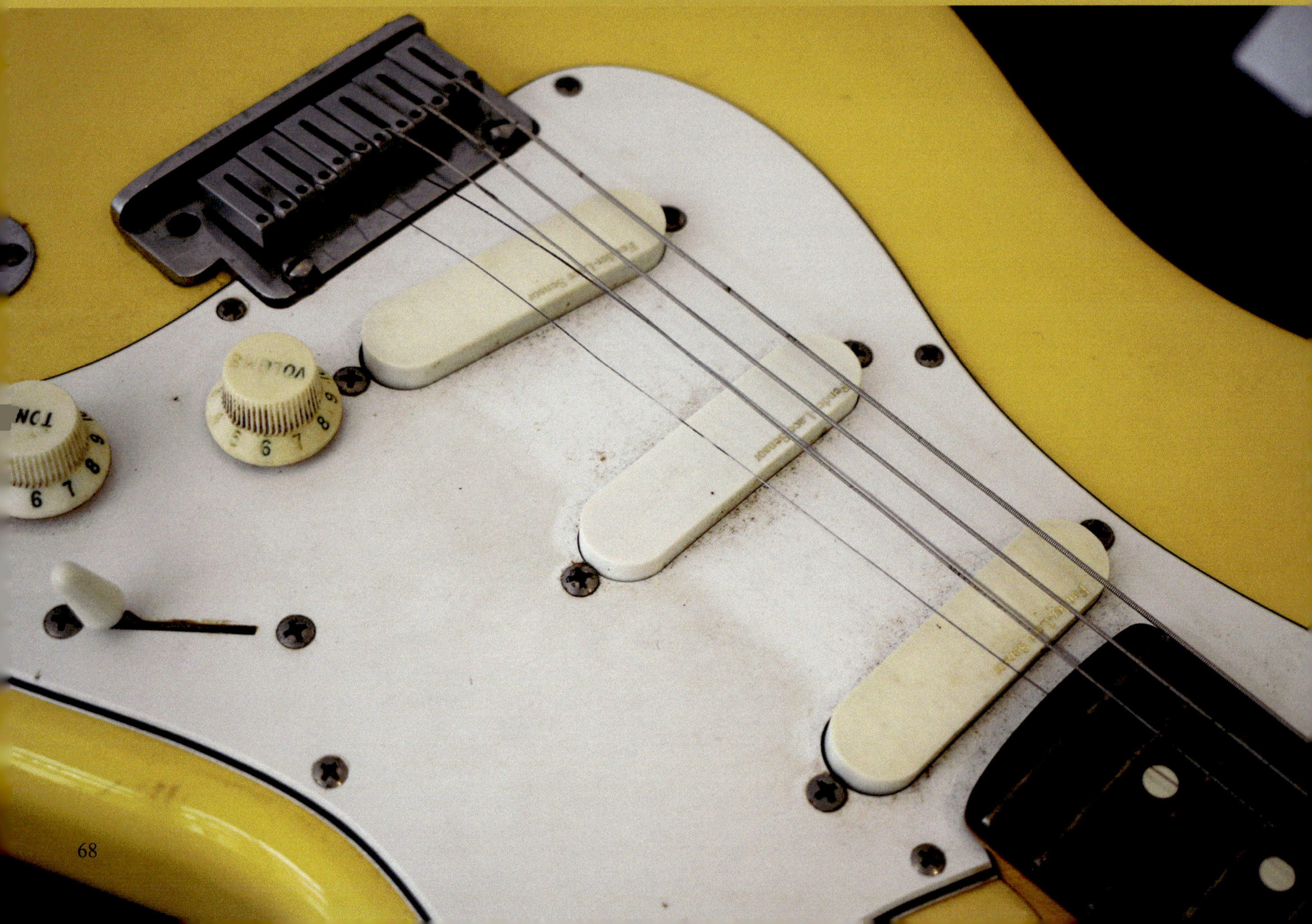

Although the Lace Sensor pickups were in development at this time, Jeff still kept his 1960's spec pickups on the guitar. The combination of parts during this time became known as the 'Strat Plus' introduced in 1987. He did not have the Lace Sensor pickups fitted until late 1989 early 1990 as a picture still shows him with the 1960's spec pickups in May 1989.

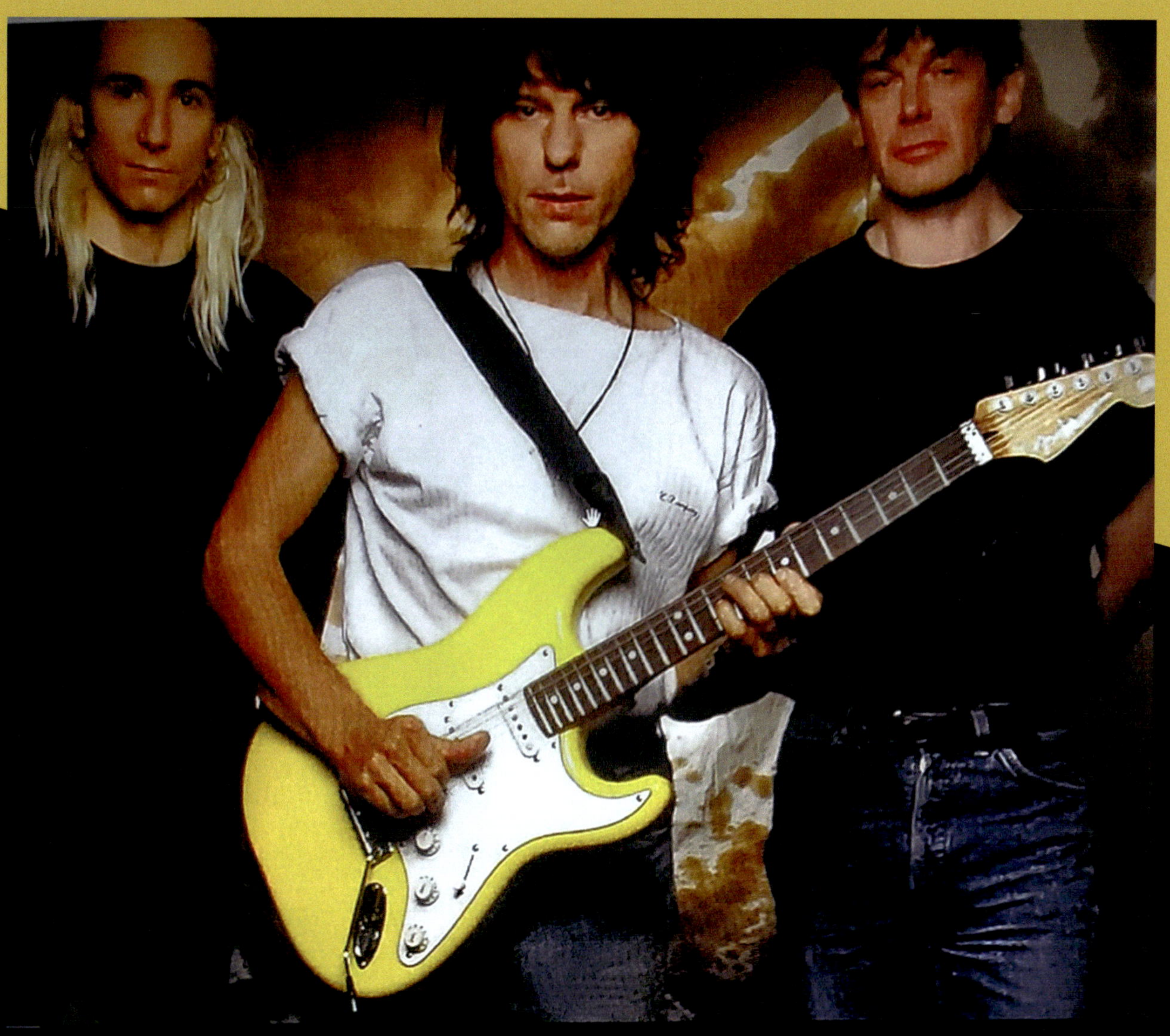

With Roller nut, 2-pivot bridge but still '62 spec pickups.

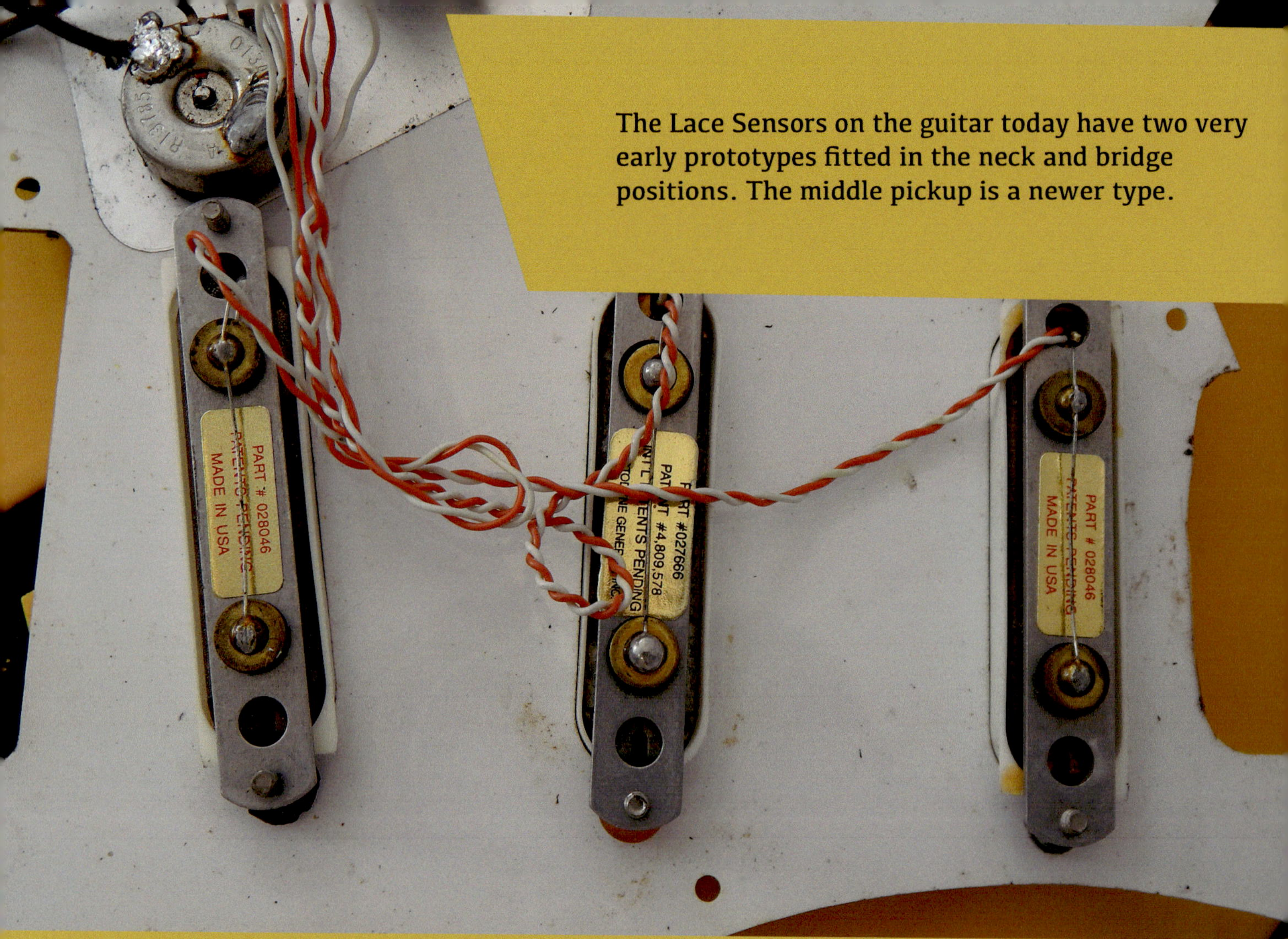

The Lace Sensors on the guitar today have two very early prototypes fitted in the neck and bridge positions. The middle pickup is a newer type.

Note: bridge and neck have squared plastic casings yet middle pickup is rounded.

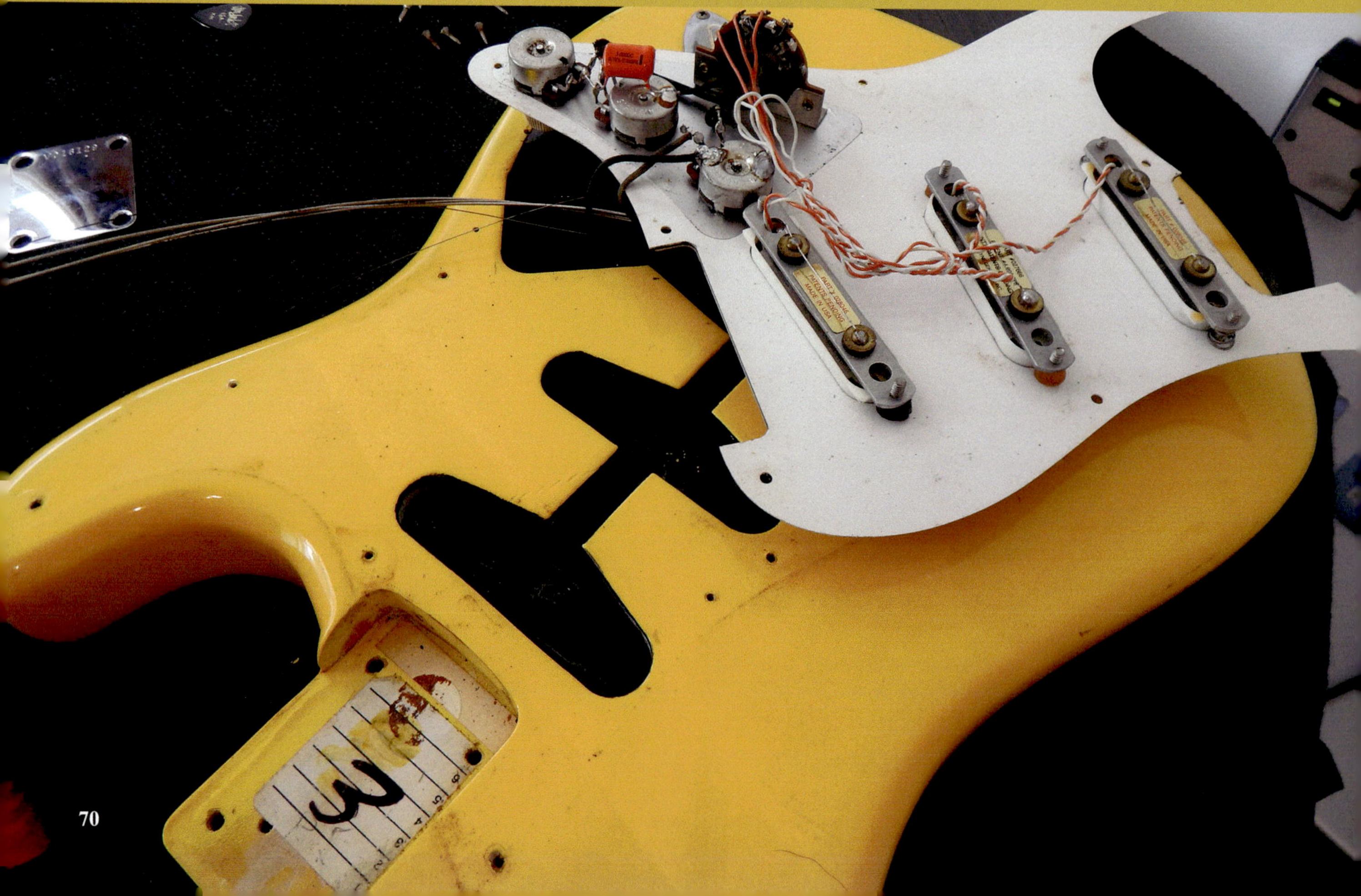

It has been said that later the guitar was again sent back to Fender due to 'finish' issues and they installed the Lace sensor pickups making it a Strat Plus. I'm personally not so sure this happened as it was known that Jeff was capable of changing things on his guitars such as necks etc and was quite familiar with wiring a guitar like this: he had a mechanical mind. On closer examination, the quality of the solder joints on the volume control seem more DIY than the familiar Custom shop style you'd expect evidenced by the picture below. Although it is pure speculation it would not surprise me at all that Jeff decided to put these in himself. Let's not forget, he was going to take the neck off the guitar (as he liked it) and fit another one for his then girlfriend to learn to play guitar.

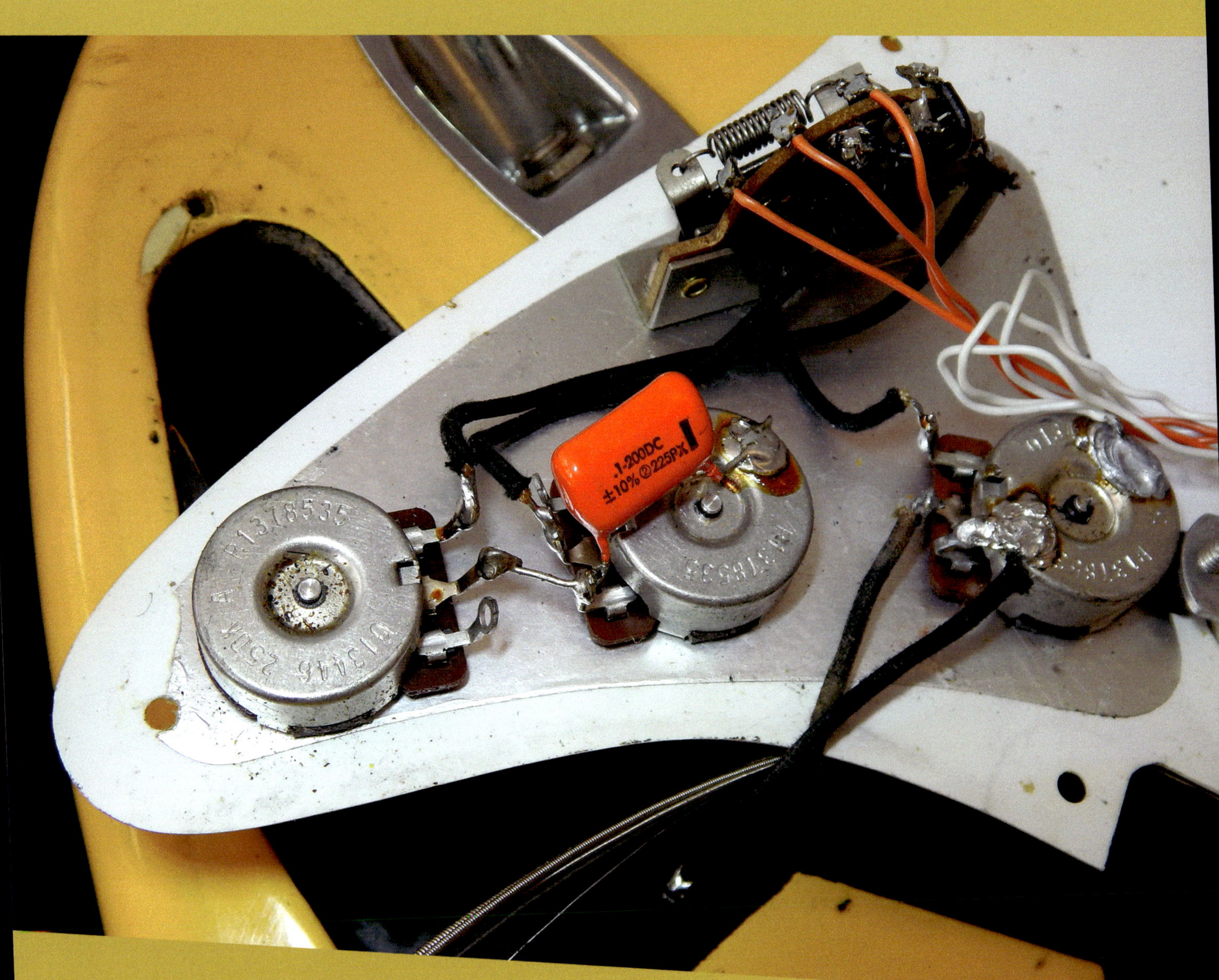

The guitar remained with Jeff Beck until 1994 when he met flying instructor Suzy O'Hara at his 50th birthday party. Suzy taught him to fly a plane at Biggin Hill in Kent, UK. During their relationship between 1994-96 Jeff wanted to teach Suzy to play guitar. He told her that the neck on the guitar was amazing and had incredible feel and if she didn't mind he'd switch it for another neck so he could keep this one for himself. He never got around to switching the neck though so the original neck remained on the guitar which was gifted to her.

Below: Jeff Beck's chord placement written on a napkin, also Morse Code from Suzy O'Hara when visiting a restaurant in France.

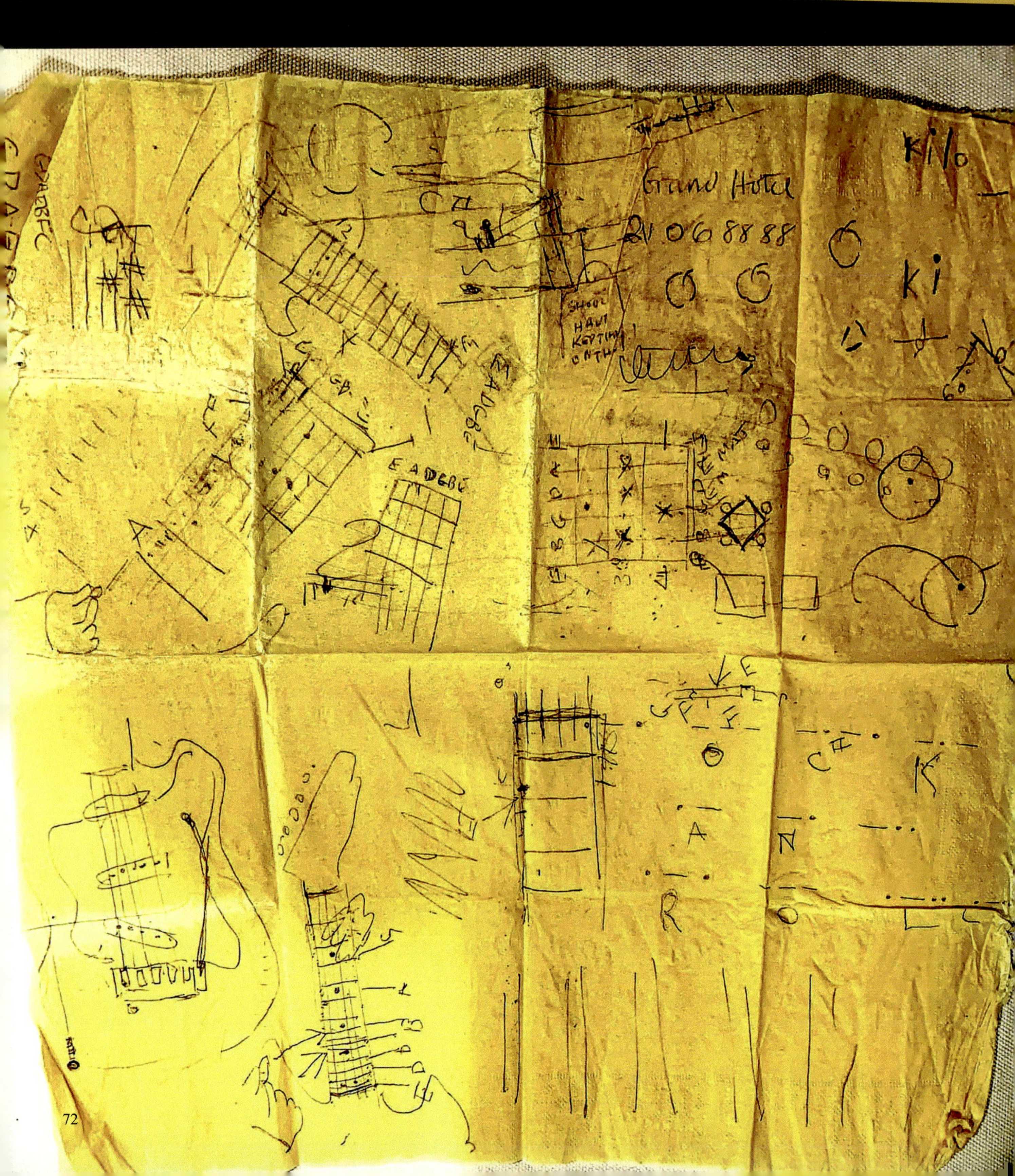

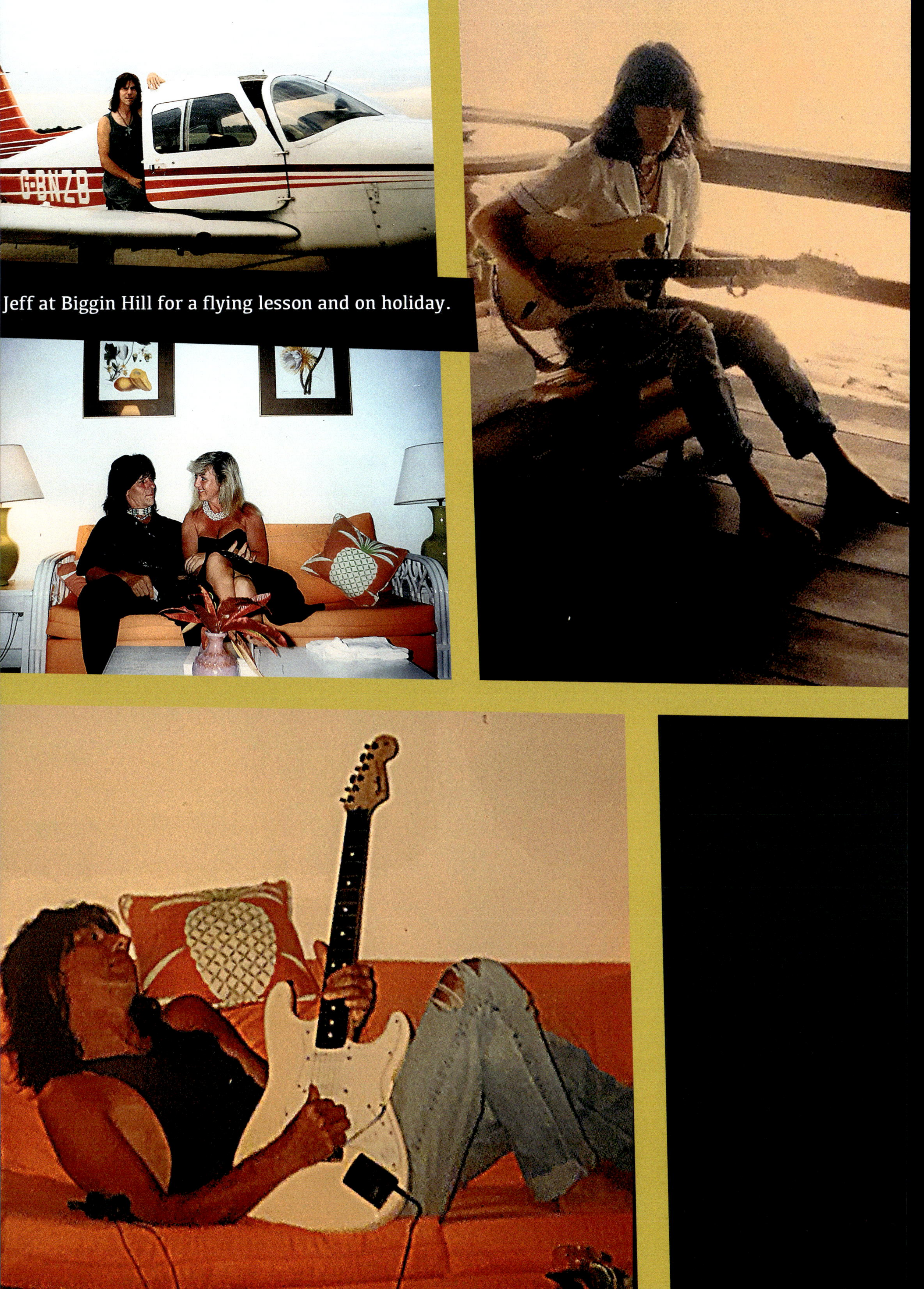

Jeff at Biggin Hill for a flying lesson and on holiday.

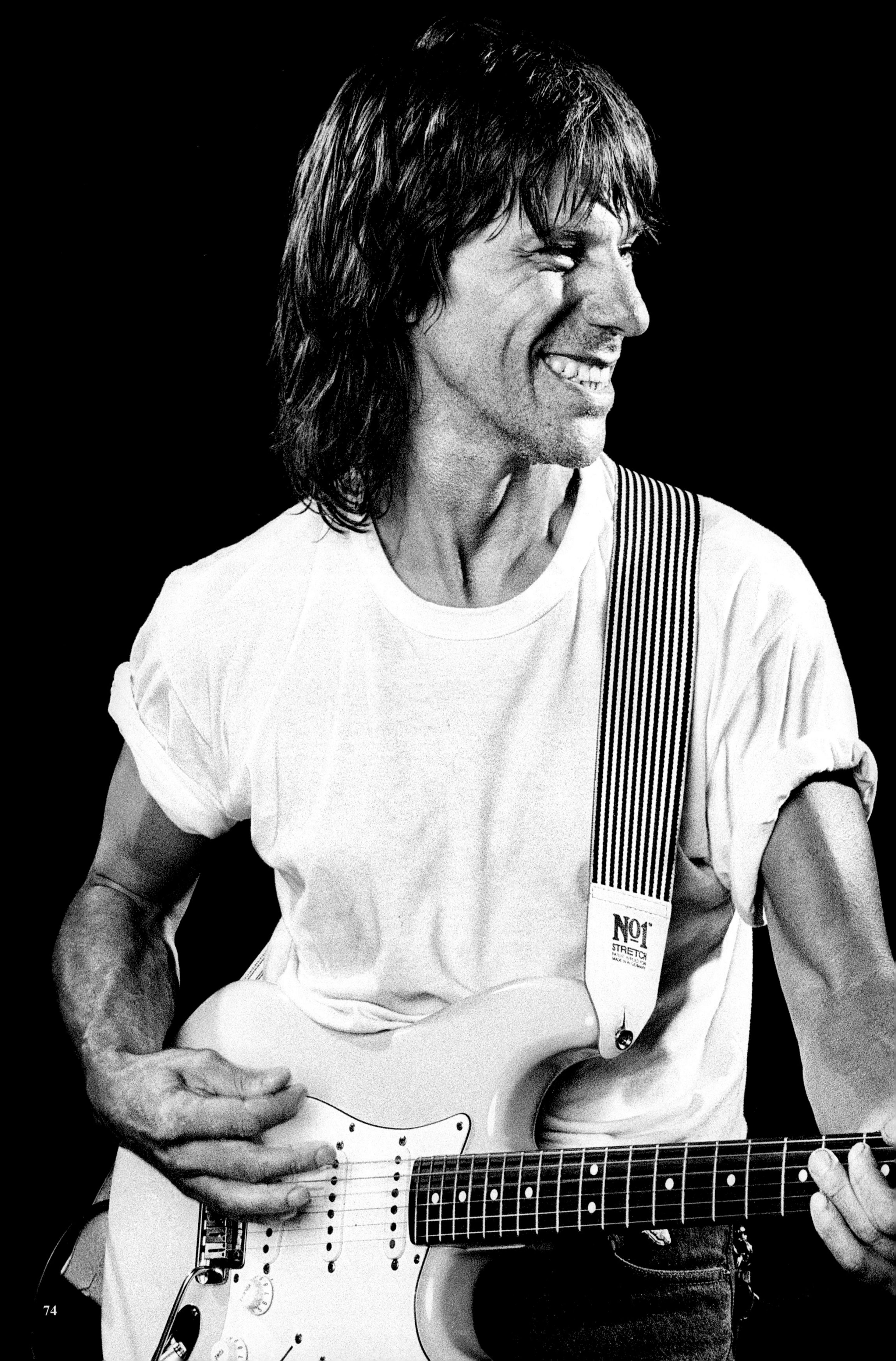
No1
STRETCH

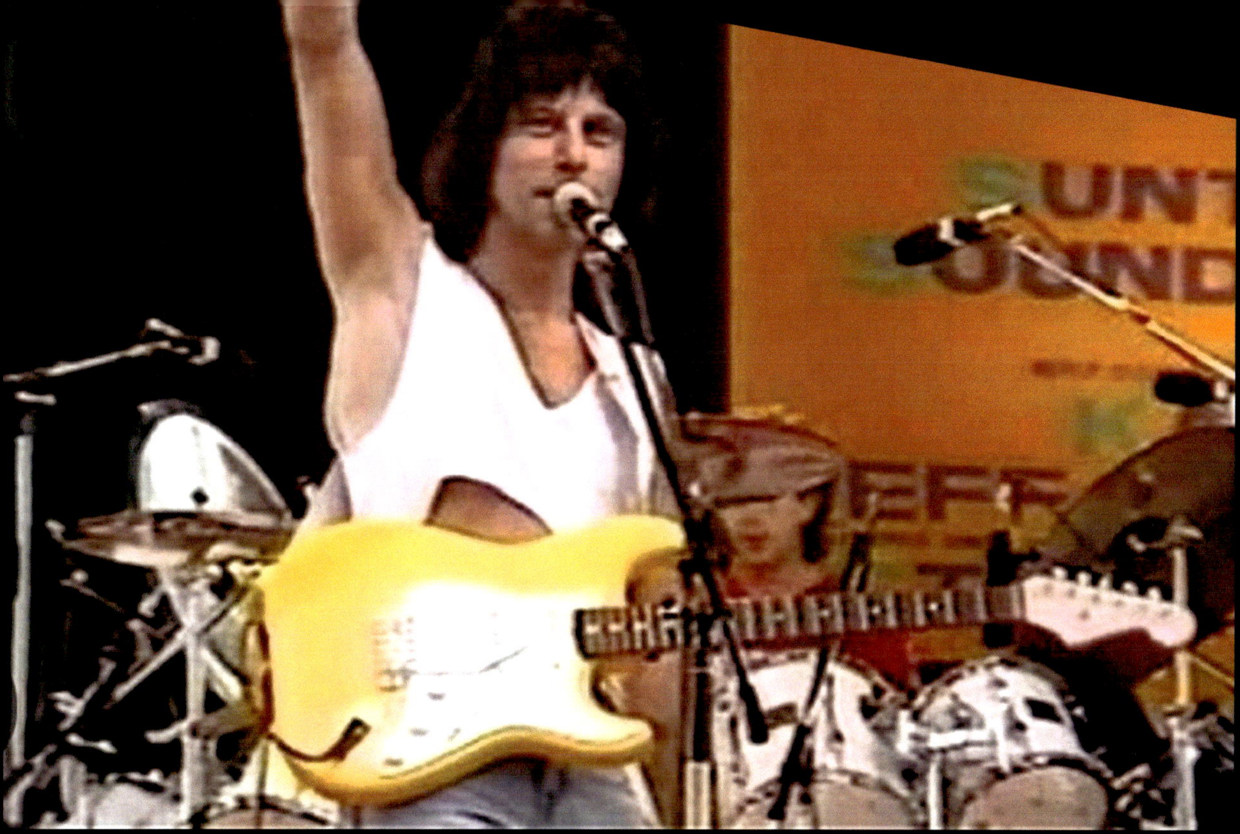

Above: Jeff in Japan early 1986 with original 1962 spec neck.
Below: With 2nd neck and Lace Sensors

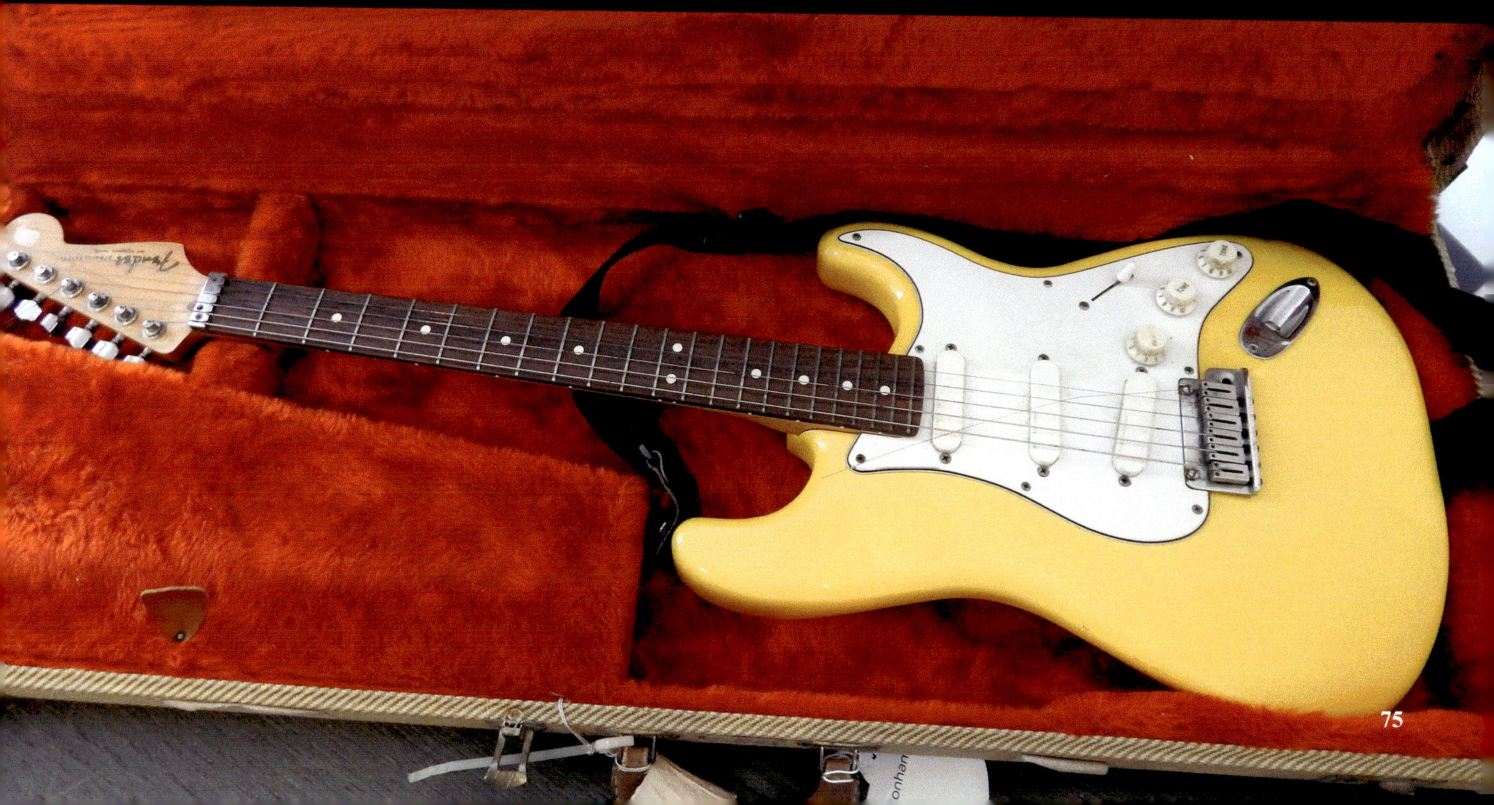

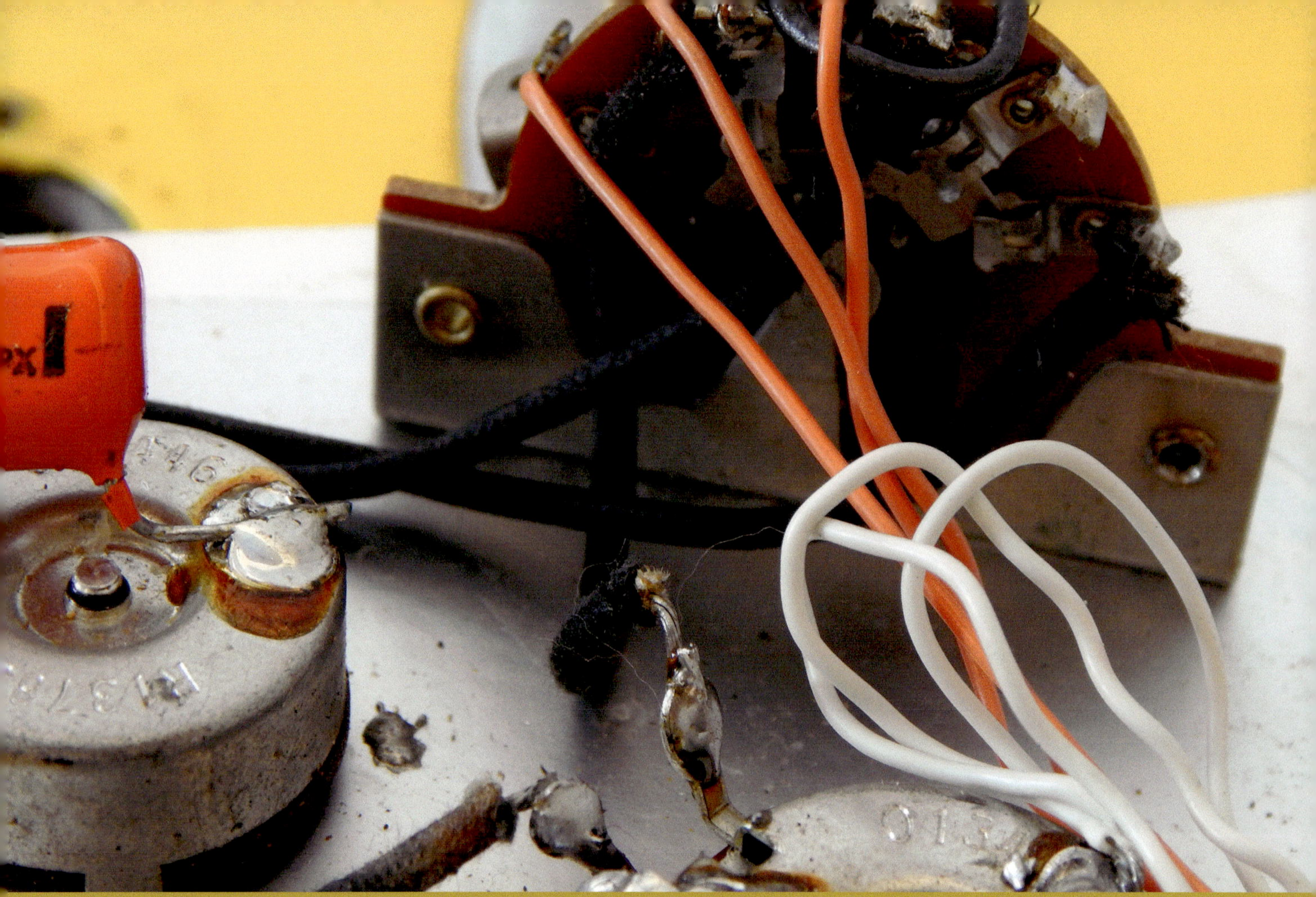

The guitar was not working when I plugged it in: there were faults with the 5-way switch and volume control, I fixed them all by end of day.

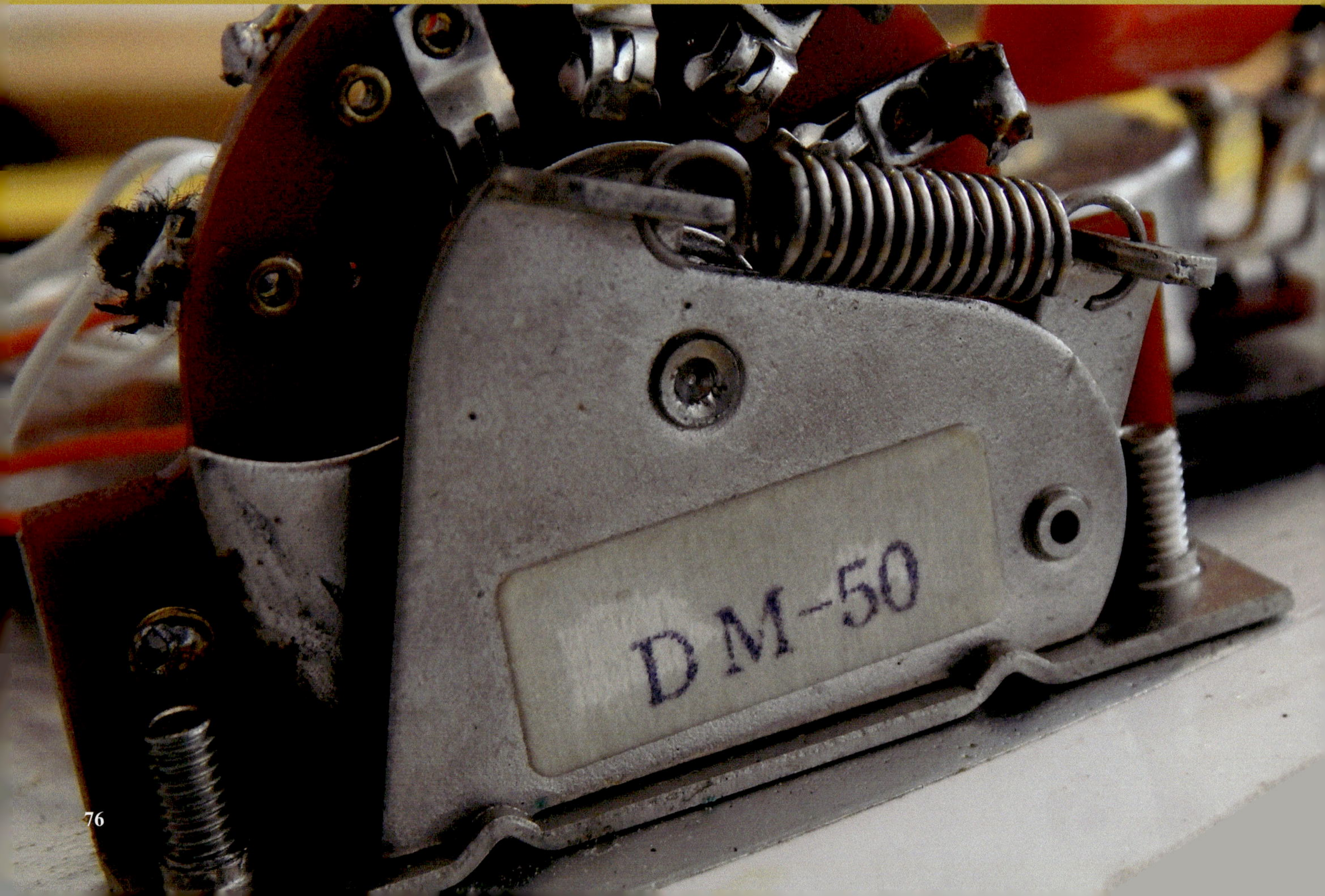

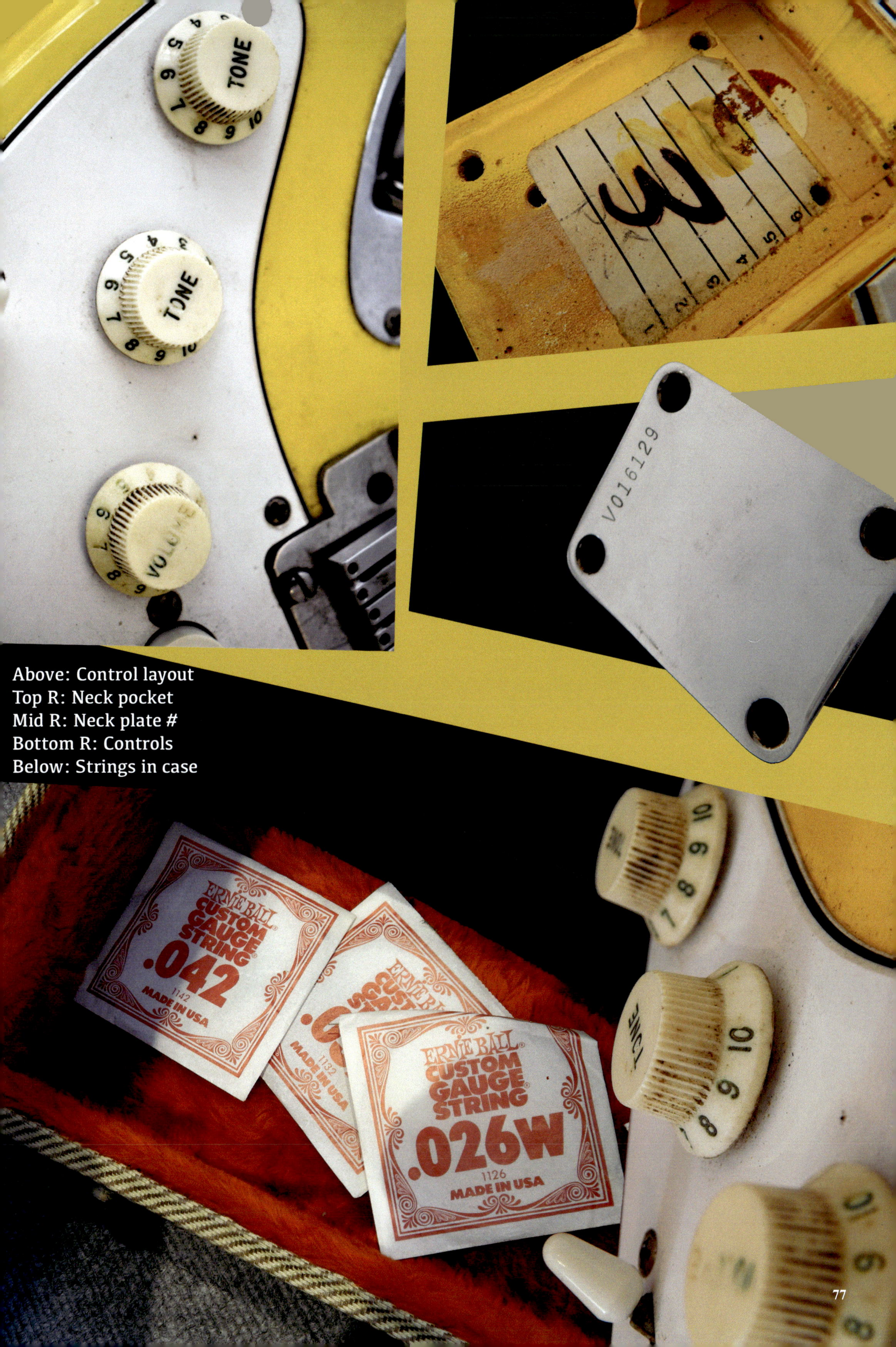

Above: Control layout
Top R: Neck pocket
Mid R: Neck plate #
Bottom R: Controls
Below: Strings in case

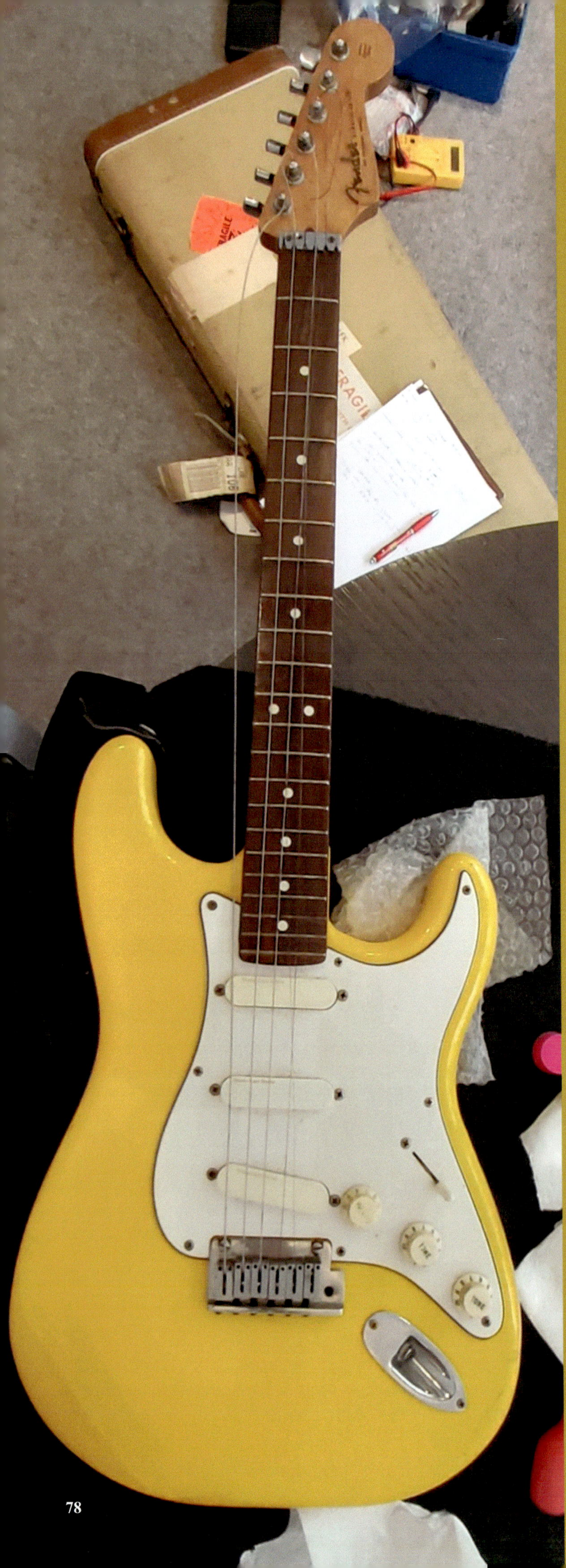

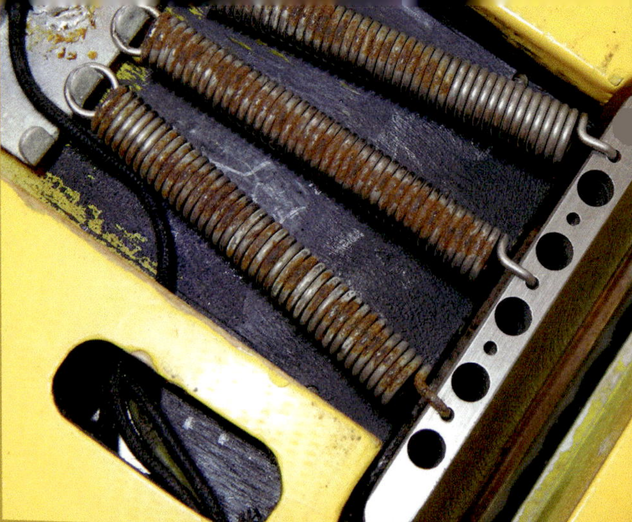

Note: Curious slot at back, would not fit a battery!

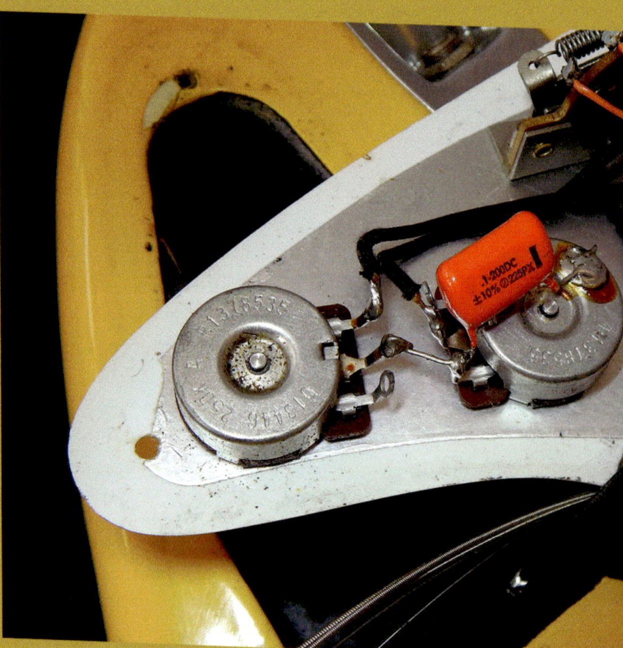

Volume/Tone dates to 35th week of 1985

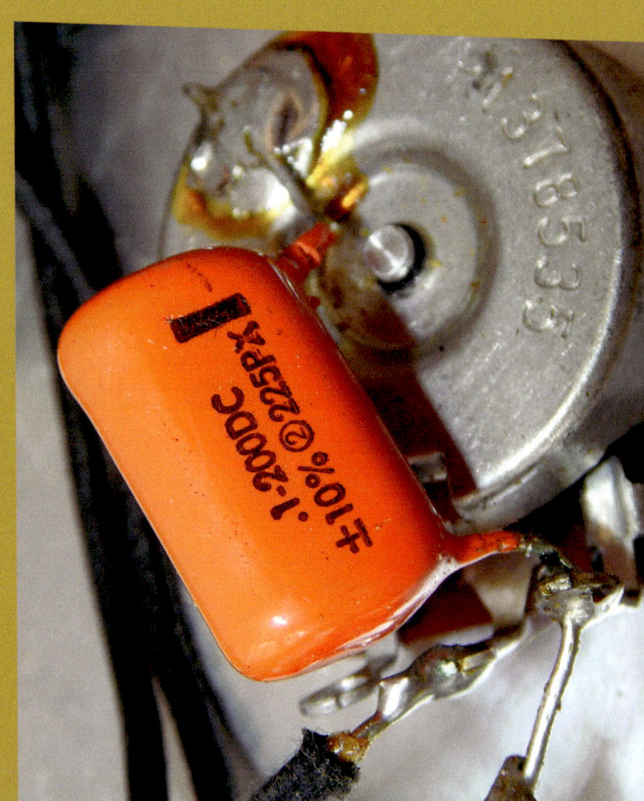

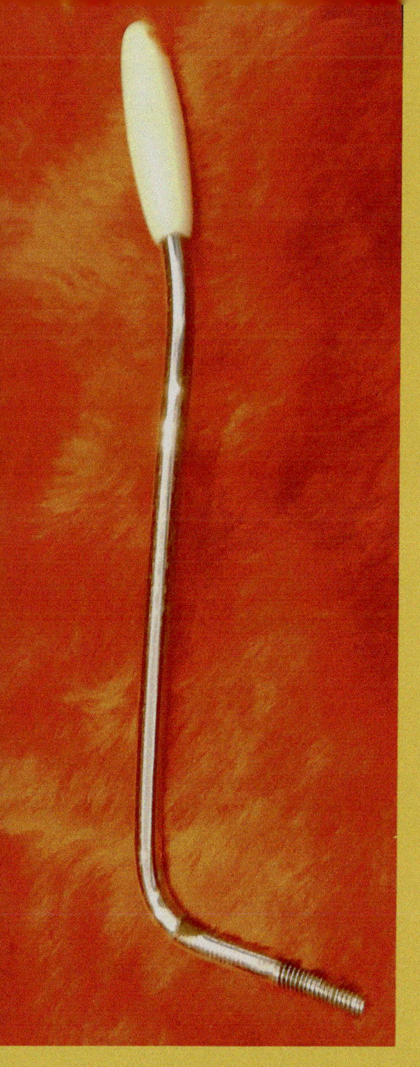

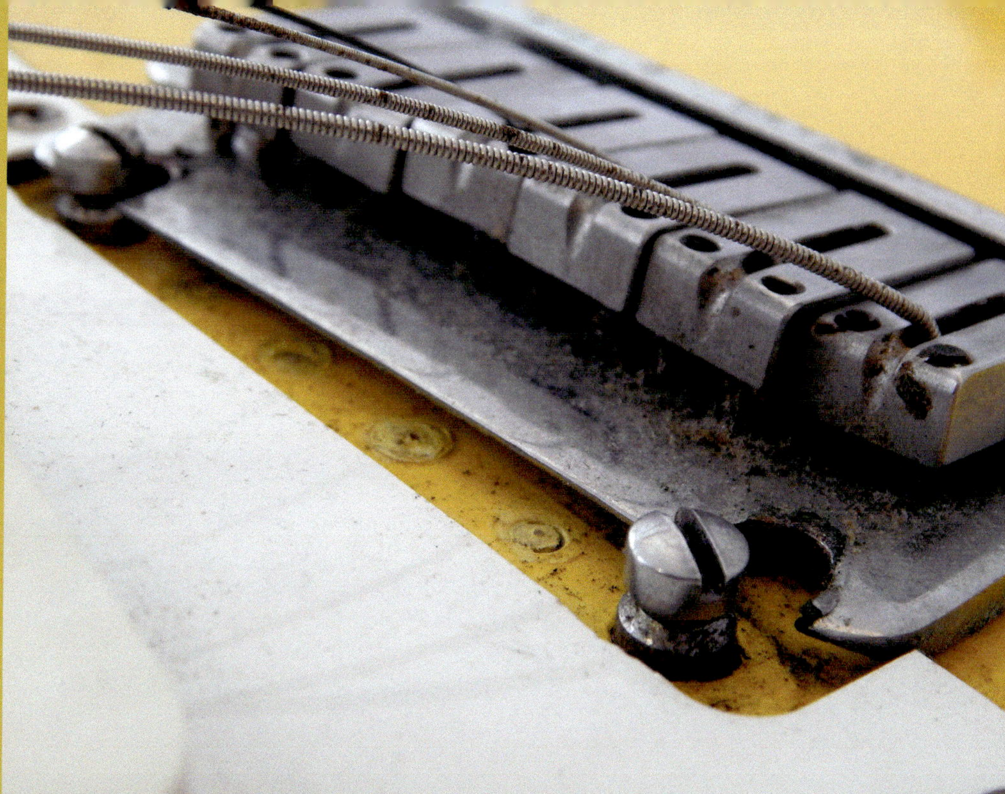

Original mucky strings

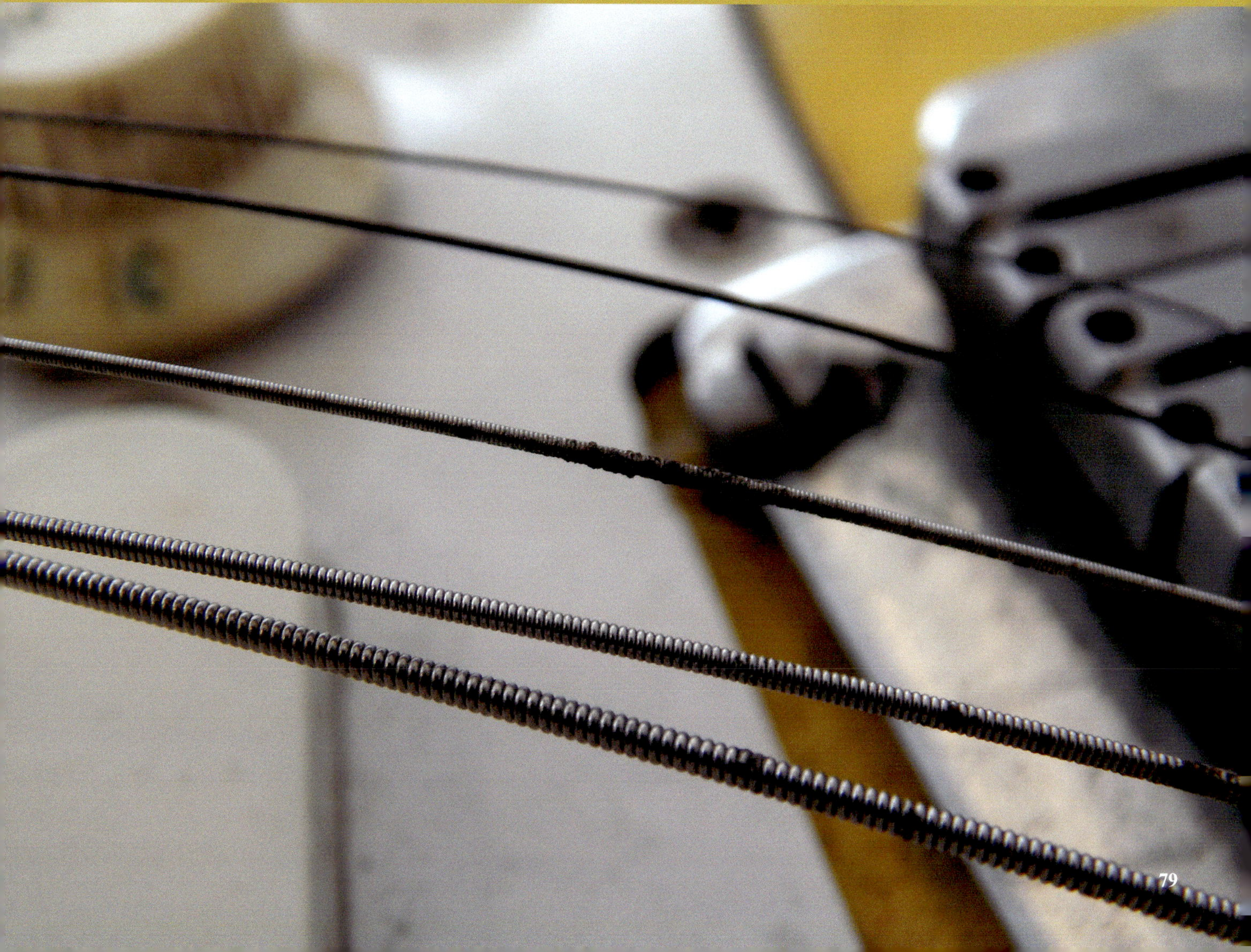

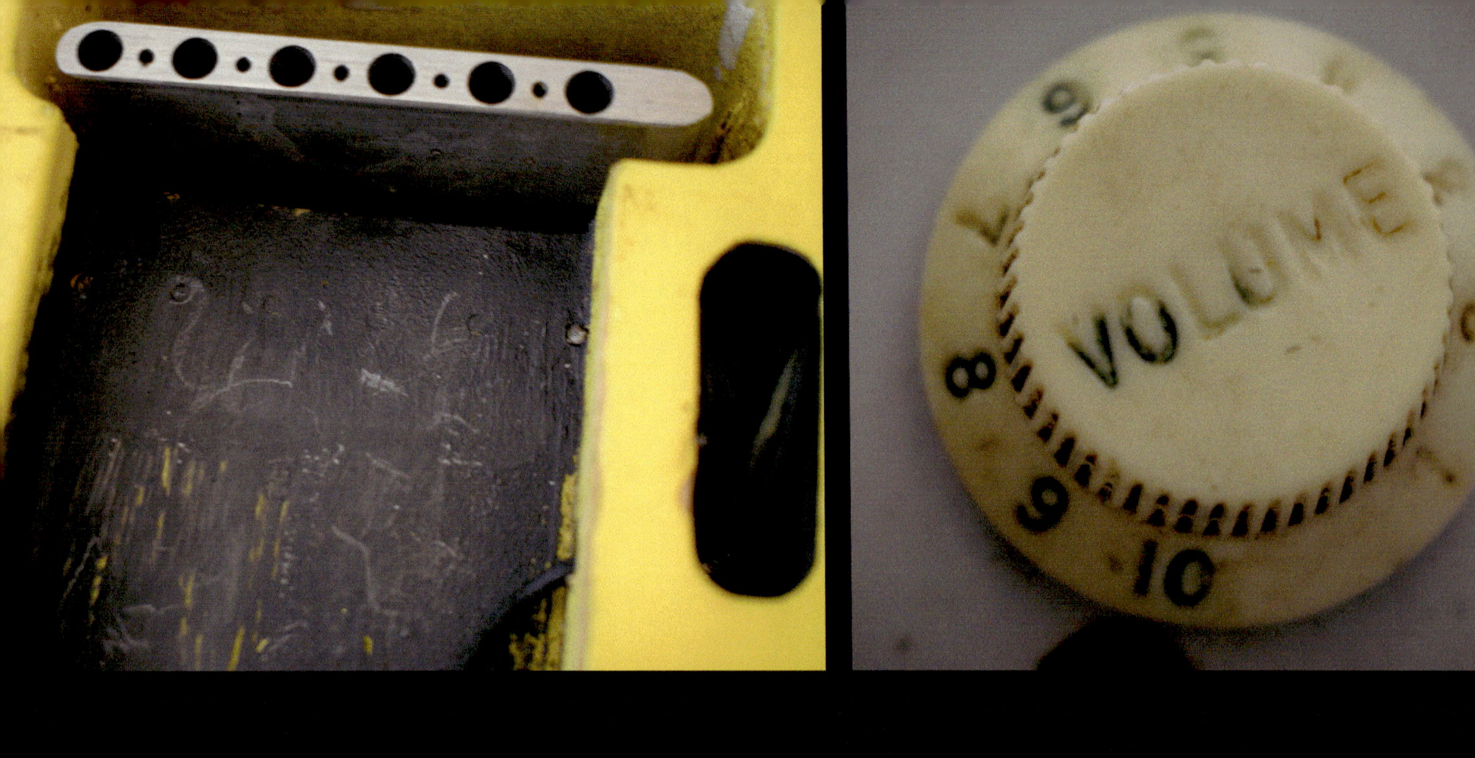

Trem cavity has been bevelled so the trem springs do not make any contact with the wood.

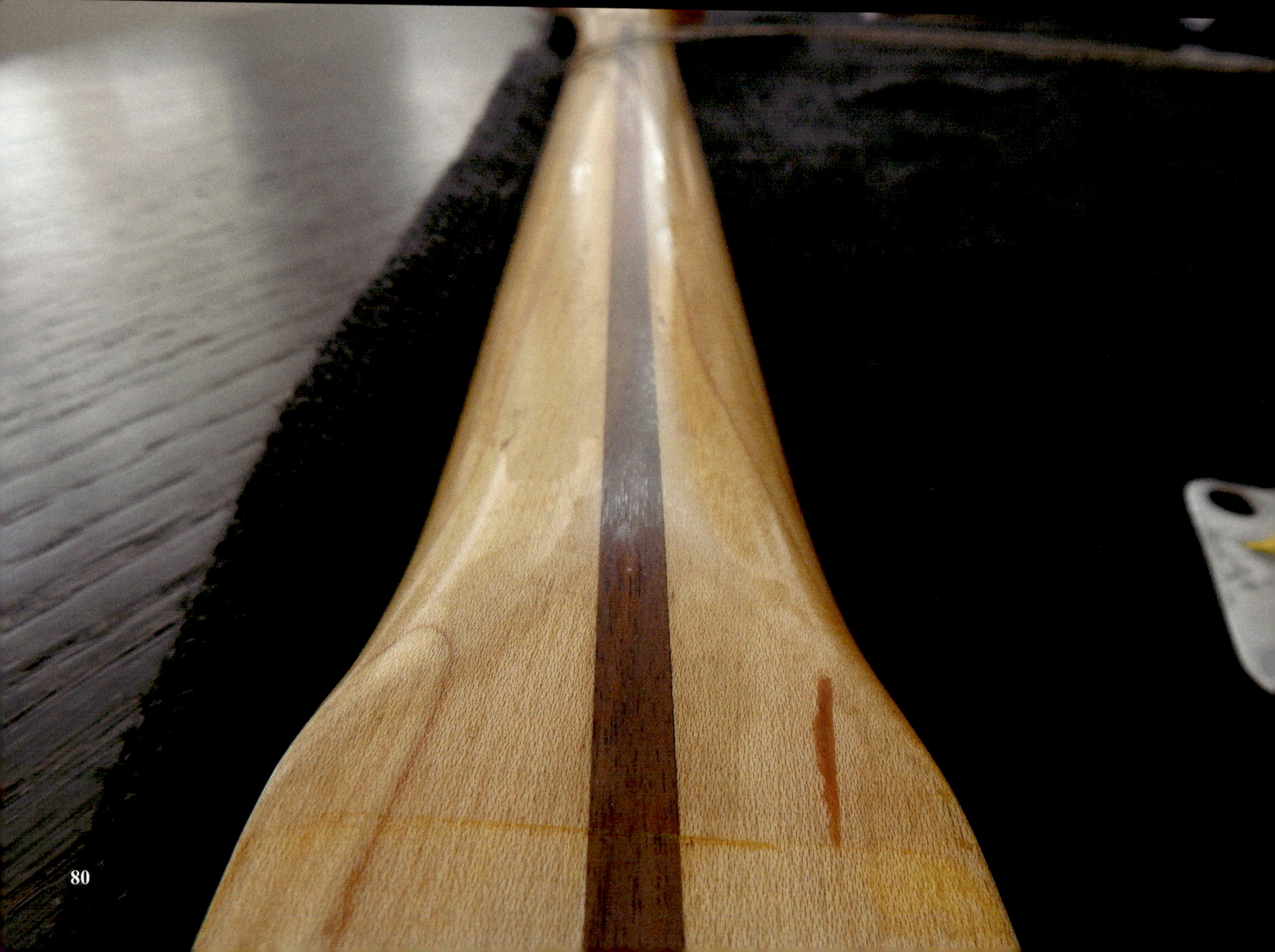

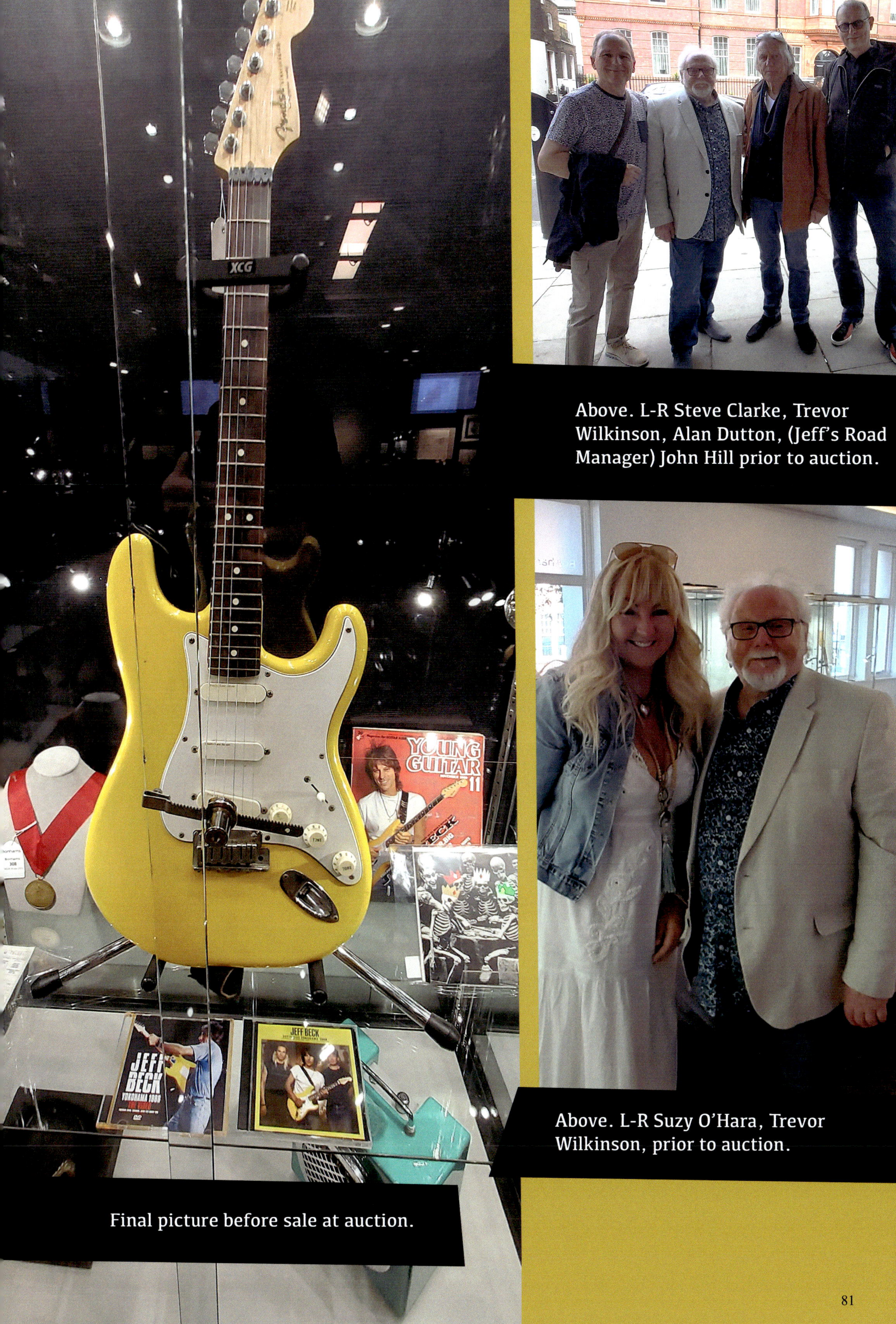

Above. L-R Steve Clarke, Trevor Wilkinson, Alan Dutton, (Jeff's Road Manager) John Hill prior to auction.

Above. L-R Suzy O'Hara, Trevor Wilkinson, prior to auction.

Final picture before sale at auction.

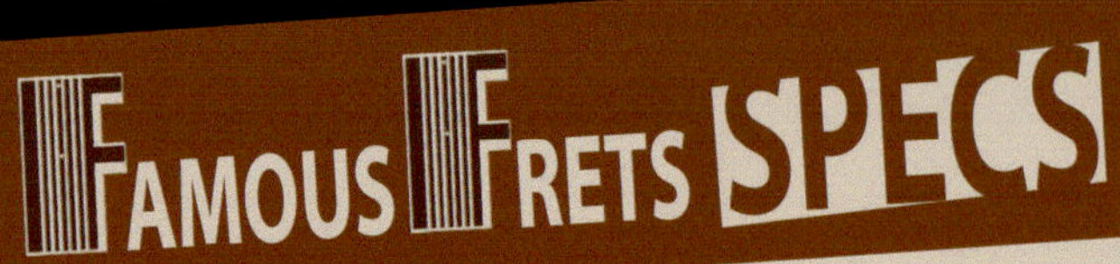

Nut: 43.47mm
12th fret: 51.52mm
Control knob at lower rim: 18.61
Switch tip: Maximum width 8.79mm
Bridge saddle width: 10.08mm
Bridge Pickup: 5.69 ohms
Mid Pickup: 5.55 ohms
Neck Pickup: 5.37 ohms
Weight: 8.48 lbs
Pot cod part number: 013446
Year code number: R1378535

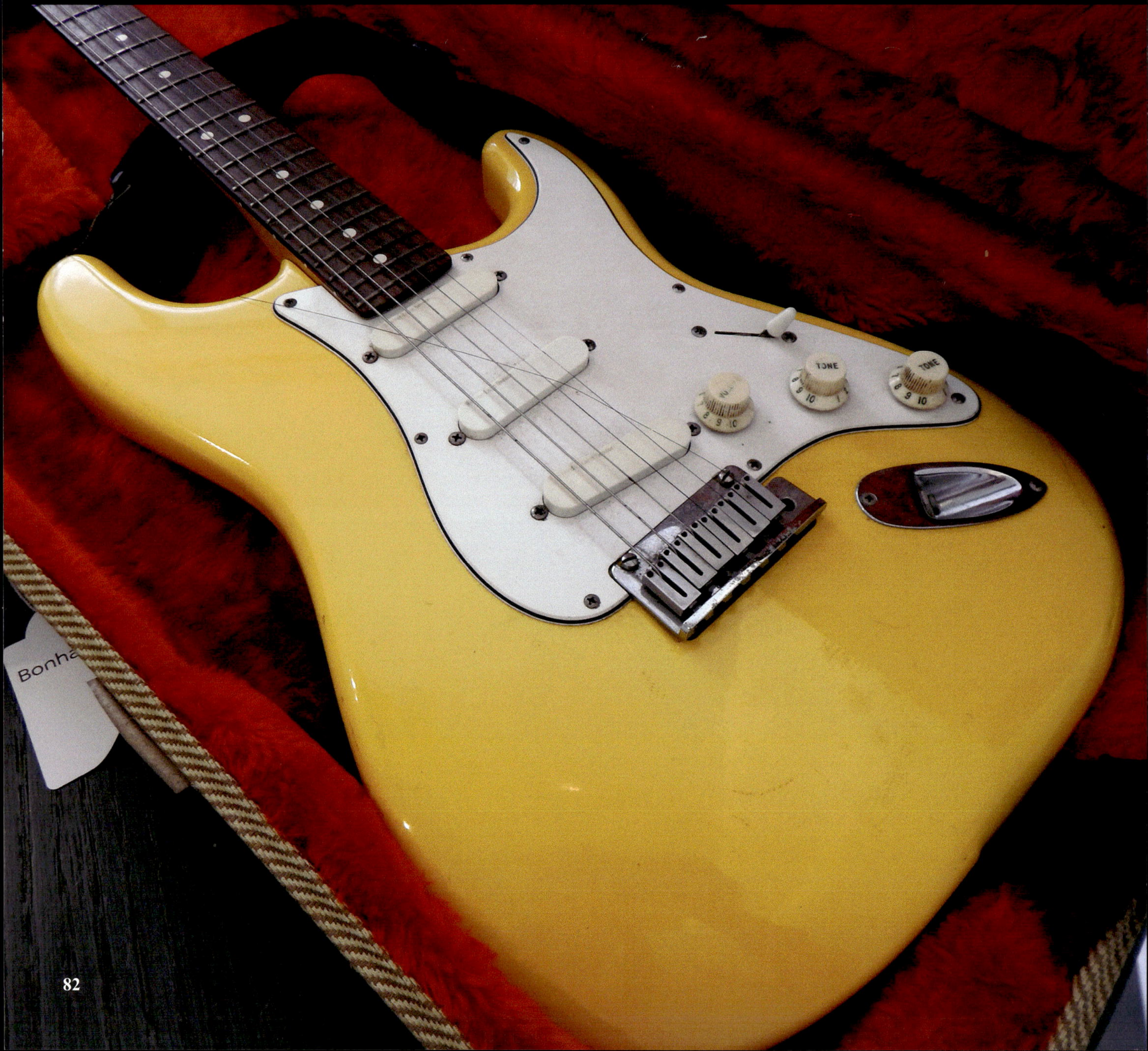

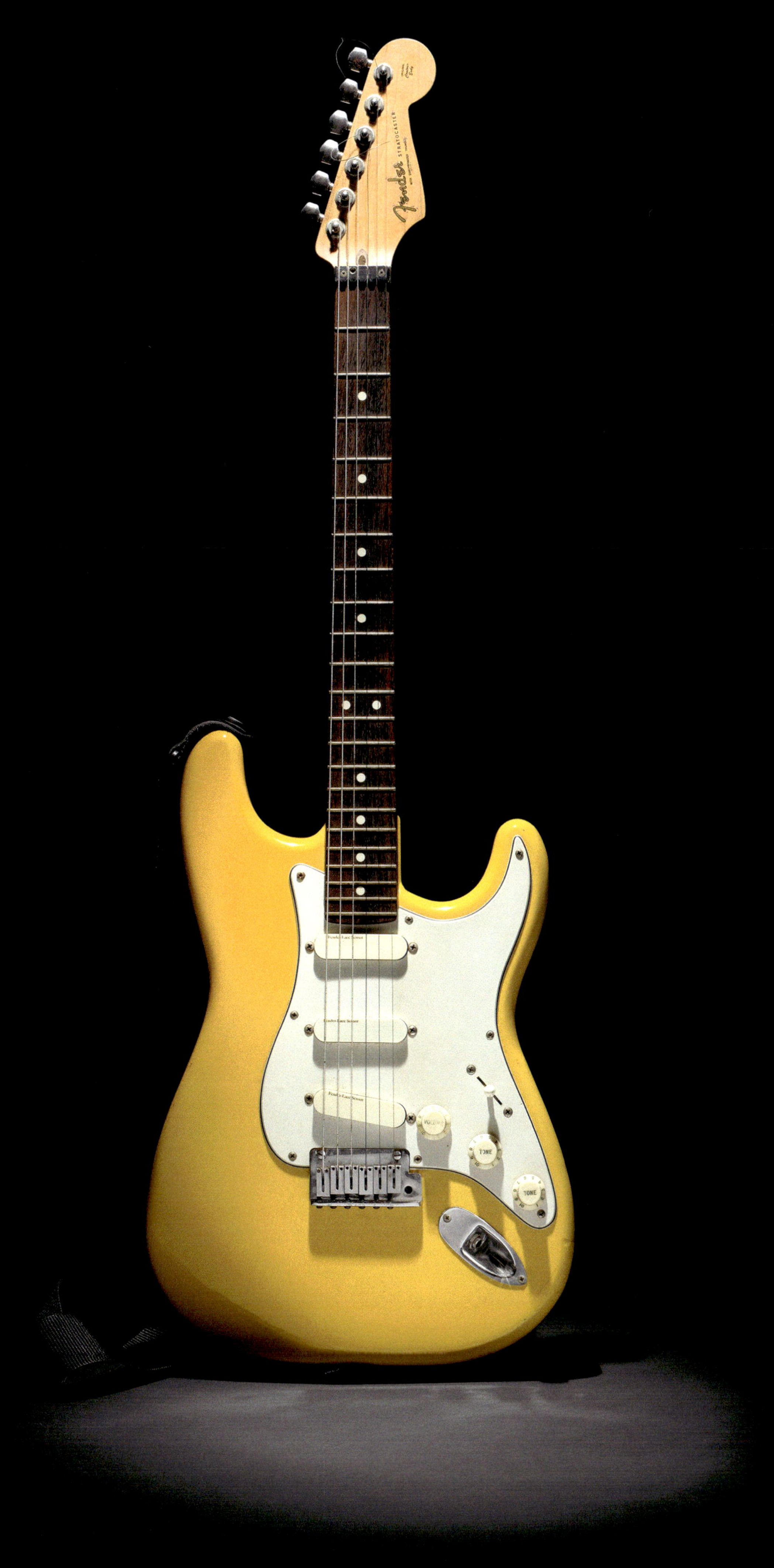

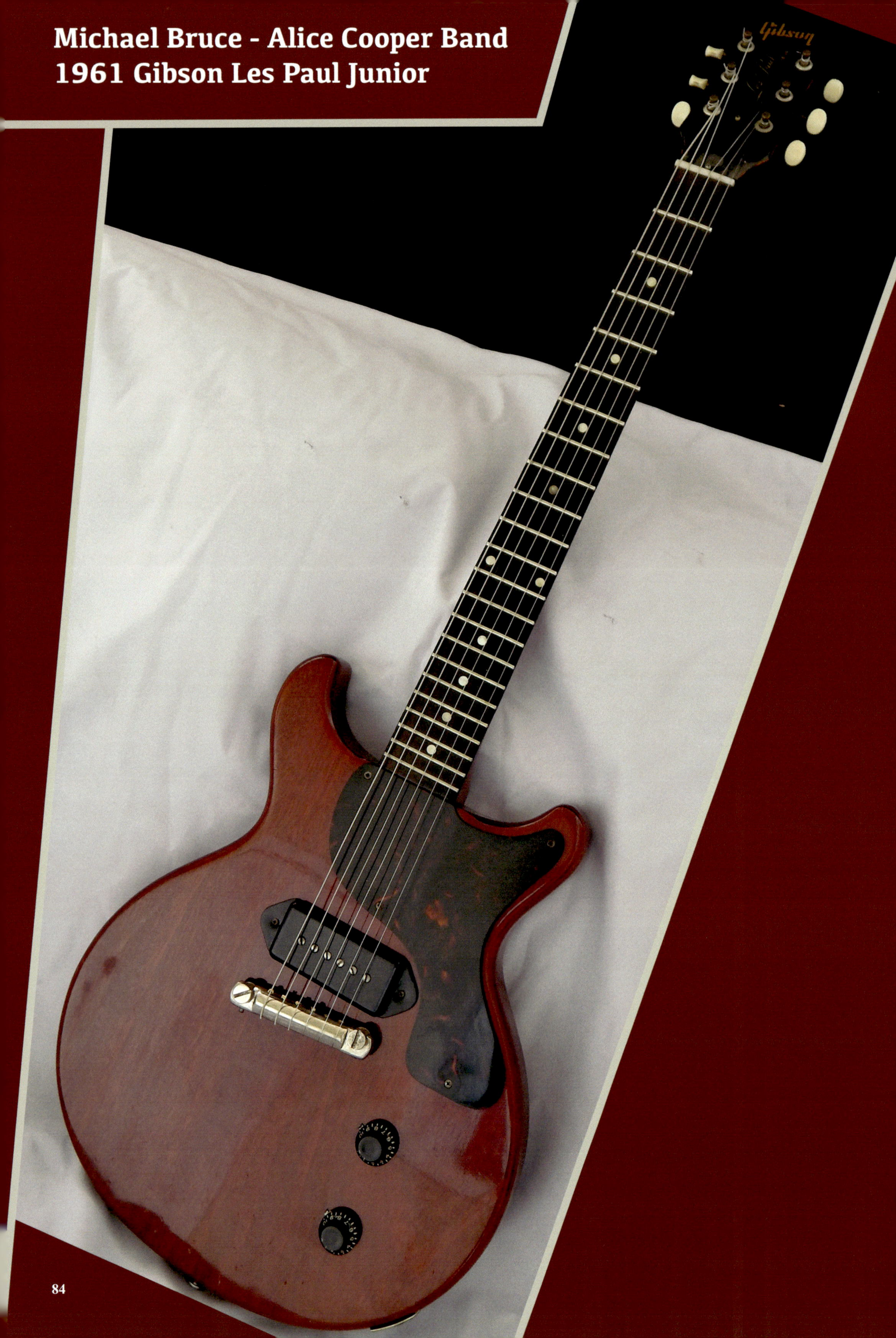

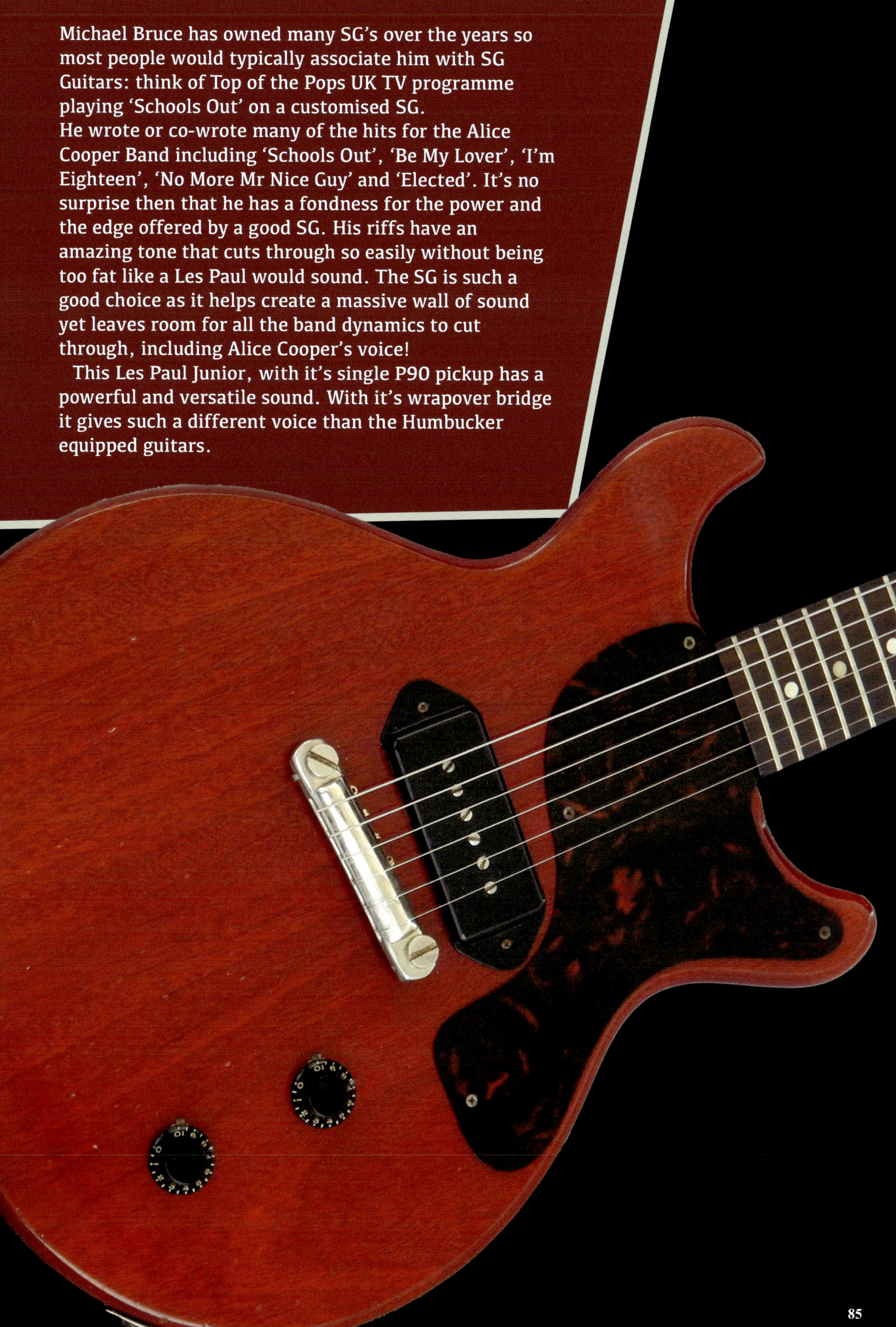

Michael Bruce has owned many SG's over the years so most people would typically associate him with SG Guitars: think of Top of the Pops UK TV programme playing 'Schools Out' on a customised SG.
He wrote or co-wrote many of the hits for the Alice Cooper Band including 'Schools Out', 'Be My Lover', 'I'm Eighteen', 'No More Mr Nice Guy' and 'Elected'. It's no surprise then that he has a fondness for the power and the edge offered by a good SG. His riffs have an amazing tone that cuts through so easily without being too fat like a Les Paul would sound. The SG is such a good choice as it helps create a massive wall of sound yet leaves room for all the band dynamics to cut through, including Alice Cooper's voice!

This Les Paul Junior, with it's single P90 pickup has a powerful and versatile sound. With it's wrapover bridge it gives such a different voice than the Humbucker equipped guitars.

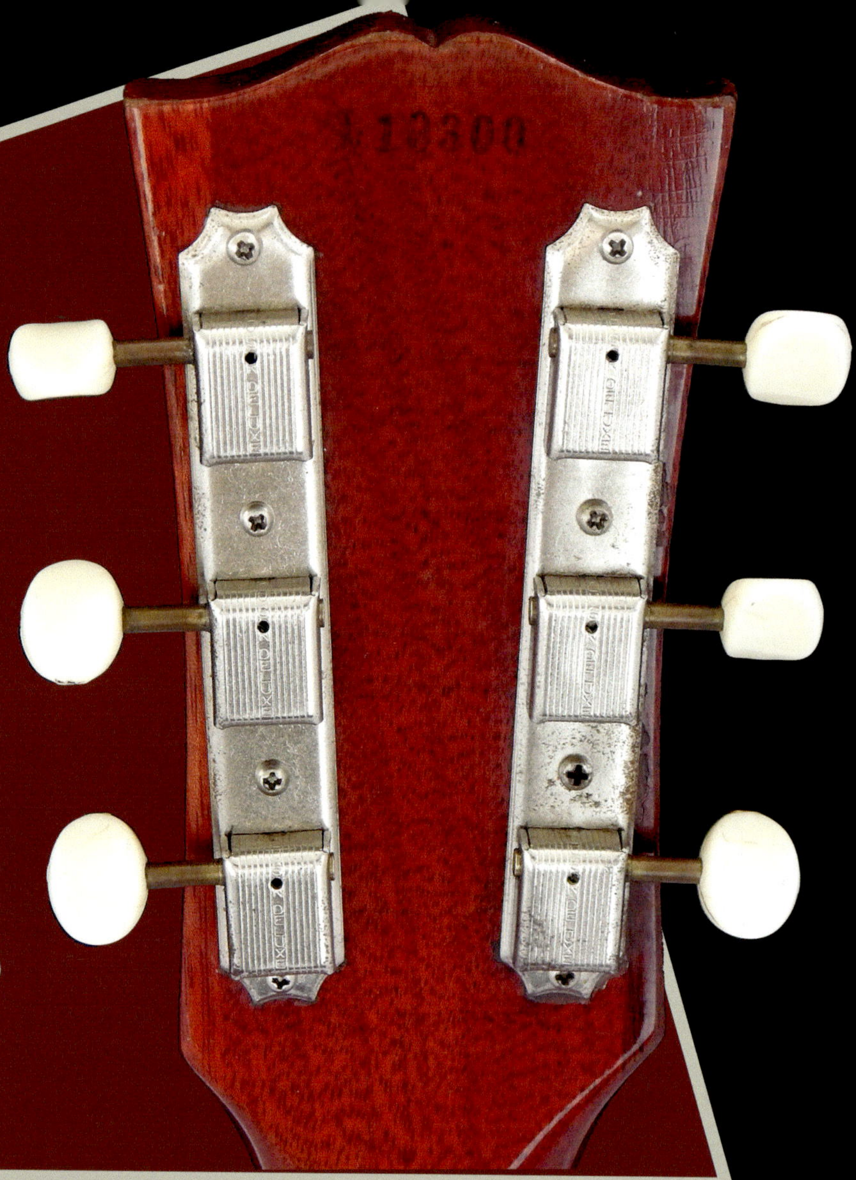

The P90 pickup measures 8.48 ohms.
(Replacement cover fitted)

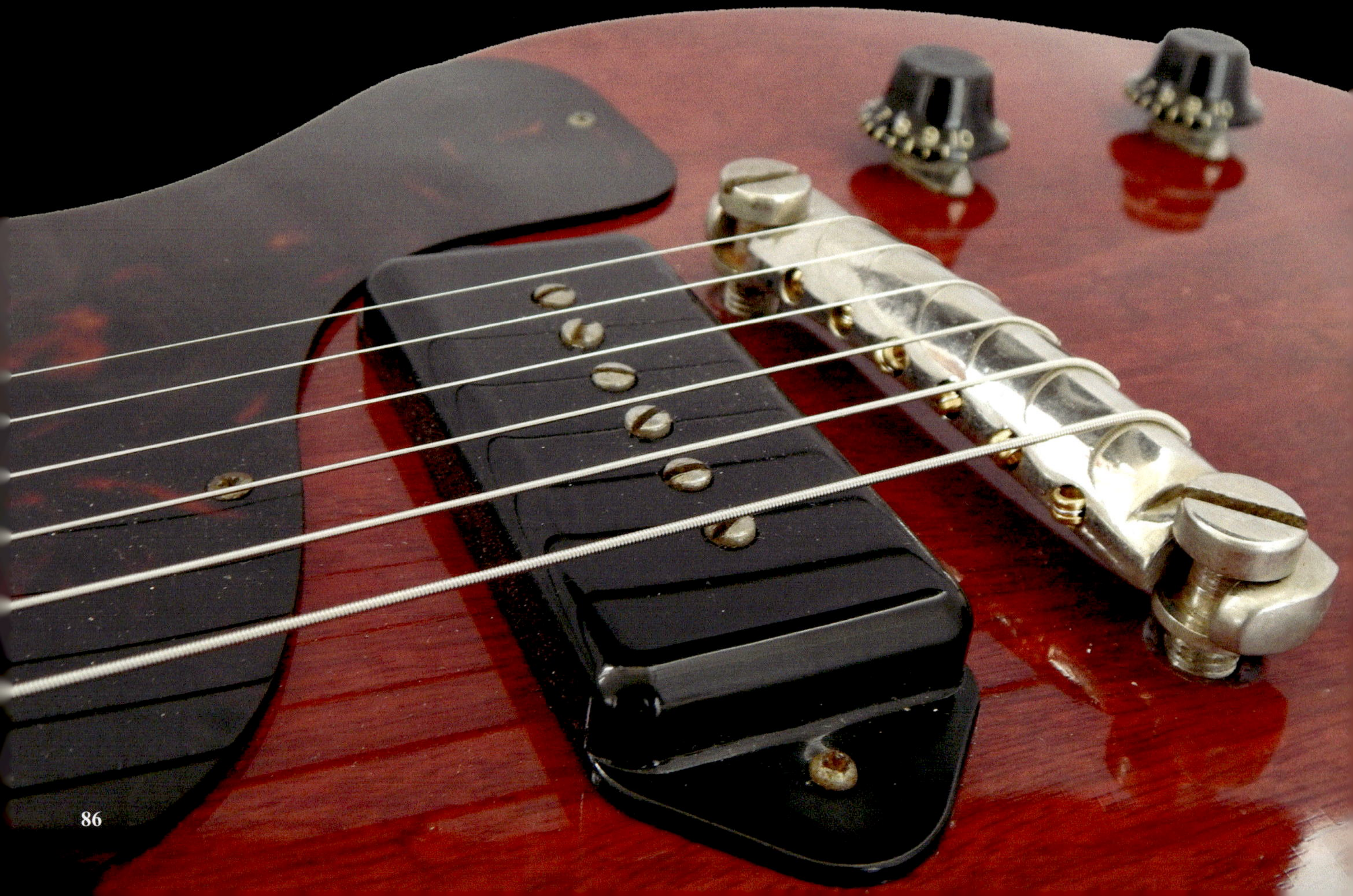

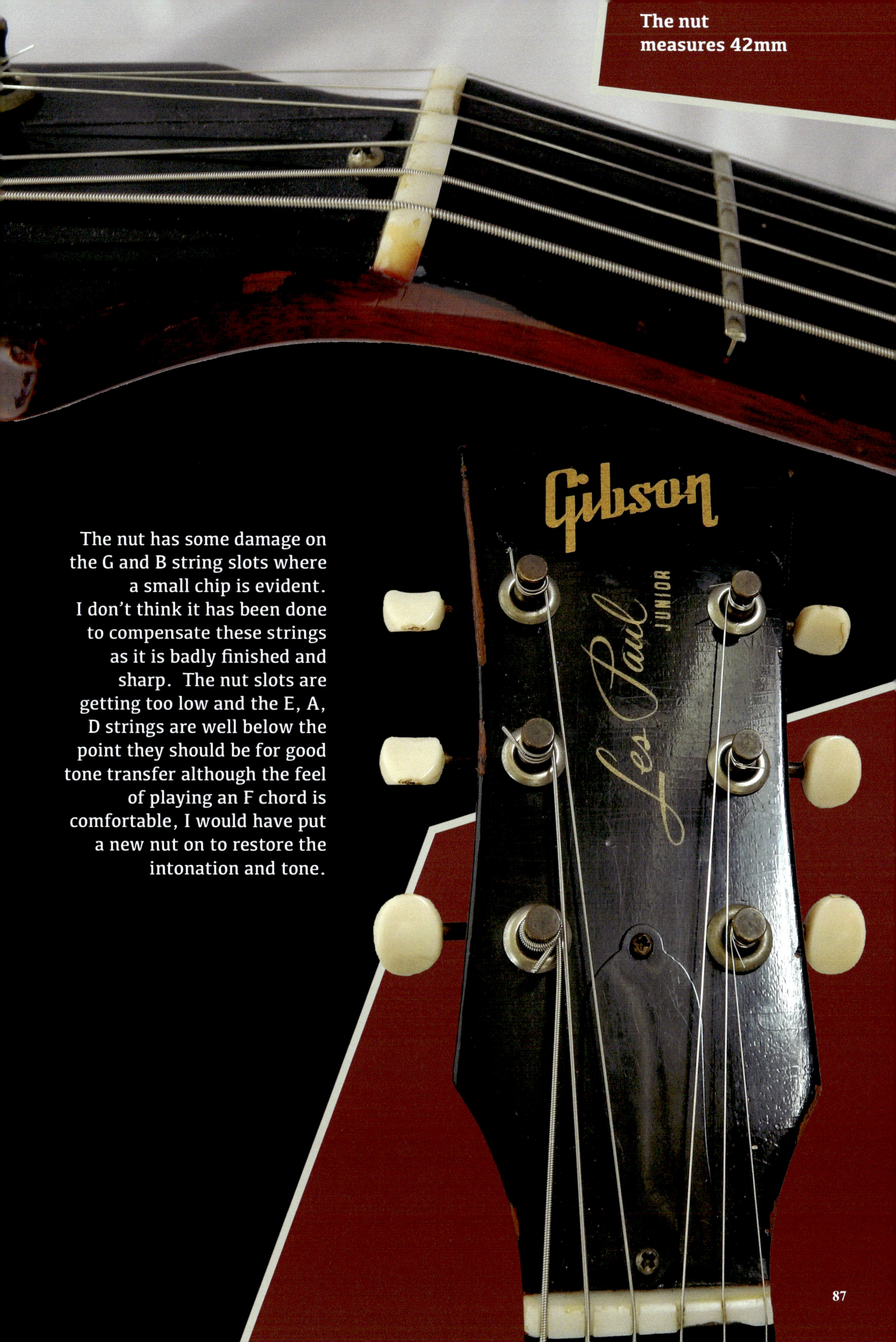

The nut has some damage on the G and B string slots where a small chip is evident. I don't think it has been done to compensate these strings as it is badly finished and sharp. The nut slots are getting too low and the E, A, D strings are well below the point they should be for good tone transfer although the feel of playing an F chord is comfortable, I would have put a new nut on to restore the intonation and tone.

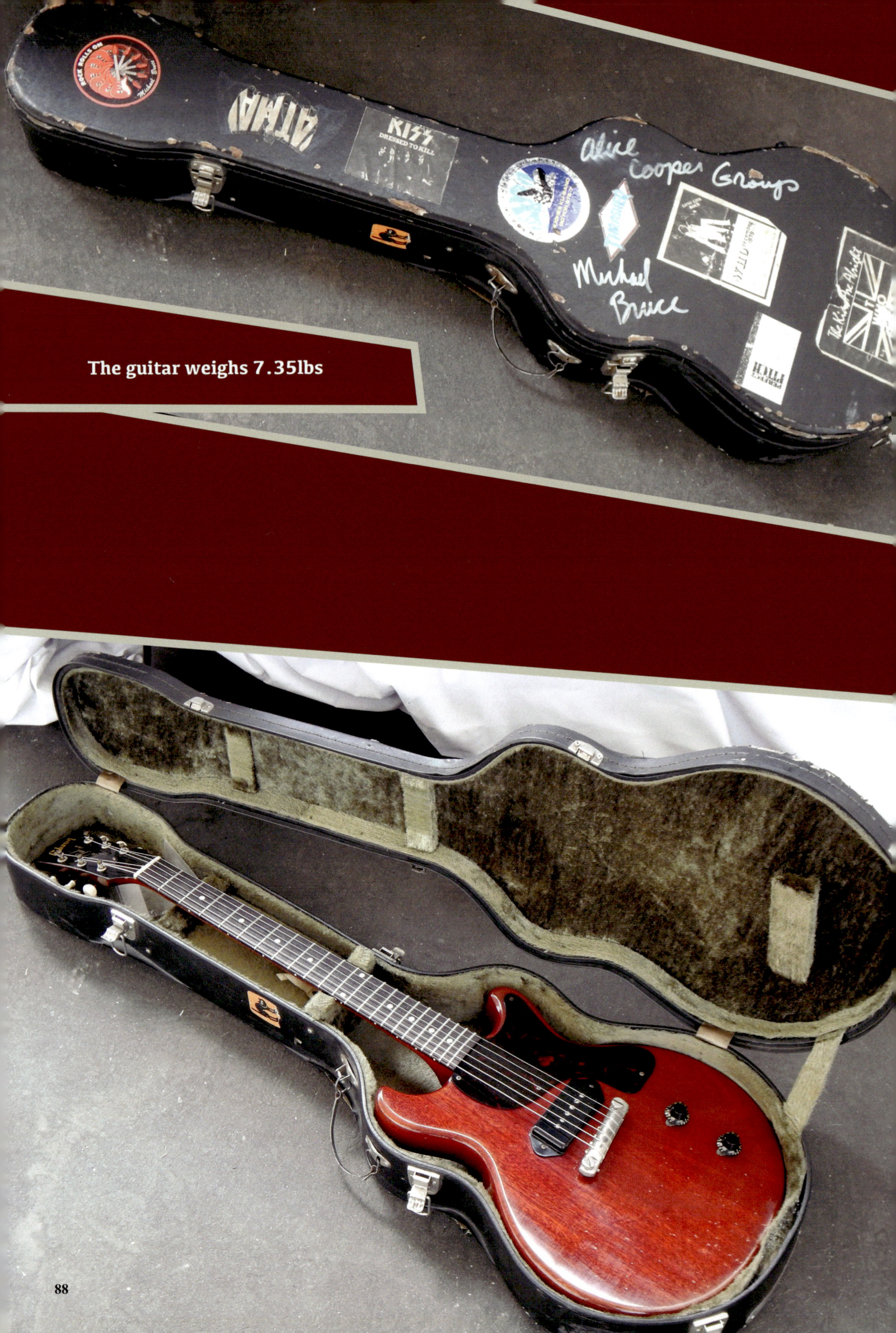

The guitar weighs 7.35lbs

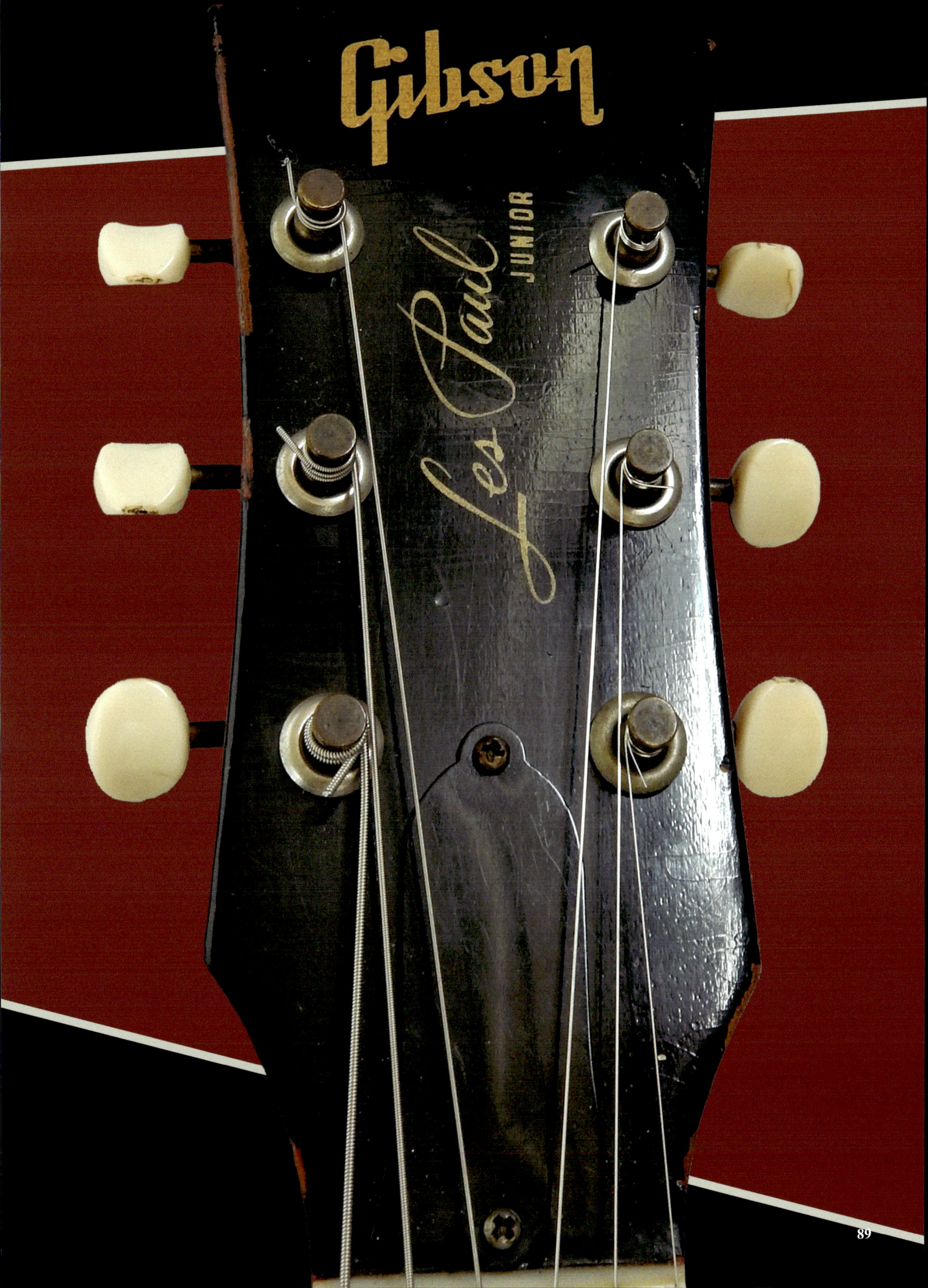

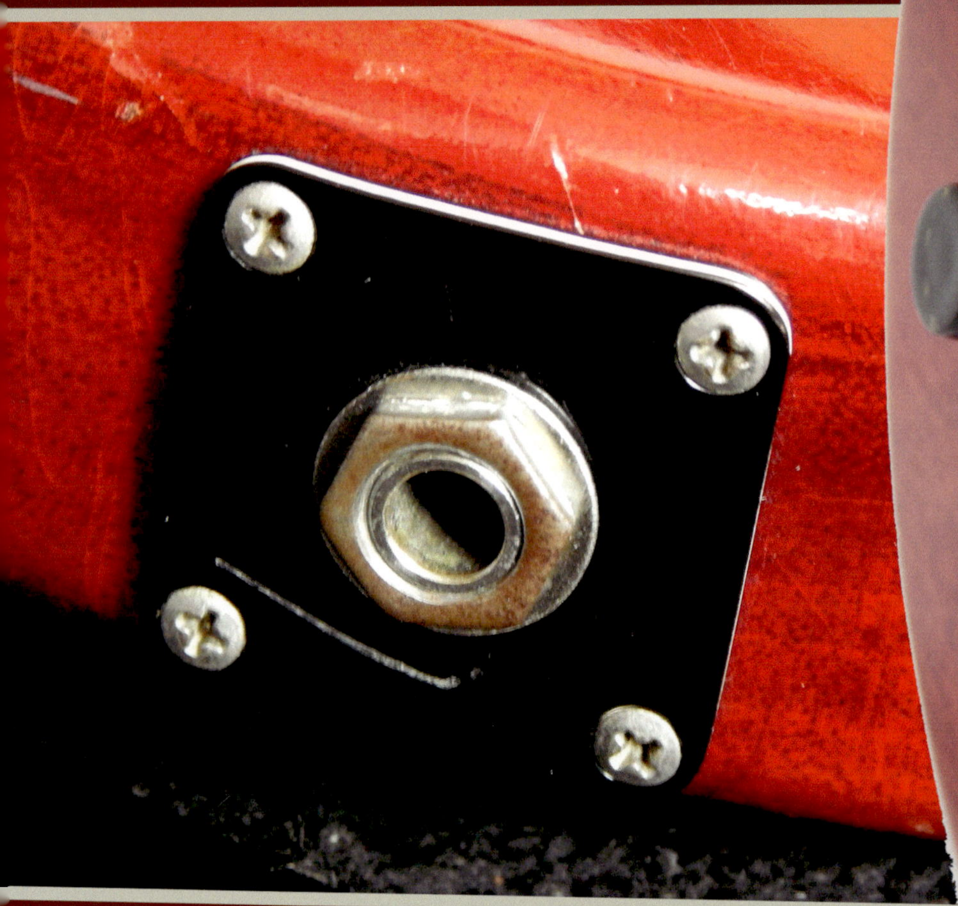

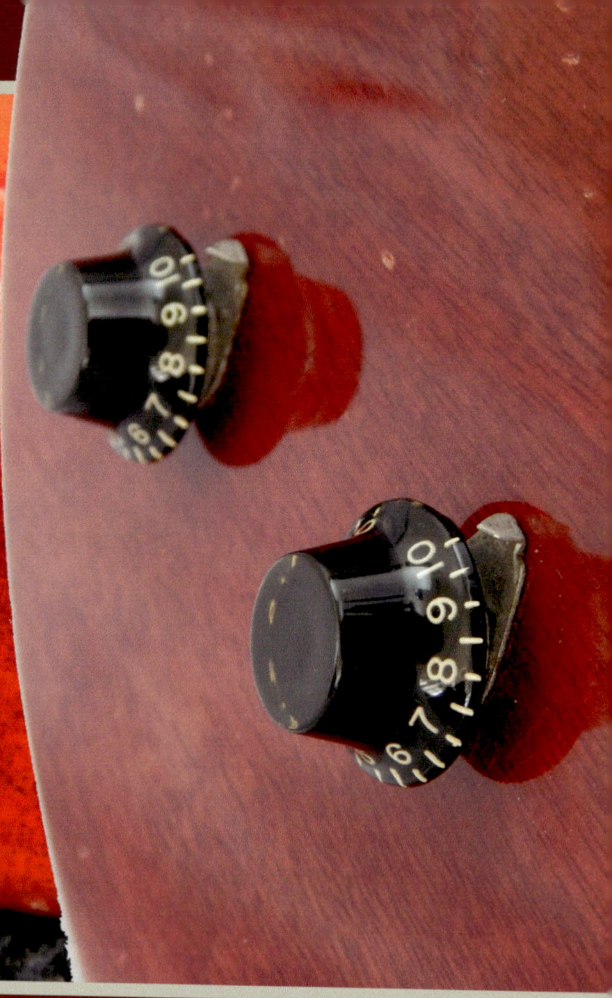

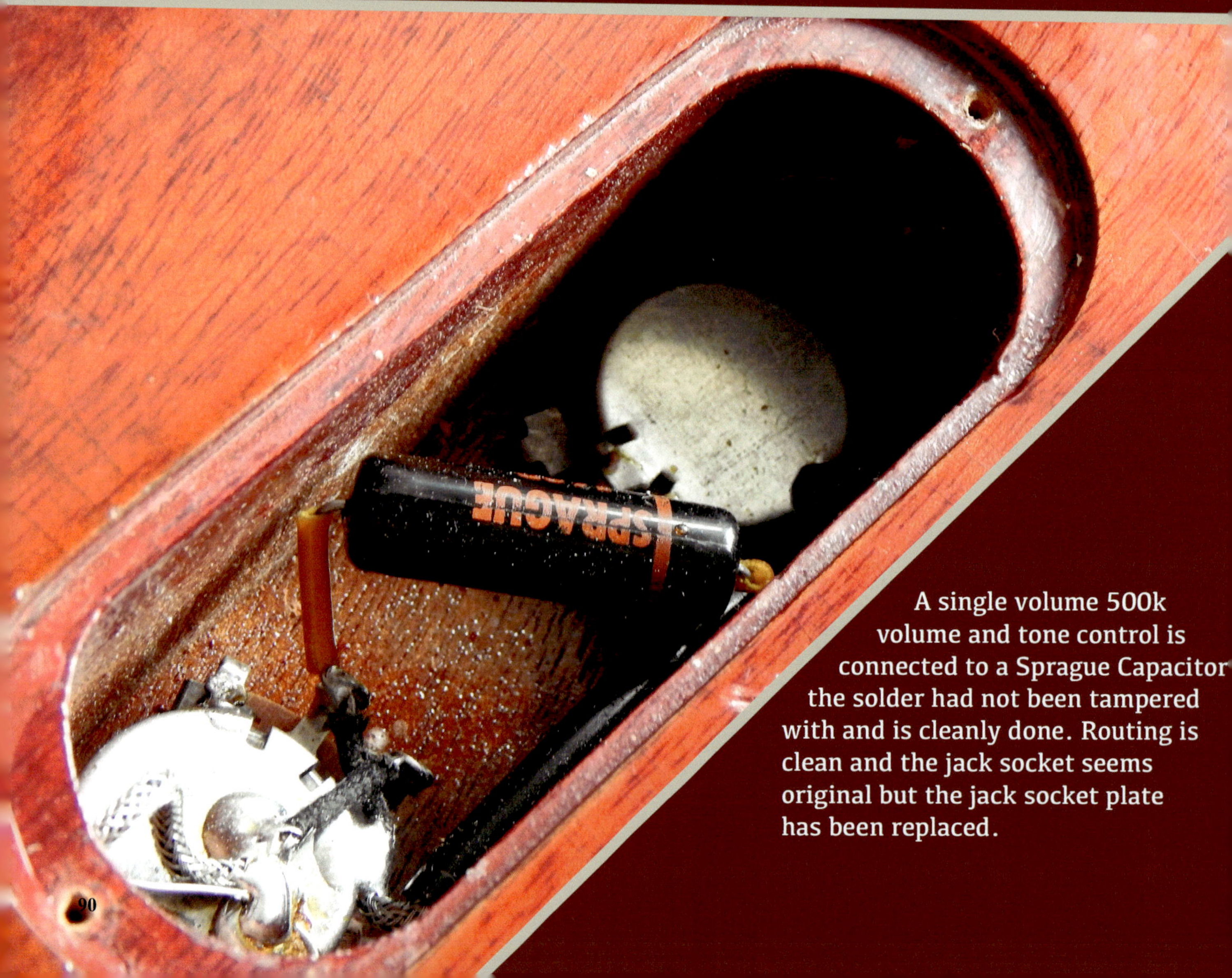

A single volume 500k volume and tone control is connected to a Sprague Capacitor the solder had not been tampered with and is cleanly done. Routing is clean and the jack socket seems original but the jack socket plate has been replaced.

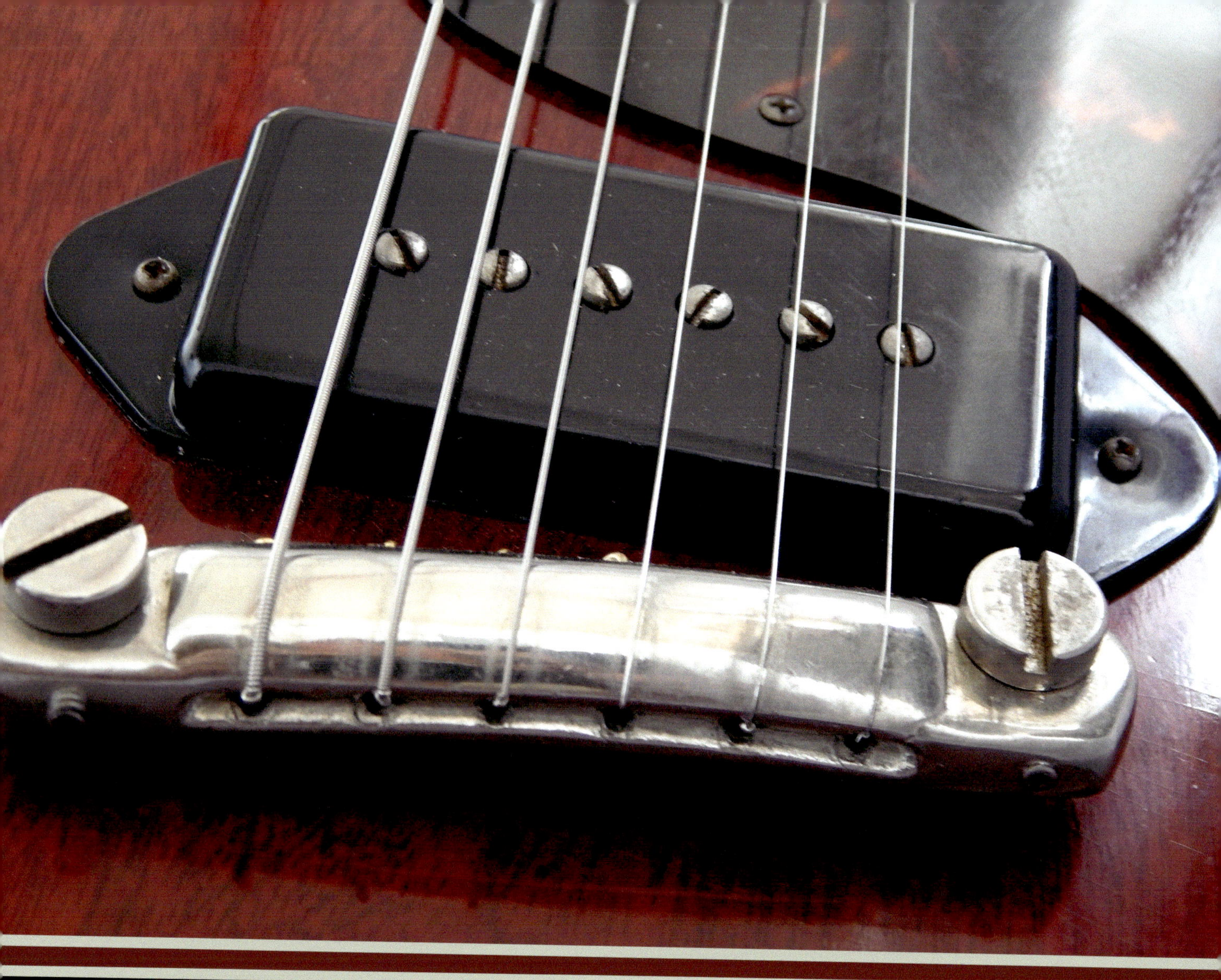

Nickel plated wraparound tailpiece anchored with two threaded studs, adjustment is via two small screws that can alter string length to intonate it. This works fine but would be improved if the frets and nut were replaced. The design of this particular wraparound is not very forgiving if there is something else needing attention: a fret dress in this case, and new nut would be essential.

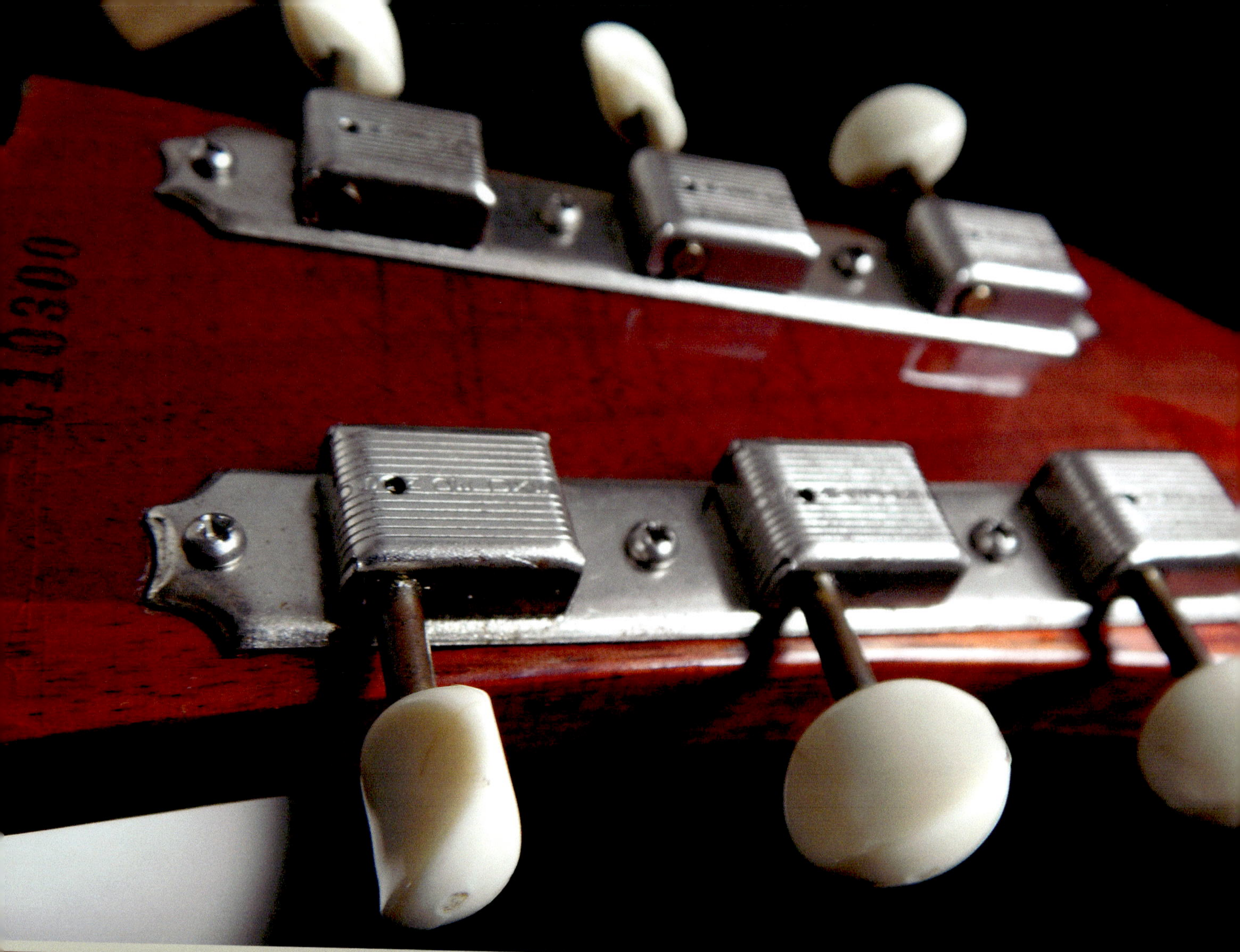

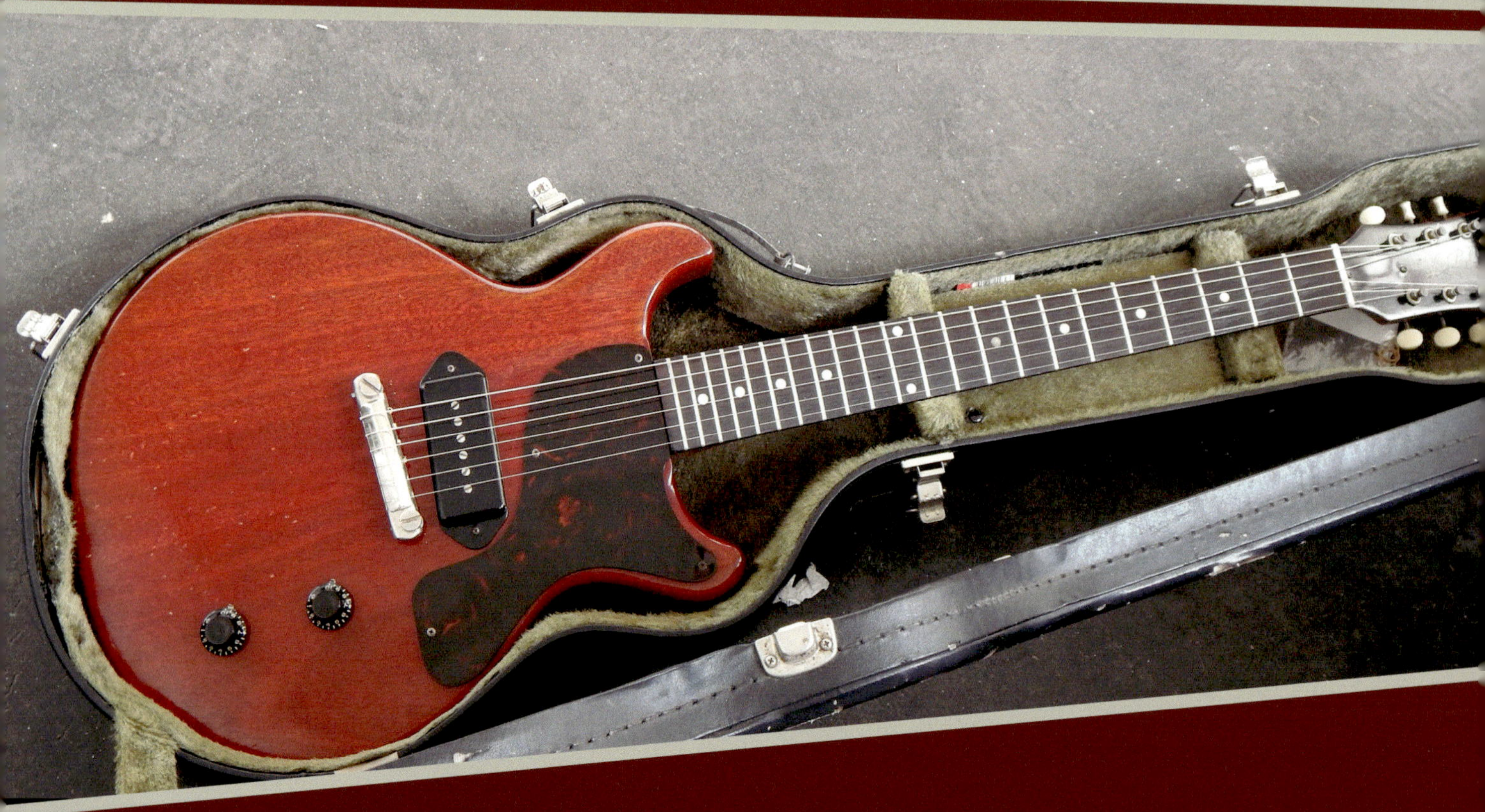

10300

Francis Rossi – Status Quo
1965 Fender Telecaster

This guitar was purchased by Francis Rossi in Glasgow second hand for £75.00 in 1968. It was used for both studio and live work for the next 47 years. According to Francis who retired the guitar in 2015, the guitar was originally a sunburst and has been heavily modified over the years with different bridges and pickups. He removed the original finish himself in favour of a natural one, but didn't like the results, he then painted it black. Unfortunately he still wasn't happy with the way it looked so he decided to sand the front and the back down and use some green furniture paint that he had to refinish just the front.

   The back of the guitar was left in a bare wood finish. The original sunburst finish is visible upon removal of the neck plate. Apparently there are several assumptions relating to the hole that has been drilled on the front of the guitars body. The most likely being that this was drilled by Francis to allow the guitar lead to be threaded through it when on stage to prevent it being ripped out of the jack socket.

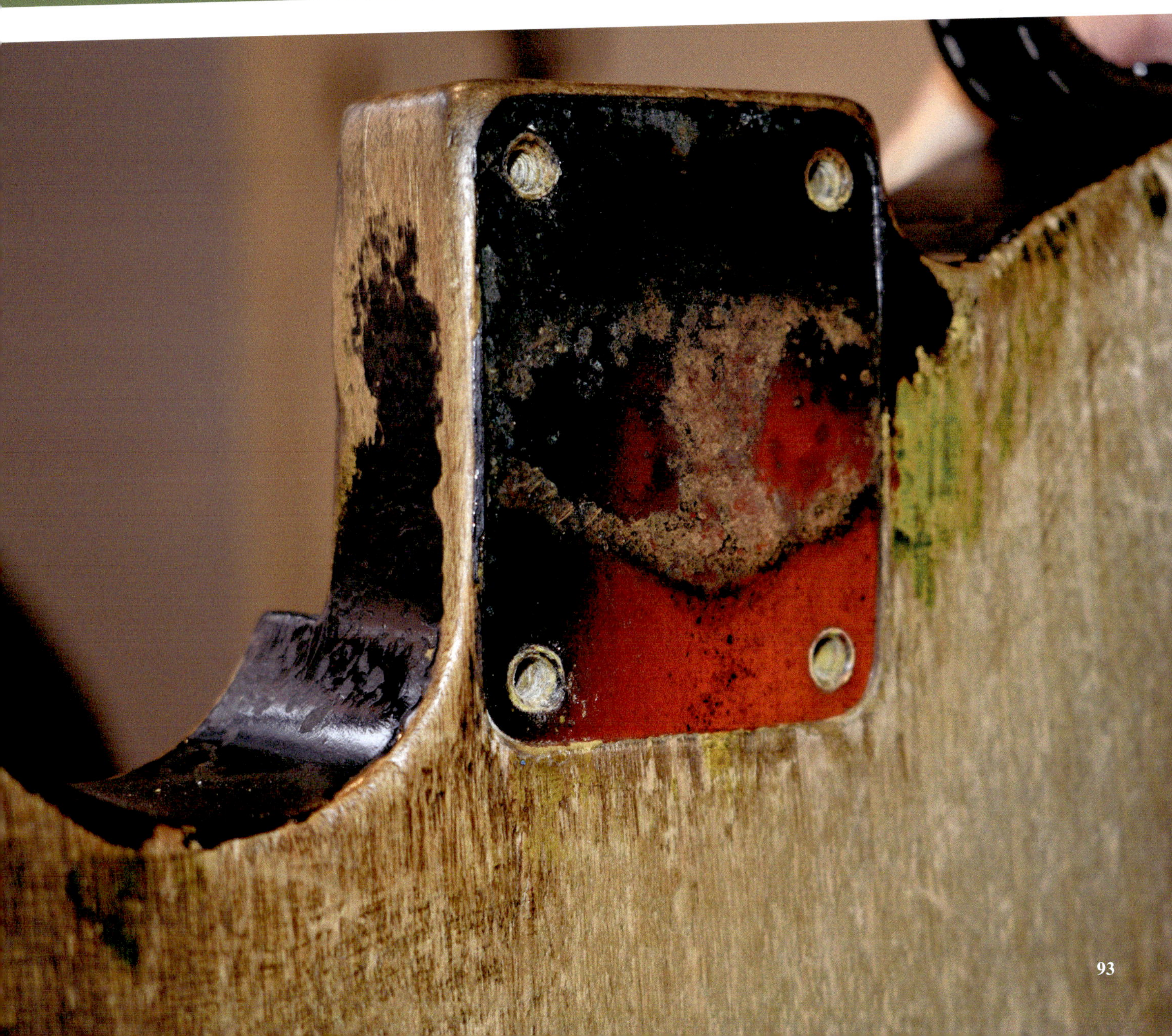

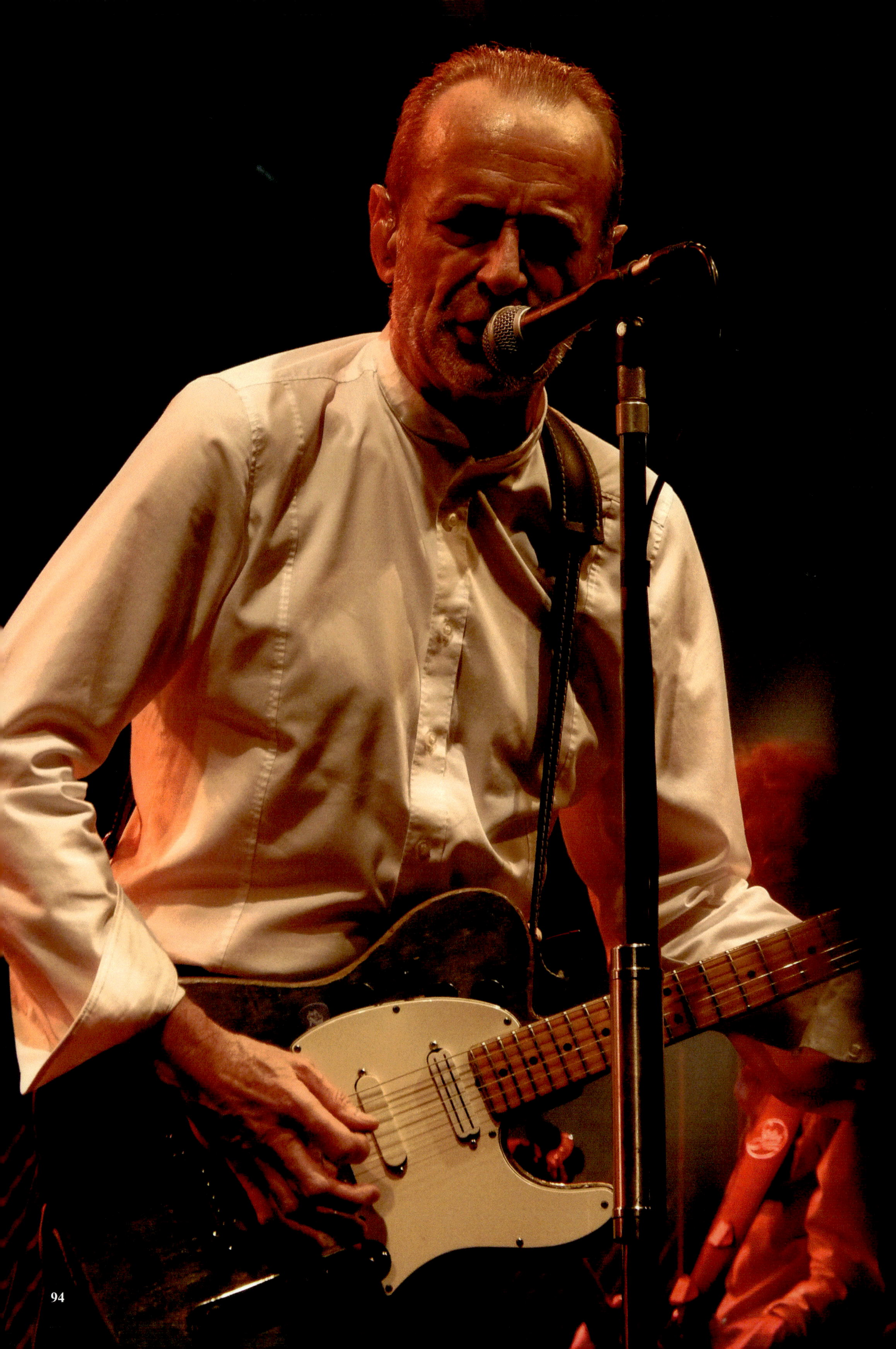

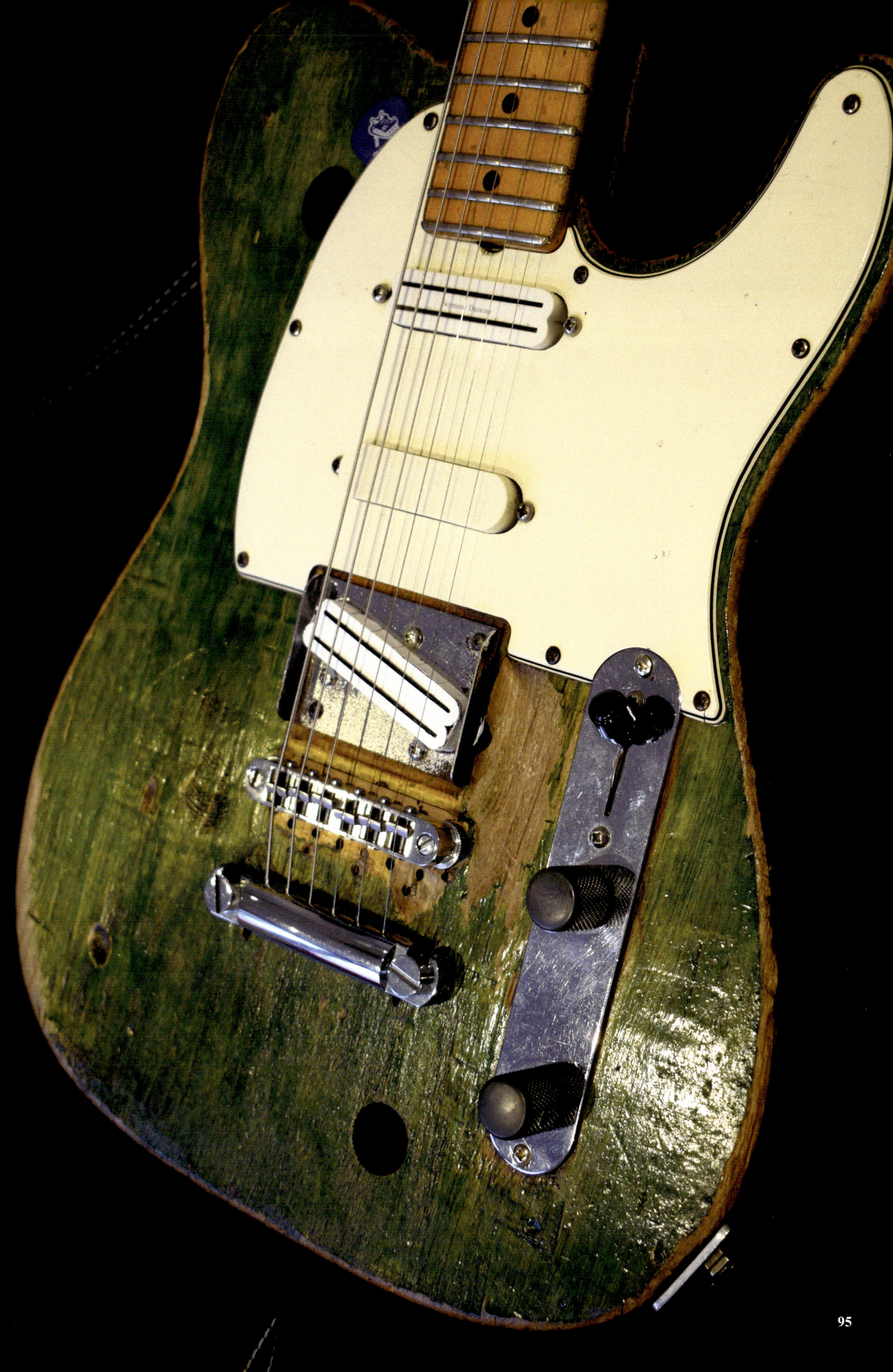

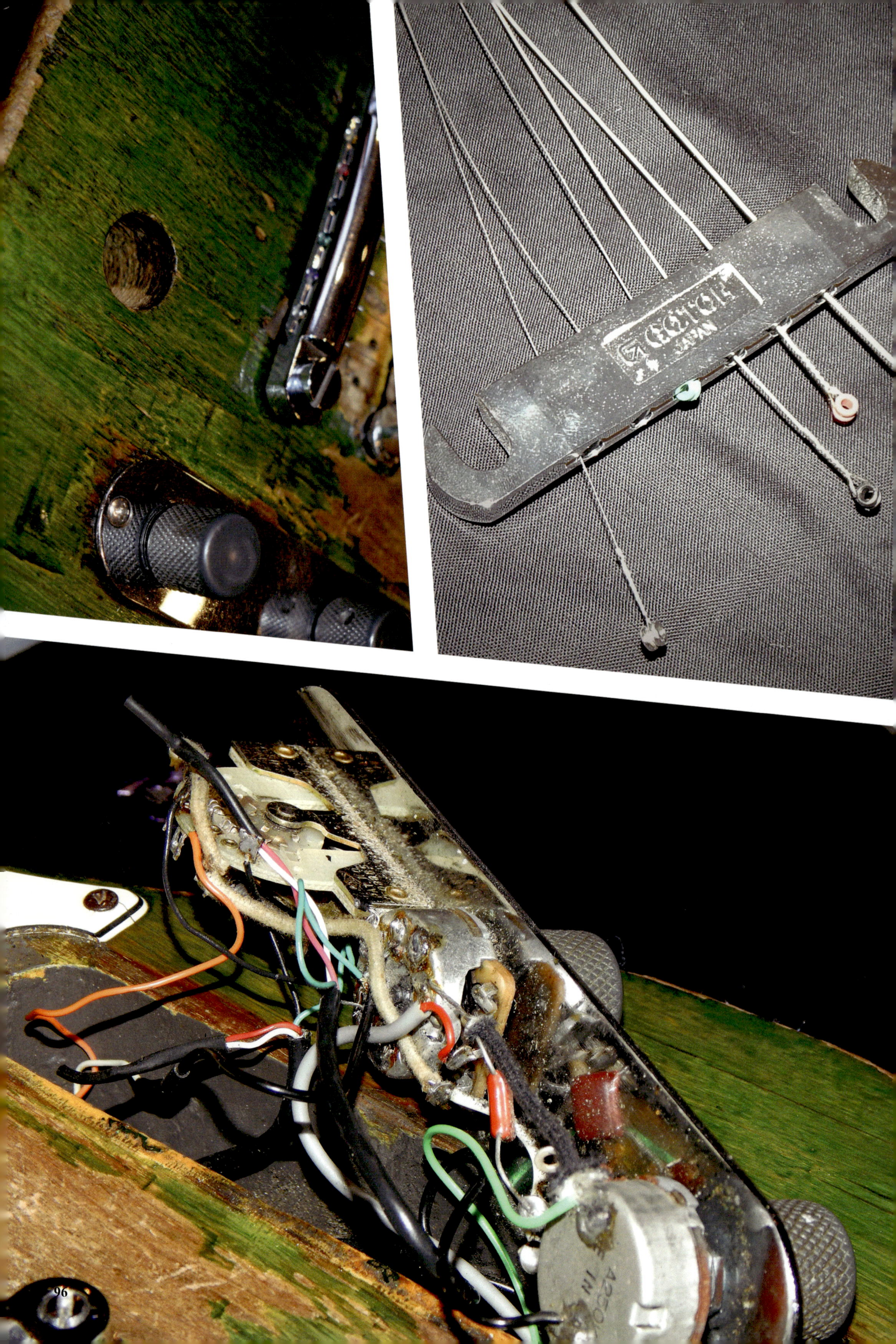

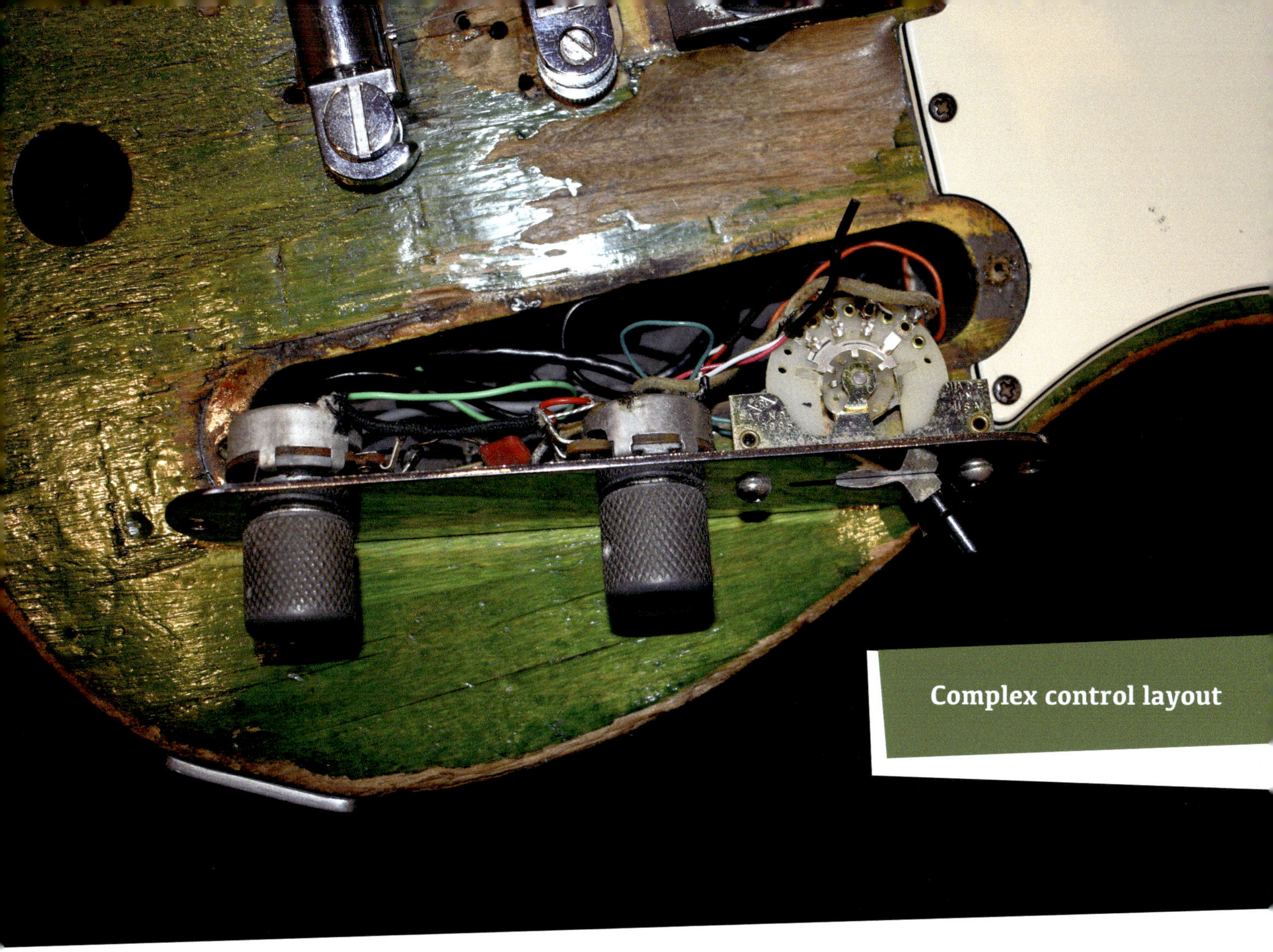

Complex control layout

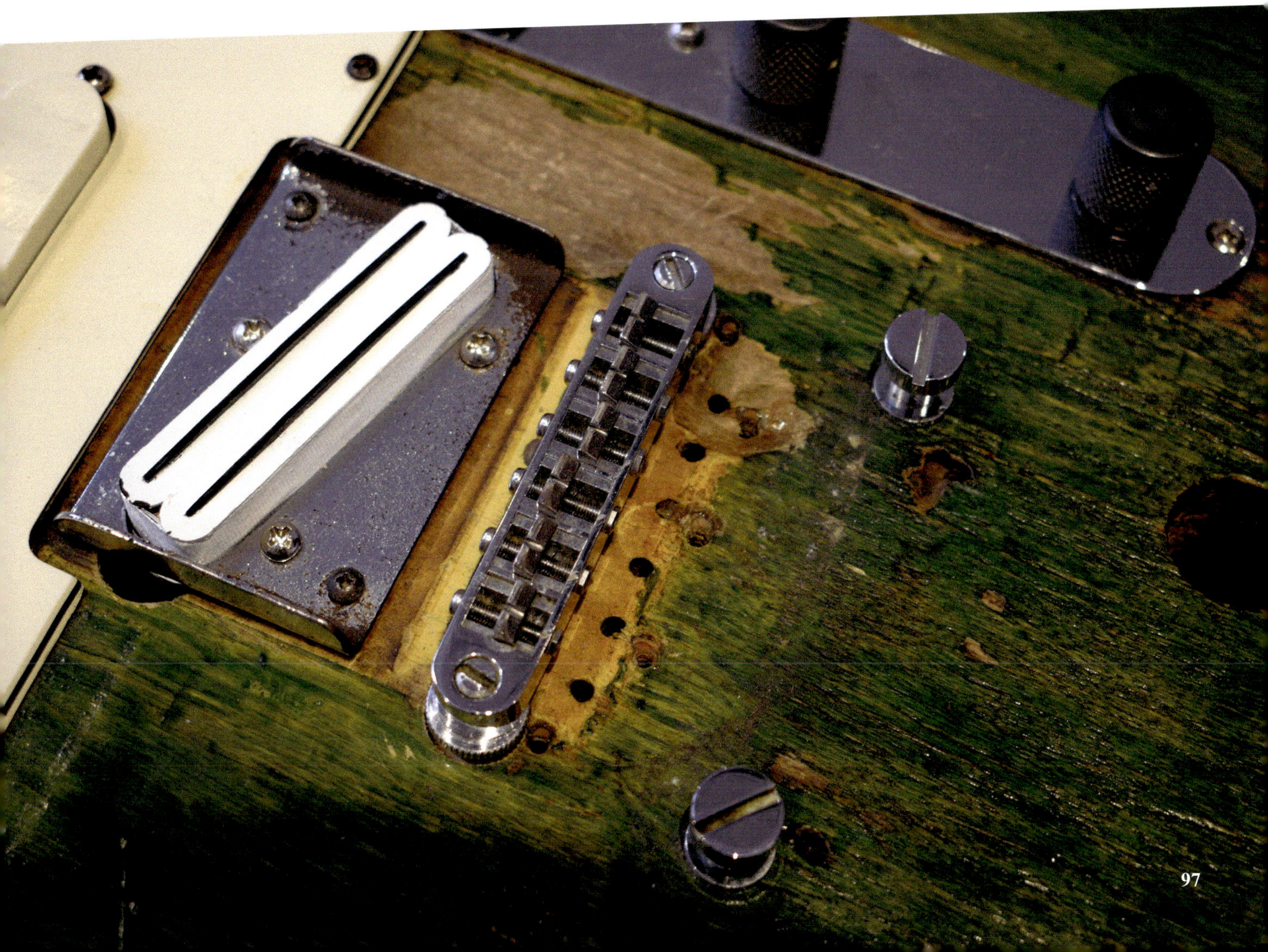

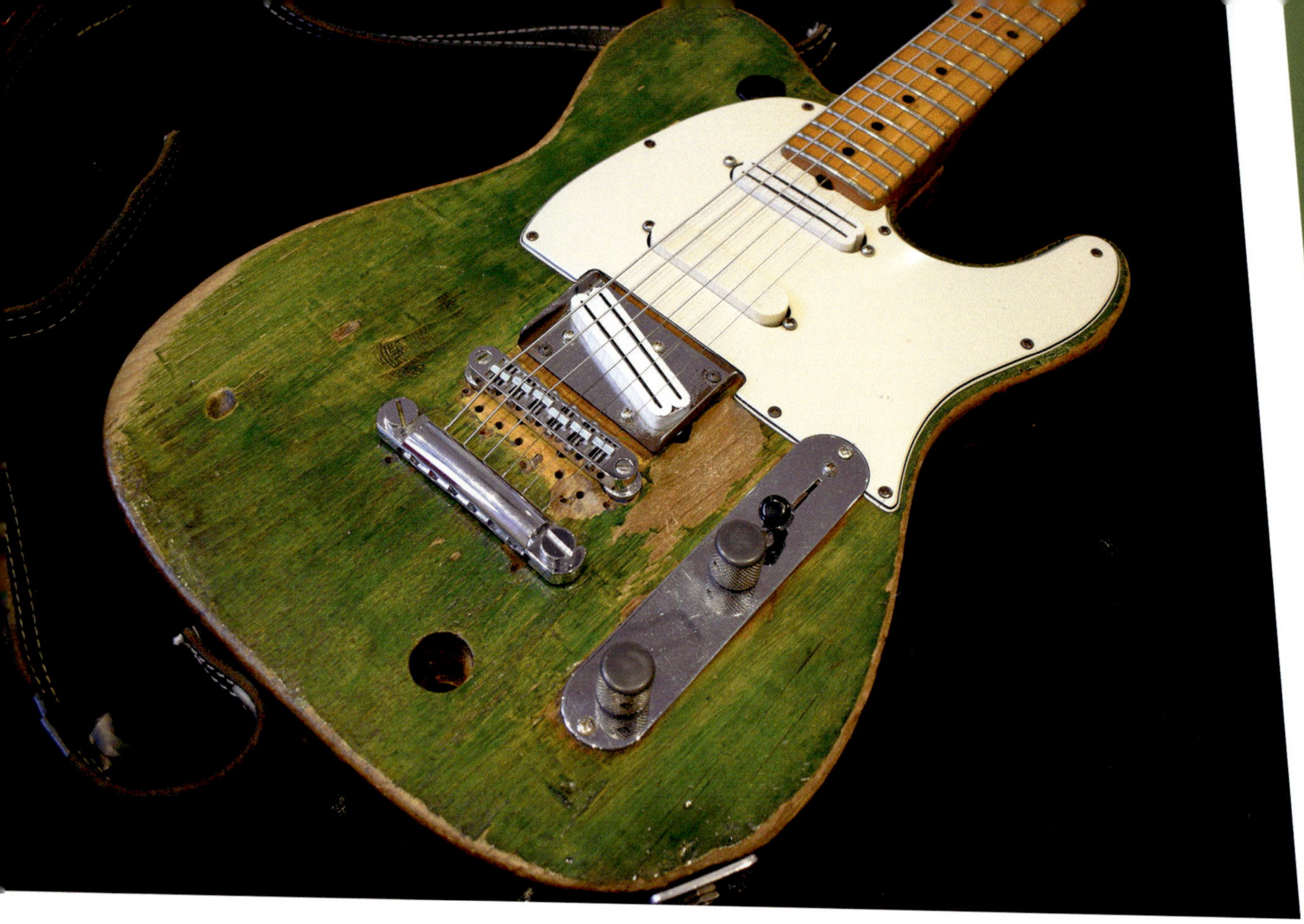

In 2011 the neck pickup was changed to a Seymour Duncan Hot Rails. Then shortly after another one was fitted in the bridge position. The Lace Sensor remained in the middle.

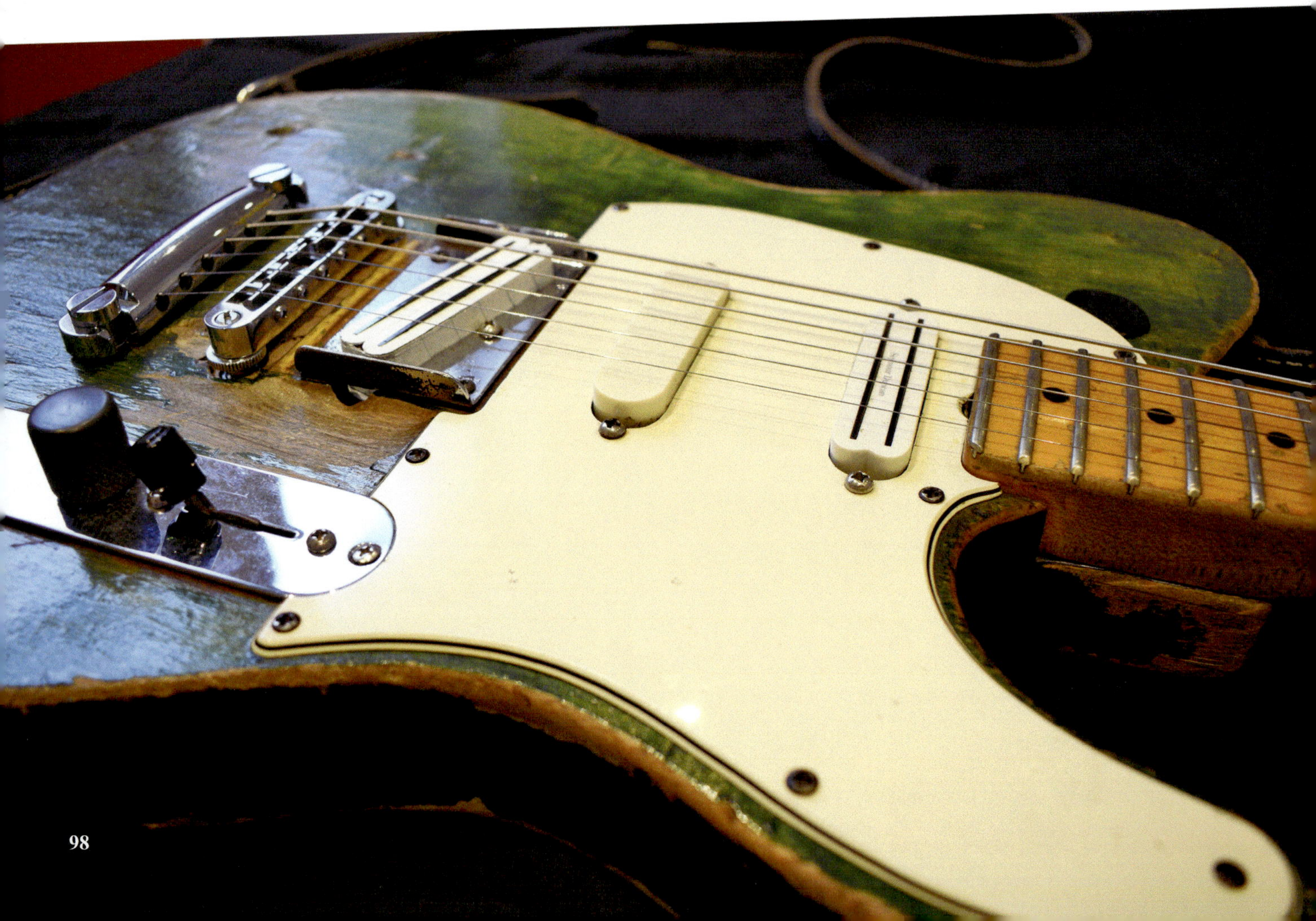

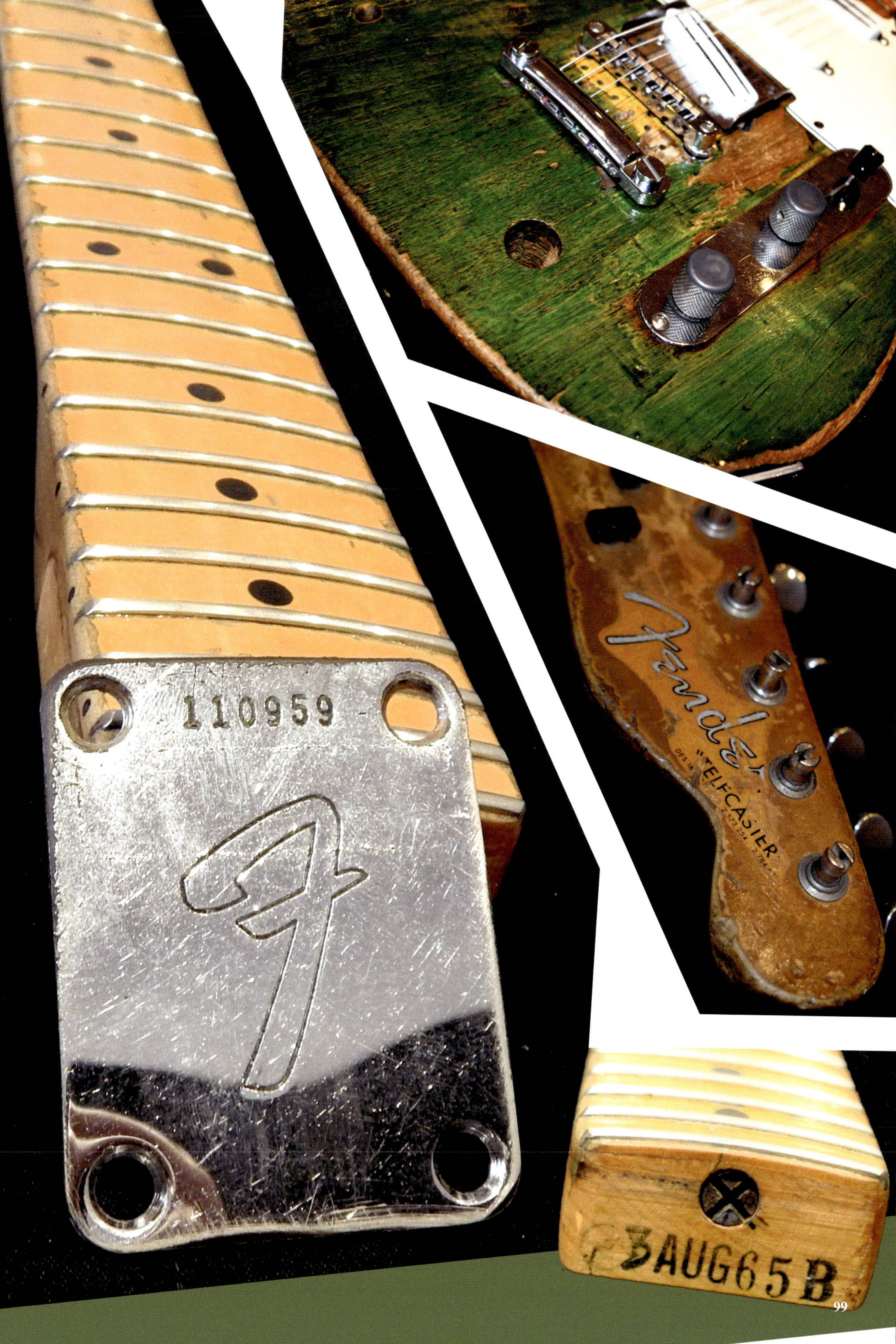
110959
Fender
TELECASTER
8 AUG 65 B

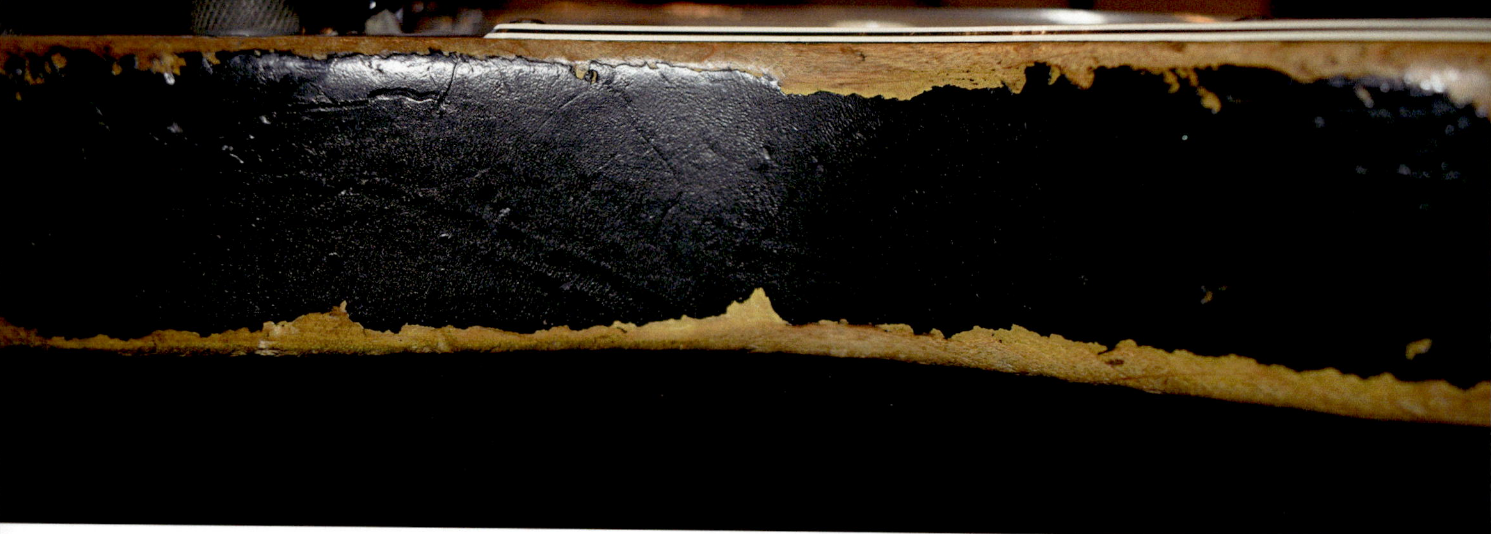

The image above shows a faint denim imprint from when Francis had painted it black but it wasn't dry in time for his gig.

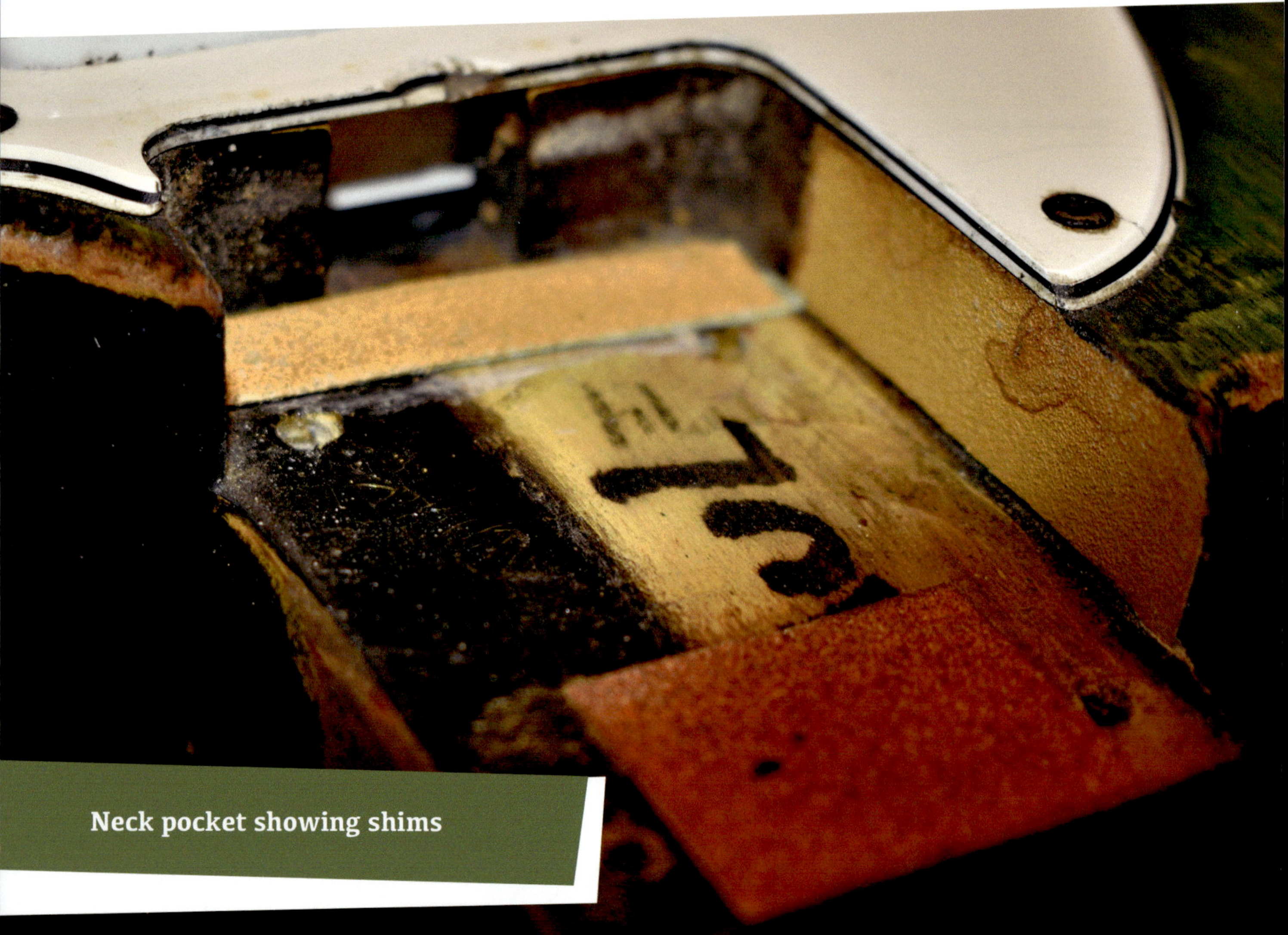

Neck pocket showing shims

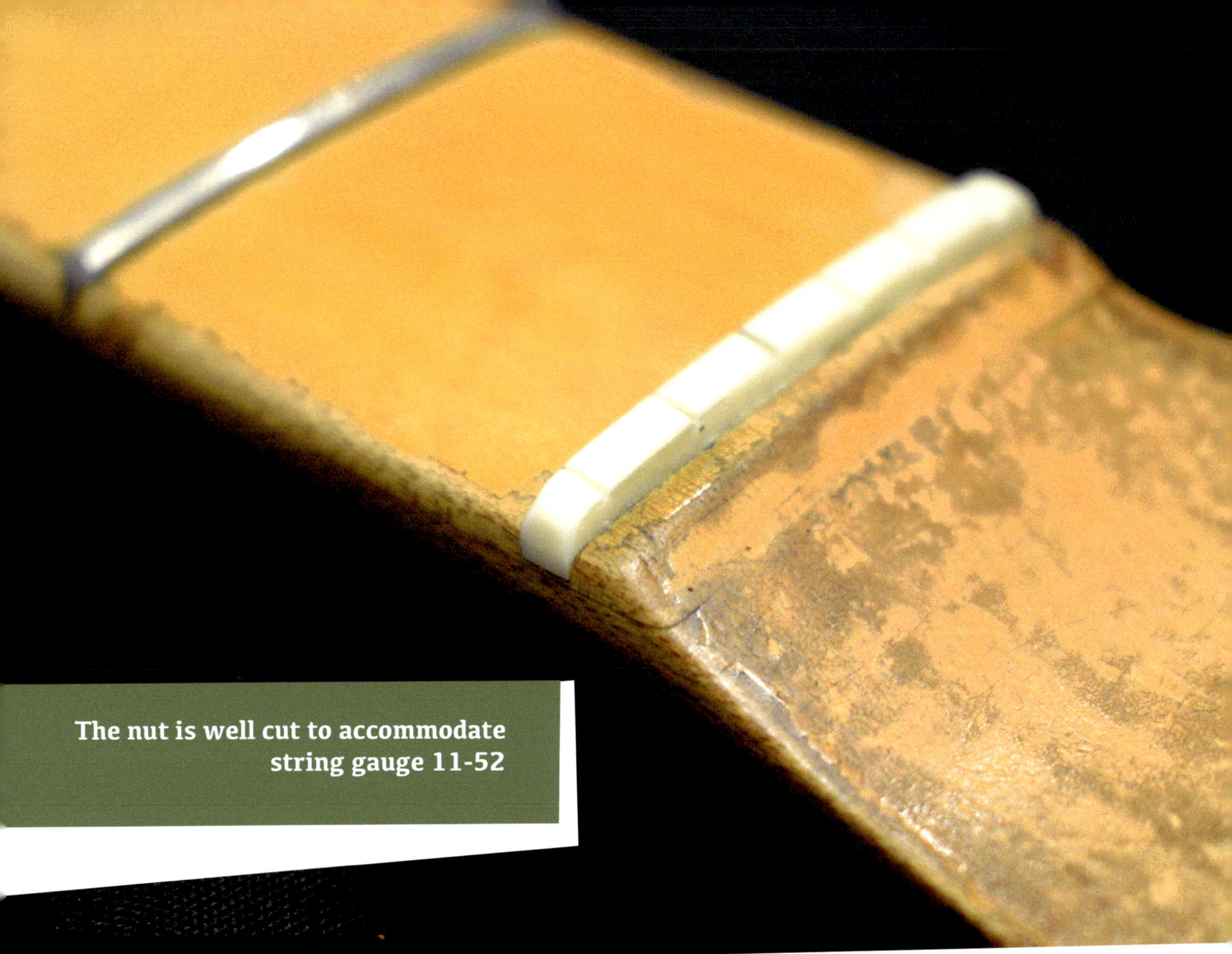

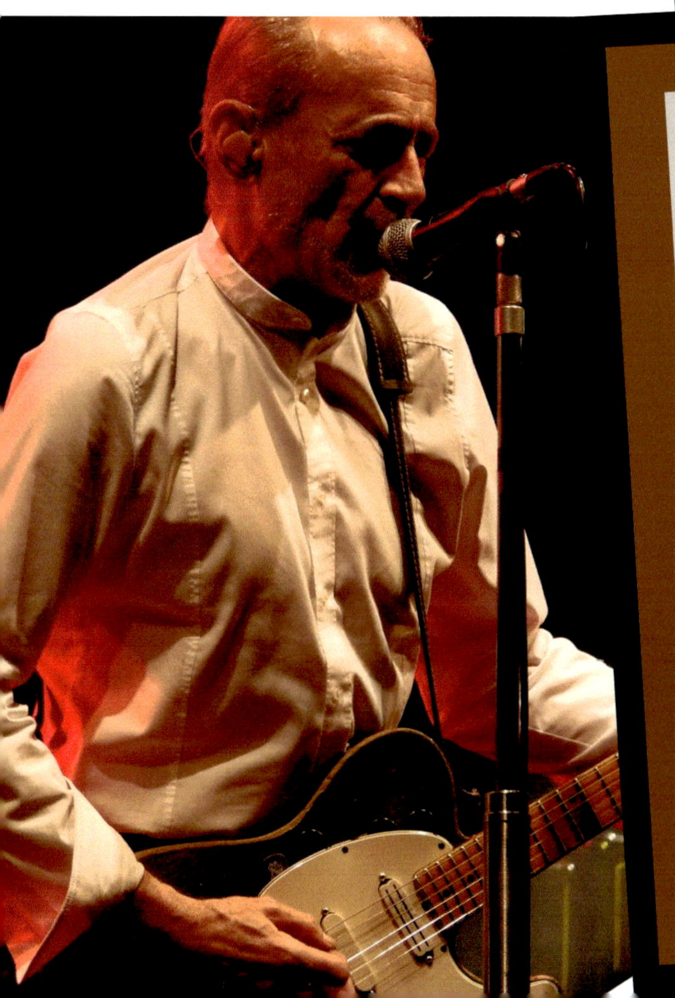

Famous Frets SPECS

Headstock thickness:
14.61mm towards the top edge
16.75mm measuring from the Low E tuner
Machine Heads: Kluson (Replacements)
Nut: 40.35mm
Frets: 2.75 Jumbo
Bridge Pickup: 15.50 ohms
Mid Pickup: 7.53 ohms
Neck Pickup: 9.65 ohms
Body thickness: 45.09mm at the lower horn
43.76mm at upper bout where the arm would rest
Bridge: 13.87mm width, 84.29mm length
12th Fret neck: 49.96mm width
Volume and Tone Controls: 19.07mm width
Weight: 7.78lbs
Tailpiece: Gotoh
Switch: Five way

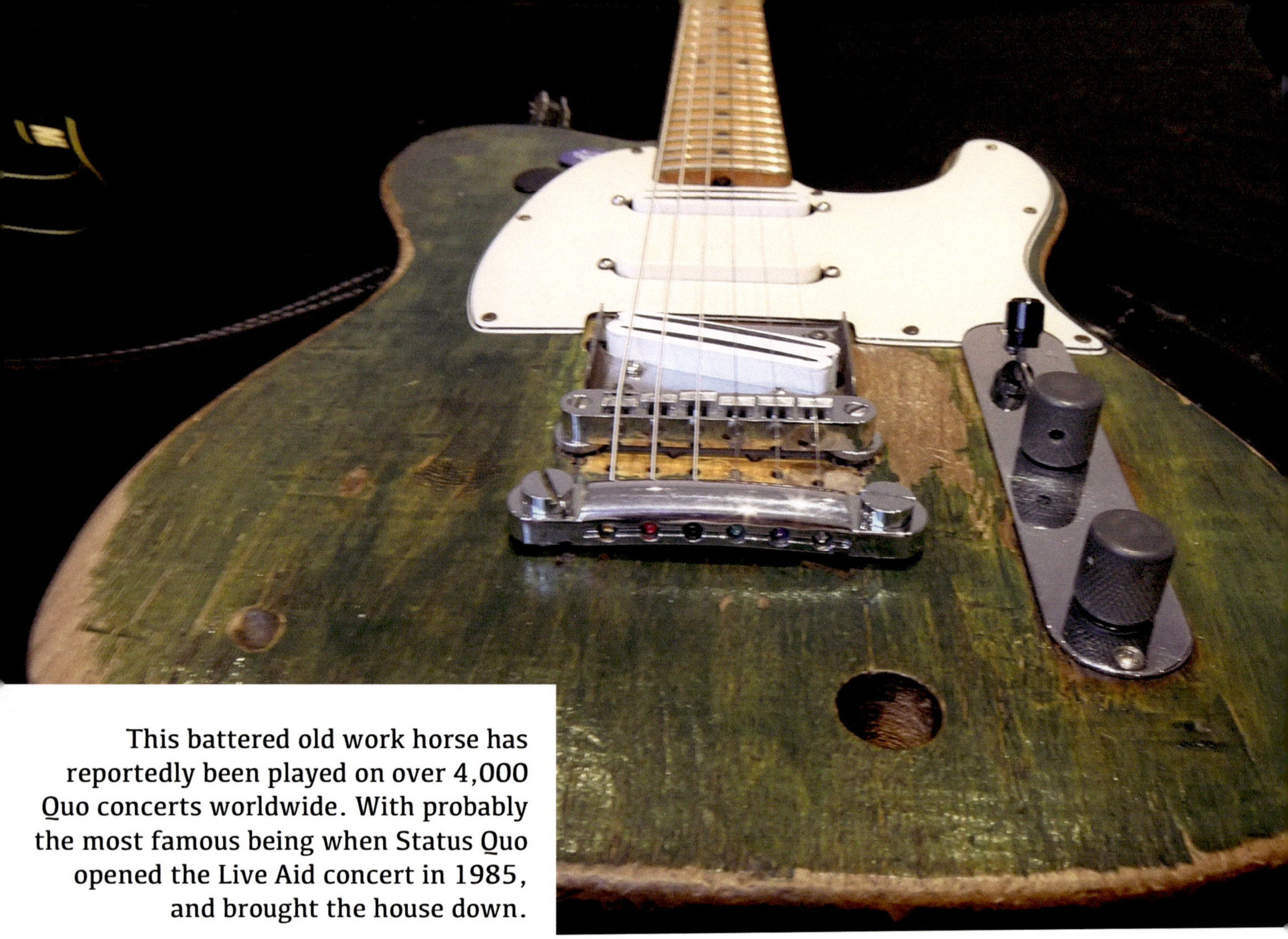

This battered old work horse has reportedly been played on over 4,000 Quo concerts worldwide. With probably the most famous being when Status Quo opened the Live Aid concert in 1985, and brought the house down.

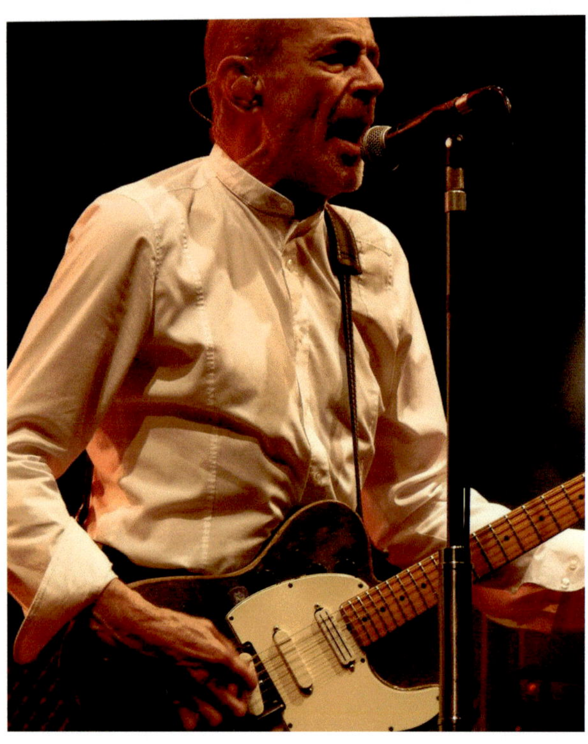

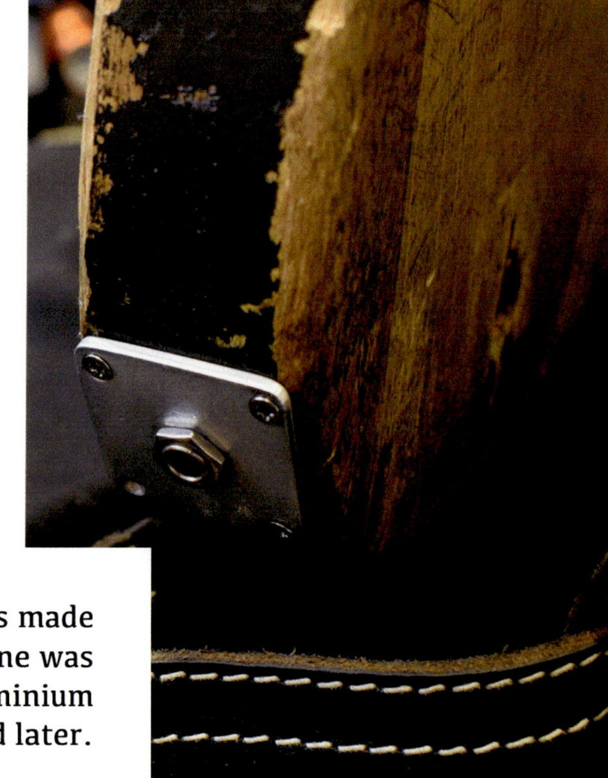

This jack socket plate (about 1/8" thick) was made from a piece of cut aluminium. The plastic one was changed possibly around 1982/83 as the aluminium one can be seen on the Live Aid concert and later.

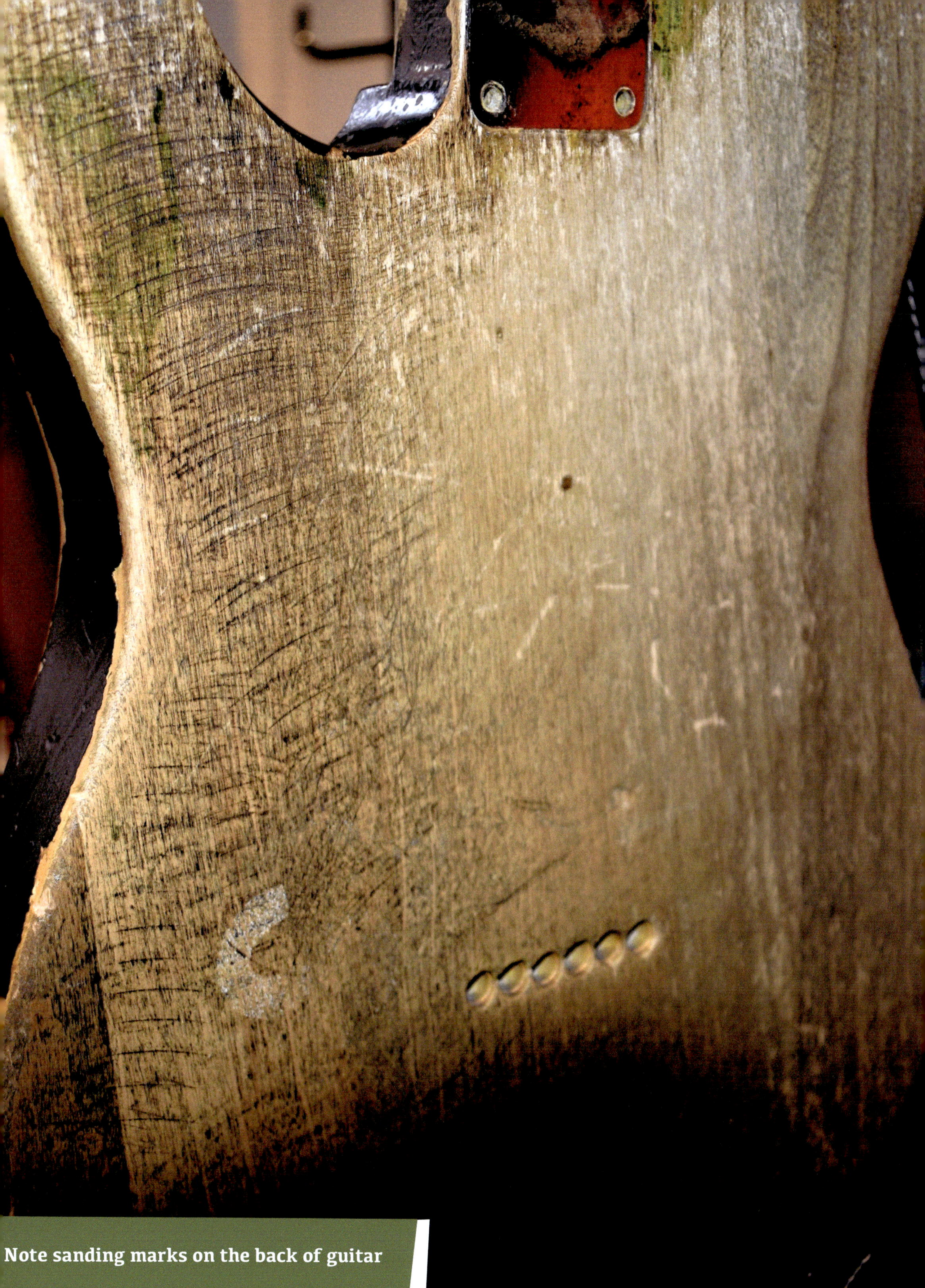

Note sanding marks on the back of guitar

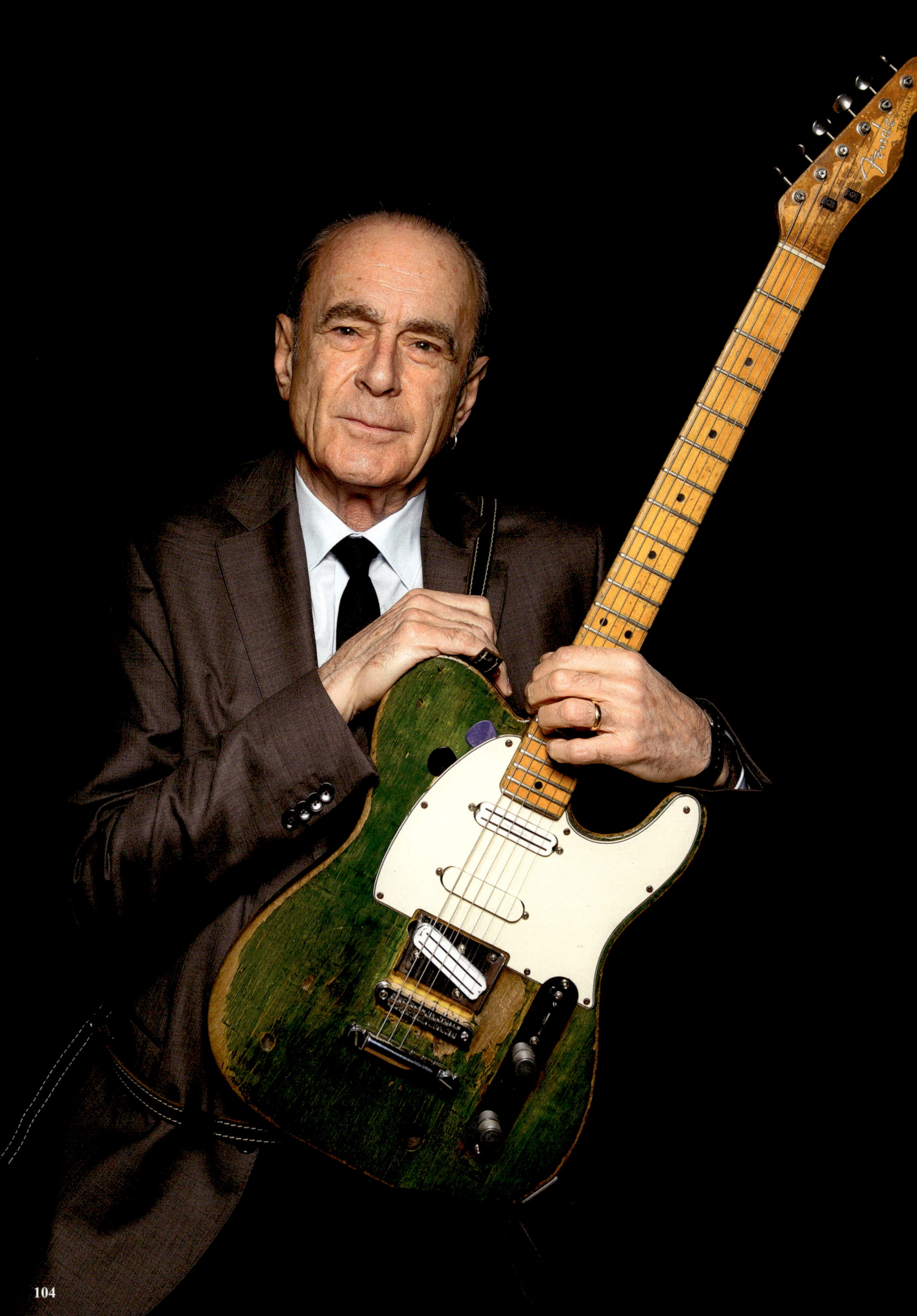

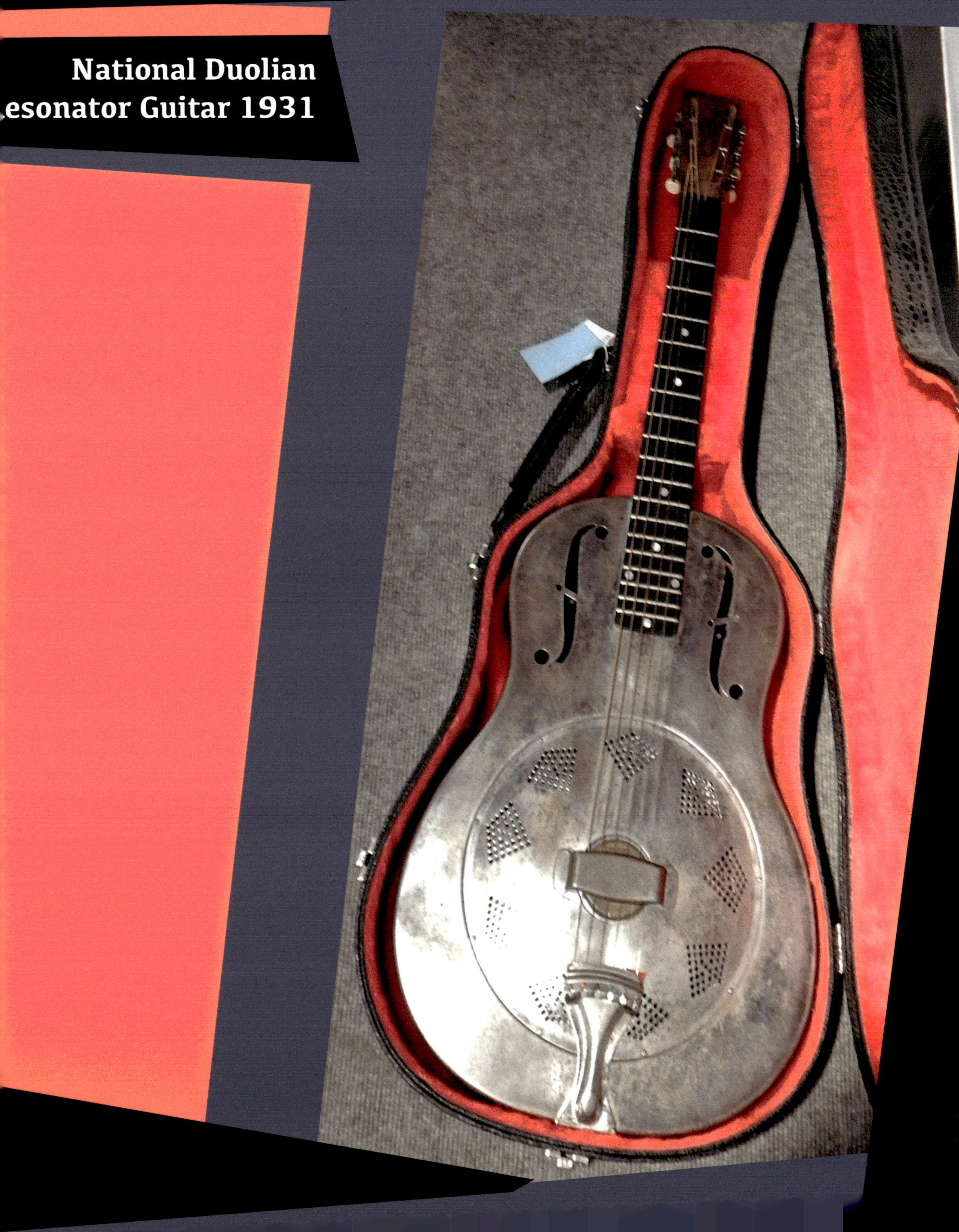
Peter Green, Fleetwood Mac

National Duolian
Resonator Guitar 1931

I was fortunate to be invited to assess and repair the entire Peter Green Collection prior to their auction in June 2023 at Bonhams, Knightsbridge, London. There was a total of 150 guitars, and also amps, mandolins, Turkish lutes etc.

This National Duolian guitar was used by Peter Green in the Splinter group era. It is also seen on the cover the 'Robert Johnson Songbook' album released in 1998. During an interview, Peter says of the guitar "I liked that this one isn't all shiny…it's a very delicate instrument to play, not like some of those Nationals: when I play it, it has a very old and original feel about it and a really old sound". This guitar was also played by Joe Bonamassa.

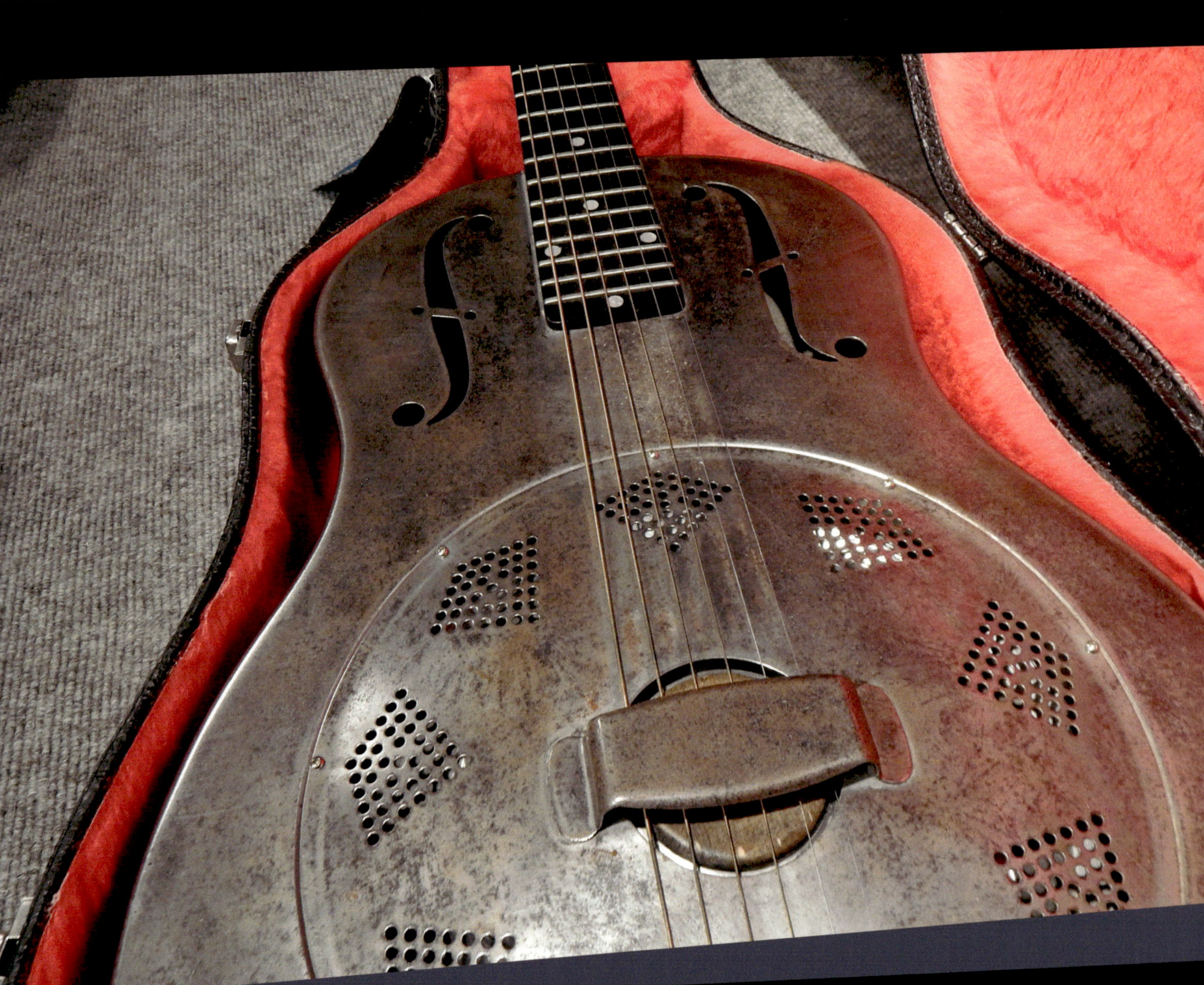

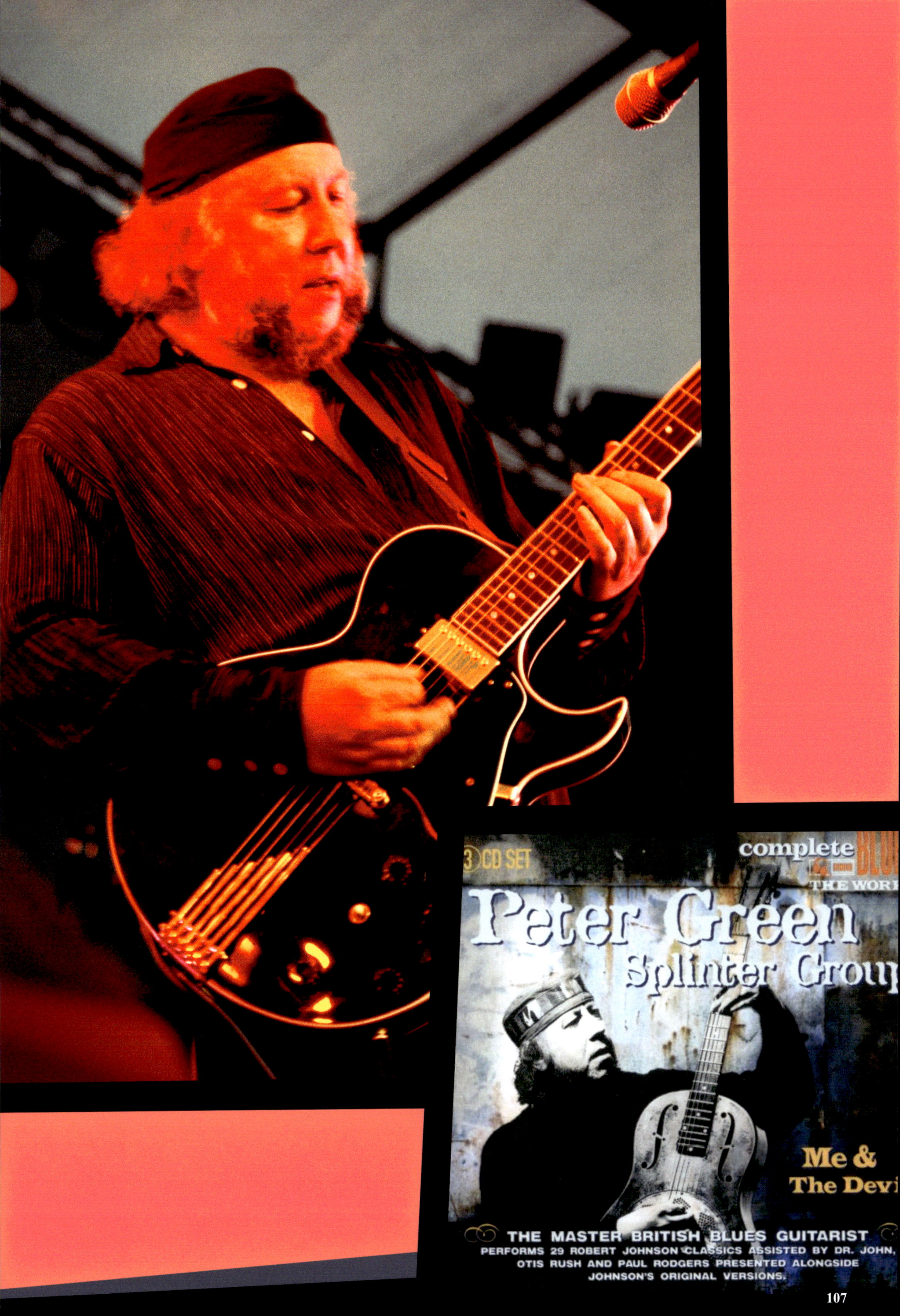
3 CD SET
complete BLU
THE WORL
Peter Green
Splinter Group
Me &
The Devi
THE MASTER BRITISH BLUES GUITARIST
PERFORMS 29 ROBERT JOHNSON CLASSICS ASSISTED BY DR. JOHN,
OTIS RUSH AND PAUL RODGERS PRESENTED ALONGSIDE
JOHNSON'S ORIGINAL VERSIONS.

Gretsch 6137 White Falcon 1968

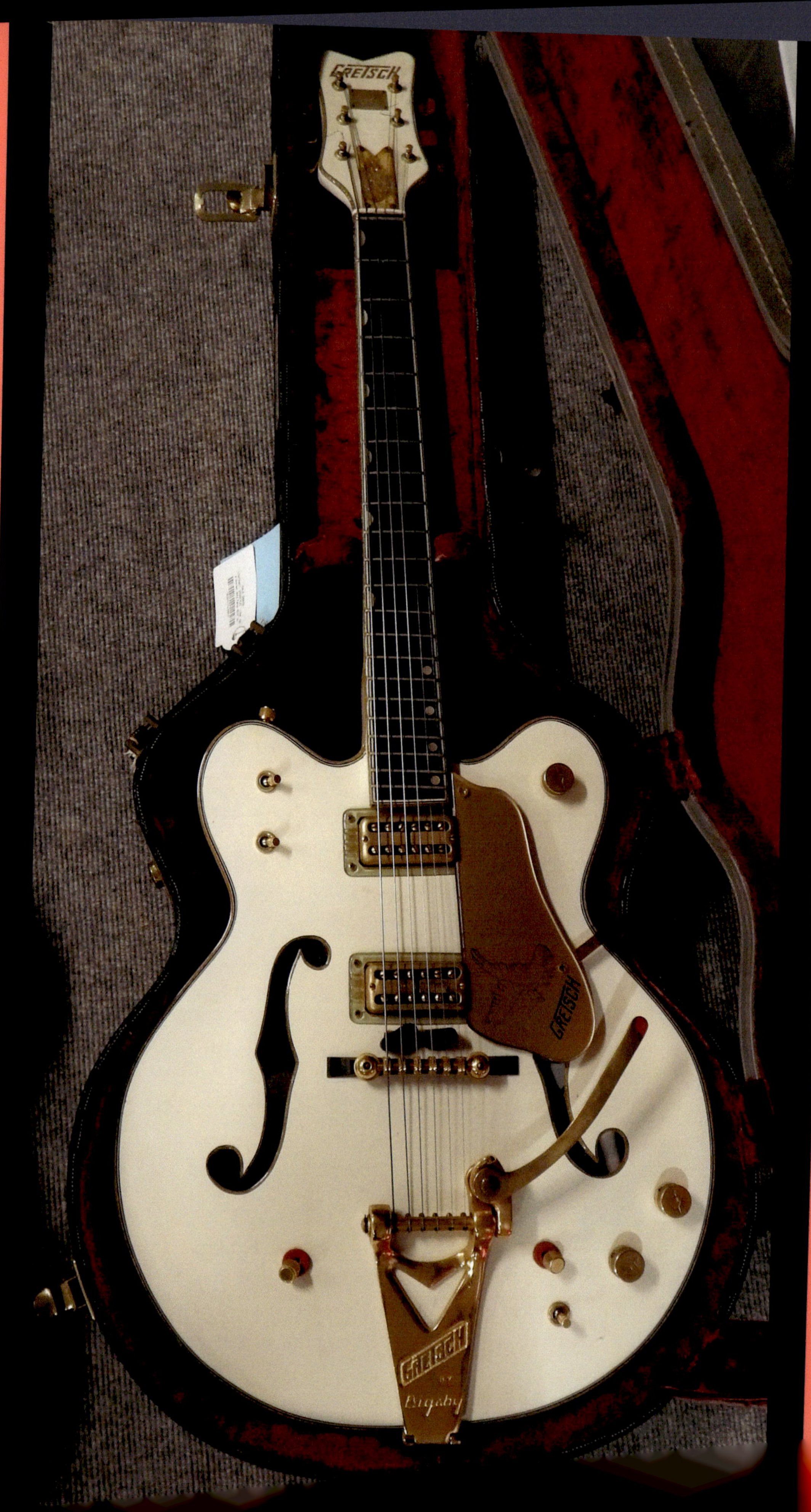

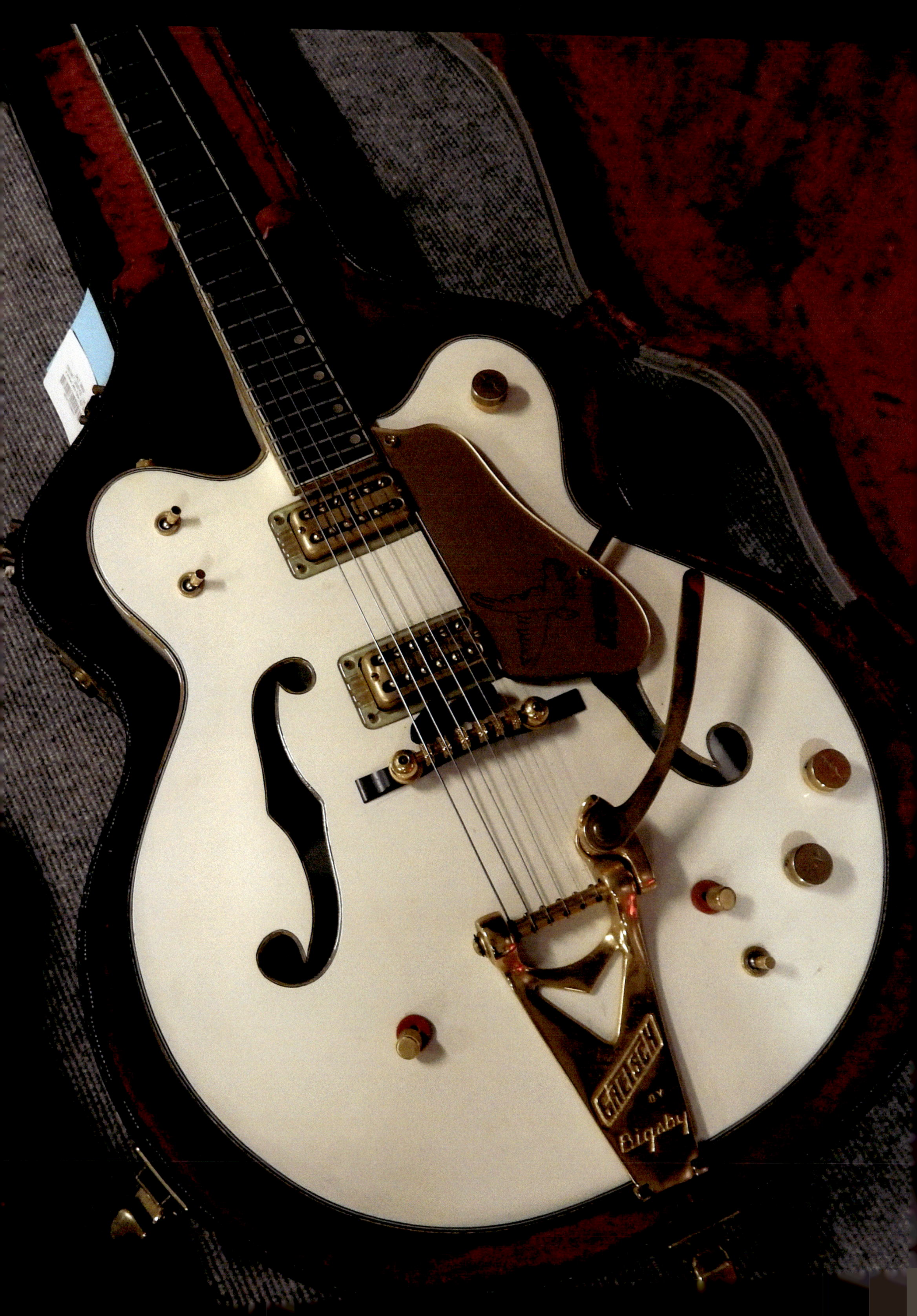
GRETSCH
BY
Bigsby

This Gretsch was bought in the mid 90's when Peter Green started collecting guitars again. It has been said that when he struck the first chord on this White Falcon he sounded like Elvis! Again, this guitar was also played by Joe Bonamassa just prior to the last date of his UK tour in May 2023. You can see an interview with Joe discussing the guitar with Guitarist magazine on YouTube.

When I first plugged this guitar in, nothing worked! The jack socket was faulty, the volume and tone controls were intermittent, toggles switches faulty. I fixed them all without having to replace any parts.

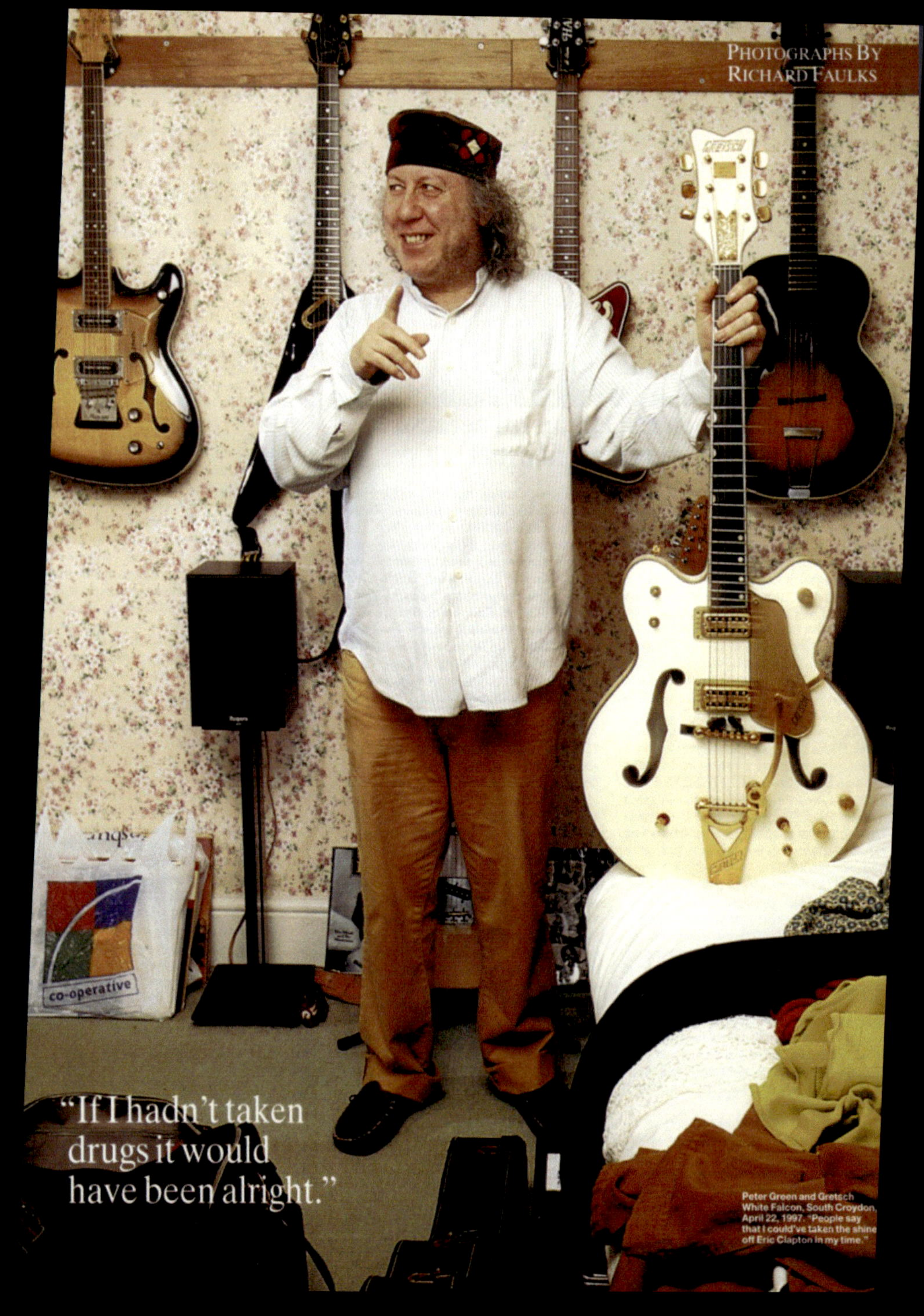

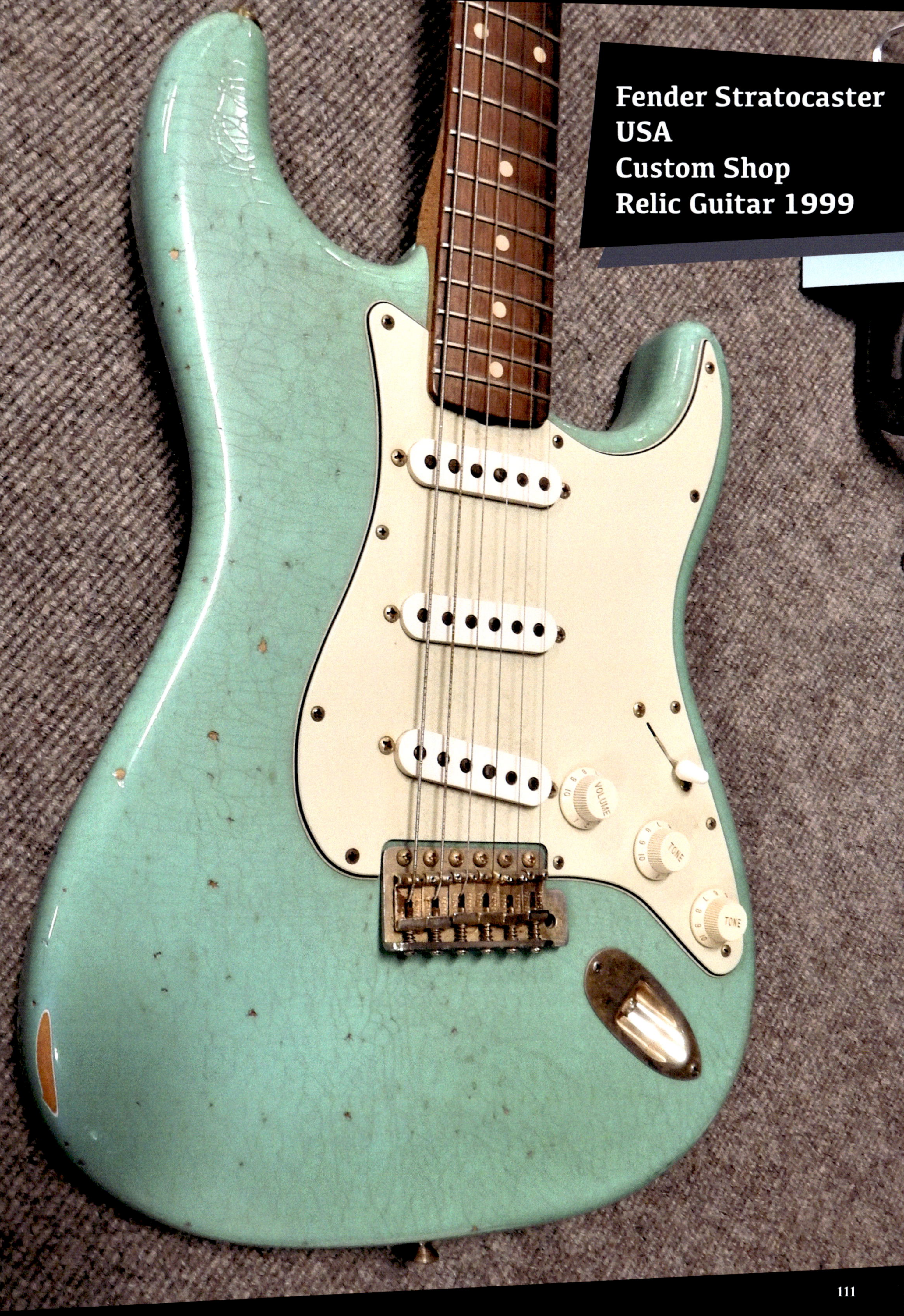

Fender Stratocaster
USA
Custom Shop
Relic Guitar 1999

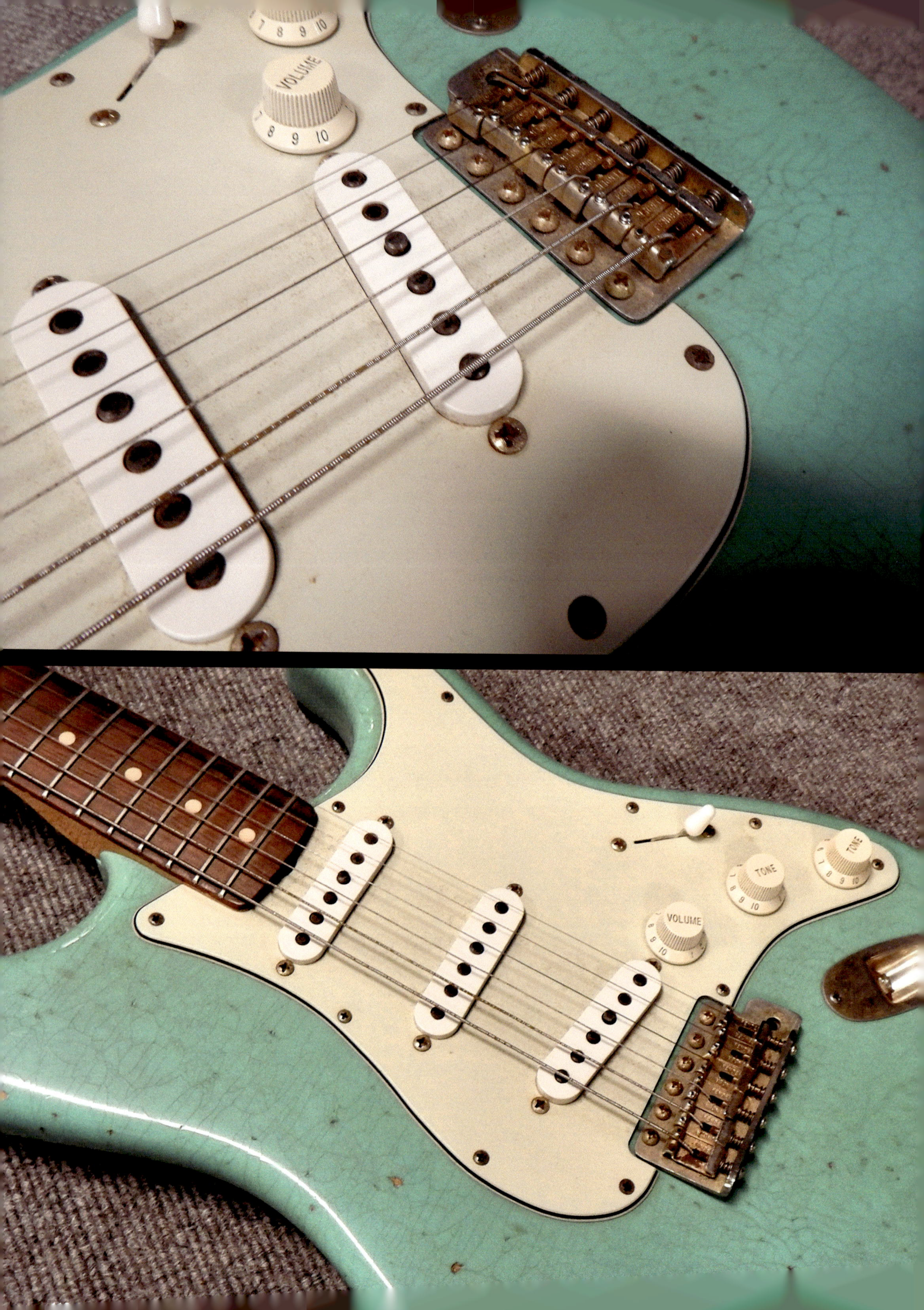

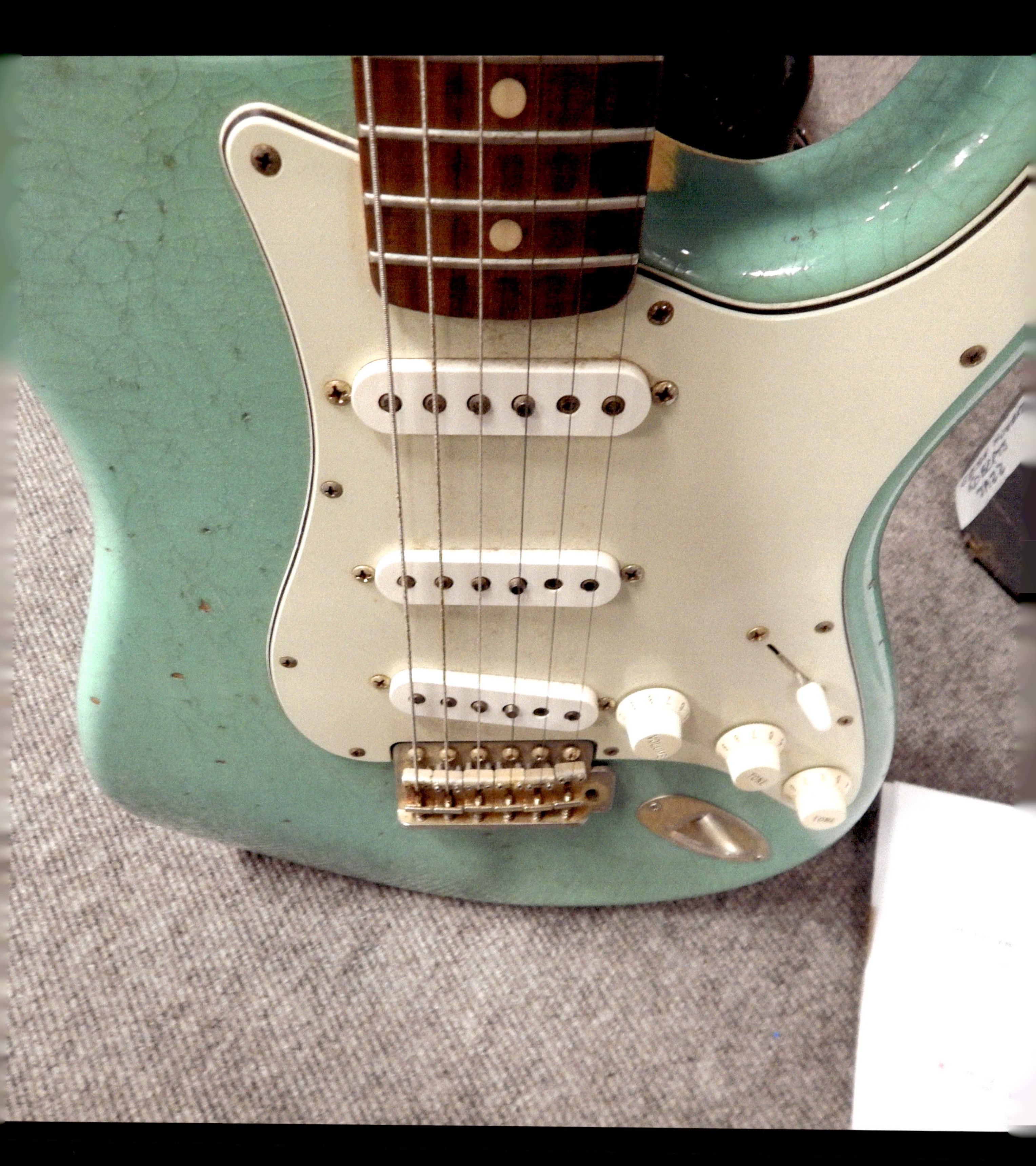

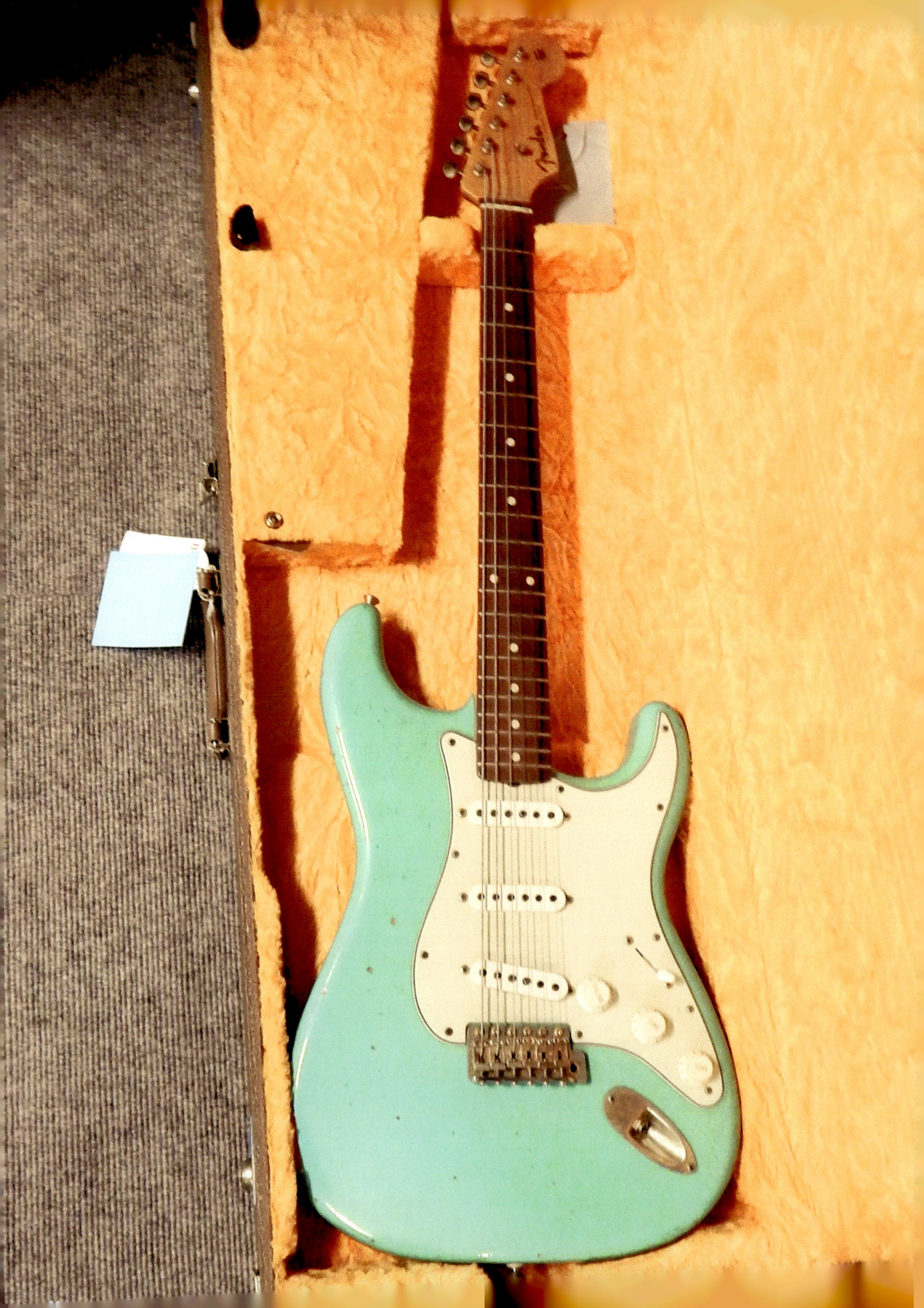

This guitar was used on stage during the Splinter group era. Also seen at the Bishopstock Blues Festival, Devon in August 2001.

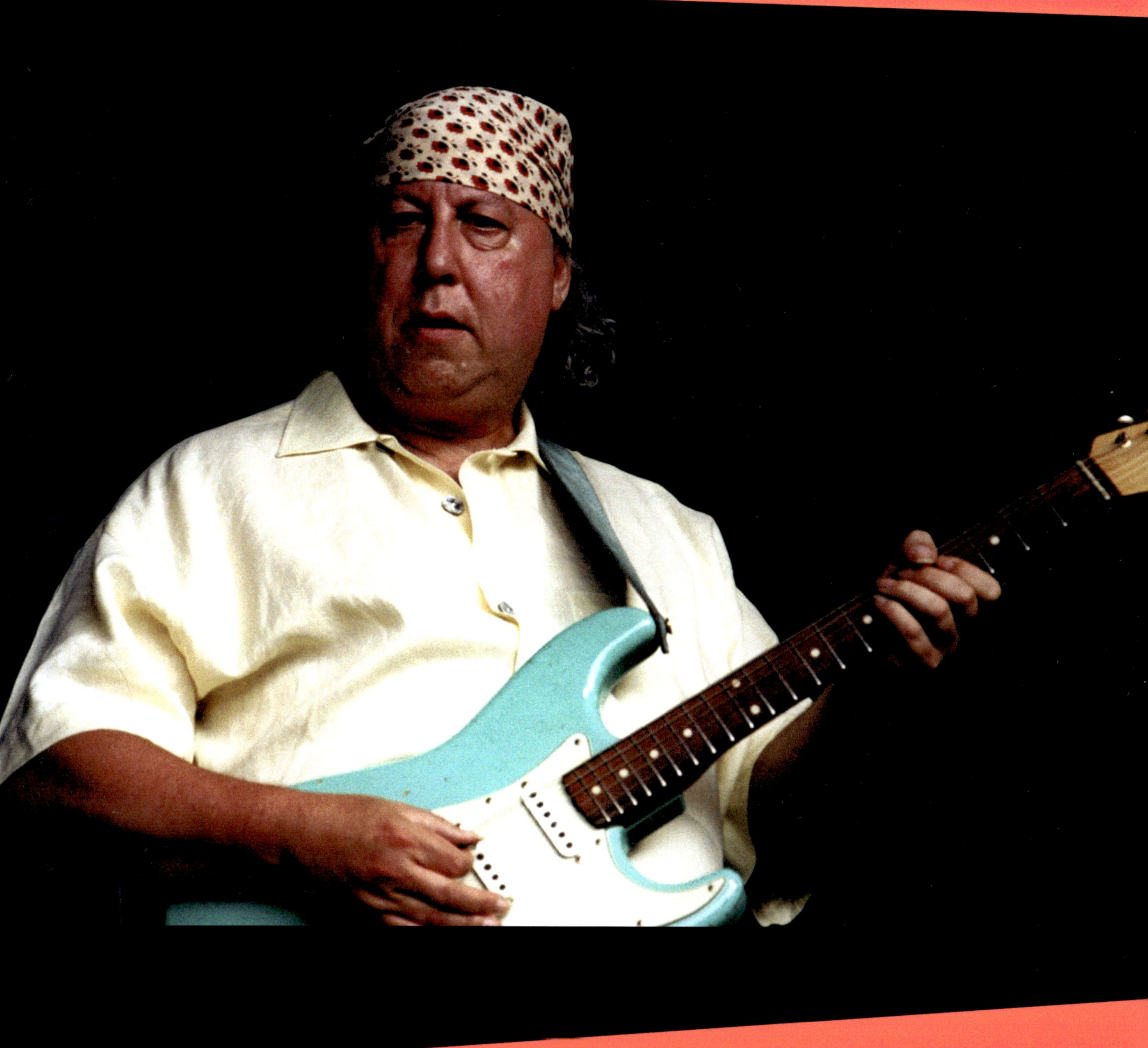

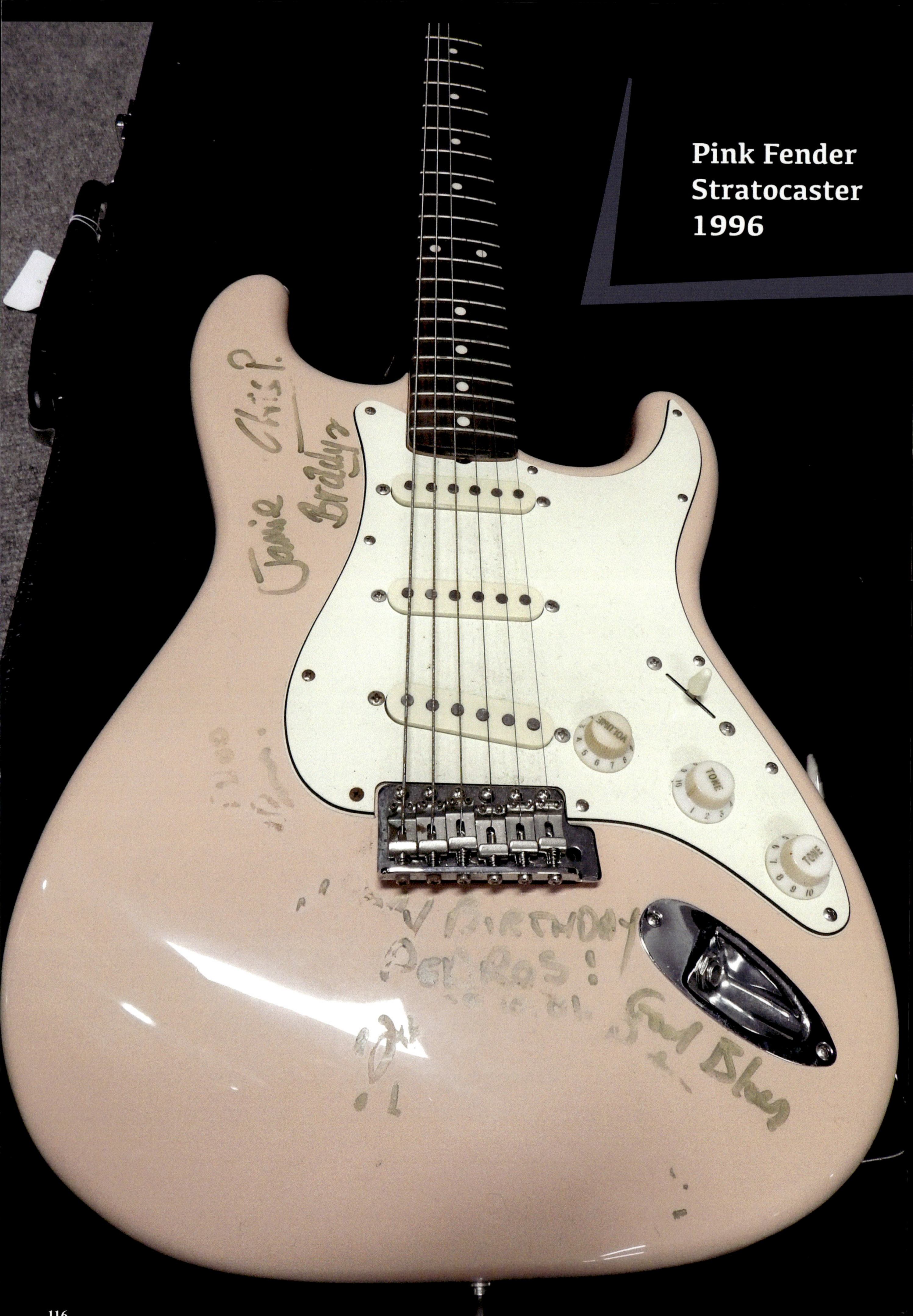

Pink Fender
Stratocaster
1996

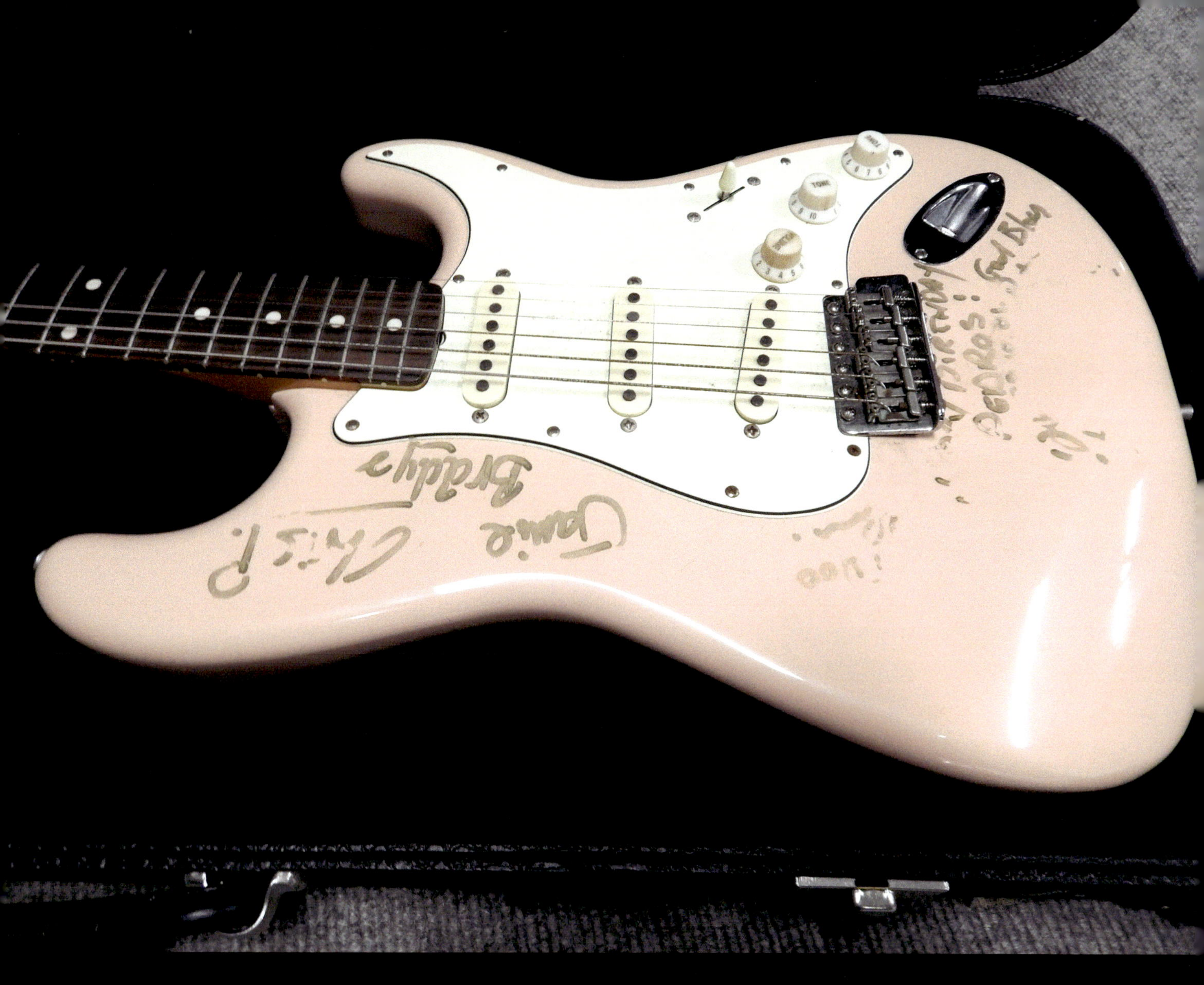

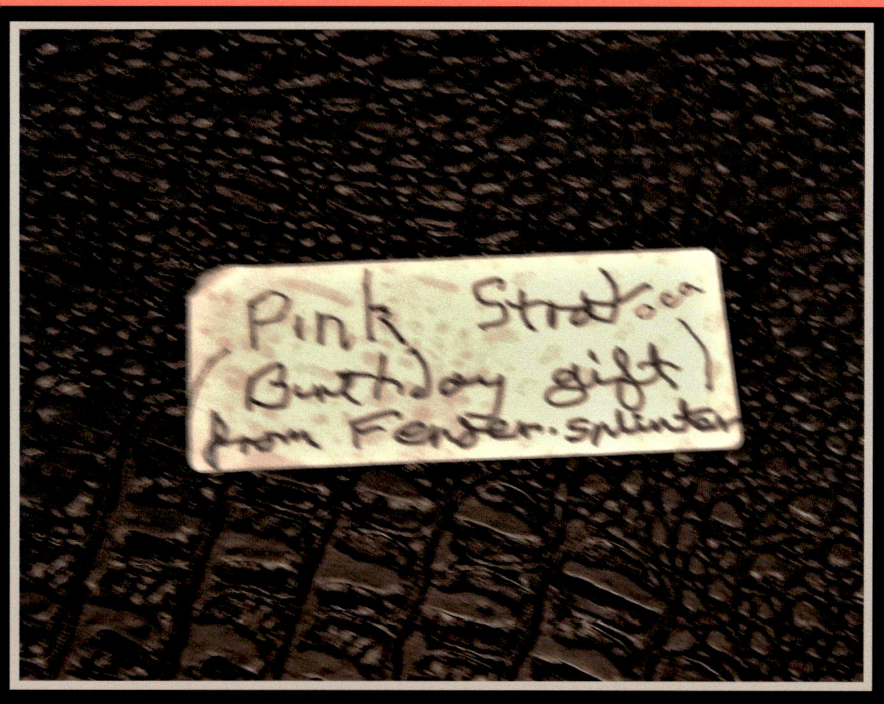

This Japanese built guitar has the body inscribed with gold marker by various Fender employees along with a message saying "Happy Birthday Pedros!" It was used many times with both Splinter Group and Peter Green and Friends. He is also seen playing 'Black Magic Woman' In Birmingham UK on 16th Dec 2009.

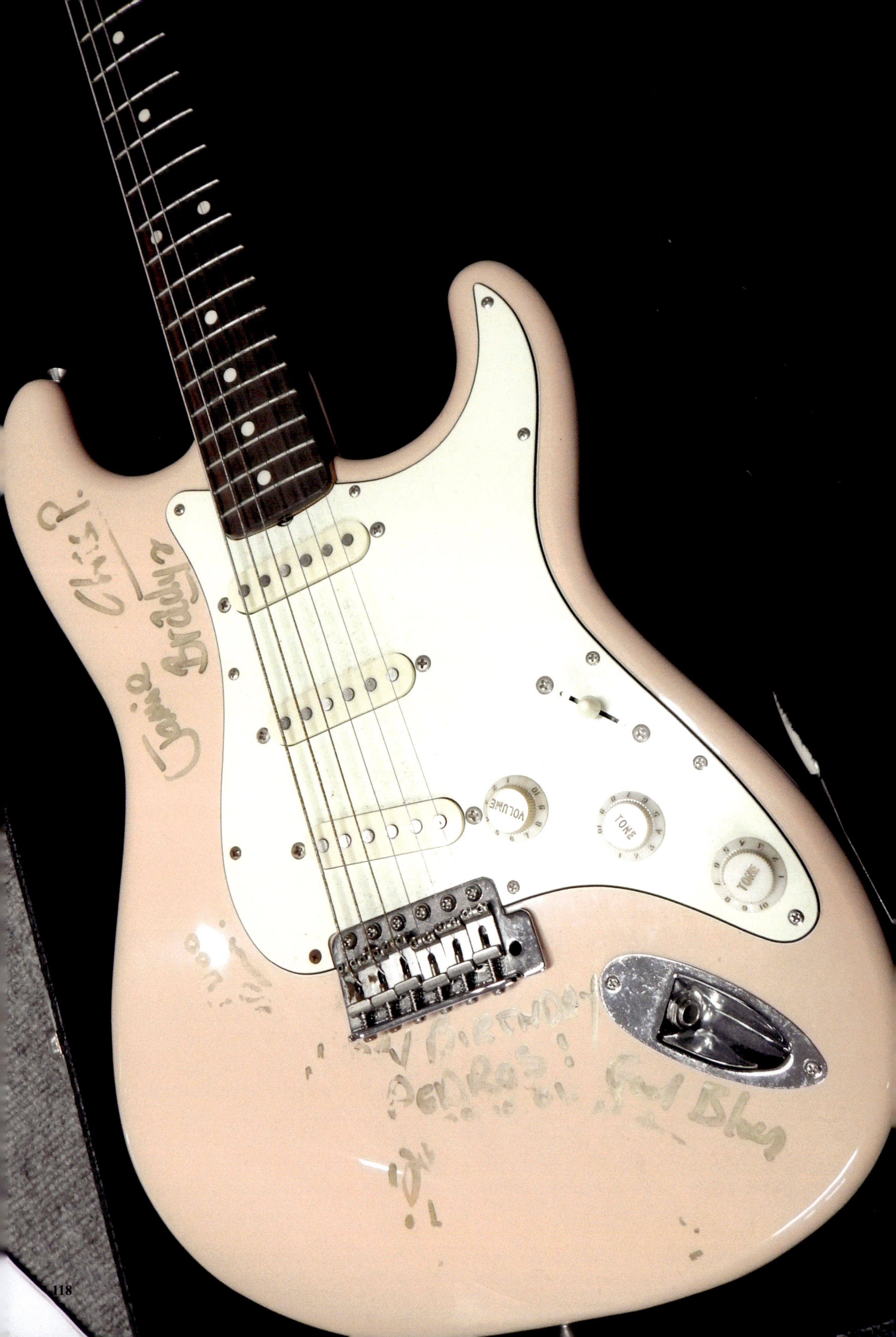
Chris P.
Jamie Braddye
HAPPY BIRTHDAY
PEDRO!
God Bless

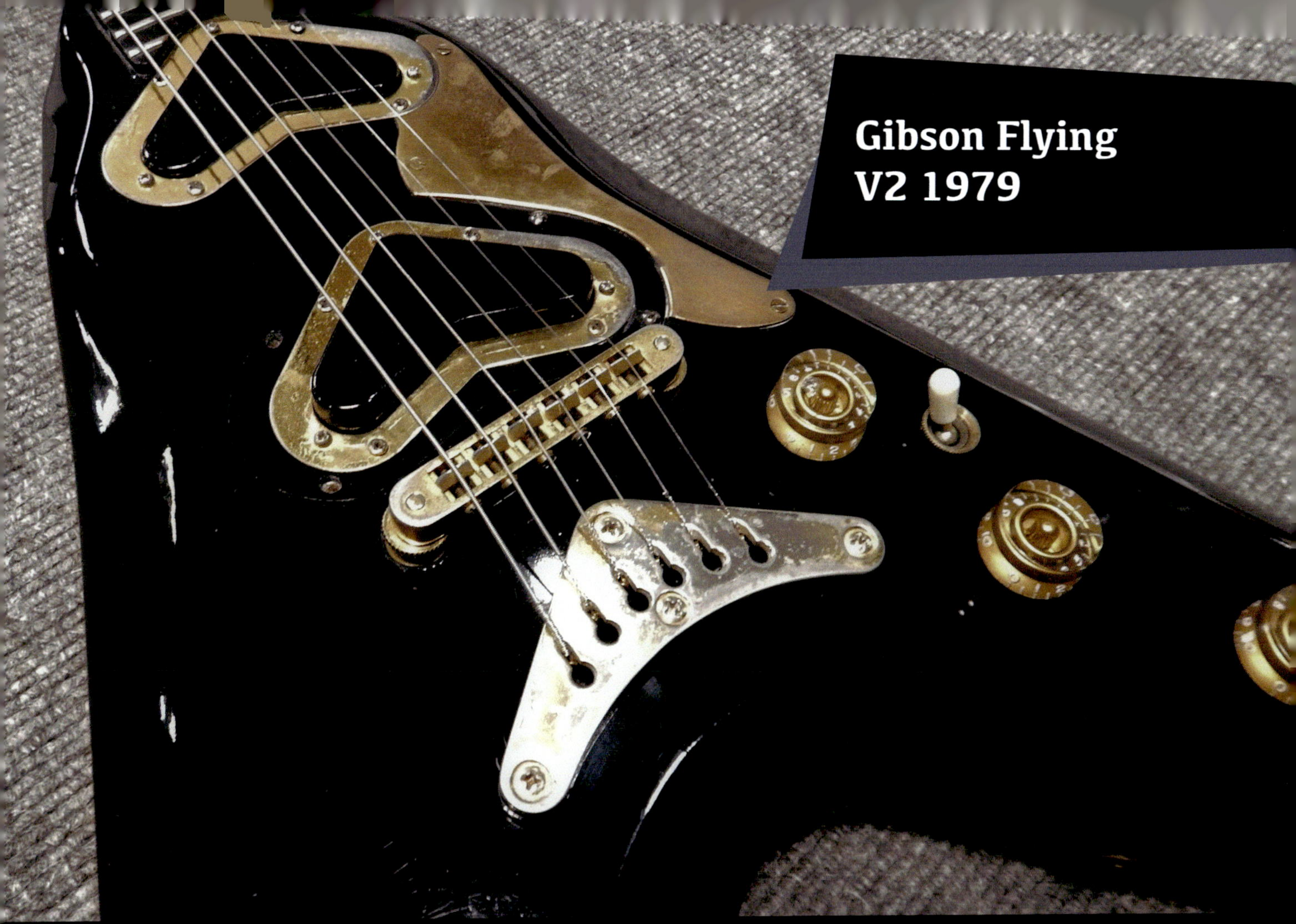

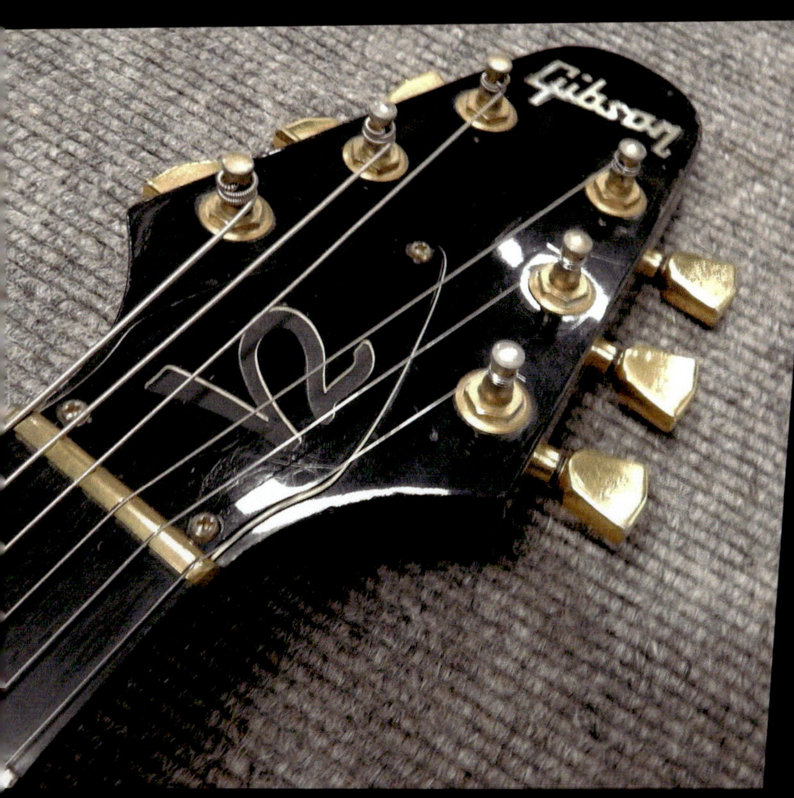

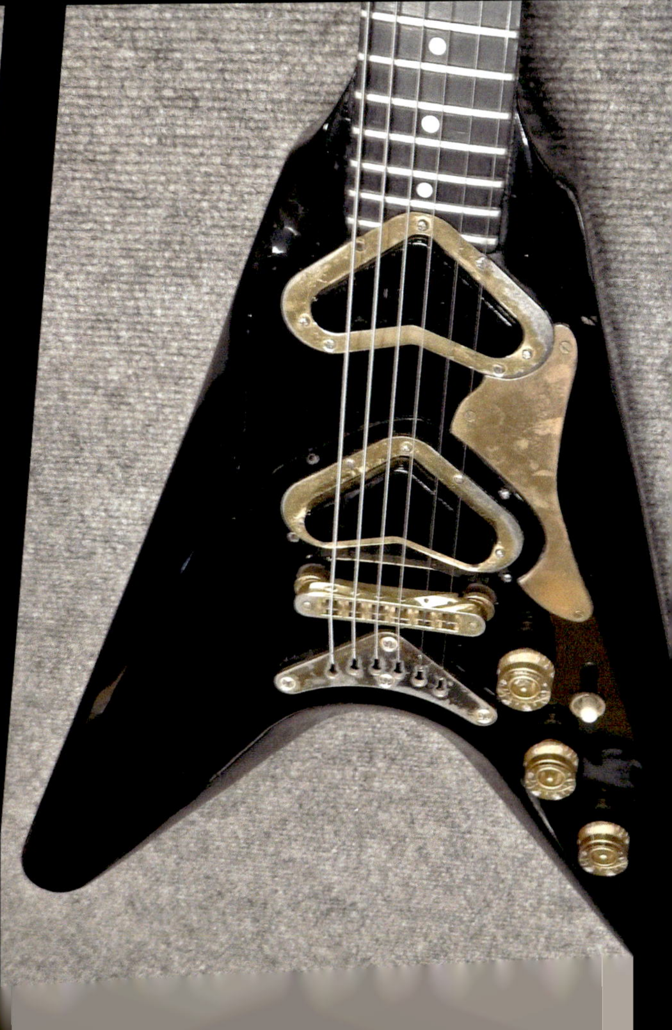

Peter Green referred to this guitar as 'Devilistic'
and looking like a 'Vincent motorbike, he bought
it because he liked the look of the black
boomerang pickups

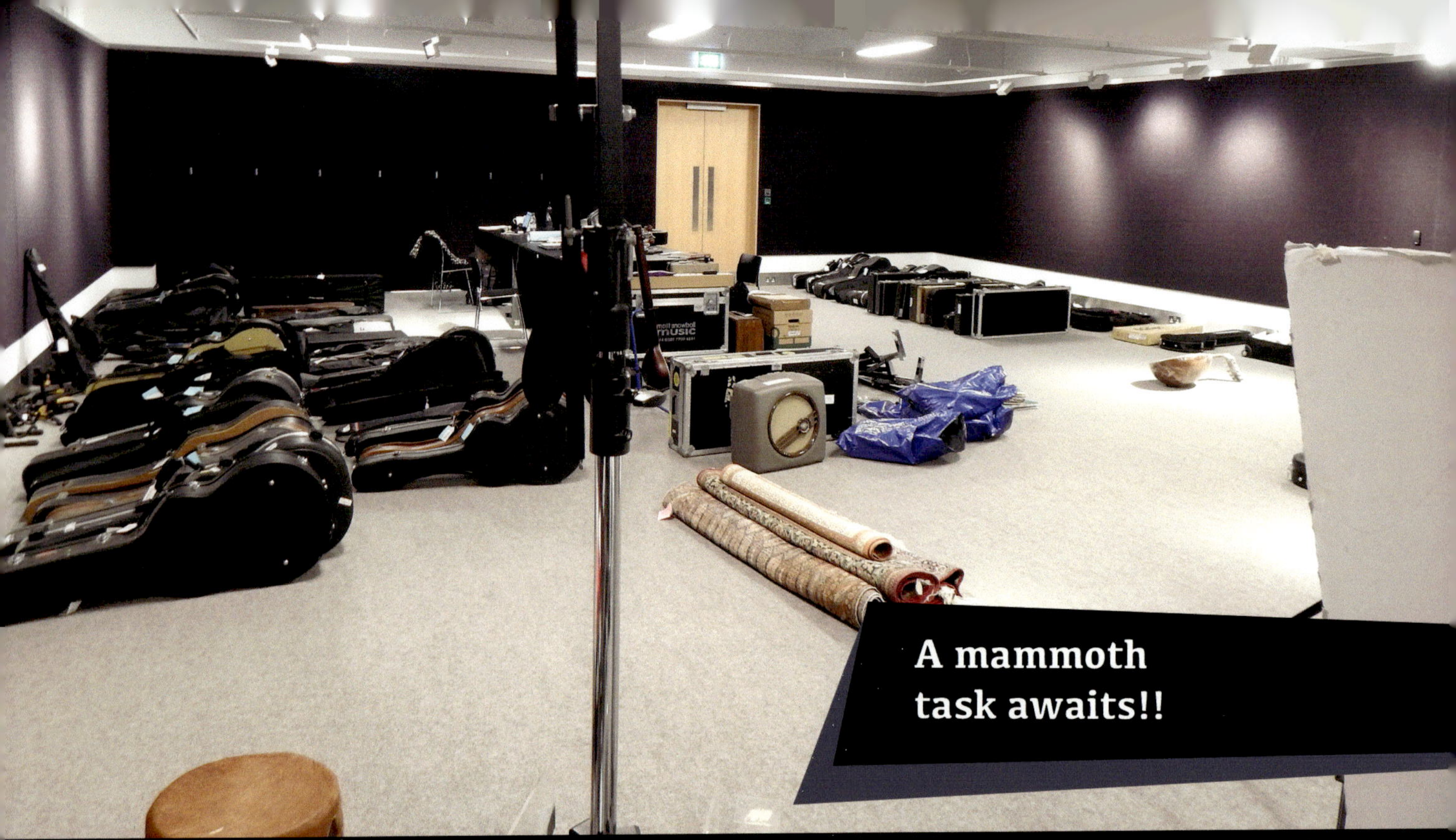

A mammoth task awaits!!

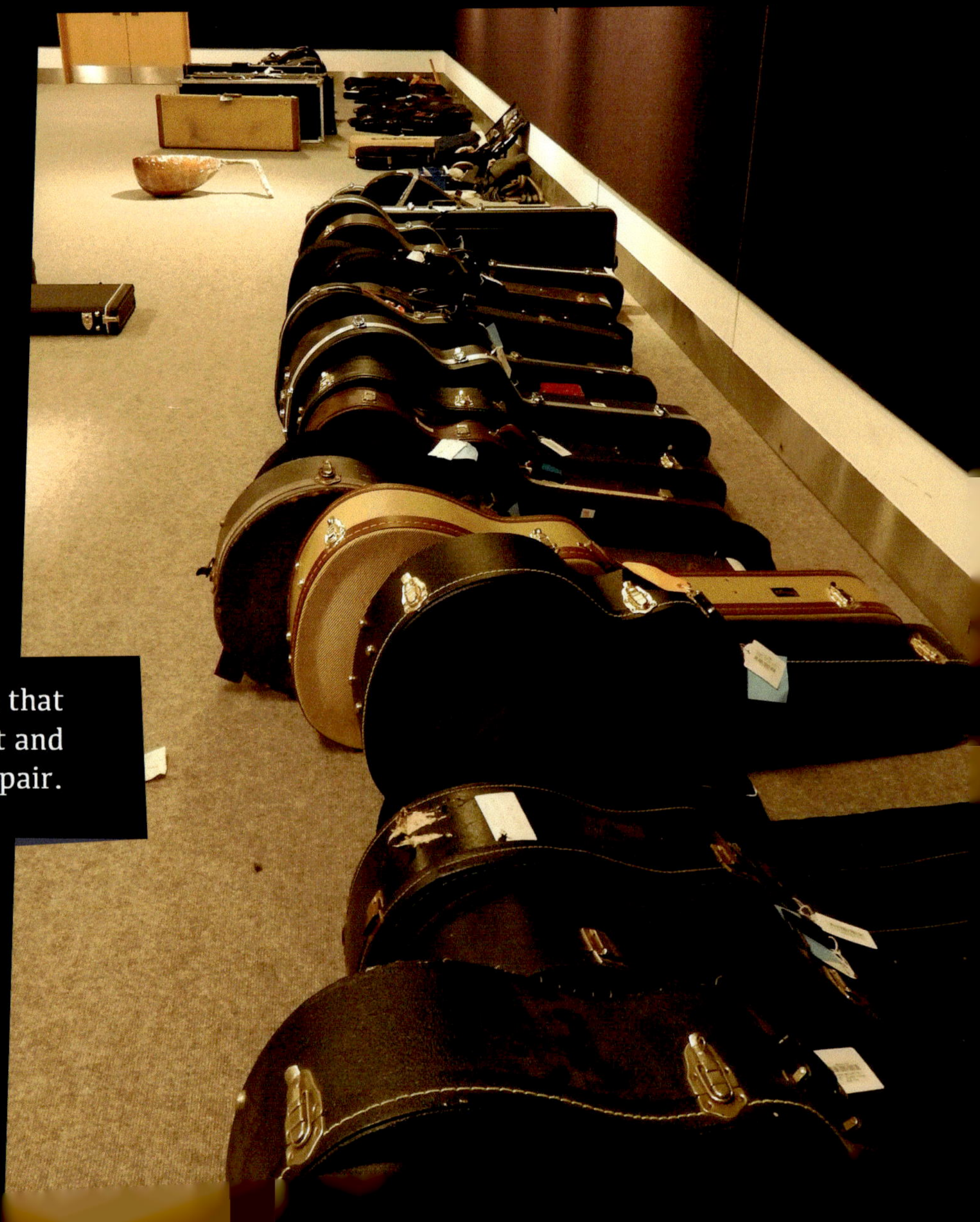

Just some of the collection that are ready for assessment and repair.

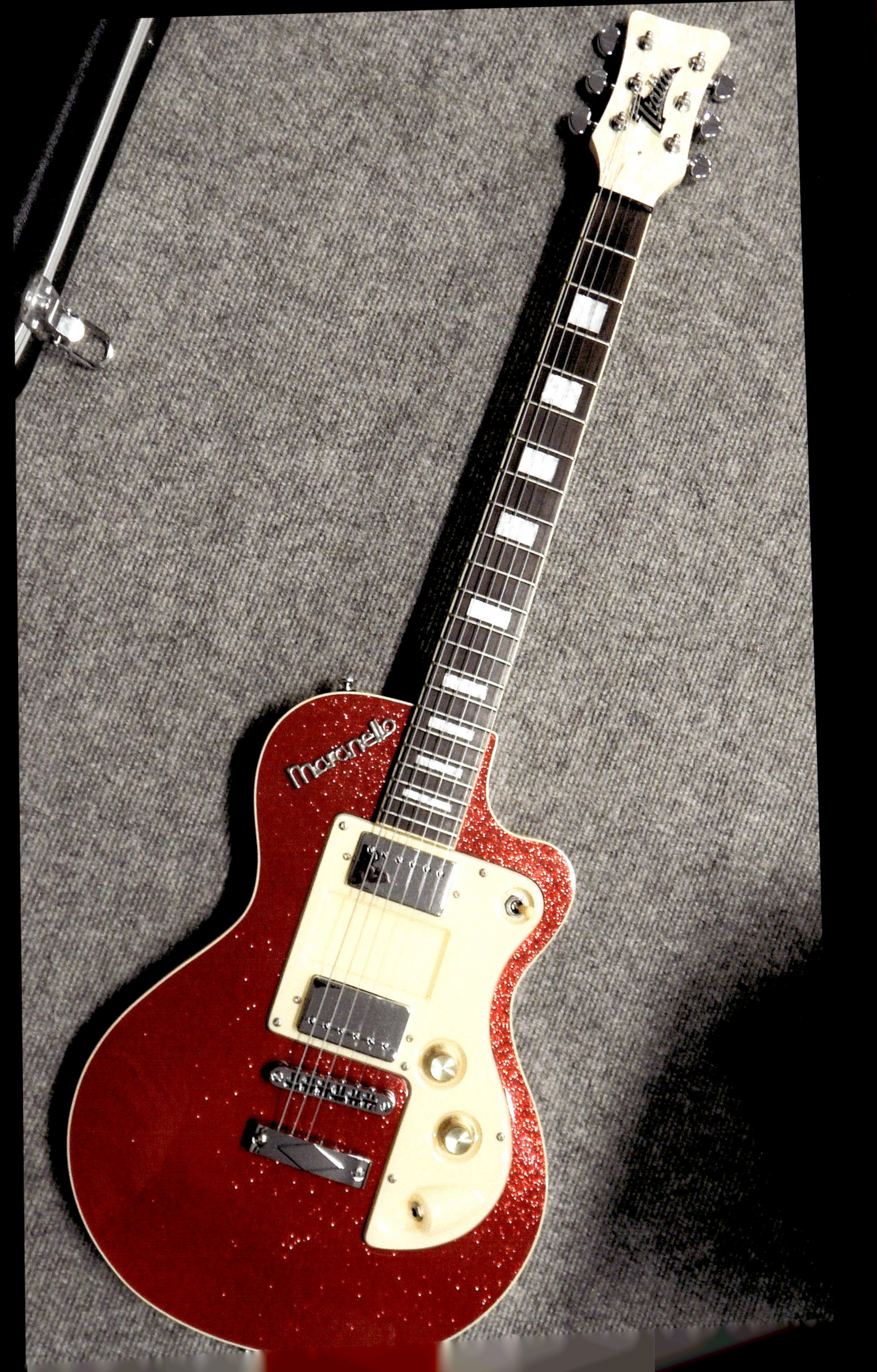

Italia Maranello Classic 'I'

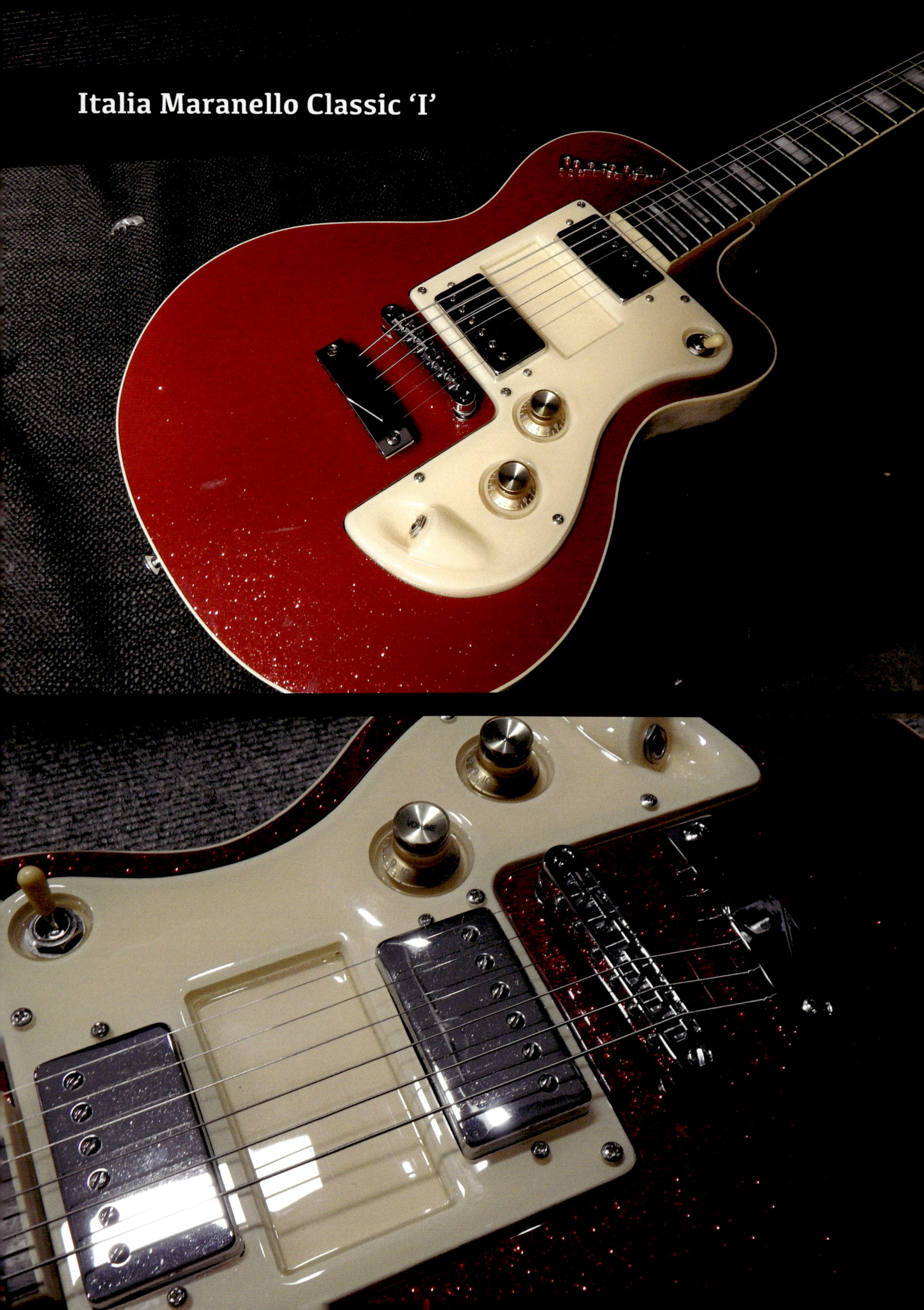

Italia Maranello Classic 'I'
VOLUME

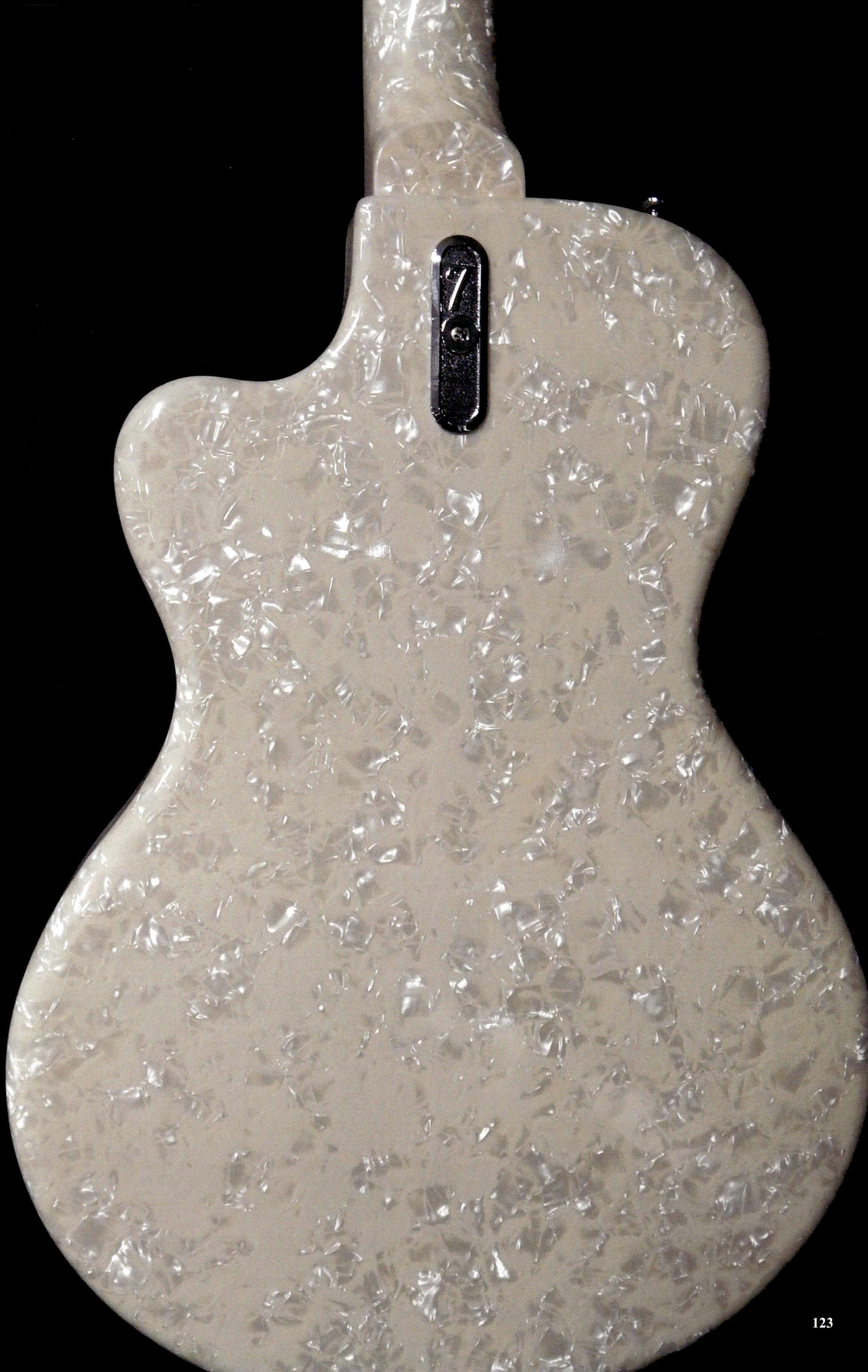

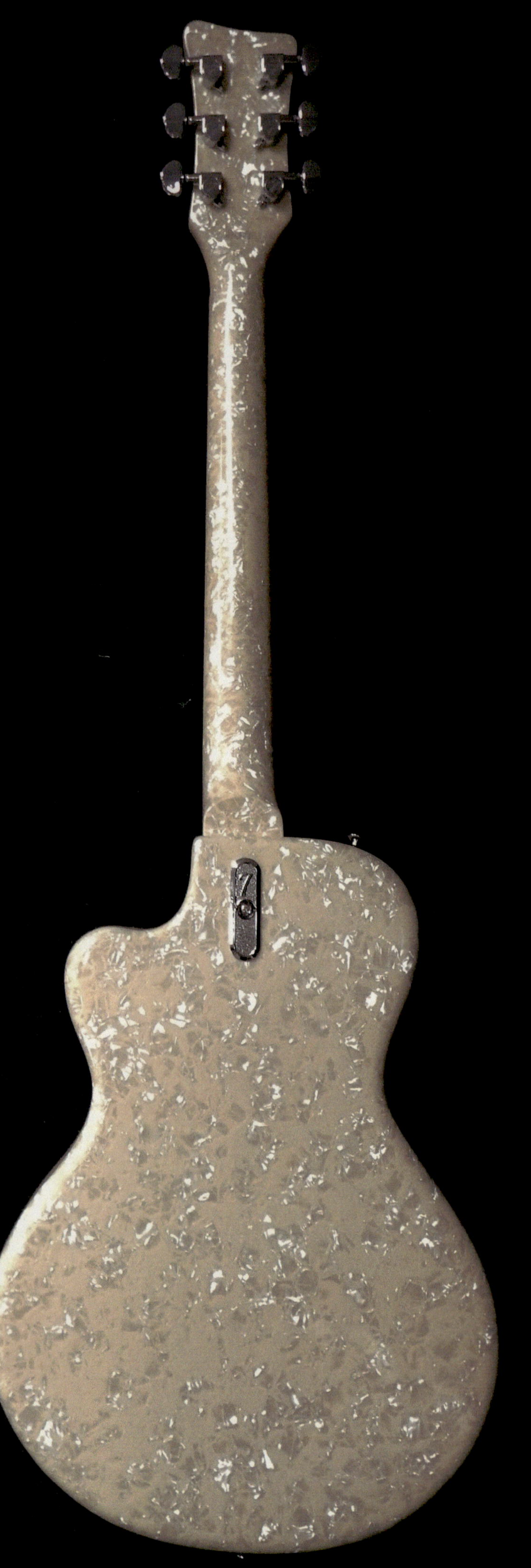

Used by Peter Green in the Splinter Group and Peter Green and Friends.
This guitar was made in Korea: the Italia brand was founded in 1998 with a line of retro-style guitars and bass's designed by Trevor Wilkinson who was inspired by guitars made in the 1950's and 60's.

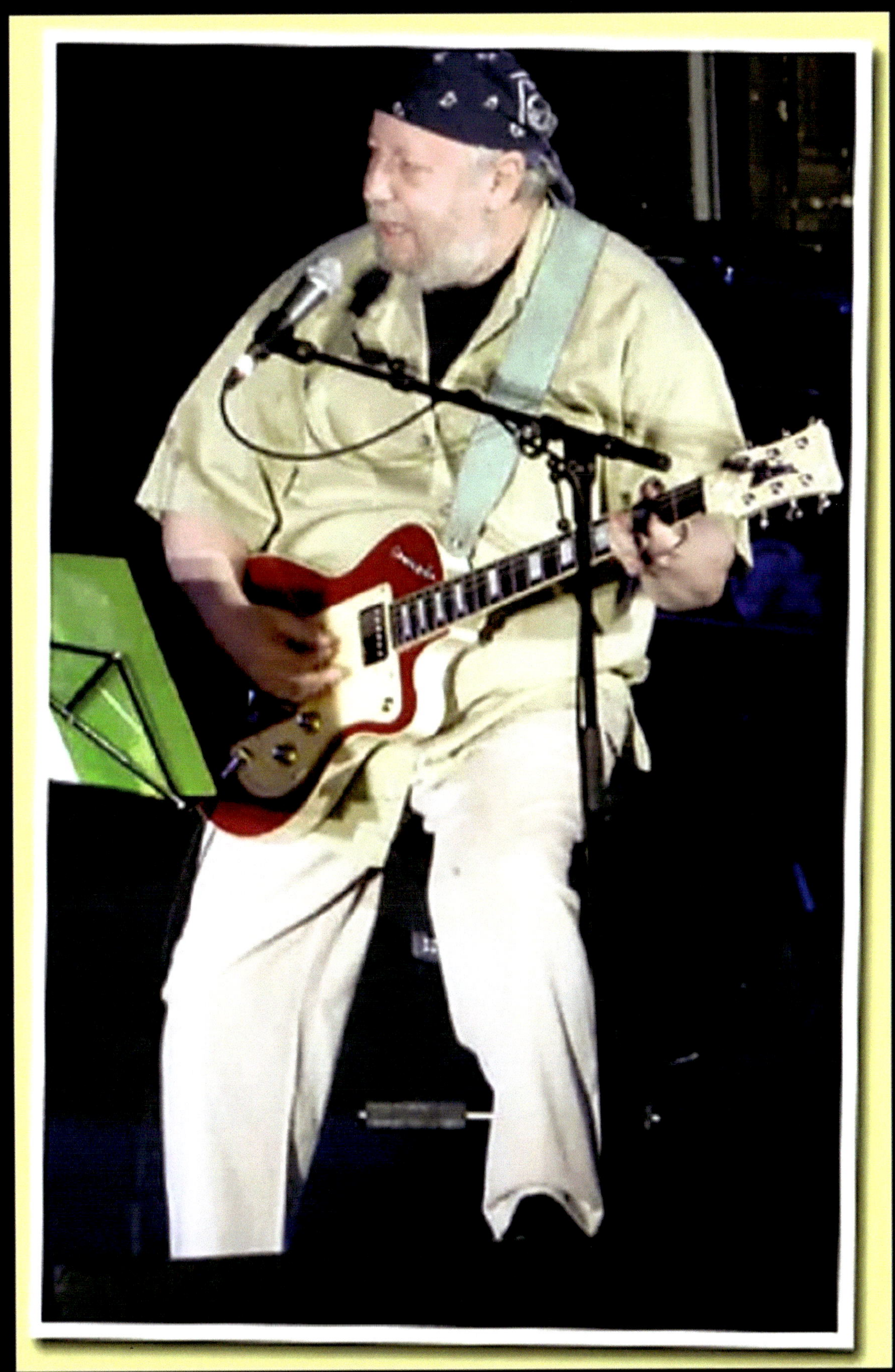

Howard Roberts Fusion III Semi Acoustic Guitar 1995

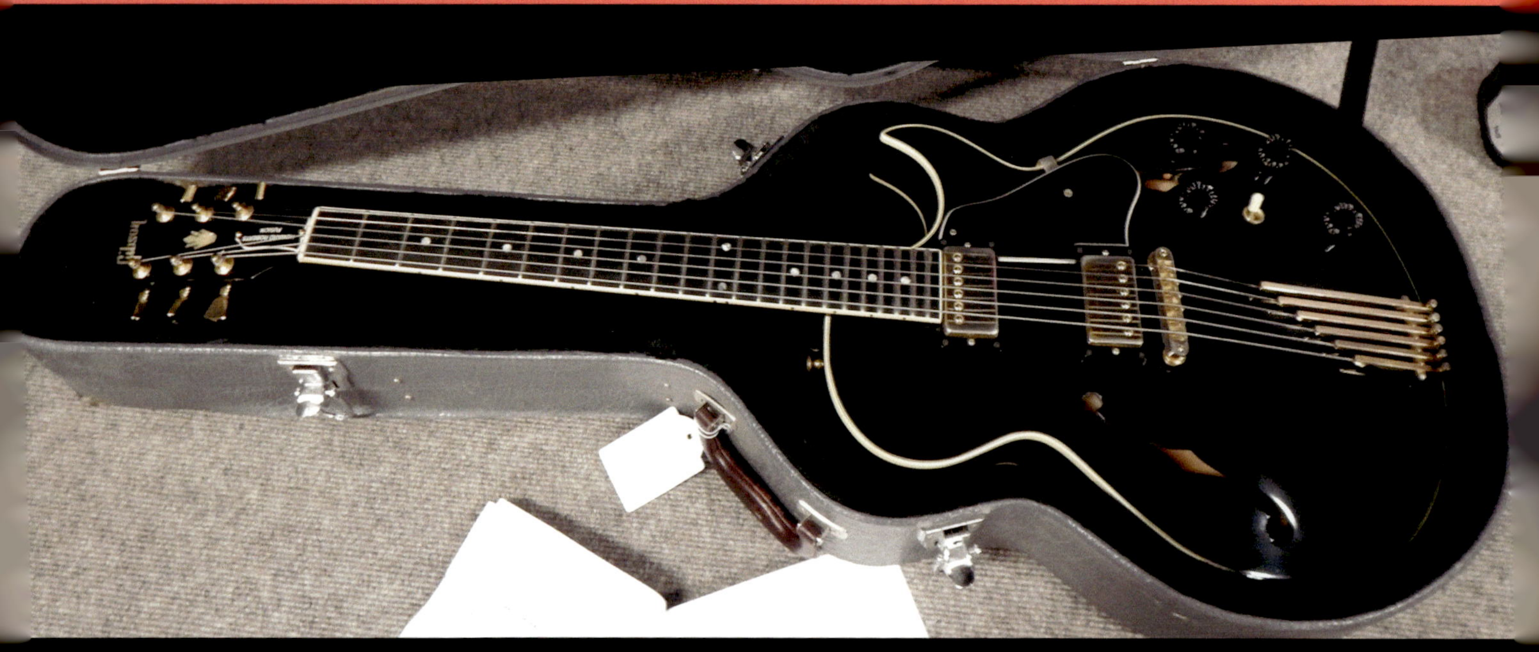

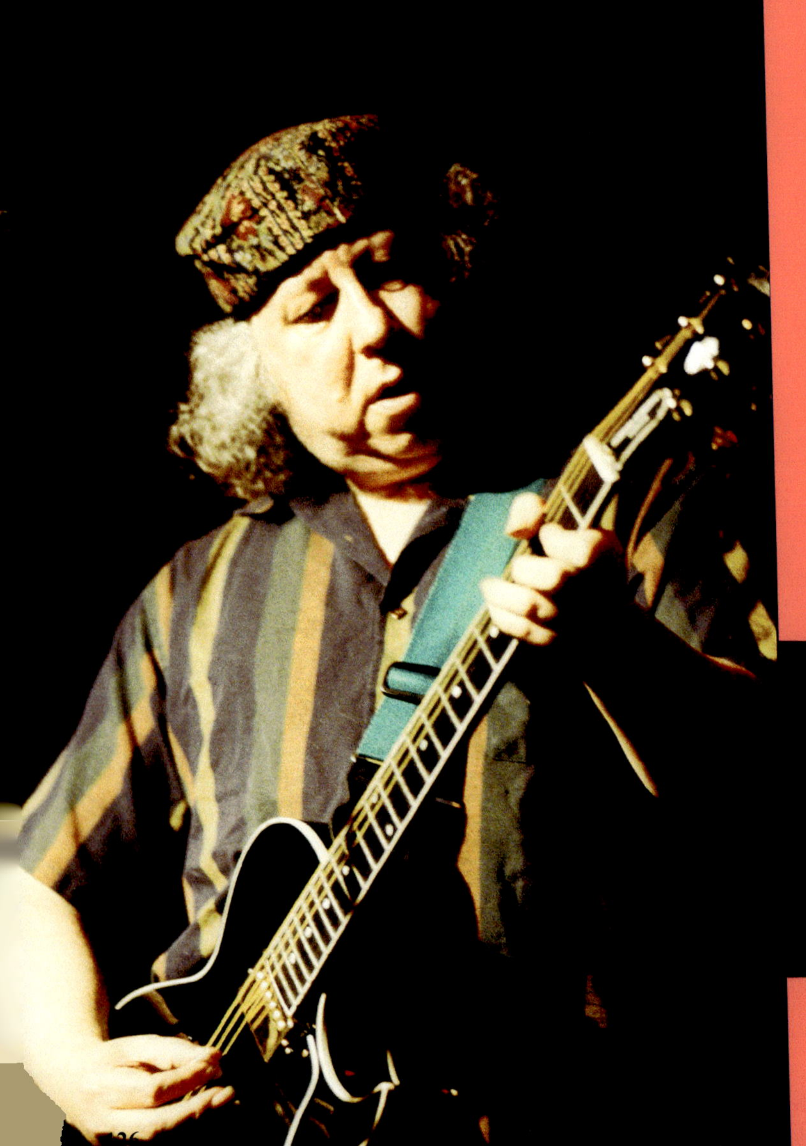

Gibson's A&R man Jamie Crompton gifted Peter this Howard Roberts Fusion III, which was Peter's main guitar during the Peter Green Splinter Group era 1996 – 2003. It was highly regarded by Peter: he took to it right away. He loved the beautiful coal black finish with gold decoration. He found it easy to play and liked its' soft jazzy sound.
He can seen playing various songs with this guitar on the televised 'Splinter Group in Concert' in Baden-Baden 28th June 1998.

Info: Two Humbucking pickups 490R and 490T. The tailpiece has finger adjustment screws. It has a bound ebony fingerboard with dot markers and gold plated hardware.

Paul Kossoff - Guild F48 1973

Paul Kossoff celebrated his 25th birthday in a hospital bed. His band 'Back Street Crawler' presented him with this fabulous Guild F48 guitar. Terry Wilson, the bass player had purchased it on behalf of the band. At the time, Kossoff was recovering from his drug addiction which had taken it's toll on him.

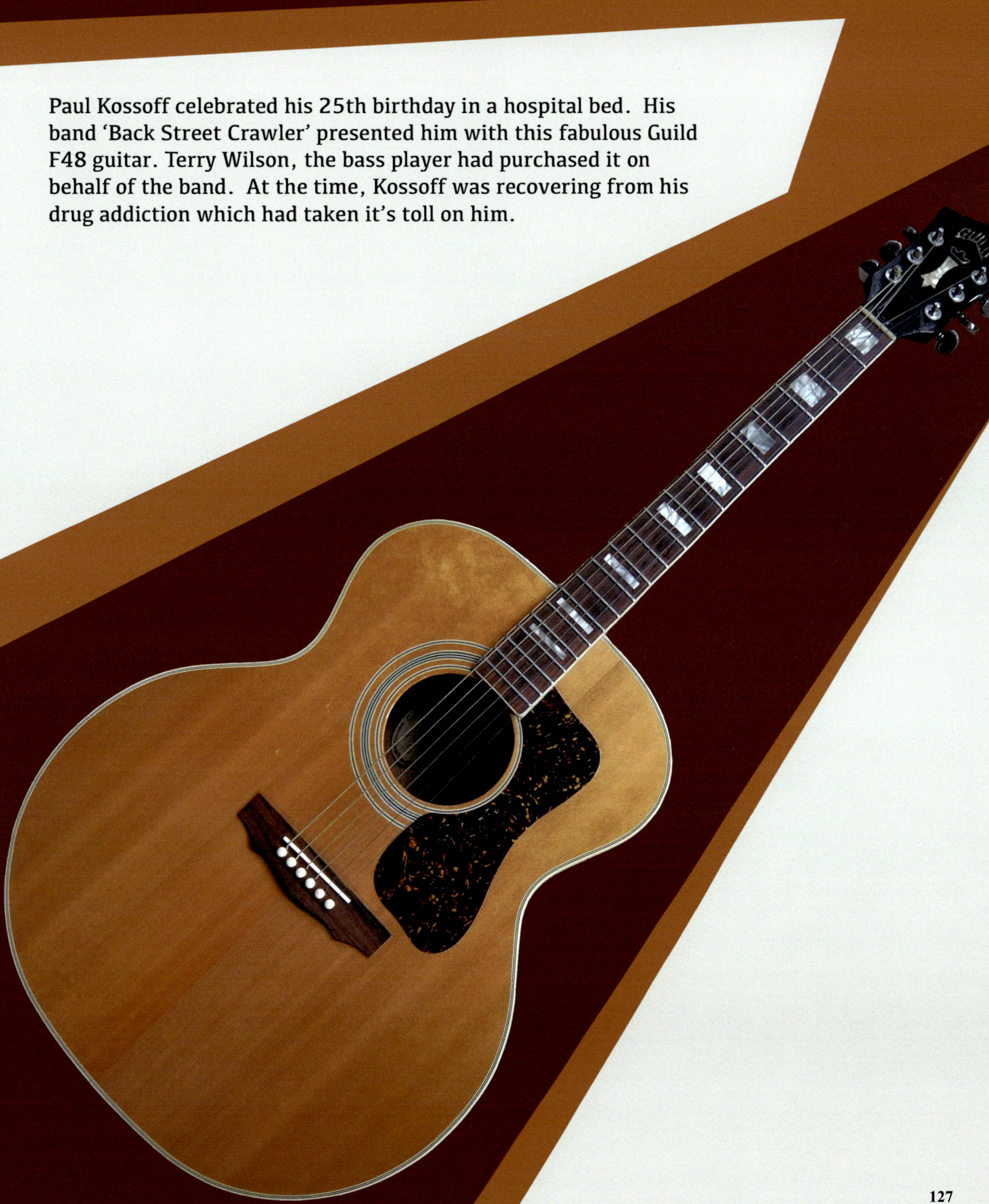

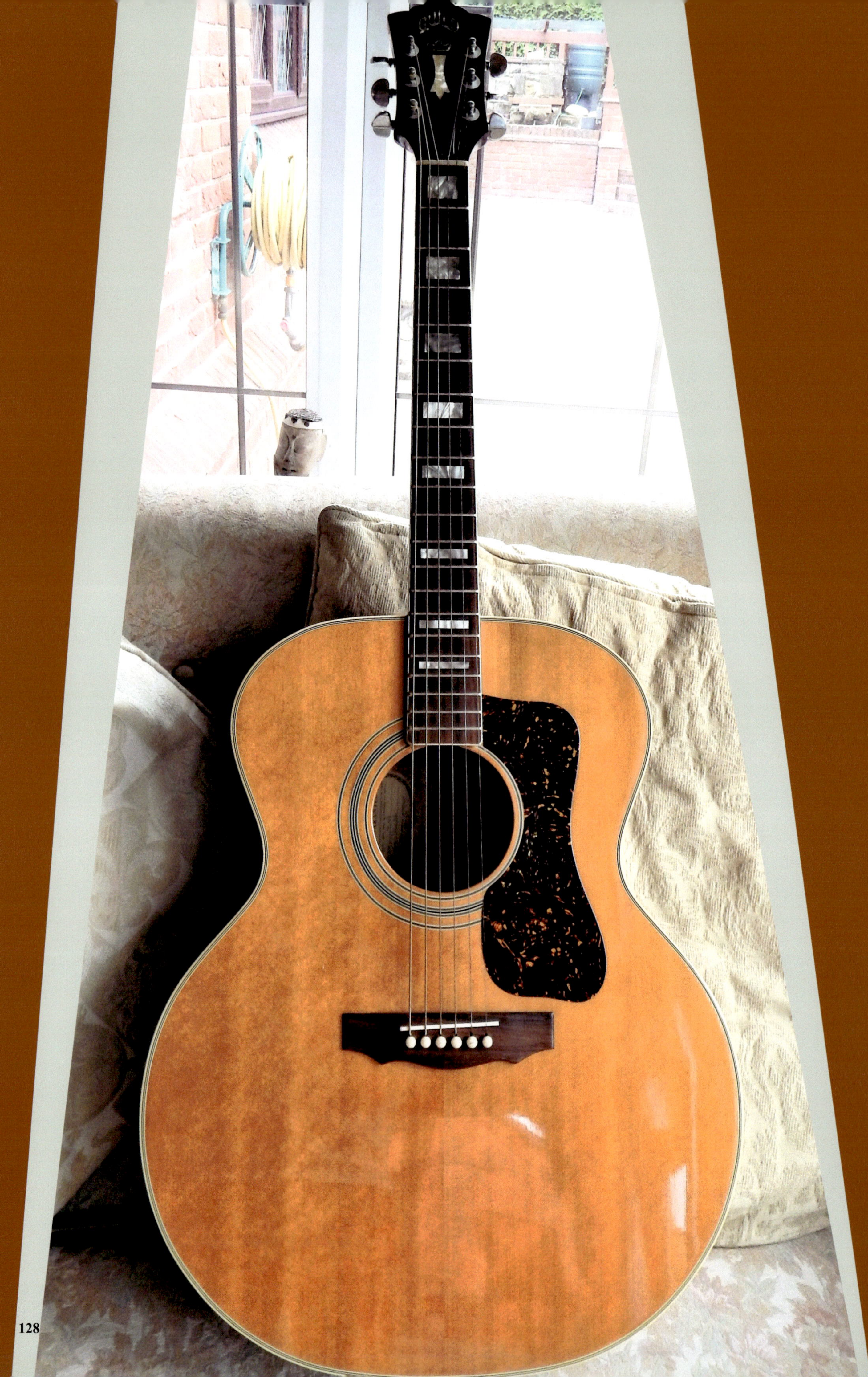

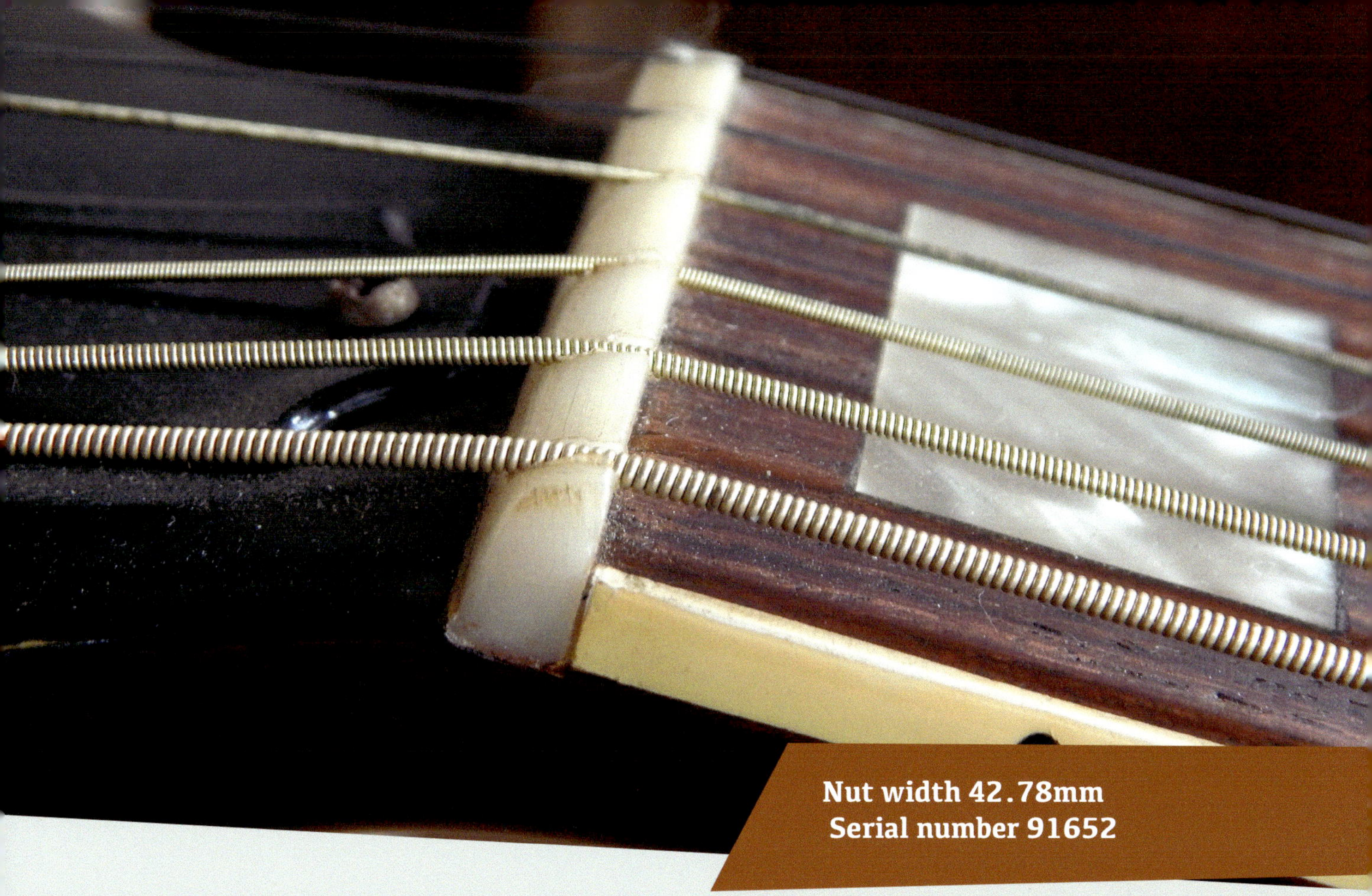

Nut width 42.78mm
Serial number 91652

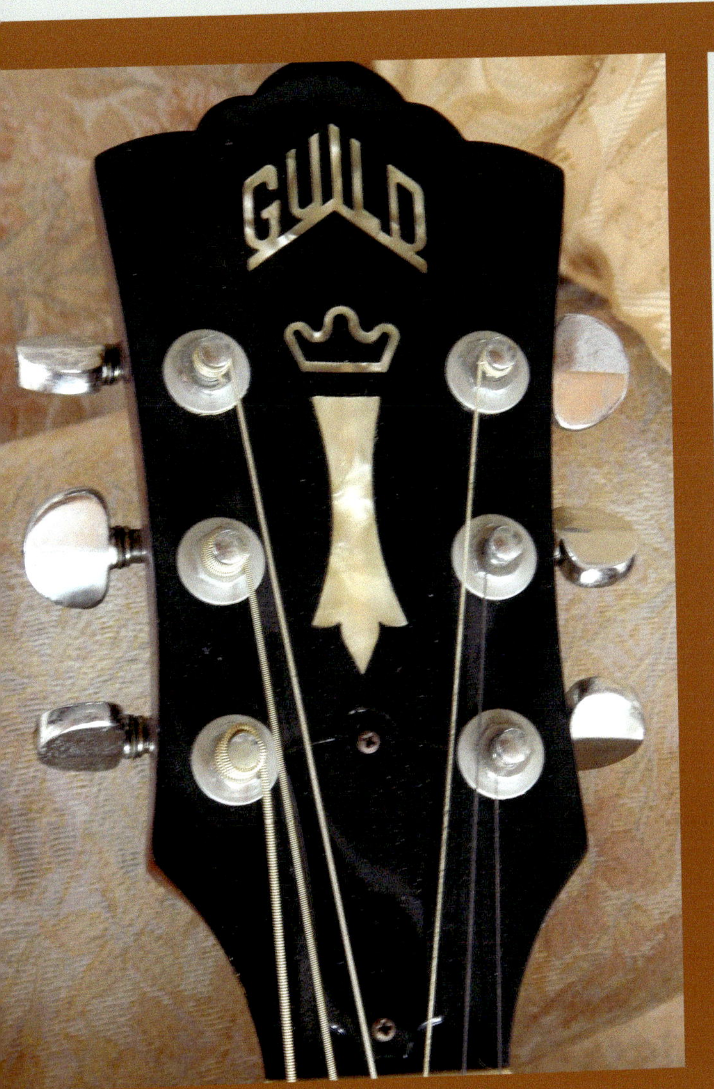

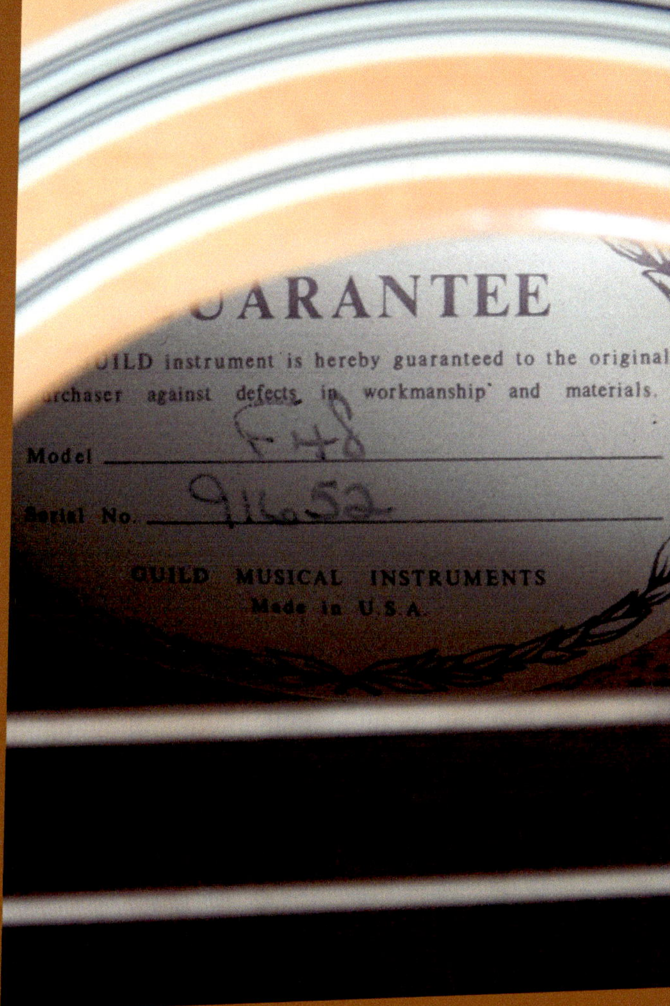
UARANTEE
UILD instrument is hereby guaranteed to the original
urchaser against defects in workmanship and materials.
Model   F-48
Serial No.   91652
GUILD MUSICAL INSTRUMENTS
Made in U.S.A.

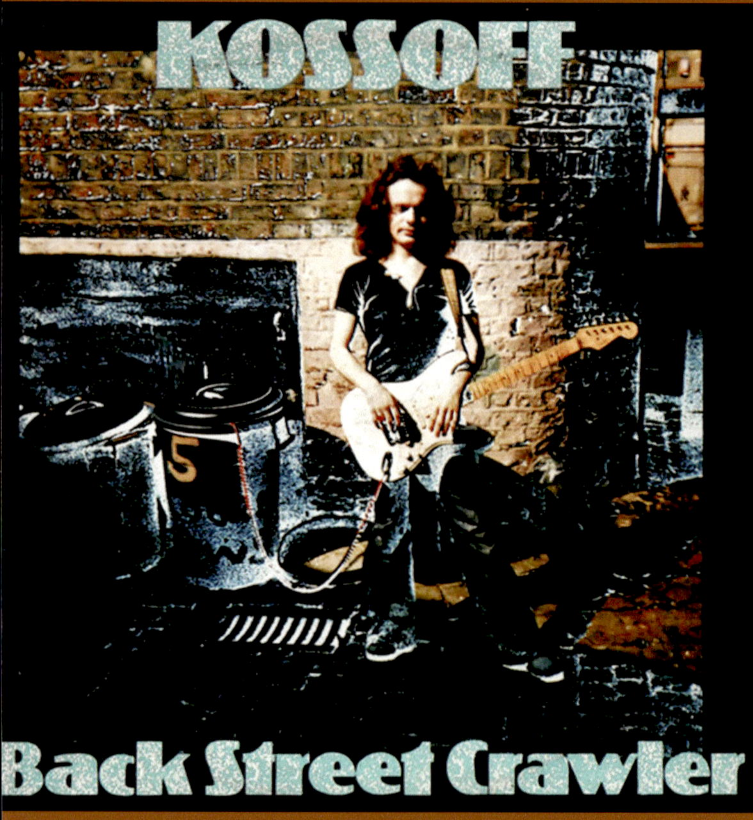

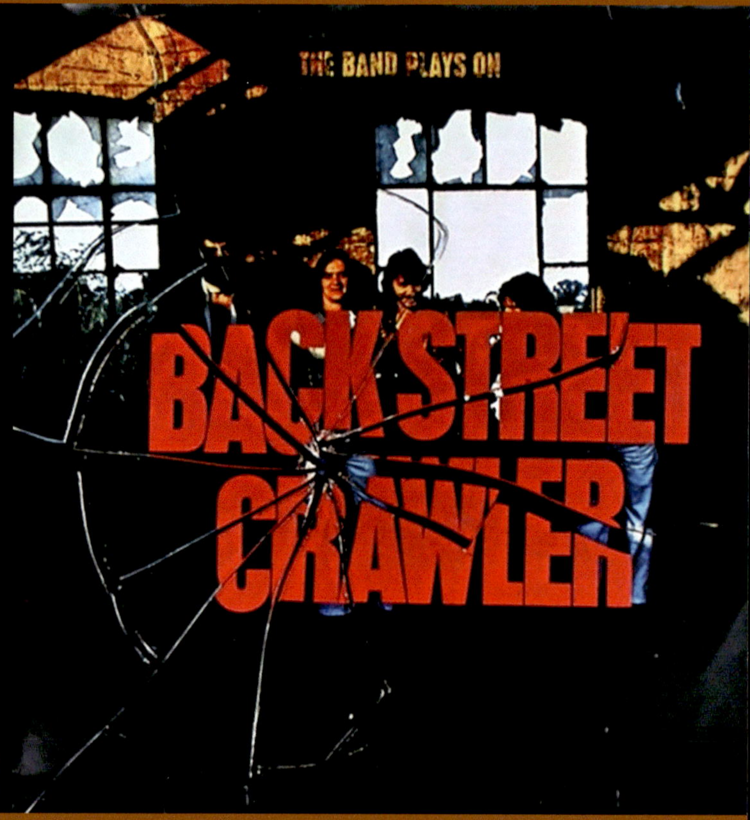

L-R
Mike Montgomery – Keyboards, Terry Wilson-Slesser – Lead Vocals,
Tony Braunagel – Drums, Paul Kossoff – Lead Guitar, Terry Wilson - Bass

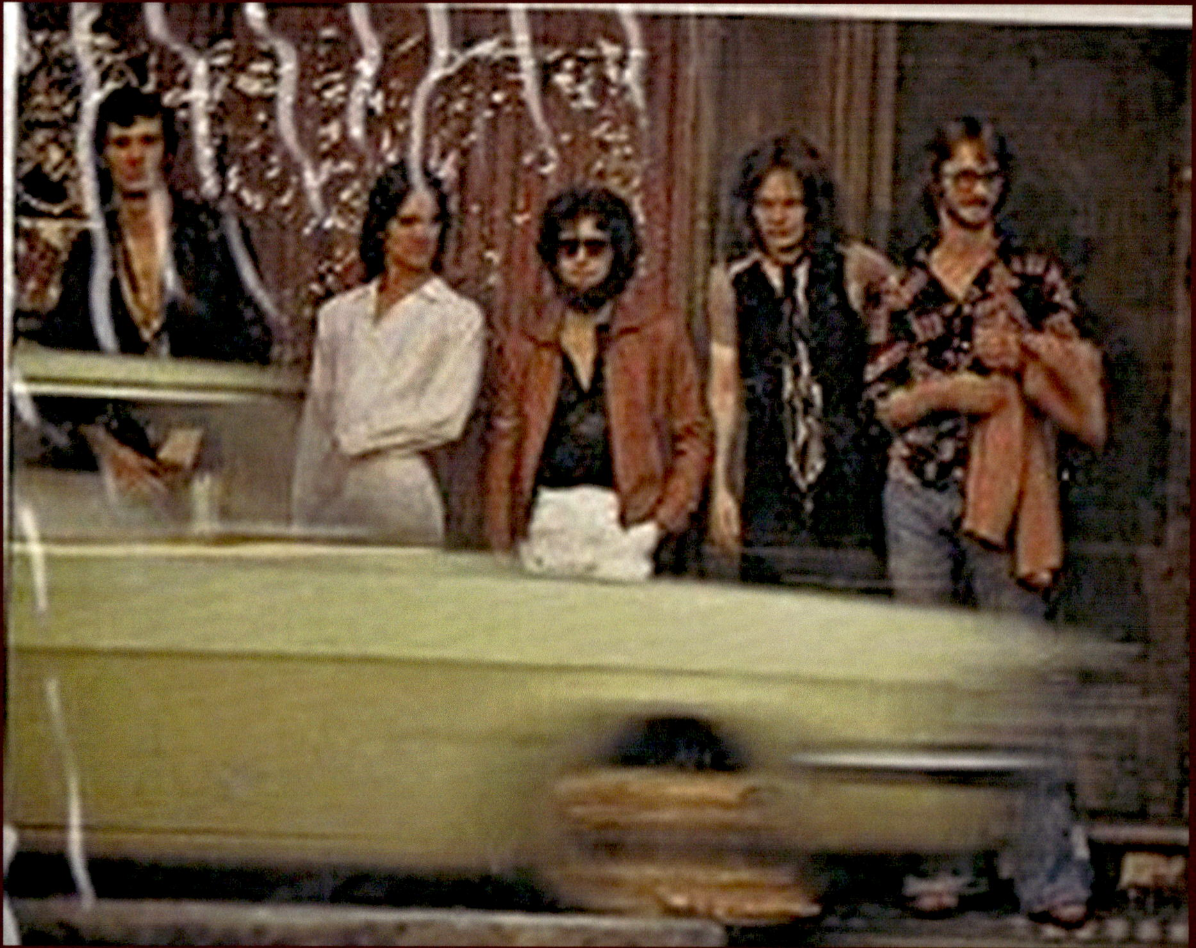

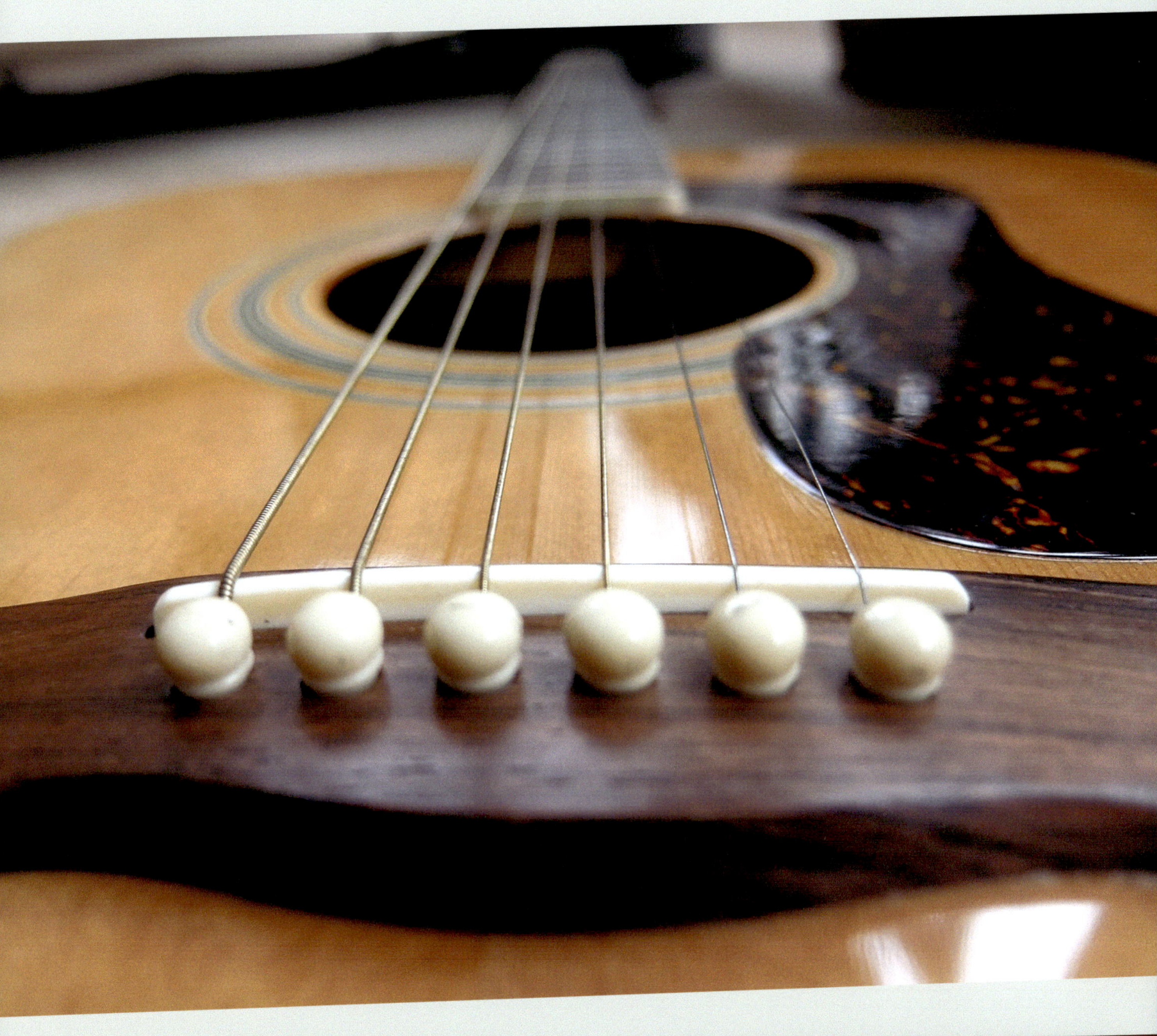

The Guild F48 had a solid Sitka spruce top, African Mahogany back and sides.
It was only produced through 1972-76. It has an East Indian Rosewood bridge and
fingerboard and Guild 'closed back' tuners and a bone nut.

The scale length from the nut to the bridge is 650mm.

The following pictures were taken when Paul's brother, Simon Kossoff visited the home of the Free Appreciation Society founder David Clayton for a book signing. Simon brought with him the F48 for me to look at which was a real treat. The Isle Of Wight Stripped Burst '59 Les Paul was also there, which is covered in my first book Famous Frets.

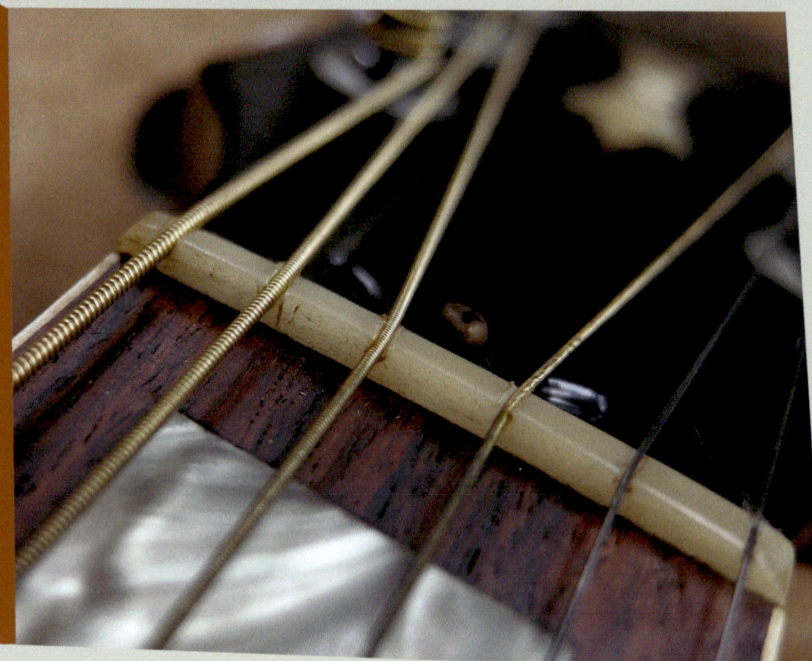

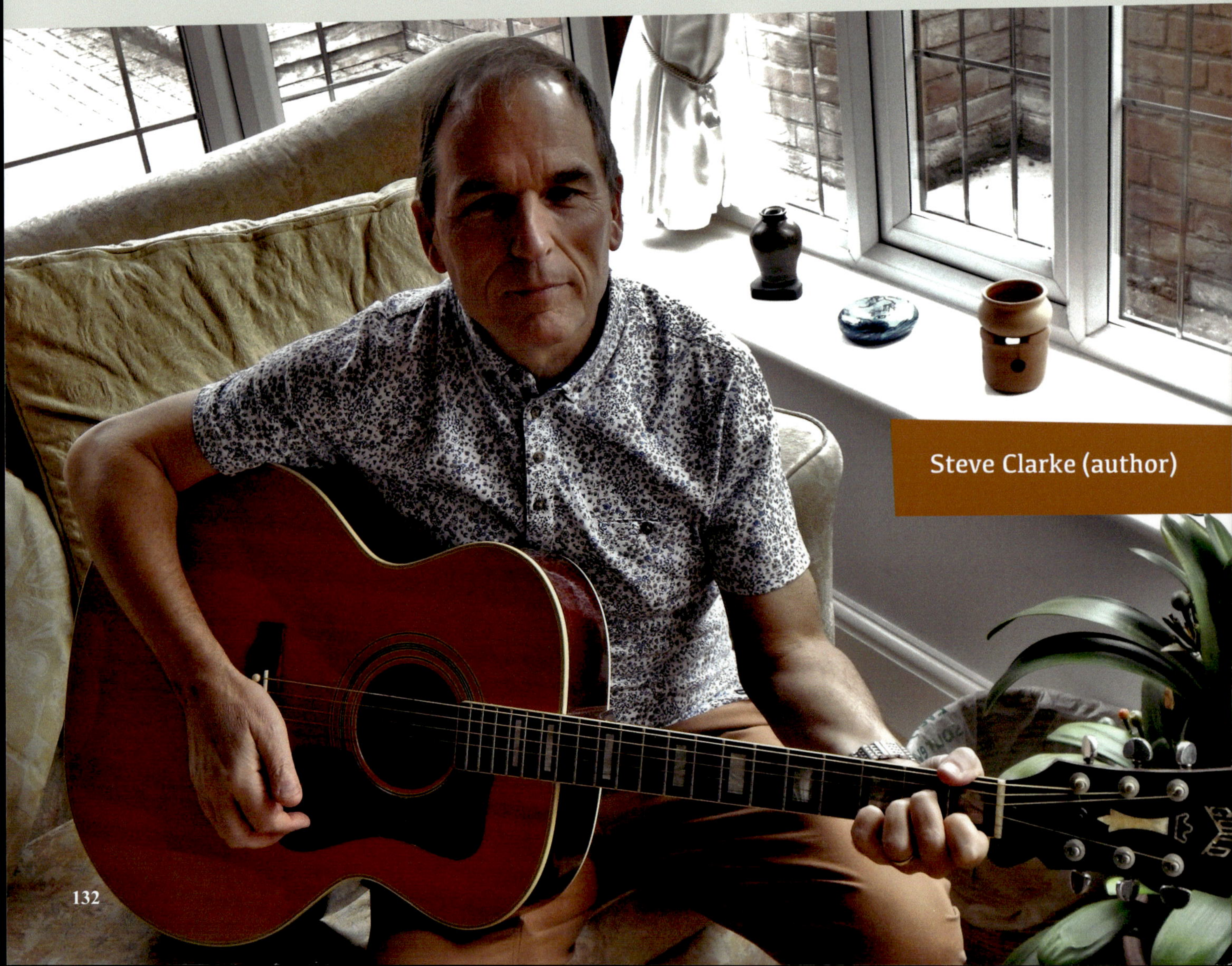

Steve Clarke (author)

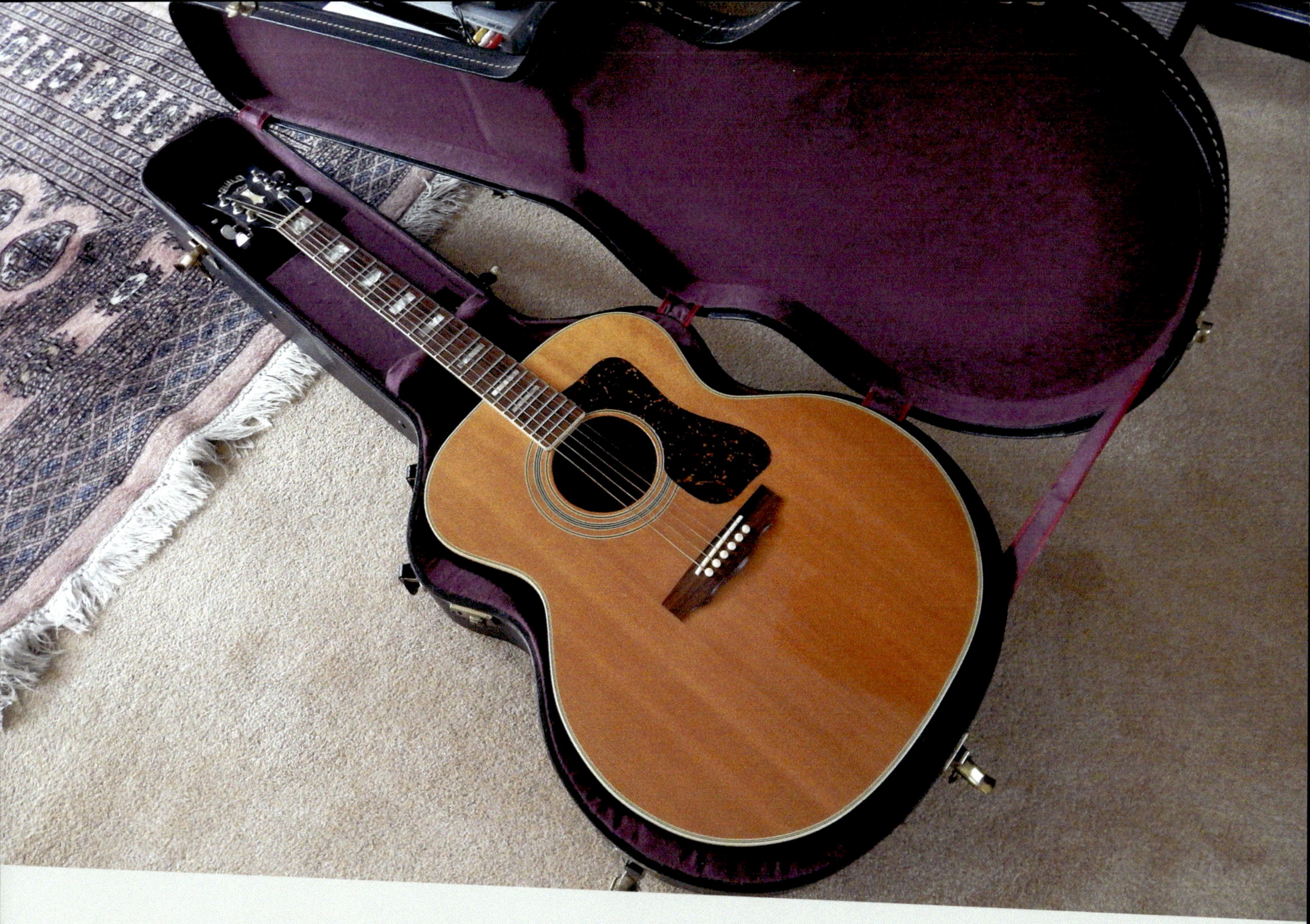

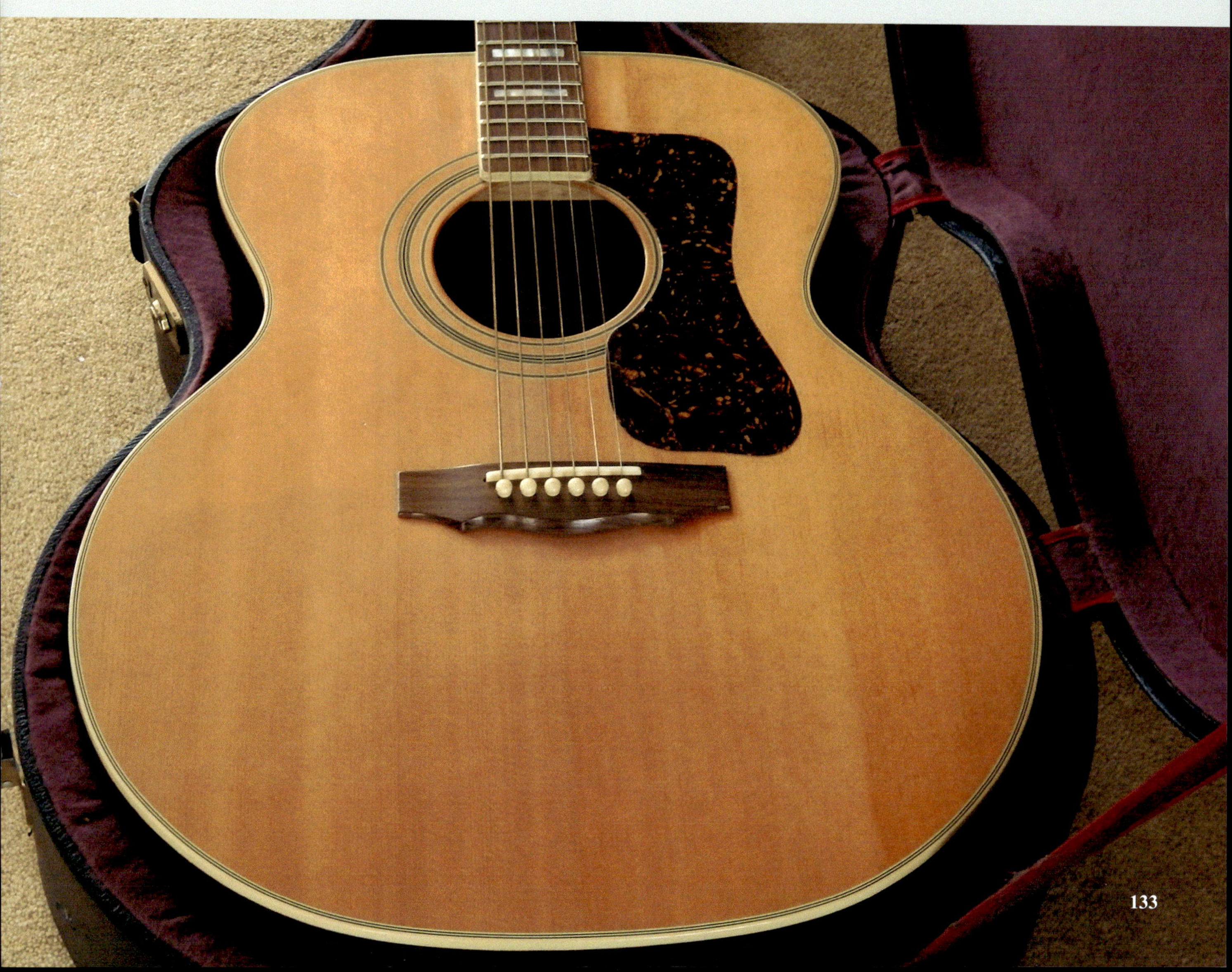

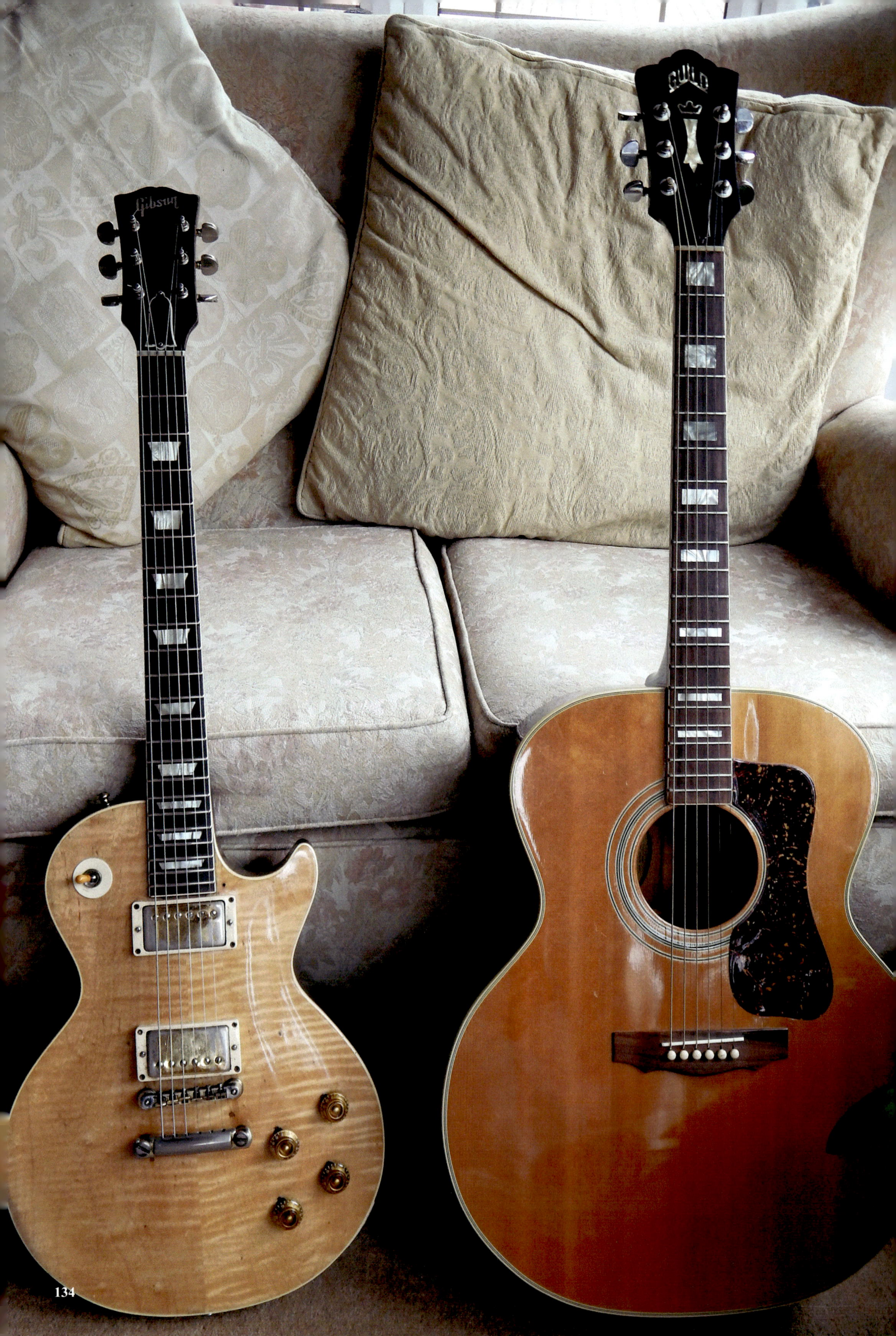